Dee Jones is a counsellor with 30 years' experience and has worked extensively in the field of Neurodivergence, particularly in Autism - in its many and varied presentations and terminology changes over the last 30 years. She has met with thousands of people over these years, as both a counsellor and a researcher, and often does public presentations on topics related to Autism. She is a mother, proud of the success of her adult children in being such amazing people! She loves reading, crafting her own stories and poems, walking, swimming, socialising with friends and especially having time with her family. A Kiwi, she has jumped *the ditch*, and now lives in Brisbane, Australia.

This work is dedicated to my family and friends, colleagues and clients, and a huge circle of fabulous people who have supported my project in so many ways – who all kept me going with the dreaded question of "How is *The Aspie Book* going"? They also kept me accountable, and inspired and encouraged me to finish writing the book. You all know who you are, so thank you, with all my heart. I could not have done this without every single one of you.

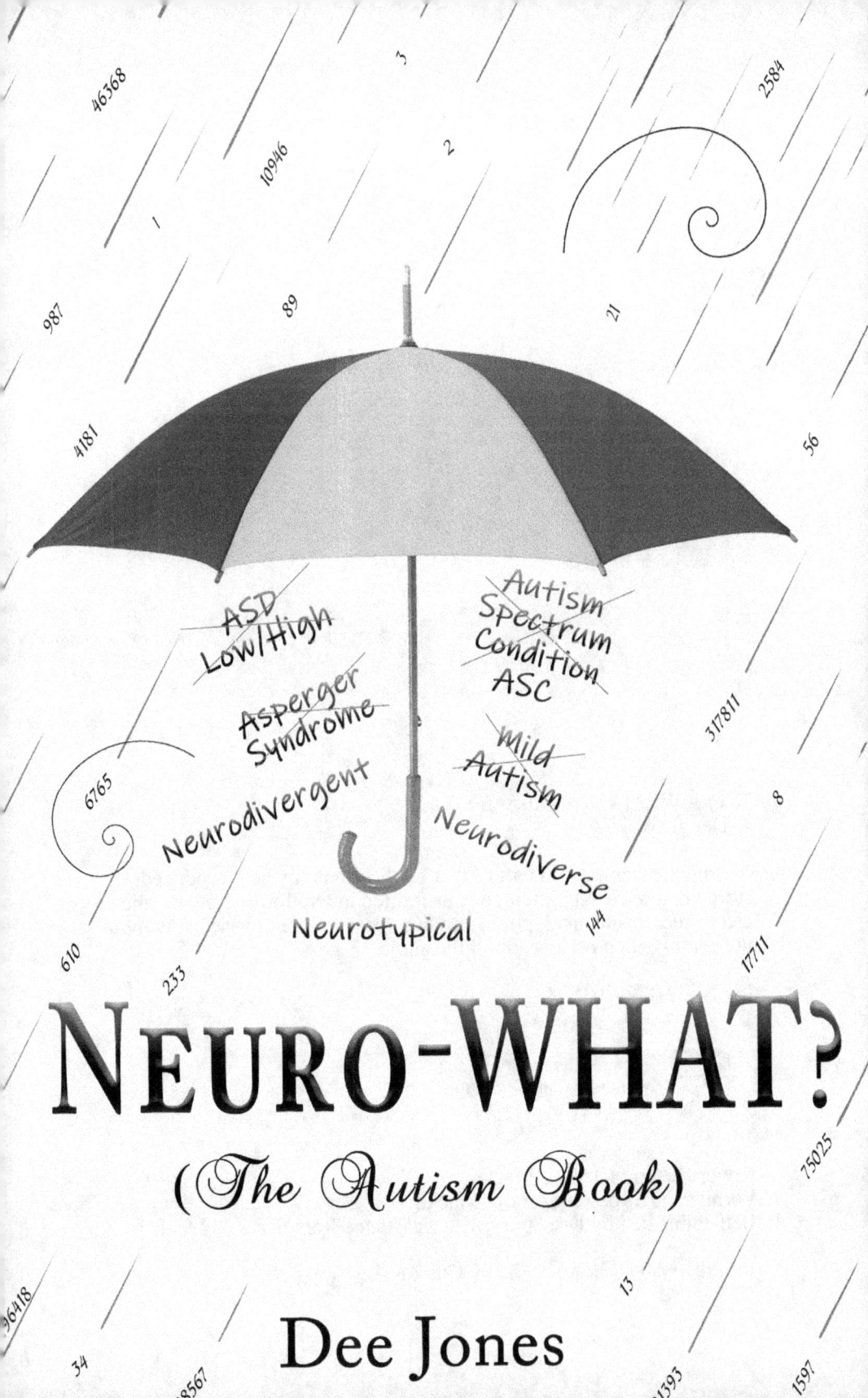

Neuro–What? (The Autism Book)
© Dee Jones 2024

All rights reserved. No part of this publication may be reproduced, stored in a retrieval system, or transmitted in any form or by any means, electronic, mechanical, photocopying, recording or otherwise, without the prior written permission of the author.

ISBN: 978-1-7635388-0-1

 A catalogue record for this work is available from the National Library of Australia

Cover Design: Clark & Mackay
Format and Typeset: Clark & Mackay
Self-Published by Dee Jones with assistance from Clark & Mackay

Proudly printed in Australia by Clark & Mackay

Again, I acknowledge the many inspiring Autistic people and Neurotypicals who wrote their stories and contributed to the book in so many varied ways, consciously but mostly unconsciously. Without them, there would be no book and certainly no last chapter! Then I need to thank my very good friend, Ruth Bartley for her eagle-eyed proof-reading, her faithfulness and unfaltering encouragement; similarly, Steve Macmillan for his thorough and complete editorial work and his massive enthusiasm for the book. His 30+ years of experience in publishing was an invaluable resource to me! I am so grateful to the two of you for giving me a sense of the validity of the project, having gone through the book so scrupulously word-for-word yourselves! It would not have got to this professional, publishable level without you two! I acknowledge my wonderful colleague and very good friend, Dr Yvette Ahmad. We worked on that research paper together which is in its final stage of refining, we picked each other brains and then went over all the information again and again and again. Your professional opinions have been so valuable in assisting with this book. I need to acknowledge my very dear friend, Debra Katsoolis, with her own sound understanding of Autism, for scrutinising my art work through my many illustrations and giving valid criticism and constructive opinions – and another ton of encouragement. I also need to acknowledge the fabulous support that I have had from Professor Tony Attwood, and his introductory foreword contributed hugely to getting publication completed. To have the support of this well-known, international author and scholar on the subject offering his time, advice and thoughts on my manuscript, and the fact that he read a nearly 520 page manuscript despite his busy schedule, is impressive!

Foreword

Dee's extensive experiences and insights as a counsellor will educate and reassure not only those who have autism, but also their families, and professionals. I really enjoyed the many case studies, quotations, and recommendations. While there are many books on Asperger's syndrome that resonate with our conceptualization and appreciation of autism, this book differs in that it includes many clever cartoons that perfectly illustrate the text and will make the reader laugh.

The book is a joy to read and explores many dimensions of Asperger's syndrome through the lifespan. The first chapter provides an engaging description of autism based on the current theoretical models. Subsequent chapters focus on the challenges and qualities of autistic girls and women, and boys and men, and the issues of being a student and employee. The chapters on relationships, being an Aspie parent, and aging explore the new frontiers of Asperger's syndrome. I highly recommend the penultimate chapter on counselling and ASD for current and prospective counsellors. The advice is wise and valuable, especially as we have extremely limited professional literature on this aspect of autism.

There will be a copy of *Neuro-WHAT?* (The Autism book) in my clinic room to recommend to clients and their families, and I will also enjoy showing them the cartoons that serve to illustrate the themes of our conversation and therapy.

Professor Tony Attwood

Table of Contents

Chapter 1 Neurodivergence/Autism/Autism Spectrum Condition (ASC)/Autism Spectrum Disorder (ASD)/Asperger's Syndrome (as a subgroup of Autism)   13

Chapter 2 Children on the Autism/Neurodivergent Spectrum   49

Chapter 3 Neurodivergent/Autistic Females   87

Chapter 4 Neurodivergent/Autistic Males   136

Chapter 5 Autism/Neurodivergence in Study and Work   168

Chapter 6 Neurodivergent Parents and Older Autistic People   224

Chapter 7 Neurotypicals   266

Chapter 8 Relationships   319

Chapter 9 Counselling and Autism   392

Chapter 10 Contributions   426

Appendix 1   485

Appendix 2   488

Appendix 3   496

Glossary   497

Bibliography   502

Chapter 1
Neurodivergence/Autism/Autism Spectrum Condition (ASC)/Autism Spectrum Disorder (ASD)/Asperger's Syndrome (as a subgroup of Autism)

Introduction

The intention of this book is that it is written in lay language, as opposed to academic text. It is a summary of my experiences and understandings, which lead to suggestions and ideas that may be helpful to anyone reading this. It is written as a simple tool for the average person on the street. There are many wonderful academic texts and biographies, should the reader want to continue and broaden their understandings. Also, many books and older works use different names for Autism and this can be confusing, so I will try to clarify this. My clients have often asked to either take *me* home (to live with them) or to write a book that they can take home. Such a book would act as a guide where there is Autism present at home. One client said, "I want what is in your head. Please write down what you know." In essence, this book is what my clients have generally asked for! But the more I wrote and write, the more there is to discuss.

Forgive me for all that I have left out!

I have worked for more than 30 years as a counsellor and for more than 20 years in all presentations of Neurodivergence – this terminology changing variously over the recent years. Human beings are on a spectrum of neurodiversity, being either neurodivergent or neurotypical. Being *neurodivergent* (also called ND) may include a range of about fourteen neurological differences compared to neurotypicals, including Autism, Attention Deficit Hyperactive Disorder (ADHD) and others. I am focusing on Autism mainly, but other neurodivergent traits are sometimes included as they can be apparent together with Autism. Neurotypical simply means not-neurodivergent, and is typical or common to most people on our planet.

There is a great movement, particularly by neurodivergent advocates, calling for the above correct name changes, and there has been much acceptance of these changes moving forward since 2020, as the previous terminology originated in the medical model which focuses on deficits and the need to 'fix'. The heading above shows the several name changes that have occurred (starting with current reference and moving back through the last 20 years). The medical model still continues with the older language and terminology.

Neurodivergent advocates work from a different model, generally known as the Social Model of Disability. This assumes that there is nothing inherently 'wrong' with disabled people nor with neurodivergent people - the opposite to a degree of the Medical Model. It works on the premise that the physical and social environment in non-accommodating to anyone who is not *typical* as is the majority of the worlds' population. It is a model increasingly accepted and growing exponentially in its acceptance, and is changing the way the world accommodates these differences between human beings. The medical model has influenced our social culture probably over hundreds if not thousands of years, and it appears that the Social Model is starting to change that. We regrettably, as a culture, still have a very long way to go though.

When I first started writing this book, we were referring to Asperger's Syndrome, which gradually changed to Autism Level 1, from the medical model. We had Autism Spectrum Disorder (ASD) which was then divided into 'low functioning' and 'high functioning'. That too, understandably, became offensive and the change was made to Autism Spectrum Condition (ASC), which was presented as having three different levels. There is currently much ongoing advocacy around this too, as this particular terminology is mainly from the medical model. Moving away from the medical model, we no longer talk about people 'with autism', as it is not an illness. The correct language is 'autistic person' or 'neurodivergent person'.

In this book, instead of Autistic Spectrum Person, I have shortened it fondly to "Aspie", with utmost respect intended, and huge fondness to my clients, colleagues and associates who even now, commonly use that terminology.

Now... this book usually refers to 'Aspies', 'Autism', 'ASD' and sometimes 'Asperger Syndrome' – because that was considered the main terminology still current up to about 2020 when I had already finished writing it. In my small community in New Zealand – we spoke *then* of 'Aspies' in a very fond way, and in an attempt to move away from all the confusing and offensive language and associations. 'Aspie" for me refers to Autistic Spectrum Person with an ending for easy speech (ASP or AS doesn't work for me when speaking aloud as these two words could have other confusing meanings!) Forgive me and please enjoy our genuine fondness of neurodivergent people when I use the words Aspie, Aspergers and ASD, with no offence in any way intended throughout the book. It was correct usage at the time of writing.

Most of what I want to achieve with this book, is to create a sound overall picture of what autism and/or neurodivergence – as well as being neurotypical – is, to those who are trying to understand. May this understanding bring harmony and community, in which we enjoy the strengths and difference we all bring to society.

History of Autism

Before the middle of the last century, there was little work or knowledge on Autism and even less on Aspergers – in fact, the terminology was not even used. Going back a bit further, the first academic and serious exploration of childhood disorders was undertaken in the 1850s and onwards. Dr John Langdon Down (from whom we get the name for the disorder known as Down syndrome) was interested in childhood disorders known as *idiocy* at the time. It seems all children's disorders were lumped together under this one classification. Most children labelled as such, or with a similar description of so-called *mental retardation,* were dispatched to institutions, where most did not survive – so there are few historical references to any childhood issues or abnormalities of this nature. I would suspect because autistic children are usually unable to explain or display that they are ill (amongst other things) – as much as non-autistic children are able to – that these children subsequently had a poor survival rate. Anyway, historically, it seems that mostly these ASD children seemed, in hindsight, to die in care and never reached maturity for several reasons. There are a few references to those who were wealthy enough to afford a caregiver and had the child, and later adult, locked away and hidden. It was very much a family secret, a hidden, shameful thing to have a child with any of these disorders. Those who functioned in society, in whichever way that looked and worked, simply must have got on with surviving.

The few that are more noted were referred to as *idiot savants*. In 1783, Gnothi Sauton described the first known scientific observation of a savant. Later, in an unrelated article on another continent, in 1789, a Dr Rush referred to man with savant capabilities yet did not seem to function socially in any appropriate recognised manner. In 1869, Mark Twain wrote an article about *Blind Tom* (a music savant but who was unable to care for himself in the most basic way), whom today we would clearly recognise as autistic. In 1887, Dr John Langdon Down described autistic children but under the current medical diagnosis of the time (usually referred to as *idiocy* or in some cases, *childhood schizophrenia*).

Two post-war Austrians in the 1940s, on different sides of the planet and who did not know each other, simultaneously and unbeknownst to each other, became aware of what we now broadly call Autism Spectrum Disorders. Dr Leo Kanner, living in America, wrote a paper in 1943, *Autistic Disturbances of Affective Contact*, after five years of observing eleven children with distinct autistic traits, which at the time were separate to any known conditions. Dr Kanner is considered to be one of the first child psychiatrists in America.

In 1944, Dr Hans Asperger in Vienna published a paper which, in translation, was titled *Autistic Psychopathy*. Dr Asperger was also a paediatrician and had observed these behaviours in his patients. Interestingly enough, Dr Asperger's work was influenced – it is understood – by the work of a Russian child psychiatrist, Dr Grunya Sukhareva, who 20 years earlier (in 1925) had published a paper on autistic behaviour – first in Russian and a year later in German.

For the next twenty or so years after the work of Dr Kanner, autism was considered to be a form of *childhood schizophrenia*. The cause of this supposed childhood schizophrenia was directly attributed to what was referred to as *cold* or more commonly, *refrigerator* mothers, who were accused of being emotionally non-invested in their children.

A significant work was produced in 1964 by psychologist Dr Bernard Rimland, called *Infantile Autism: The Syndrome and Its Implication for a Neural Theory of Behavior*. By this time, his own autistic son was about eight years old. He challenged the current medical thinking. It radically changed the thinking of the time, moving away from the false accusations of emotionally cold, distant and dissociated mothers to a more neurological developmental model, which completely debunked the schizophrenia link. Dr Rimland spent more than 40 years working and specialising in the field of developmental disorders, and he coined the term *Kanner's Disorder* or *Kanner Syndrome*, for the more debilitating, low-functioning end of the autistic disorders.

Because Dr Asperger's papers were all in German, his work was not discovered until the 1980s and was then explored in the significant work of Dr Lorna Wing. Lorna Wing was herself a psychiatrist, and apparently after her own daughter was born with autism, she specialised in child psychiatry while making the field of autism and Asperger syndrome her specialist areas. It was also her work that gave the name of Dr Asperger to the separate condition – that seemed part of autism – and hence Asperger syndrome was born as a separate entity to autism.

Since then, a significant amount of research has been undertaken and some leading names in this field currently include Professor Tony Attwood, Professor Simon Baron-Cohen, Dr Leanne Holliday Willey and Dr Temple Grandin – among many significant others who continue the research.

In recent years, it has been mistakenly alleged that Dr Asperger was part of a senior medical team in Hitler's Nazi regime and that he signed the death warrant of a significant number of children whom he considered unfit for the Aryan political model. These children, who had a wide range of disabilities, were all put to death, and some, cruelly, were used for human experimentation. Dr Asperger *saved* the ones that he perceived as highly intelligent and who became subjects of his study and observation – and these would all be diagnosed as *Asperger Syndrome* or today would be on the *Autism Spectrum Disorder*.

This new discovery of the history of Dr Asperger rocked the academic world in the field, many of whom no longer wanted that name associated with children today. For lack of agreement as to better terminology, most academics seem to have resigned themselves to now talking about being *on the spectrum* of Autism.

What is Autism and Aspergers?

The term *Autism* was first coined in the 1940s. Since then, it has come to be realised that autism is a spectrum which ranges from lower end, almost non-functioning, to what is now known as high-functioning autism. The *functioning* part basically refers to how capable a person is at looking after themselves and how closely they can live or simulate being in our neurotypical society. *Low functioning* implies that the person will usually need to be cared for by another adult, whereas *high functioning* means that the person is fully capable of living independently as an adult and functions *normally* to a large degree in society and daily life.

Psychiatric diagnosis is dependent on the current DSM. DSM stands for the Diagnostic and Statistical Manual of Mental Disorders. These are updated every few years and reprinted under a numbered and sub-lettered system. The latest edition is known as the DSM-5. Psychologists use a number of diagnostic tools, one of which includes the DSM-5.

The diagnosis of Asperger's Syndrome was first published in the DSM-IV in 1994 by the American Psychiatric Association. This was followed by the DSM-IVR and then the DSM-IVT. But by the 2013 edition of the DSM-V, Asperger syndrome as a diagnosis had been completely removed again and the range of autism/Aspergic disorders were all re-classified under ASD – Autism Spectrum Disorder. Not all professionals and academics – especially non-psychiatrists – agree with this. There is still argument whether Aspergers is part of autism or not and its prevalence. Despite the fact that *Aspergers* no longer exists as a formal diagnosis in the psychiatric diagnostic manual of the DSM-V, most academics and professional people working in this field hold on to the term, and at the time of writing, there is still huge international academic contention on the subject.

Clinical psychologists use a variety of diagnostic tools to diagnose ASD, and they also refer the DSM-V as one of the relevant guides to look to.

Another tool that is used is the WHO ICD-10. This stands for the World Health Organisation International Classification of Disease, and they are currently on the 10th upgrade. In this ICD-10, Aspergers is described as being a subset of autism and in itself is not recognised. Asperger Syndrome is described in this manual as *nosological*, which simply means that it has no classification.

My Terminology for the Purposes of the Book

I generally refer to Asperger Syndrome, although when I am being more broad and inclusive of more High Functioning Autistic traits, I will refer to Autism Spectrum Disorder (AS or ASD). I sometimes just use the first word on its own, as in Aspergers.

I mainly use the internet appellation of *Aspie*, which is still commonly used and especially so in non-professional circles. For me Aspie is a shortening of Autistic Spectrum Person – and ASPie looks wrong to me!

I mostly refer to neurotypicals as neurotypicals throughout the book, although there are lots of variations and shortenings for this too.

When writing to overseas colleagues, I have sometimes been fiercely corrected with an insistence that I use their terminology in only one absolutely correct but their way over time has also since changed. I try to respect them when they have pointed out their concern and simply use their terminology for the sake of keeping the peace when dealing with them.

Some people add an apostrophe and say Asperger's syndrome (which is probably grammatically more correct).

So even in the naming of the syndrome, its presence and later removal, there is not a cohesively single correct way in which this is labelled – but there remains a broad consensus amongst academics.

My own choice of words are the ones that I commonly use and how we speak locally. It is used with respect and with no intention of causing any offence anywhere in the world!

Diagnosis Key Terms and Background

A cold does not have a single symptom, yet a cluster of symptoms together can indicate a cold. Add some further variations into the cluster, and flu may be diagnosed instead of a cold. Aspergers does not have one defining trait. It has a large cluster of traits that operate together and the formation of the clusters can vary widely.

In general, ASD is a *developmental disorder* – this means that a child is thought to be born with the condition, which remains or is apparent through most of the developmental stages as the child is growing. A developmental condition is one that appears in childhood (usually early childhood) while the child is obviously developing over the years into their adult state. Some development conditions can disappear by adulthood, but ASD seems to remain throughout life, with different periods developmentally of it being more noticeable.

Tony Attwood has mentioned that some people who have been diagnosed on the spectrum and who have had significant support appear to lose the traits in adulthood. I wonder whether:

- Some people have been closely trained to appear neurotypical to fit in better but retain their thinking style.
- Some people have become very good at masking their difference.
- There are no elderly adults diagnosed in childhood so we cannot make any comparative assumptions or statements.
- In the light of the statement above, some academics have said that as people on the spectrum get older, that some of their traits of childhood come to the forefront strongly again.

Autism is a condition that *affects communication and effective social interaction*. Language can often be delayed and may not develop fully even by adulthood. Then again, other children speak early and often in full sentences and would therefore be considered more *high functioning*. Social skills are poor for most of those with ASD, with varying degrees of difficulty and success.

They *often have obsessive interests and they may often have repetitive, obsessive behaviours* that are unusual and distinctly noticeable in a social situation. People who are described as fully autistic and low functioning can generally not live alone as adults and usually need some level of care – especially if they are considered severely *low functioning*. On the other hand, being *high functioning* with autism, means that the person can generally function in a neurotypical world. *High functioning* is also a limiting qualification to some degree because many people may be *high functioning* but may have social difficulties and inadequacies.

Asperger syndrome is less obvious developmentally and even experts can miss the symptoms. I think it was Professor Tony Attwood (considered internationally as an expert in this field) who did not recognise that his son was on the spectrum until this own son was about 34 or 35 years old! And I believe that it was his adult daughter, a kindergarten teacher, who pointed out her brother's diagnosis to their father!

In Asperger syndrome, language can be normal, early and fluent, or late but in full sentences. Asperger syndrome is more noticeable as the child gets older. The main observable traits manifesting as social difficulties within groups and in relating to and understanding others. Females are even more likely to slip through the proverbial diagnostic nets because it seems that they are able to mask their social symptoms from an early age.

Asperger syndrome is also not usually distinctly noticeable until the child is getting older and the noticeability is often in varying social situations – in which the child shows a difficulty in coping socially and misses social cues and social contexts. Other clues are a child's sensitivities to aspects of the world around them (or over-sensitivities) or some obsessive repetitive rituals and interests. Often it is difficult in the early stages for an observant parent to even begin to identify the problem – it is initially often just a vague social discomfort that they are aware of around their child and some unusual but mild idiosyncrasies in their child.

Another key trait is the *obsession on at least one particular area of interest*, such as trucks or insects for example – an exception being that some people never find, until quite late in life, their area of interest, for example, an interest in genealogy or growing magnolias. Obsessions can be enduring, meaning that they continue through a lot of their growing years and life, while others can occasionally change. An obsession lasts a long time and is not a childish momentary fad. Dr Lianne Holliday Willey writes of her father being on the spectrum. In his declining aging years, he had a carer. If he became distressed in any way, including by his carer, he would revert back to his obsession of trains, by focussing on his train memorabilia or talking rapidly about some area relative to this interest.

Thereafter, one will often notice *sensitivities*: usually a hypersensitivity to sound, textures, light, tastes, movement, and sensory – all of which vary in intensity and make it difficult for a parent to specifically notice unless their child is particularly reactive. In adults, these sensitivities are fully formed and noticeable, and the Aspergic person will take deliberate measures to avoid whatever they are sensitive to or learn to manage it. This is extremely stressful and exhausting. Forced to endure whatever they are sensitive to as adults, it can be the cause of enormous distress. Not all Aspies, however, have sensory issues. Some may have only one; others may have multiple sensory issues.

Thereafter, all the various authorities differ only in semantics: trying to define in varying terminology a more specific diagnosis. Perhaps the reader can see now why it is so difficult to diagnose.

Another closely related diagnosis for people, especially children on the spectrum, is Pervasive Developmental Disorder and sometimes PDD-NOS (Pervasive Developmental Disorder – Not Otherwise Specified). These diagnosis, with the additional one of Rett syndrome, are now all lumped together under the diagnostic title of Autism Spectrum Disorder.

Asperger syndrome is sometimes also referred to as Mild Autism, or alternatively, High Functioning Autism. In the latest DSM-V, Asperger syndrome itself has been withdrawn, and as a diagnosis specifically in the field of psychiatry, no longer exists – but not in the field of psychology, it seems.

So you can see that if professionals quite often have difficulty with all the varying terminology and recognising the patterns of Aspergers, why lay people (non-professionals) have so much difficulty understanding the condition, recognising the condition and struggling to get the right kind of help.

It is also very important then, when seeking a diagnosis, to be sure that the professional is a relevant expert in the area. I have worked with many psychologists and psychiatrists who, despite their best intentions, have missed this diagnosis because it is not their speciality area. I once saw a clip on YouTube, in which a mother described struggling for three years to get a diagnosis for her daughter. She went from one specialist to another, until she met a new one who was able to diagnose the daughter in ten minutes – the daughter's symptoms were that obvious to this particular professional because of specialised experience and knowledge!

My Very Simplified List of What Is Autism, including what was Asperger Syndrome, ASD. ASC or HFA

- <u>Development disorder</u>
  - It appears in early childhood
  - It seems to stay for life but becomes milder or better managed as insight develops
  - Girls are more socially aware, so symptoms are more masked
  - Girls are better at mimicking appropriate social behaviour
  - The babies are either *very good*, or extremely fractious and easily upset by their various sensitivities
  - Often have digestive issues

- <u>Social disorder</u> (it is actually known primarily as a social development disorder)
  - Do not seem to seek company of people
  - Often long for a good friend but do not know how to go about achieving that
  - Prefer objects or animals
  - Poor eye contact
  - Poor at responding socially
  - Struggle with chit-chat or small talk
  - Poor at reading others' body language or tone of voice
  - Poor at reading social cues
  - Don't get conversational or communication sub-scripts
  - Seem to not recognise social hierarchies
  - Not self-aware of how they use social space (proprioception issues)
  - Interrupt conversations
  - Difficulty functioning in a group
  - Such as taking turns to speak
  - Having group discussions

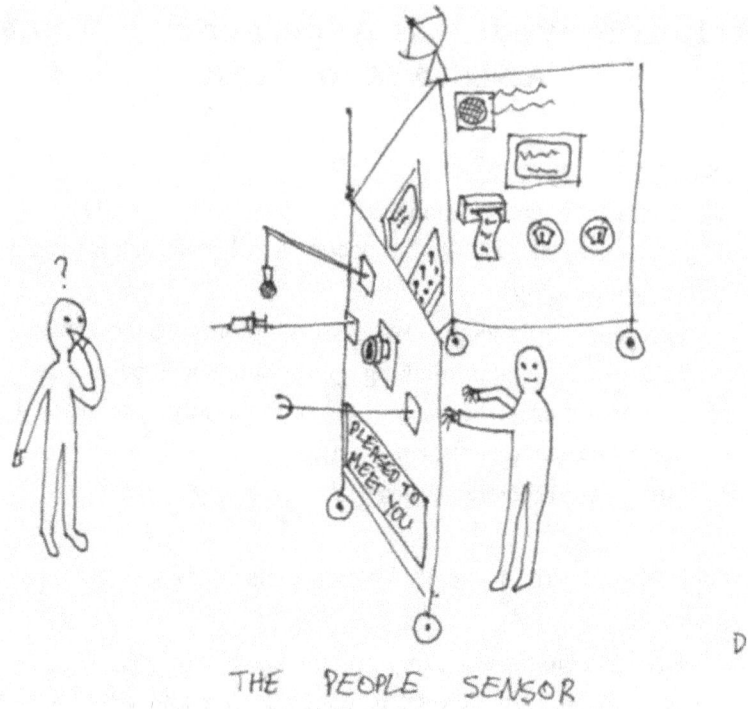

THE PEOPLE SENSOR

- They may be part of a small social group when they are younger, but as they mature, they seem to be increasingly isolated or look for one-on-one situations (except for the rare extroverts)
- They need more time alone than neurotypicals
- They have difficulty expressing empathy appropriately
- They have difficulty *reading* another person and seeing where another person is coming from in the conversational give-and-take – especially around recognising the perceptions, emotions, reactions, intentions and beliefs that the other may have.

For this, Tony Attwood uses the term lack of theory of mind. It is an old term that comes from studies around cognitive development by Piaget but is later first fully coined in a 1978 study of apes and chimpanzees, in terms of reflecting on how they socialise. Similarly, Simon Baron-Cohen refers to mind-blindness in a similar way. Both in the context of ASD, refers to the difficulty that people on the spectrum have in reading the emotions and intentions of others and responding appropriately or empathetically.

Most children are born with mirror-neuro systems in the brain. These mirror-cells literally act like mirrors and is the tool by which children often mimic behaviour. For example, we learn to knit or hammer or cook by observing when we are very young. Or we may mimic nursing our doll or pretending to be truck drivers. It is thought that neurologically, these cells are damaged or not fully formed for those on the spectrum – hence they do not learn to mirror social behaviour. The lack of social mirroring may also be due to the lack of eye contact and acute observation more common in the development of neurotypical children.

It appears that neurologically different parts of the brain are activated (often referred to as "light up" from the terminology used in brain scans where an active part of the brain lights up on a screen that monitors the brain). In one study, the same story was read to Aspies and neurotypicals. The story intended to explore the level of Theory of Mind of participants, so that the subjects of the study had to use Theory of Mind to work out what the protagonist of the story was thinking and intending. On the scans, the neurotypicals lit up in the prefrontal cortex, which is the part of the brain that uses insight, reason, and understanding around relationships. In Aspies, a segment of the frontal cortex lit up, which is the part that does problem solving.

- <u>Obsessive Behaviours or Interests</u>
  - Singular focus
    - Very good for study
    - Develop huge facts-base of knowledge
  - Need routine
  - Do not like change
  - Have a narrow interest range (if they are lucky enough to find one)
  - Have very set ways of doing things
  - Easily upset if they cannot access their interest object
  - May repeat certain movements or sound
  - Don't like it when rules are bent, particularly rules about their specialist interest area
  - But will bend rules when being creative and will work laterally
  - Good at problem solving non-social issues
  - Can be extremely creative especially around their area of interest

- Heightened Sensitivities
    - To sound, visuals, touch, smells, tastes and textures.
        - Includes seams and labels of clothing
        - Food colours and textures
        - Sprays and deodorants in the air

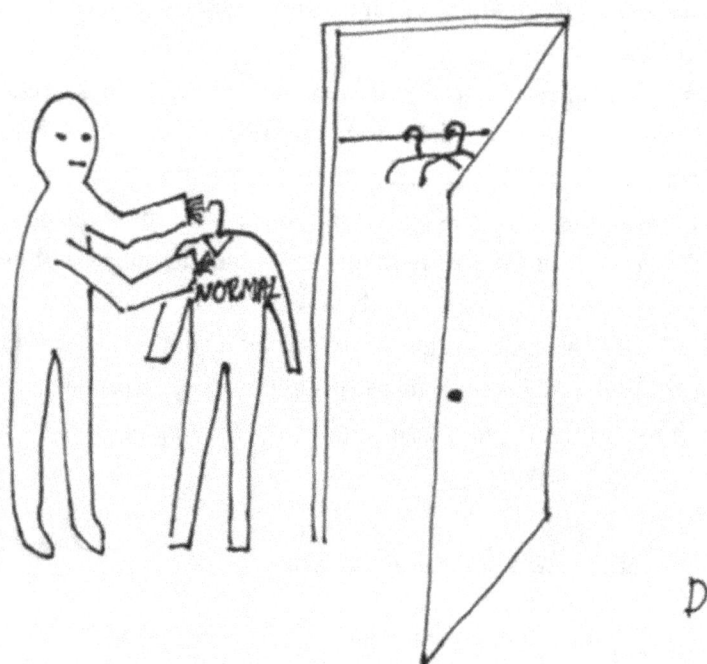

        - Other people chewing
        - Difficulty sleeping if a room is not dark enough
        - As teenagers and later adults, to perceived criticism
        - Develop anxiety due to a lifetime of criticisms

My Additional Observations

- Socially, females generally cope better than males
    - Due to having a more female, and hence, social brain, they can intuitively pick up the rules of social behaviour
    - They mimic social rules to look what they consider to be *normal*. This is often referred to as 'masking' or 'social masking'

- They stress more about social expectations than males as they are aware of social performance expectations
- Often females particularly can have such delicate rules, that they may appear to change on a whim to neurotypicals, so that neurotypicals can become a little wary in relationships.

On the same topic as above, some can, on an apparent whim – although when challenged can distinctly and clearly explain their steps – end a relationship, move to a new house, change jobs, change hobbies and so forth. These are big changes that most neurotypicals would often have processed aloud in social circles. I have noticed that in these circumstances, they (Aspies) will often say that they always wanted to do this but couldn't before this apparent opportunity arose. Considering their narrow range of interests, one would have thought that this would have been expressed. Many neurotypicals are blind-sided by this and are usually left confused and angry, and sometimes distressed. This unusual Aspie behaviour may also be due to mind-blindness, on the assumption that others close to them may know what they are thinking.

- Females appear to often have a spiritual understanding or sixth sense in relation to social performance and expectations
- Both males and females are more likely to be faithful in long-term relationship. Unfaithfulness is not common.

- <u>Socialising</u>
  - Aspies often prefer more alone time than neurotypicals. Some may deliberately isolate for long periods
  - Aspies socialise best through a shared interest
  - Aspies generally prefer one-on-one socialising or at best, small groups
  - Aspies do not generally enjoy crowds and will avoid crowded places where possible
  - I have found that Aspies are usually quiet in most social circumstances unless they are the rare extrovert, or are experts in a field and can hold court as such.

- They appear to not enjoy environments that have uncontrolled or unpredictable elements, such as being jostled in a crowd or unexpected noises
- In social environments, Aspies often only communicate with words whereas neurotypicals may use the whole additional range of communicating skills such as body language, tone of words and subtexts – all of which the Aspie will often miss.
- Because of their (often) lack of facial expression, it is hard to read when one has unintentionally upset them. Although they snap rarely – when they do it seems out of proportion to the issue. This makes people a little wary around them
- They can have multiple personas if need be, one for each different social interaction (this is more of a female invention to cope socially)

> I have seen many variations of the following story.
> One young man I know gave himself different names, and hence different characters for different social situations. He was extremely shy and needed these name-roles to help him cope with different social situations. He used his birth name at school and used a different name when he started working part time in different jobs as he felt that he had to be a different person for each job. When he went to university, he gave himself a university character and a name that he liked, and then went out and acted that person or role out and coped there too. This new character worked very well at university and he quickly had a good social circle around him. As he matured, he was able to integrate these several different ways of being, and went back to using his birth name, but with some excellent social skills learned in the process!

- Cognitive strengths and differences
    - As adults, they are often hard working and focussed and can concentrate well on their work tasks if they have the correct environment and few interruptions. They are also quite determined and will generally complete the work correctly and in time.
    - They can be very objective and analytical
    - They generally do not seek attention, are non-aggrandising and don't look for praise

- They are often intelligent or at least highly knowledgeable on a few subjects
- Often highly intelligent in certain areas, particularly – but not always – the STEM (Science, Technology, Engineering, Maths) subjects. Some academics refer to STEMM subjects, and add Medicine
- There often seem to be *gaps* in their thinking, as if they have missed something (usually a social cue or subscript) but not in their STEM fields
- They are usually very literal
- Sometimes ordinary things have to be explained very clearly and simply, despite that an Aspie often has higher intelligence. This is because there are disruptions in their executive functioning (in their brain) causing overwhelm or thought interruptions.

> One frustrated Aspie mum asked me how I managed my housework, so I had to break down my daily chores and system for her to imitate. She couldn't seem to make a plan or system herself, despite her high intelligence!

- Very detailed and notice details
- Can fixate on topics
- Often take idioms literally

> An example of how literal Aspies can be is as follows, with permission from my dear Aspie friend to use this example. I was selling a piece of land privately and asked my Aspie friend who had worked in advertising to check the wording and layout of the advertisement for me. The land was bordered on the one side by large trees, known as *Mexican Elders*. She went to the website where it was listed, read it through and approved of the wording. She then surprised me by asking if I would miss the elderly neighbours and mused that it must have been hard living next door to them with all the yummy Mexican food smells coming over the fence. She literally thought I had two elderly people who were neighbours on the nearest boundary, who – in her mind – were of Mexican extract (*Mexican Elders*)!

- They are generally quite literal with very concrete thinking. They do not hint, have hidden agendas or have conversational sub-texts.
- Have difficulties with self-identity

- Will often create a persona and act out that persona to cope with a social situation. It is almost as if they are temporarily wearing another borrowed, or acquired, identity for each event
- Great observational skills (except for interpreting social behaviour, and especially so in Aspie males)
- Often have difficulty with abstract concepts unless the abstract concepts have predictable rules (e.g. mathematics, social policies)
- Poor short-term memories
- Excellent long-term memories for facts and details

> One young woman told me that when she was a child, she believed that her mother knew her so intimately that she believed that her mother could see what she was thinking. She said it was only when she was about 16 years old that she realised that her mother could not see what she was thinking. She felt quite alone and bereft after that. It took her many many years to learn that she had to express her relevant thoughts to others.

- Difficulties managing time
- Can regularly be late due to poor time management and awareness
- Alternatively may be rigid with time management
- Both of which annoys neurotypicals!
- Need processing time
- Often have difficulties understanding the give-and-take nature of conversation. Conversation is often a tool that they use minimally until they recognise (through insight or training) that they have an active part to play in social situations.

- There is a need to STIM (self-stimulatory behaviour that soothes or helps processing as they do the repeated behaviour)
- Difficulties with self-identity
- They can be unpredictable and can snap at others quite easily

• Emotional reactions
  - They seem to have much deeper emotions
  - They have difficulty expressing their emotions in words

The Emotion Processing Centre

An explanation of the drawing below, for those who may not get the artist's intentions or meaning, the artist saw her thoughts like mice, scurrying, squeaking, noisy, very active and busy – but especially hard to catch. She hoped that she could train her thoughts to go into a *machine* that would sort, process, order and tidy them up into neat little packages that could be held at the end and would be more easily worked with. (This drawing is not in any way meant to be some sort of cruel statement about processing literal/real mice!)

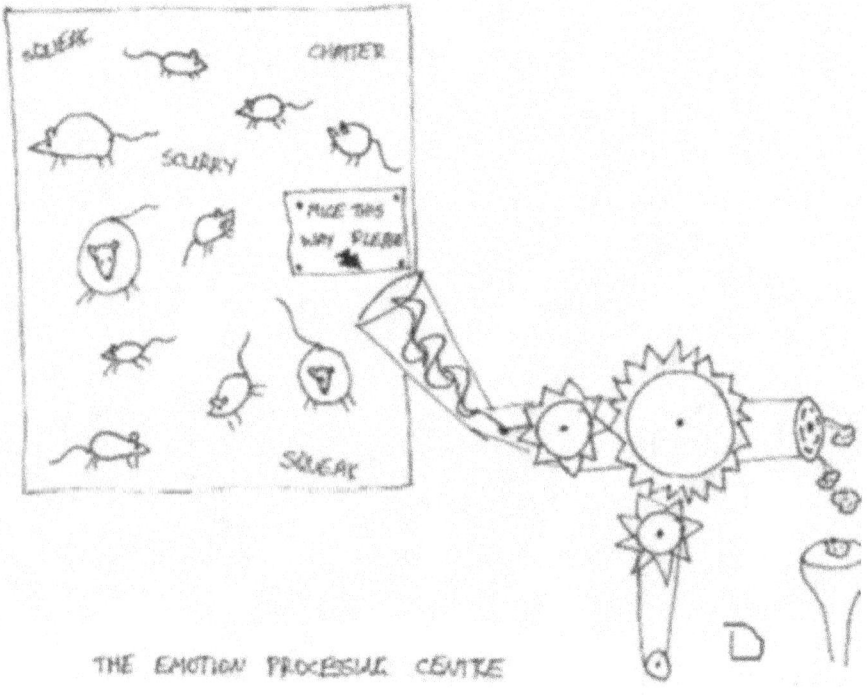

THE EMOTION PROCESSING CENTRE

- Aspies are often described as being emotionally detached, cold and aloof. I believe that this is because they cannot express themselves with facial expressions.
- I have also heard people say that Aspies do not have emotions. This is decidedly untrue!
- To me, it seems that Aspies have greater emotions than neurotypicals. I describe these emotions as being dammed up somehow, with only a straw to release the dam and pressure of emotions.
- Which explains why when they have a breakdown, it appears that a flood of emotions escape
- In a stressful situation, I have found that Aspies often freeze mentally and sometimes physically. The Amygdala (the survivor

freeze/flight/fight centre) according to Temple Grandin is apparently larger than that in neurotypicals. This is in the middle of the emotional centre (the Limbic Centre) in the brain.

- When they freeze and go silent, neurotypicals interpret this as them withdrawing and no longer engaged or responding to them. It causes a vicious emotional and social cycle that leaves both feeling stressed and bewildered.
- I have found female Aspies particularly compassionate about any cruelty experienced by others, especially animal cruelty. I have had Aspie females sob in my office about a cruelty that they had read about, usually in the media. Many are active in organisations to prevent ongoing cruelty and to rescue harmed animals.
- They have difficulty expressing their emotions with facial expressions.
- When their emotions are *opened up*, they are often distraught, and it is difficult to close them down again once they are surfaced.
- When distressed, they seem to be obsessed about that emotion that is causing distress.
- Extreme distress can look like a psychotic episode or breakdown.
- Due to being misunderstood, they are often single, with a few (or many) relationships that have ended.
- If they are overwhelmed by stimuli or by emotions, then:
    - ☐ As children they are prone to tantrums, sometimes excessively
    - ☐ Adults and children may then externalise their distress
    - ☐ They may have impulsive aggressive behaviour
    - ☐ Adults can have major meltdowns

One man I know was extremely anxious about driving for many reasons; others were unpredictable on the road, too many stimuli were occurring simultaneously and he did not feel confident as a driver. When he was pulled over by a police officer for a routine breathalyser test, this man became so distressed at being pulled over and not understanding why he was pulled over that he became aggressive and was nearly arrested, despite being sober!

- Processing and stimming
    - People on the spectrum need time to process their thinking and emotions. This is usually quiet downtime.
    - Often, they need to STIM while doing so. STIM, usually written as a verb as in *to stim* or *stimming*, stands for *self-stimulatory behaviour*. Stimming is a repeated behaviour that seems to me to still the brain, much as what we do in trauma therapy when working with clients who are traumatised. By letting a trauma client stroke a sensory cushion, or even better, a cat or dog if they can tolerate that, it seems to break through the freeze-flight-fight response. In trauma, this stimming helps the client's brain to *stay* in the room and not trigger the amygdala and the stress associated with the aroused amygdala. I believe or intuit that something similar happens to people on the spectrum when they are stimming.
    - Many professionals believe that it a soothing behaviour. This is because the client is observed to be visibly calming down when they stim.
    - I believe that stimming is a healthy dissociation from the present, during which the person who is stimming tries to process and make sense of whatever is happening internally for them.
    - Poor filtering of stimuli
        * Most seem to find filtering stimuli difficult
        * It seems that all stimuli have equal demands for attention
        * Most neurotypicals can prioritise what is important when faced with multiple stimuli. Many can block most stimuli altogether.
        * For those with ASD, the ticking of the clock, passing traffic outside, the movement of a fan, the change of light through flickering blinds, the texture of the seat, the texture of their clothes, all demand as much attention as a conversation.
        * Sudden changes in stimuli can overly startle.

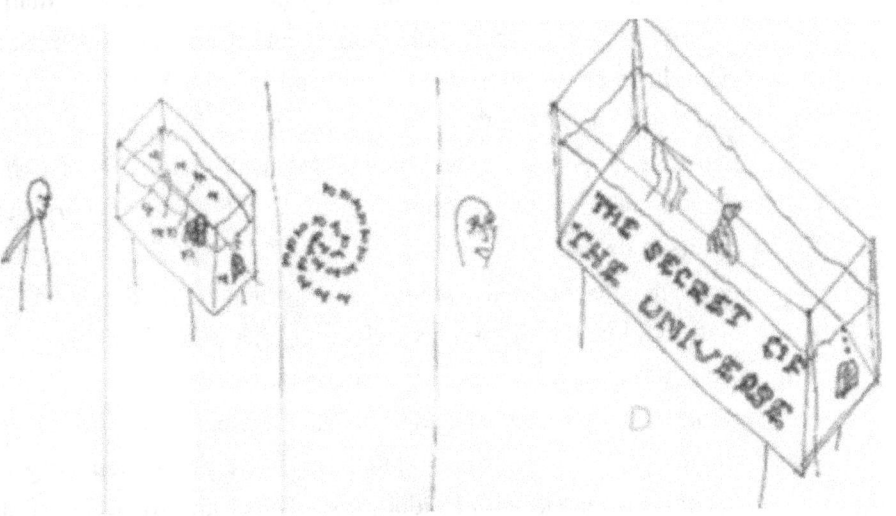

* Many Aspies tell me that they will look at a fish tank, or over some busy activity (for example, they will enjoy looking at a construction site). They tell me they do not physically look at the fish in the tank but at a point far beyond the tank so that the fish appear to swim across their vision, rather than being a central focus. The artist cleverly (in the drawing above) is precisely doing this, and the fish cleverly cooperate and spell out the *answer to the universe* for the artist.
* Given enough time for the situation, I have found clients able to eventually articulate what was happening for them, which they could not do in a stressed state and prior to stimming.
* For those who are stimming, who are ASD, the stimming itself can take many forms. If the ASD or autistic person is *low functioning*, care needs to be taken that they do not injure themselves, for example, in banging their head or tearing at their skin – sometimes they may simply run without stopping. Stimming at an Aspergers level of HFA (High Functioning Autism or Aspergers) can be more calm and may involve a leg being jiggled, finger and thumb rubbing, moving the hand regularly along the fabric of their sleeve or trousers, playing with an object such as a Lego toy or clicking a pen, when not too distressed. Some people like to hide in a dark room, cupboard or under a stairwell, while some like to roll themselves up and cocoon in a duvet. I know a brilliant intellectual

Aspie who at times of severe need to stim, pulls on an adult diaper – with no other behaviours that would lead one to consider infantilism or variations thereof. The need at those rare times is to feel tightly held. Another Aspie stimmed by getting a fresh roll of soft toilet paper, and slowly and methodically tearing it, stacking it or shredding it. Stimming, regardless of its many purposes, seems to definitely be a comfort.

* Some people stim daily, or after a stressful event, or to prepare for a stressful event. Some may only stim once a week. Others may only stim once a month after an accumulation of stress.

* Some develop a public and a private stim, which differs widely. In this case, the public stim is temporary. The public stim may be listening to music with headphones to block the sound of others eating. The private stim may take the form of going into their own private space and rocking either on a chair, or simply sitting on their bed. As adults, many learn stims like reading, watching old movies, sifting through their marble collection, letting some sand trickle through their fingers or playing online games. Stimming is completely different to having a hobby, but sometimes they can overlap.

* Many adult Aspies can be taught to stim by doing mindfulness exercises or yoga. Some can be encouraged to do adult colouring in pictures. Some may get lost in a favourite hobby. I know some who do artwork at these times, with fine details. Another lady on the spectrum that I know may watch an eight series detective DVD over and over again. In fact, many Aspies like to watch a DVD or movie in which they know practically every word and have watched many times before, because it is safe and predictable and deeply familiar. To me, they are actually not watching it but seem to be focussing and then processing at a point well beyond the moving screen pictures.

Other Observations

- They are at higher risk of being:
  - Bullied, mocked or taunted on a regular basis (usually by neurotypicals)
  - Sexually abused
  - Financially hoodwinked
  - Cheated of their rights
  - Victimised
  - Lonely
  - Deeply misunderstood

  (All possibly because they miss social warning cues)

- Parenting issues:
  - Less likely to move far away from parents
  - Less bonded emotionally to children but may be obsessively attached
  - Males are sometimes poorly attached to their offspring, and may have low emotional connections with their children.

- There is a higher incidence of
  - Sexual identity issues
  - Anxiety
  - A minimal sense of personal identity
  - Crisis of identity

THE MIRROR

- Not reaching social milestones such as
    - Getting a driver's licence
    - Holding down paid employment on a regular basis
    - Late in developing relationships

- Cognitive rigidity
    - Despite intelligence, can be inflexible at times
    - Want things done repeatedly the same way
    - Rigid around change
    - Poor short-term memory
    - Become anxious around unexpected change
    - Become anxious around change even if warned
    - Need prior warnings of change in routine or different people
    - Need to be prepared for moving to a new house, moving school
    - Rigid beliefs at times that they adhere to regardless

- Can't quickly change from subject to subject. It is understood that when neurotypicals have a conversation, at least 13 parts of the frontal cortex (the *hard-drive* in the brain) are working simultaneously and are all connected. These connections seem to work in series, so that if one doesn't work, the others cannot work or work ineffectively. It is thought that Aspies have these parts of the brain not at all functioning; hence, they often miss the backstory and the interpretation of many communications. It appears to be one of the reasons that Aspies sometimes miss the punch lines in jokes.

> On their way to a wedding, an elderly Aspie man was driving a vehicle in which there were two passengers. They were driving on a busy main road in a city. They had just entered a five-exit traffic circle, when the sirens of a racing police car behind them were coincidently at this time, switched on. This elderly man braked hard and stopped dead still in the traffic, nearly causing a major accident! His rules for five-exit traffic circles and give-way to a police vehicle when demanded clashed, and he could not proceed normally!

- Aspies often have difficulty processing two separate bits of information at once, especially if they are complex emotional ones.
- Aspies are quite often very distractible and have difficulty focussing and concentrating on one thing at a time, very similar to the pattern found in ADHD (Attention Deficit Hyperactive Disorder). Lorna Wing, in the early 1990s, came up with a theory around the Reticular Formation of the brain. The Reticular Formation is near the top of the brainstem, not far from the Amygdala (the fight-or-flight system) and runs down the back of the brainstem for about 4–5cm. If this were a fibre-optic cable, then it would be an extremely dense and highly complex filtering system. If the filter does not work efficiently, then distractions would not be able to be filtered out and hence the difficulty in concentrating and focussing when Aspies face a lot of stimuli simultaneously. She did a lot of work in this area, and some of her therapies appeared to have made positive differences in this regard.

They are more likely to experience

Misophonia
Repeated noise (like chewing) causes anger and affects the ability to think
Synaesthesia
Sounds can make a visual pattern, or tastes can be visual
Misokinesia
Repeated movements like a flapping flag is distressing
Dyspraxia
Difficulty when coordinating movement and coordination
Prosopagnosia
Face blindness: an inability to recognise other people by their faces
Dyslexia
Difficulty with words, symbols and letters despite normal intelligence
Eating disorders
Anorexia, bulimia, difficulty with certain foods or food textures
Selective mutism
Mainly in childhood
Anxiety
Depression
Gender issues
Obsessive Compulsive Disorder (OCD)
Digestive and Gut issues
Tourette's syndrome

Diagnostic Difficulties

One of the biggest issues about Asperger syndrome (or as now known as ASD) is the difficulty in recognising it and diagnosing it – as described before. Most teachers, counsellors, doctors, psychiatrists and often psychologists do not recognise it – especially initially – unless they have undertaken specialist interest in the field or have had someone in the family who was on the spectrum. Because Aspergers is a social development disorder, it is of course not too noticeable in the early stages of life, until social situations are then increasingly occurring.

Because those with ASD are more factual neurologically, they seem to not learn social behaviour like neurotypicals (by almost a process of osmosis) do. Instead, they seem to learn social behaviour as a series of rules. The rules then become quite dictatorial (as can the Aspie be, especially as a child!), but the principle of *should* appears to dominate in their thinking. This rule making is eventually extremely stressful as it is a means of controlling unsafe situations and acts as a social and personal driver – but eventually, it becomes a force of its own.

After a period of consistent time, the little traits start becoming apparent. Some ASD people completely withdraw socially and emotionally. Some may become selectively mute due to stress. Because girls are so very good at masking and hiding their Aspie traits through mimicking social behaviour, they often and realistically, usually slip under the radar but often have extreme difficulty coping and suffer high internal anxiety, which is unknown and unseen, except by themselves. Being social – which means anywhere where there are people around – becomes a constant strain and source of anxiety. Also, because those on the spectrum seldom show facial expression, others assume that all is well but when the Aspergic person no longer copes and is completely taken by surprise as the proverbial wheels comes off for them. Others who may live with them fail to comprehend a subsequent meltdown in any way. So the distressed Aspie is then often treated in a derogatory, disdainful, minimising way by others, who then make comments about their mental state – and another vicious social cycle ensues.

There are also problems with diagnostic tools on the whole. So far, there is no agreed diagnostic tool for females and even the ones used for males have their limits when used for testing females as well. It is very helpful to have a third party (for example a mother, an adult sibling or a spouse) available who knows the person being tested very well. The interaction of the client, the third party and the assessor is also critical to this process!

Furthermore, there seems to be insufficient consensus as to what Asperger Syndrome actually is or which *test* is the most accurate – such a *Gillberg and Gillberg*, amongst others. Tony Attwood has mentioned that he prefers the *Gillberg and Gillberg* diagnostic tool – inferring that it is clearly and simply laid out. There are also a few free online tests, one of which is the EQ (Empathy Quotient) test put together based on his research, by Simon Baron-Cohen.

Another important factor often overlooked in diagnosis is that the teenage and adult clients with Asperger syndrome have often developed co-morbidities. In simple English, that means that they have developed other problems, often mental health ones, indirectly, because of their Aspergers. This group of people commonly can become depressed or extremely anxious, while some develop addictions and eating disorders, usually due to no longer coping. These are just a few examples. When one is dealing with an alcoholic *for example*, it is difficult to see past that to the underlying possibility that Asperger syndrome could also be lying underneath, cleverly concealed and hidden under all the other symptoms.

We need to change the way we work when dealing with somebody on the spectrum. We need to change the way we are doing schools and education (and this can be done at no great cost). We need to change the way we are doing human resources. We need to utilise all people's skills in a healthy way that works for both the person employed and the employer. We need to stop expecting such a large portion of our society to only conform to our neurotypical world – we need to adjust around others who have spent a lifetime adjusting around us.

Further Background Comments

I particularly like the work of Professor Simon Baron-Cohen. He did a lot of specialising in Asperger syndrome and/or Autism Spectrum Disorder and significant work on the differences between the male and female brain. He made an interesting statement some years ago in that he referred to the neurological wiring in ASD as being like a *double male brain*.

Research indicates that the male and female brain operates quite differently at times and that up to 83% [this statistic varies up to 87%, depending which author one reads] of males think and act like males – and similarly for females. Different centres in the brain dominate differently between the genders or are interconnected with different systems.

In males, it is far easier to recognise Aspergers as operating typically in a *double male brain way*. ASD males appear more literal, less emotionally connected, more analytically wordy, more rigid both mentally and physically, more fixated on rules and I find them more dyspraxic than the average male.

Unfortunately, we cannot relate the same pattern to females and the female brain. It is not so clear. Women often have a level of intuition and many Aspergic women often have an innate highly developed *sixth sense* and can often be quite spiritually inclined. If you combine this female Aspergic intuitiveness with a male brain, you get a very different kind of thinking. For predominantly this reason, amongst others, many females are not easily picked up as having ASD. They can intuit when something relationally is not right but often cannot identify what that *something* is. Also, by observation, they are often great social mimics and can mimic their way through a situation so that they look like neurotypical females – something that a male on the Aspergic spectrum cannot replicate in a male world.

The majority of Aspergers or ASD definitions that have been written are often done in psycho-speak – that language of the academics, which is truly fine for academics but hard for the ordinary person on the street to grasp. Some typical examples that would be difficult for non-academic people to understand follow:

- Tony Attwood has a description in concise academia in which he talks of lack of theory of mind and refers to Asperger syndrome as a social development disorder.
- Temple Grandin talks about her research specifically neurologically and refers to the different wiring in the brain (known as *neurology*).
- Simon Baron-Cohen talks about a double male brain and mind-blindness.
- The latest DSM-V has a complex diagnostic set of tools designed with relevant variables along six axis, ignores Asperger syndrome altogether as a separate entity but includes its symptoms within its diagnosis known as High Functioning Autism, which is often referred to as HFA.
- The WHO ICD-10 speaks of Asperger syndrome as *nosological*.

These are all very learned people (whom I think are pretty wonderful for their work) who have researched and have been passionate and hard working in this field, but it can be difficult to understand, especially if you are looking for help and are not particularly academic.

Misdiagnosed Clients

Let's get something clear! Most professionals are wonderful in their jobs. When someone is behaving psychotic and is suicidal, or at risk in anyway and is presented for treatment – especially at an Accident and Emergency wing of a hospital – there is no place for a rational conversation or the time to explore the possibility of Asperger syndrome. Furthermore, just as a cardiologist cannot easily and immediately tell the difference between an extreme panic attack and a heart attack, it is very difficult to recognise an Aspergic overload meltdown from a psychotic episode – especially in an emergency room or in a medical emergency ward at a hospital. Fortunately, most of the misdiagnosis does not happen in an emergency ward.

Over the years, I have worked with that many Aspergic clients (mostly female!) that have been misdiagnosed and have been given mental health conditions that are incorrect. I no longer am able to remember or count how many there have been. Sometimes the client has only one symptom for the mental health diagnosis that they have been given! Unfortunately, this often-incorrect diagnosis creates a mental health record for the ASD client, which can subsequently prevent them from possibly entering certain professions, and they often end up on some very strong medications (including anti-psychotic medications) which, in my humble opinion, are not required long term for Aspergers or ASD! This even more so when there are no comorbid mental health diagnosis.

Many Aspie women have been diagnosed as ADHD (Attention Deficit Hyperactive Disorder), ADD (Attention Deficit Disorder), Bi-Polar or BPD (Borderline Personality Disorder). BPD is more likely to – it seems to me – often be diagnosed after a mental breakdown in which the Aspie may have self-harmed or attempted suicide. When my clients have explored the recognised criteria for their (mis)diagnosis, they are often aghast, as they do not fit the vast majority of the criteria, often only having one symptom!

The males I have worked with have often been heavily sedated and labelled with schizophrenia, Schizoid Affective Disorder and/or dysthymia, when they were clearly and obviously Aspie. The diagnostic labelling happened after emotional breakdowns or suicide attempts. Thereafter, they faced a regime of anti-psychotic medications, which left them almost zombified (for a lack of better expression). One man came off his antipsychotic cocktail of medications over a protracted period and discovered that he had no memory of the thirty years he was medicated and in the mental health system. This took him into a period of deep grieving for his perceived loss of life.

The issue around diagnosing females on the spectrum is well known academically, and most specialists, especially *the big names* in the ASD field, are looking into it.

Whether you are male or female and suspect that a diagnosis is to be made, please ensure that you confirm that *your specialist person is very familiar with ASD* and able to undertake this diagnosis.

Understanding the Human Spectrum, and the Neurodivergent-autistic Spectrum

The human spectrum of people come in a wide variation of shapes, skin colours, hair types, sizes and so forth. And all of them are widely within a *normal* range. It is unusual to see a woman nine foot tall. It is unusual to see someone who weighs 800 kgs. Most people are within a wide range of what is considered normal.

Let's use a metaphor for the spectrum for human beings. On one end of the spectrum, you may find people from Sweden. They generally have blue eyes and are blonde. This is quite typical of many people throughout Scandinavia – in fact, it would be the norm in Scandinavia (excluding immigrants). On the other end of the human spectrum, we could perhaps compare people from Papua New Guinea. These people are extremely dark skinned, have dark eyes, extremely short tight-curly hair, which would be quite coarse in texture. Generally, somebody from Sweden will have fine, soft, blonde hair. Both groups of people have completely different diets. Both groups of people have developed a different culture. Yet if you walk down the street of a cosmopolitan city and saw a Swedish person or somebody from Papua New Guinea, one generally wouldn't blink an eye. Because both groups of people are incredibly normal!

I believe both Aspergers and neurotypical are *normal*, and they are each an important part of the human spectrum (which is obvious, of course!). I have made up my own little theory, which is purely experiential and unscientific but based on my observations over the years. I guess it can be called *anecdotal* observations.

When working with predominantly heterosexual couples in couple therapy over nearly three decades, I have noticed how females often seem to process information but seem to include a significant use of some sort of an emotional filter as well. Men seem more analytical and seem to engage their emotions less as a filter. They seem to bandy words and shift them around, while women respond with emotionally loaded language. I noticed that Aspie women often respond the same way as the men do in therapy. I had long had this musing when I came across Simon Baron-Cohen's assertions regard the male-female brain and ASD, which complimented my thinking.

By then I already had a picture in my head, which I have drawn to illustrate the pattern I seemed to be experiencing in the counselling room. I think the illustration in the diagram above is quite clear.

When looking at the table below, I have given Aspergic traits more prevalence than the general statistics around the world indicate. When researching the international statistics on Asperger syndrome or ASD, there is a large variance. This is mainly because Aspergers itself doesn't exist in the psychiatrist manual anymore. Many adults, especially the elderly, have missed being diagnosed; people have been misdiagnosed; there is no standard definition of low functioning or high functioning ASD (which terminology in itself causes offence), and many do not yet agree exactly what constitutes a diagnosis or which diagnostic tool to use. The only consistent thing in the statistics of Aspergers or ASD is the huge non-agreement.

For autism and ASD, statistics vary from country to country, where some claim a ratio of 1:59 and others 1:167 – but there is no defining how they came to those conclusions and how the autism was diagnosed. There was a health article from Greece that suggested 25% (!) of Greeks had Asperger syndrome, but I have not been able to trace that again. There was another semi-serious – but still tongue-in-cheek article – that I read some time ago which suggested 40% of Scandinavians had traits! A Ministry of Health document last updated April 2017 suggests that the statistics in New Zealand is 1:100 children. These included children already diagnosed and across the whole broad ASD spectrum.

Even more misleading is seeing people with distinct traits but not enough for them to be diagnosed on the spectrum. (Having significant traits but not enough for diagnosis means that people still have social difficulties – many times these apparent traits became apparent in couple counselling. I reviewed my years of counselling and records, removed clients who were diagnosed, removed clients who thought they may be on a spectrum, and I would suggest that the figure is maybe closer to 1:20 or even less (traits) out of what was left. My favourite hairdresser was distinctly on the spectrum, as was the guy who fixed lawnmowers and bicycles, three librarians, people and their children among my friendship circle, children in my children's classes – so I was able to put together quite a long list. *But this armchair-type diagnosing is dangerous, and we will not go there anymore!* As my good friend (a registered clinical psychologist) said, "Everyone is on a spectrum somewhere."

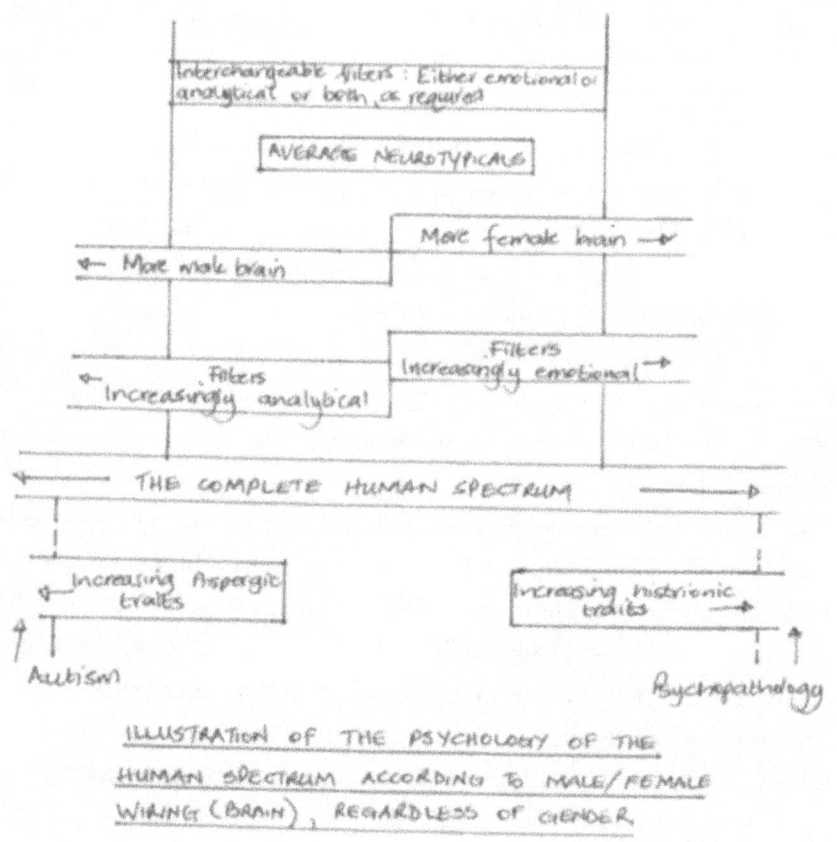

ILLUSTRATION OF THE PSYCHOLOGY OF THE HUMAN SPECTRUM ACCORDING TO MALE/FEMALE WIRING (BRAIN), REGARDLESS OF GENDER.

The Best News Ever

Aspies are super-humans in my opinion. Healthy Aspies are generally highly intelligent, have a great sense of humour, are warm and friendly and fiercely loyal. Once they trust you, they are always glad to see you, without fail. There are no mind games. There is no judgement – just genuine, unconditional regard. They are often objective, so make wonderful sounding boards. They usually always remember important things about you, like your birthday. They keep forgiving you when you don't. They are blunt and direct. When discussing topics, they don't get emotional if you disagree with them. In their field, they are hugely knowledgeable and factual and often very useful to know as they usually remember all the facts and have them readily available!

Chapter 2
Children on the Autism/Neurodivergent Spectrum

If you are reading this chapter out of choice, especially if it is the first chapter that you chose to dip into, then be encouraged – you are already a good parent, teacher or caregiver. Well done! You care and you want to help and are looking for tools.

Please be aware that he and she is used interchangeably in this section.

Mostly, all children flourish when they are nurtured, loved and cared for. Children on the ASD spectrum or who have Asperger syndrome, similarly, in a nurturing nourishing environment flourish and in an unkind or uncaring environment often end up loners or function poorly in most ways but especially so in their social environments.

It is not always easy to diagnose children on the Aspergers (ASD) spectrum. Even professionals who work full-time in the field are often unable to fully, easily and confidently make this diagnosis, and even then, with some caution and difficulty. The main difficulty is due to the many different presentations and variations of Aspergers, that Aspergers is not a single or small group of criteria but is a cluster of behaviours that can be very broad in range, and the child's age and limited ability to communicate with insight into their behaviour, thinking and responses (which of course, is the same for any child and even for many adults).

With the wonderful tool and insights of *retrospect*, it is often easier to diagnose! It was the child who didn't settle easily. It was the child who didn't make much eye contact. It was the child who would not settle if their routine was upset even in some small way. It was the child who spoke early and spoke in good sentences, or it was the child who didn't speak until full sentences were mentally formed before being voiced. It was the very good baby who didn't seem to want for much. It was the irritable baby who fussed and cried his sleepless journey to toddlerhood.

In retrospect, we notice the absence of imaginary play. In retrospect, we notice the general absence of the echolalia phase. In retrospect, we had observed the absence of parallel play at a young age, but at a much later stage, we notice that they prefer to parallel play and don't get involved when similar aged children have moved on to group play. In retrospect, we notice that they were fussy about food textures. In retrospect, we notice they didn't fit in easily in social situations or at play centres and children-focussed activities. In retrospect, we saw that they didn't rush off to play at children's parties and would often hang around cautiously with Mum – or they occupied themselves separately from the partygoers. Of course, there are always exceptions to these observations, which certainly compounds the problem of recognising and diagnosing. These differences are also generally more pronounced in boys, and of course – generally completely missed in extroverted Aspergic girls. Perhaps you can now see why even professionals and specialists in this field are often cautious and confused – and reluctant to make that diagnosis!

It is important to consistently remember that the diagnosis of Aspergers is not due to a single symptom or characteristic. What comes below is common to many children, not only children on the spectrum. As I will say often in this book – a cold is not a symptom – it is a significant cluster of symptoms. It is the same with Aspergers, in which we are looking at, around and for a cluster of symptoms.

I have often noticed that babies suspected to be on the spectrum seem either a little more passive – meaning they appear to be less actively involved in life or expressing their needs or are distressed day and night and are seldom at peace. They don't make much eye contact, if any. If they do make eye contact, they appear indifferent to that person, almost as if that person were as inanimate as every other object in the room. As they begin to move around and get a little older, they may touch objects and become fascinated by some objects (as a toddler their new baby sibling may be carelessly handled as if that too were another object). They may become unusually attached to an object. We certainly know their presence when they are overwhelmed or out of routine or there's too much stress within the family. They then cry and stiffen and are very (very!)

difficult to soothe. At other times, they are the overly good babies, who are quite placid and seemingly undemanding.

They're often not very aware of themselves or their needs, and I have sometimes considered them similar (only in this one regard) to *anorexics* in the sense that they don't seem to be aware of their self or the needs of self – or can't or maybe don't feel they have a right to make demands

> I spoke with one mum who reflected on her child. She had a moment of epiphany that something wasn't quite right one day when she did a small *experiment* with her 14-month-old *different* daughter. The mum wanted to check for Aspergers as she had some suspicions. This child was partly breastfed and at this stage was still refusing most solids. The mum sat in the lounge and put her baby at her feet, surrounding her with various objects and toys. She could crawl but was slow to learn to walk – as if she were simply not interested rather than physically unable to do so. The baby hardly interacted with the toys and just seemed to look around at dust motes and at the light. The mother did not engage at all with the child for six hours. The mother read her book waiting for the child to demand something…the child did not ask for a feed when she was hungry and her stomach was clearly rumbling. The child did not seem to ask for anything. She seemed to only sit there but was placid and externally appeared relaxed and not in any way distressed. Finally, the mother could not bear it any longer and with some tears, lifted her little girl onto her lap and fed her. Other babies would have been bored within about 20 minutes. They would have cried and fussed. They would have wanted their nappy changed. They would have demanded to be fed. This was obviously, the more placid Aspie baby.

One of the things I have often observed within Aspergers is the extreme polarities of behaviour with little middle ground. The children are either obsessed or completely disinterested. They grasp at arithmetic or reading, or completely don't absorb it. They are either talking for hours at you or appear totally shut down.

As young children, they will treat other children and even babies as if they were inanimate objects. They may stick a finger in the other one's eye or touch parts of their body – but it is from sheer curiosity and not maliciously motivated.

A firm explanation not to do certain behaviours is usually sufficient, although it is a good idea to stay on guard as there might have to be several reminders (we are talking about little children!).

Because Aspie children often treat others as objects, it is often difficult for others to bond with them, beginning the huge cycle of isolation for Aspies. As much as anybody else, they want friends and want to belong. They often cannot express their feelings, which makes them *appear* emotionless and unresponsive and socially that makes them less easy to bond with.

> I remember being at the local airport. There were two boys there with their mother, and I knew the whole family. The older boy was about 11 and his brother was nearly 10 years old. The older boy had been diagnosed on the ASD spectrum. The mother was going away for two weeks to another city for a specific career training and her partner was to look after the boys. The younger boy was red-eyed and still weeping, demanding enormous amounts of attention, affection and comfort from his mother. The other boy (the ASD one) was wandering around and appeared fidgety. He was touching things abstractedly and often talking to the other waiting passengers. Because he knew me, he came over and talked to me a lot. By his restlessness and by his speed talking on various subjects, the anxiety in his hand gestures over his chest and his eyes darting everywhere, I could see his telltale signs of distress – so I engaged with him as much as I could (I was seeing my own son off). Yet this boy's expression showed no signs of distress that anyone in the general public could read. It was fairly expressionless – most peaceful – except for the occasional frown or smile as he socially engaged – and even those were few. A few weeks later, when I was able to talk to him again, I asked how distressed he was feeling. With difficulty, he explained his sense of isolation and distress, the feeling that his mother would never come back, the anger that he couldn't find a way to express what his brother was feeling, the sadness that he couldn't get comfort from his mother. His mother, who was in the room and part of our conversation, listened in a state of shock and then felt enormous subsequent guilt. It was a good learning curve for everybody. Lately, I have been hearing him say, "I love you, Mummy," from time to time, and she affirms her affection for him, back to him.

Primary Aged Children Factual Thinking and Lack of Theory of Mind

Their minds are quite factually and reality based, and imagination is very difficult for them. Generally, they prefer facts or non-fiction. They also often have difficulty applying themselves to a topic that does not interest them, yet can deeply research and understand enormous amounts of data from their own research or observations (unlike neurotypical children) or even recall facts that they have been told. It is rare to have a naturally creative Aspie (in a neurotypical way), and if they are creative, it is often in a specific area that has fully caught their attention and become an obsession. For example, they may enjoy playing with words and enjoy creating stories or pictures from them – but it is the sheer joy of words. They like to shuffle words around the way a child may shuffle wooden blocks around. Their creativity is also from a range of lateral thoughts and are often unique. They are often not limited by the more controlled neurotypical rules of creativity.

Random multiple thoughts are running all the time (again – unless it is an obsession), and it is very difficult for them to remain focussed and maintain the thread of a single dominant thought. It is almost impossible and takes a great effort to reign in their thinking and for them to learn to have a semblance of focus (unless they are obsessively focussed).

Turning thought into words is also another difficulty – unless they are particularly language focussed. When I talk to Aspies (children and adults), they often seem able to explain what they are thinking (providing they trust that their listener has the patience to wait through an often-convoluted description) even though they are filtering multiple thoughts at a time. It seems that Aspies – children and adults – are often able to explain their thinking or to answer a question in a patient environment. Yet doing the same process in writing can be very difficult, especially for children. This is often referred to as having problems with executive functioning.

Conversely, once (or if) Aspie children and adults learn the ability to write down their self-expressions and thoughts, they are often able to express themselves better through writing and prefer that form of communicating. I would guess that this is because they only have to deal with the communication and not a person as well.

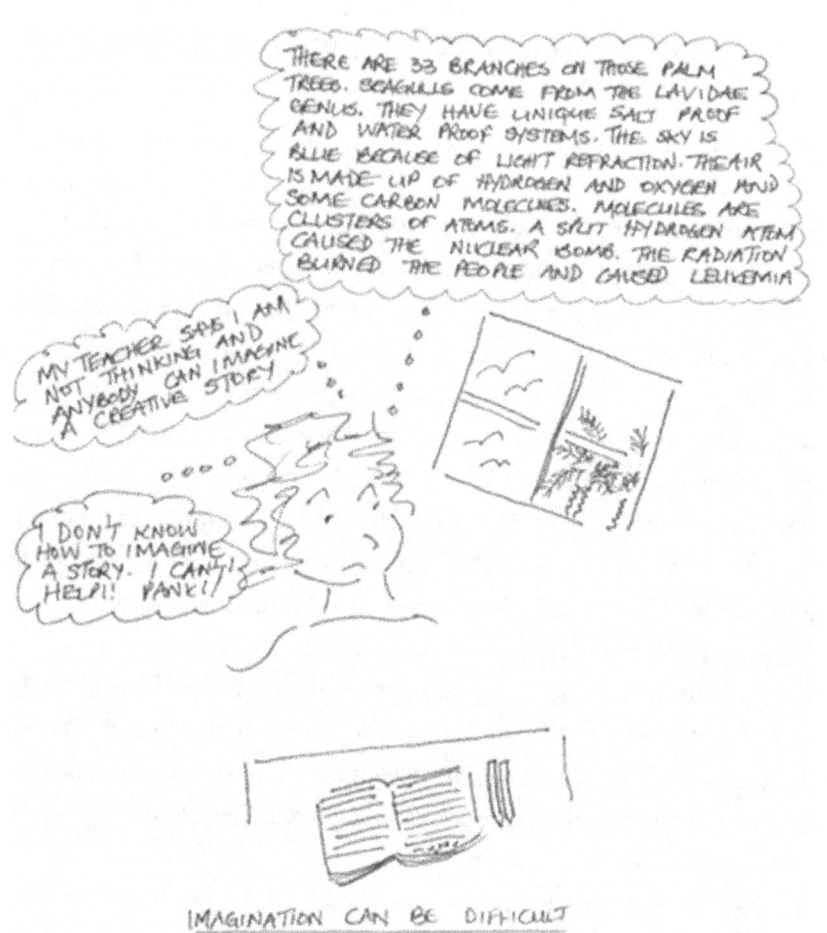

IMAGINATION CAN BE DIFFICULT

But at the moment – we're on the topic of children only! It often seems as though they have many thoughts trapped and they seem to be unable to get them out of the *word-safe* so to speak. It is as if they don't seem to have the password into the *safe* where the words are kept, despite often knowing the words and even generally being able to spell them out when tested.

Neurological links between the brain that does creative thought and converting that into pathways that become writing seems to be delayed and often for some it seems like it never happens – hence the difficulty expressing themselves in writing as children.

Some researchers have theorised that the part of the brain that has thought is not – or is only partly – linked to the part of the brain that expresses thoughts or converts thoughts to marks on paper. This has at times been discussed as a neurological failure rather than a lack of intelligence.

Imaginative play can therefore be quite tricky for these children.

> I observed the following at a day-care.
>
> I remember watching one scene unfold between two little friends who were three-and-a-half and four-and-a-half years old. The younger one appeared to show a few traits on the spectrum, but surprisingly, she seemed to be the dominant friend, who made the decisions about how their play would look. They never played pretend games with dolls for example – the younger one would have none of that! The younger one gave an instruction to gather all the little chairs and stools in the room, which they then carefully lined up. There were about 14 seats in three or four little rows. When all the seats were ready and the younger one was satisfied, the two girls perched primly in the middle two seats of the front row and sat there staring ahead in absolute silence. I eventually had to ask what they were playing. "We are pretending to be mummies in church," the younger one said.

It is not uncommon to find dyslexia in Aspergic children. For some unknown reason (at this stage), it seems that the neurological part of the brain that deals with written words does not seem to connect efficiently. If this is the case, some patient, old-fashioned teaching of phonics and grammar rules is often successful – if it is sustained and maintained over a very long period. You are then teaching a different part of their brain about words and Aspies relate very well to rules. Realistically, rules are often factually based, so it is a common-sense approach, in my thinking, where the child is having difficulty in this way.

Although their thinking is primarily factually based, they seem to be able to play with the facts quite literally and will come up with very unusual thinking. If they are very communicative, they can be quite vocal and ask endless questions. These questions will include: "how do clouds work?", "how do worms know how to find their way out of the ground?", and "who made up the word *poo*?" They might also play with the thought that a lawn could be blue if you painted it. They will play with the thought that you could make a giant sparrow that would be scary, but they won't create stories the way neurotypicals do. Neurotypical fiction often involves emotion, something that is very difficult for even an adult on the spectrum to express.

Something that comes up strongly in diagnosis is the diagnostic criteria formally referred to as *lack of theory of mind*. Basically, this means the inability to perceive another person as having their own thoughts and emotions and that others are self-contained human beings (not moving, emotionless objects). Aspies are often very surprised when people react, especially when the Aspie had no prediction that they would. An Aspie child may state a fact that you have spots on your face – and they are ugly – and are then quite shocked when the person is offended, upset or angry in response.

A lack of theory of mind generally means that there is an inability to apprehend how another may be thinking or feeling. Using an old expression, without theory of mind, we will find it very difficult to proverbially *walk in someone else's shoes*. Theory of mind is the key and core of social interaction for neurotypicals.

Summary

- Factual thinking
- A lateral creativity around facts
- Difficulty around imagination
- Not limited by neurotypical limits
- Difficulty getting thoughts translated on to paper into written words.
- Lack of theory of mind

Overcoming Unique Hurdles

Aspie children have unique hurdles that other children do not have. Aspie children literally may not like a particular colour, and I have heard of a few who were particularly resistant to the colour brown.

I know of one family who had a daughter on the spectrum. They had a long-awaited holiday arrive and off they went in their loaded vehicle to the rented beach house, with much anticipation of pleasure and holiday downtime. When they got there, the house was painted *brown*. The child (aged about twelve at the time) refused to get out of the vehicle and had a full meltdown if they even parked near the house or where it was visible. (I need to add that Aspie children often do not cope with change and holidays are usually difficult anyway). Eventually, after midnight and after several hours of her crying and screaming, they packed up the car and returned home. Her siblings were very angry, and the parents were very disappointed – it was a very glum trip back home.

A further example I have heard about that particular colour follows. A loathing of a colour; in this instance, it is brown again, means every area of their life may be affected, including what they wear or even eat. It means they won't eat brown food – for example, toast, meat, barbeques or pizza.

> One child with distinct Aspie traits only ate white food – as in white bread, white pies (crust only not the filling), white chicken breast – and especially not *brown* or any other colour for that matter (e.g. blue, red, green or yellow). He would not eat meat but would eventually tolerate carrots as his only coloured food. Strangely and selectively, the rest of his diet was chocolate, including all colours of Smarties and fried, orange, puffed crisps.

(At this point, most neurotypical adult readers are cynically critical of the child or the *indulgent* parents of the child.)

If you have the patience to unravel the child's unique hurdles, you can actually make a lot of progress with them. They are often willing, keen learners and they love to please. This is a key and very critical point – *they genuinely want to please* (at least most of the time). Other hurdles may include noise in the classroom.

> I have heard of one boy who is in a class of 24 children. Most of the time, he works outside of the classroom. He says he can sometimes hear 20 conversations at once and they mess with his head. This boy would probably be about ten years old.

Summary

- Overcoming unique hurdles
- Unknown limiting obstacles to ordinary learning
- Difficulty coping with change including holidays
- Children on the spectrum generally want to please you and do what you expect of them

Inability to Prioritise

Aspie children have multiple thoughts running around in their head at the same time. They, and adults on the spectrum, tell me so often. They are unable to prioritise thoughts, nor are usually able to work out and sustain the chief thought that they need to run with. They appear externally to be daydreaming and unfocussed despite an internal sense of panic and distress, especially if they are under time or performance pressures. They often do not respond when called or talk to when in this state. If they are stressed, then this dissociation will be even more heightened. It appears that they seem to freeze, not proceed in anyway with their work and get further and further behind. At this point, they become extremely stressed. If the bell should then ring for another lesson, the child may well have not completed all or most work or may not have done anything at all. Then it's off to the next classroom and the whole process begins all over again. This is often an area in which a speedy false diagnosis based on this one symptom is made, especially for girls, and the child is considered to have ADD (Attention Deficit Disorder).

After a day at school like this – if the child manages to make a whole day – the child will be extremely stressed (with often no obvious external symptoms) and will come home and have a meltdown almost immediately. This is where an observant parent can step in – preferably before the meltdown and help the child de-stress.

Another Aspie child may be very diligent and force themselves to stay focussed and will keep doing work. As they finish a task, they will do another that the teacher passes on to those who have completed the work. They appear quiet, docile and diligent. The child comes home shattered and cannot focus the rest of the evening, may cry easily and often – and may not be able to sleep (probably due to an overload of adrenalin). These children are rule focussed and the rule is to obey the teacher, but they will do this to their own detriment.

Unable to filter or prioritise multiple thoughts

> One parent I know asked the teacher to not push their child so hard and to give her breaks between papers while describing the issues for the child at home. This child worked faster and more diligently than any other student in the class, and when she finished a task, the teacher would give her extra work. The teacher told her that her daughter was a model student at school and experienced none of the signs the parent described, therefore she obviously had parenting issues at home. She advised the parent to seek help for her parenting issues!

If this overload stress is not checked, particularly in a school situation, the child will then often develop a secondary disorder, namely an anxiety which increasingly and potentially builds to rather concerning levels throughout their development.

Summary

- Multiple racing thoughts
- Difficulty in prioritising thoughts, intentions or instructions
- Similar to ADD in this one regard
- Leads to stress and the beginnings of anxiety

Difficulties Understanding Language

Aspergic children require to be spoken to in short sentences, preferably with one verb. They also need to be addressed with one issue or statement at a time. It is also important not to wander off the topic in circuitous distractions and explanations, then come back to the point. You would have left the Aspergic child behind and conversationally lost them a long time ago.

They also do not understand idioms and clichés that we commonly use. As you can see the drawing says: "how do I read between the lines?", and "if he didn't have a bag, then how did he let the cat out?". These are common idioms that we use often, but Aspergic children have great difficulty understanding these. This is one time when it's really important to hold onto the *kiss* principle – which is *keep it simple, stupid*.

Aspergic children often do try to look between the lines – literally – when they are told to look *between* the lines for an answer, meaning the gap between each line of type on the printed page. It is also important to be aware of what we are saying to the children. One five-year-old was enormously distressed on his first day of school (and I have heard this story several times). He was told, "Sit here for the present." And he sat very still. He was distraught after he got home because he did not have a gift.

Dealing with idioms and various English language expressions is very difficult.

Conversely, Aspergic children may often have extremely adult language, but they still do not understand it despite being able to be quite articulate. Remember that they can only explain facts generally. They cannot deal with or understand hints or emotions, except their own emotions and even those they don't really understand. (To be fair – most children do not, but children on the ASD spectrum are even less self-aware.)

Summary

- Absence of understanding idioms, or language nuances
- Keep to simple sentences with one focus and one verb

Reaching Overload With Subsequent Meltdowns

Mention of meltdowns has been made repeatedly. An Aspergic child will have a meltdown when they are over stimulated, overwhelmed or distressed in any way. Meltdowns are far bigger than temper tantrums and unlike a temper tantrum, the child is not wanting anything – they simply can no longer cope!

It is also important to have conversations with your child – if you can and when you can – about situations that do overwhelm them. These conversations need to happen when all is pleasant and peaceful – in the car on a journey for example (which has the added benefit of not needing eye contact either!). You can teach yourself some strategies. When these are successful, you can teach your child the strategies that the child may find useful to repeat in these situations.

A meltdown can look quite scary. They may scream, cry, break things, throw things, bang their head on the concrete floor, pull down curtains, be extremely distressed and appear inconsolable – like a tantrum of an over-tired child but far worse. They may also look like they are in extreme pain (they probably are *in extremis* in some form). In adults, this meltdown can look quite psychotic and very disturbing. After a meltdown, it will be as if all their circuitry is shut down – they can seem quite numb, blank, unresponsive, dissociated – usually until after they have had a good long sleep. However, it can last a few days, especially if their situation has not changed for the better in any way. Try to have some strategies in place to minimise this experience for them and for you.

Try this experiment. Look at the picture after this paragraph. Read the words in circular speech, turning the book round and round to your right so that you can read the words *aloud* but at the same time turning your body around, spinning towards your left. While this is happening, have the TV news on really loud and try to focus on the visual and the sound and the content. Do this for five minutes. Stop and immediately list the first three articles on the news in detail. Or even more difficult and closer to the Aspie overwhelmed feeling, recall what was standing directly behind the person interviewed in the second news article.

"THE MELT-DOWN"

Imagine doing this under extreme pressure knowing that you will get into trouble if you could not accurately capture the details. This experiment is just a teeny-tiny taste of what it is like to be Aspergic in a very busy environment where there's lots of stimulation – and we haven't even discussed their sensitivities yet!

Perhaps now you can have a little more compassion. Perhaps now, you can learn to simplify things with your lovely Aspie child or student who, when she is safe and happy, is delightful and only wants to please you. Of course, this is true for most children too, whether they are on the spectrum or not.

They Are Literal

In the drawing, you can see that this happy little Aspie girl (probably about 11 or 12 years old) has triumphantly circled where x is literally on the board, when actually the teacher intended her to solve the value of x mathematically. It is only the slightest shift in semantics but what a huge difference it can make! This child would then have had a growling from the teacher for being cheeky, or the class may have laughed at her – resulting in a very embarrassed or upset Aspie with no idea of what she did wrong!

THEY CAN BE VERY LITERAL

Aspies are often accused of being smart, cheeky or rude. When accused of this, especially at moments when they are trying their hardest, they will be quite stunned by the accusation when they are well intentioned to be helpful and accommodating. Usually at that point, they will become quite dissociated and not respond to you at all, as they try to work out what they did wrong. Of course, this is even worse when you (and perhaps the whole class) laugh at her misunderstanding, and she has become the butt of the joke. The child will usually be standing still and feel quite shocked and physically frozen (like being a neurotypical and being blind-sided), and it will seem like they are then ignoring your next instructions to sit down in a seat (and if the teacher's assumption is that the child is increasingly badly behaved, then the teacher will react even more negatively and so the drama goes on). I think the Aspie might be able to hear your next instruction but not be able to process it and follow through at that point. I always say that at that point you have lost them (meaning that you have lost your ability to connect with them for a time).

Try using their literal thinking proactively. The self-awareness of how you are choosing to use your words is essential. Remember, you are the adult leading the child. Be clear in your wording, directives and intentions – they rely fully on you!

Again, an initial gentle reaction and rephrasing of the question may be all it takes to keep them focussed. Of course, if this is how you normally work with all people, you will naturally be well liked and your students or your child will be cooperative on the whole – and you would probably not be exposed to this kind of issue. So keep up the good work!

> I was told of an incident in which a young man of about 14 or 15 was being assessed. The occupational therapist who was telling me the story said that she had described to him that he had to make a choice of one of three different numbers (0=easy, 1=hard, 2=intensely difficult, 3=impossible), which would be the indicator reflecting closest to the degree to which he struggled with an issue. She would read a question to him and his response would be to indicate the relevant number 0, 1, 2 or 3, which indicated how strongly he felt about the issue, and she would double check that he understood what was expected of him. She read the following sentence to him, "I have difficulty with relationships." He immediately told her how sorry he was for her, and he wondered how you could help! She struggled to get him refocused after that, even though she had been direct, clear and gentle with him from the beginning (and she had not laughed at him or embarrassed him in any way).

The Joker or Class Clown: a Possible Strategy for Group Acceptance

A lot of our life discoveries are made by accident. A well-loved but mostly misunderstood child will see laughter as a positive affirmation. When one of his *faux pas* have met with laughter, he will often repeat this faux pas, sometimes *ad nauseum*. So, in simple English, he accidently makes a mistake which elicited fond laughter from an audience or from a group of boys he would especially like to be friends with and be included in their circle, then he will repeat, he will repeat, he will repeat, he will repeat (get the message?) exactly that behaviour. When that behaviour is no longer funny, the boy will try something similar. For example, he may realise that if he says something considered rude to a teacher, he will try a different rude word or statement.

INAPPROPRIATE HUMOUR CAN BE USED TO COVER SOCIAL DIFFICULTIES

The audience of young students gasp with delight, waiting to see the teacher's reaction and the unfolding consequences, but the student is delighted because smiling people (the student/s whose attention he is seeking) means that they like him, or so he interprets it. The sad cycle can escalate, with the child being seen by the teacher or adult in whose care the child is in, as poorly behaved, uncooperative and extremely irritating. This preconception follows him from class to class and sometimes in his reports from school to school. The future does not look bright socially for this lad.

> One boy I know would get restless and was probably overwhelmed in class one day. In his need to get away and as his anxiety increased, he slid off his chair in class and started belly crawling under the desks in an attempt to find some sort of quite space. He would then accidently touch people's feet as he slithered past them, so you can imagine the classroom rumpus that ensued. Because a lot of children – especially the boys – encouraged him with "GO! GO! GO!" and clapped and laughed and yahooed; another part of this boy latched on to this as something he could do to get these boys approval. Eventually, it became a rather annoying habit for the teacher to deal with. Fortunately, there were few students in the class, which made the situation a bit easier to quickly remedy, but even so – it is not what the teacher needed! Nor was it what this boy needed. He needed a better and more helpful strategy. In actuality, some understanding would have helped and that could have allowed him a quiet place to deal with whatever was overwhelming him. Then a conversation could ensue and the issues could have been worked through.

On the other hand, I have seen some very sad outcomes based on this same strategy. Aspies generally, and when children especially, have no deception in the them: there is no guile, no cunning, no mind games. In fact, there is a remarkable and noticeable absence of this human trait in Aspie children. Aspergers of course – and this a reminder – is a *social development disorder*. This means that they cannot read social situations very well – and especially as children. They are gullible innocents and are often the butt of practical jokes and worse. Some of these *jokes* are cruel and leave the victim with no dignity to rescue themselves or the situation. The Aspie becomes the subject of bullying and repeated ridicule.

If they are not the victim of a practical joke, they may have to be the nominated person to do a deed against a teacher or adult, in order to gain acceptance in a coveted group. They are completely set up, with no supports. They are willing to pay the price of group acceptance, never realising that there will be dire consequences, or that they will probably never have acceptance to this group anyway.

This is the child who joins a group of boys to egg a house, or throw stones from a bridge on a train, or throw rocks on a house below road level. Not only will the Aspie child be placed in the most exposed position, the child will not realise danger until it is too late. This child is most likely to be the one that is caught as the others would have seen warning cues of *danger* (an angry adult looming!) and have scarpered early in the piece. This is the child caught with stones in his hand, eggs in her hand, or surrounded by fallen stolen fruit under a tree. This is also the child who has poor social cues and responses and couldn't talk their way out of a paper-bag (if you are an Aspie, that means *is unable to tell even a simple, easy lie*). This is also the child that faces the punishment.

To not get their new *friends* in trouble, the Aspie may try to hide their part and take all the blame himself. Unfortunately, these are not good friends, so the Aspie will be trapped again – or if he refuses, then become the subject of further rejection, ridicule and bullying. As we are talking about children at the start of their lifespans, this is not an auspicious beginning!

Sensitivity

There are a lot of words to describe intense sensitivities. Below are just a small select few of them:

Allodynia is a heightened sensitivity to touch. This is also known as tactile sensitivity.

Misophonia is a condition in which a person is overly sensitive to sounds, like chewing.

Photophobic means having an extreme sensitivity to light.

Hyperosmia means having an abnormally acute sense of smell.

Misokinesia means being aware of repeated movements that intensely annoy and distract, such as a flapping flag, or the pendulum of a grandfather clock, or a Neko ornament (the Fortune Cat that often waves its paw and is found in Asian stores).

The average Aspie child (and adult) has some level of most of these sensitivities, if not all of these sensitivities.

This means that your Aspie child perhaps cannot stand the smell of the washing powder that her clothes were washed in – inhaling the highly perfumed perfume makes her feel dizzy; she is irritated by the texture of the paper that she has to write on and she tries to write without touching the paper and then stresses because the paper moves; she cannot bear the intense ear-searing scratching of her pencil and the overhead lights in the classroom with their brilliant luminosity or their flickering as they are maybe gas tubes. The label of her school shirt is sharply rubbing against the back of her neck and scratches her repeatedly so she tries to hold her head extremely still so that the painful rubbing does not happen; the seams of her singlet are also scratchy but are a constant irritation she tries to ignore; she is sure that you have given her luncheon meat on her sandwiches and she cannot stand the sight, smell, texture or colour of the luncheon meat and she knows you will be angry if she does not eat it; she has to face the catty girls outside at lunchtime and the boys who repeatedly *accidently* kick the ball at her and when she seeks solace in the library, the kindly librarian sends her out in the glaring sun *to get some fresh air*. Now she additionally and separately, to all of the above, has to get through her myriad of thoughts and concentrate only what her teacher, scout leader or police officer (who is testing her to see if she can be an after-school lollypop helper!) is saying and focus on only one thing – the subject that she is writing about.

And you wonder why she comes home shattered, drained, uncommunicative and maybe cries? I think it's a miracle that she gets through every day and still does so well.

Because some children have difficulty coping when their sensitivities are triggered, say by a noisy environment, their mothers are always alert and hypervigilant to sensitivity issues. They don't want an upset child. They don't want a public meltdown. And they don't want to deal with the aftermath. It really will help if the parent or parents actually teach the children how to cope and give them some skills for potential unexpected environment triggers that they are sensitive to. Our job as parents is to teach our children how to cope with life, however that looks, so that they can function as best as possible as adults. This training may need to start when the children are very young.

Some sensitivities are manageable – for example, not going to rock concerts, or not insisting that their children wear clothing made from wool or fabrics that may irritate the Aspie child, or removing clothing labels because the child is sensitive to that. Other things in the environment are not always as manageable, and so the child needs to be taught skills to cope with both kinds of situations.

Not Usually Athletic, Nor Team Players

Generally, your ASD child is not sporty or athletic. They are seldom involved in sports and are not good team players (although they usually try very hard), mainly because they don't get the social signals but also because they are generally not into sport. In fact, they are more likely than not to be uncoordinated and clumsy.

It is also not uncommon to find an Aspie child who is dyspraxic. In more academic terms, there are usually issues around gross motor control. This means controlling the muscles in your body. They often have poor posture, have very limited stamina; they generally do not have good balance and have poor muscle tone. They are generally not good at sport. Please remember that these are generalisations. They may develop an obsession for a sport, but it is more likely to be about sport figures and games scores, than the actual physical engagement and involvement.

They may perhaps enjoy a sport that has a non-competitive option and in which they are the solo player – for example, swimming or horse riding where they can use these options. They may learn badminton or squash because it is the *done thing* to get in amongst the peers they wish to be with – and they will play a technically perfect game once they have learned it – but it is highly unlikely that they will end up on the international sports scene. If they get involved in something like ballet, they will strive to be technically perfect, but they are not usually a *natural*. There are exceptions, so please forgive my broad statements. Regardless, your child will be so willing to belong, and to help his team, he will try his very best, his enthusiastic utmost.

Sadly, I have often heard of, or seen, this child in the following school setting. A teacher picks two team leaders who have to pick their team. This one child is constantly and deliberately overlooked or ignored. Sometimes the growing team will discourage their leaders to also not consider this member. The child is increasingly humiliated and embarrassed until the teacher makes a unilateral decision and assigns the last unchosen few children to a particular team. The team leader of the sports team then assigns this child to a spot where they will be least likely to be needed (or least likely be a hindrance to the team).

> Once, and I have to say this – bless her heart – a girl who was obviously on the spectrum had enthusiastically joined a soccer club for little kids, and she had waited a long time to be assigned a game. She was given the position of left midfielder and everyone was secretly hoping that she would never get to the ball. She was probably about seven or eight years old. It was near the end of the game; the scores were evenly divided and the two teams were playing furiously to gain that last goal. The ball came flying towards her to where she had run up to be near her own goal to defend it. She enthusiastically and gallantly threw out a powerful kick, and the ball ended

> up in the goal and she was grinning with sheer delight. Unbeknownst to her, she had kicked the ball into her own team's goal. She was unaware of this and then was surprised as her team berated her. Of course, she simply shut down and could not face playing after that, although she stayed on as reserve for the rest of the season. Her team lost the game that day, as she had scored this last goal for the opposing team.

Also, alongside the difficulty of fitting into a team, they have difficulty working in a group. They work far better on their own. In group work, they may miss social cues, or they may forget or mistake their particular part of the group effort, which will infuriate the group. The other alternative is that they may often be selected for example, in a STEM subject, in which the group or the peer will freeload off all the Aspie's work. Even playing board games in a group of children including one Aspie can cause problems for the Aspie. Care needs to be taken appropriately by adults wherever there are groups of children that your Aspie may be involved with.

Difficulty Looking in the Eyes of Others (Issues with Direct Eye Contact)

As a neurotypical (non-Aspie), I am extremely uncomfortable if someone does not look me in the eye when they are talking to me. I interpret that there is some level of dishonesty happening or that the other party is shifty and hiding something. As the conversation goes on over time, this becomes increasingly uncomfortable. At the very extreme, the other person may be extremely shy, but even extremely shy people have a little *peep* from under their eyelashes. Aspies don't!

The reverse is true for Aspies. They are hugely uncomfortable, some describing it as *painful* to look another person in the eye when they are having a conversation. This is as uncomfortable, or even more so, when the reverse happens for us neurotypicals. How do we solve this? Assuming that you as the reader is the adult here, then remember this chapter is about children. How important is it that they look you in the eye? This minute? Right now? Can you sometimes leave them be? You will get a much better conversation if you play alongside them, or help with their homework, or even their chores – again alongside them. That reduces the need to do the eye-to-eye thing either way and nobody is uncomfortable or on edge. That is a healthy solution where everyone benefits.

Of course, when we are responsible for raising or working with children, we also have to teach them to cope in the real world. If your child is on the spectrum and is avoiding eye contact, you can teach them that it is a social *rule* of the majority (the neurotypicals) to make eye contact when they are talking, and that they ought to try sometimes.

COMMUNICATION DIFFICULTIES, ESPECIALLY AROUND LACK OF EYE-CONTACT.

Aspies can relate to rules. Help them to learn when this eye-contact-business is appropriate and when not. And have an open discussion with them as to how they can manage this social custom more comfortably for themselves and for the other party. Some of my clients choose to look at the point of a cheek just under an eye, others look and focus on the eyebrow – all little tips that make it easier for the Aspie and the neurotypical won't even detect that slight variance of eye focus!

Another hint that may help your Aspie child is to rehearse this with them before any particular event (see the next sub-section). I believe that Aspies can make very good actors if you give them the correct helps. If you are worried that they need to *genuinely* make eye contact, then that belief is your problem – this is never going to happen voluntarily (or consistently) very often for your child.

Cognitive or Executive Function, Difficulties

As explained in the first chapter, Aspies have several cognitive issues or differences when compared with the more common neurotypical wiring. *Cognitive* refers to our thinking and processing. In children, this happens primarily in the frontal cortex, as the prefrontal cortex is not fully developed until the early twenties in most adults, whether on the spectrum or not.

Aspie children can have *cognitive rigidity.* This means that they have difficulty changing from one subject to another, especially so if speed between the changes are of essence. Or they have difficulty in switching backwards and forwards between two or more subjects – such as building a Lego construction and having to stop and greet grandma who has just arrived. Or they may not be able to do what is expected of them, and they will simply freeze. If they do not have a *brain-freeze* in which they seem unable to proceed at all and have gone blank, they may instead have, at the very least, a significantly noticeable cognitive delay. These can accumulate and make focussing on school subjects increasingly difficult as the day goes on.

Aspie children often have limited executive functioning, neurologically. So, Aspie children can have difficulties with getting organised and often need an adult to make a daily or schoolwork *roadmap* for them, when their peers or siblings are managing to be more organised, independent and autonomous. Their cognitive organisation is often poor because the brain circuitry does not seem to be fully connected. This is of course, common to all children, but Aspie children are either painfully meticulous (which is more rare) or more usually, extremely disorganised. It appears that the cognitive processes to make events sequential and flowing, often has neurological gaps in Aspie children. This is despite them frequently being highly intelligent. They can be top in maths but forget to eat their lunch (in their lunch break when the other students are eating their lunch) and be oblivious as to why they later have no energy and are feeling tired and listless.

Lorna Wing, the earlier pioneer in Asperger syndrome, suggests that Aspies have incomplete pathways and poor screening activity in the part of the brain that is known as the Reticular Formation. This part of the brain helps to combine important activities and filter out those not needed at the time. Some of its job is to coordinate muscles in walking for instance and may be the reason Aspie children often are dyspraxic, or at least have poor muscle coordination. Reticular Formation also acts as a filter and helps prioritise what is important. A neurotypical child can filter out what is not a priority and can, for example, ignore what is happening around him. The Reticular Formation is very useful as it stops us getting overwhelmed, if it is working properly.

Reticular Formation is also the part of the brain that helps us to create priorities and ignore distractions. As a neurotypical, I can often focus on my client and their presentation and my Reticular Formation will filter out the hum of the air-conditioner, or the ticking of the clock, and certainly the fabric of my clothes and the feeling of the seat that I am sitting on. In fact, mindfulness is very popular as a therapy and for stress management, in which neurotypicals are taught to be *aware* of all their senses and surroundings! This is ironically the complete opposite of what I often have to teach Aspies and Aspie children! The poor functioning of the Reticular Formation is therefore another reason why your Aspie has difficulty focussing (unless they are in a closed obsessive state) and sometimes act as if they have an Attention Deficit Disorder!

Aspie children lack empathy, again because the brain wiring for creating an empathy circuit often has missing links. But an Aspie child can be taught to have a level of empathy. Some Aspie children (mainly female Aspies) appear to have empathy but have no way of expressing it and seem to shut down. A later explanation may tell us what was happening for them at the time, but all we saw was indifference at its most positive.

Empathy is often described as being on a spectrum, with neurotypicals high on that spectrum and Aspies low on the empathy spectrum. Simon Baron-Cohen seems to suggest that Aspies, and Aspie children by default, appear to have *zero degrees of empathy*. I have noticed Aspie children treat people and even babies as if they were other objects in their environment with no recognition that *these are people* and not objects! I believe that Aspie children can be taught *cognitive empathy*, at the very least. They can be taught to think about what something may feel like for another person, even if they may never develop *emotional empathy*.

Aspie children also have cognitive difficulties regards *reading* the context of a situation. Neurotypical children as young as five will understand to not pick their nose in public, yet I can have a twelve-year-old Aspie child who will be talking to me and picking their nose at the same time. This is called context blindness. Little neurotypical children can also have context blindness but are quickly corrected by their (sometimes embarrassed) parents. Aspies may have context blindness well into adulthood and throughout adulthood. Early teaching is important to help the child. Context blindness is often behind the incidents in which Aspie children speak out bluntly and inappropriately, or spill family or friend's secrets. They do not seem to realise which is an appropriate context and which is not, and seemingly are sometimes not even aware of any context.

It is good to understand that Aspie children have different cognitive wiring. It is not wrong. It is not a sickness that can be fixed. It is just not neurotypical, which is the dominant thinking of the world's population.

> Being on the spectrum is, "Different, not less," says Temple Grandin.

Working for years with Aspie children as I have, I have found that they can be taught different ways to react and relate. They are never too old to learn, just like neurotypical children. When I work with Aspie children, I try to make a game of teaching them the secret codes and passwords of neurotypicals. At the same time, I always emphasise that we are going to keep their Aspie strengths. I say to them that they are going to be the best Aspie that they can be, but they can also learn to be fluent in neurotypical. I use the metaphor of being fluent in one language and that learning a second language doesn't change the person but simply makes them better communicators to more people.

And then, focus on what your child is good at. I would encourage parents and teachers who are neurotypical to learn to speak and communicate in Aspie. It really is a two-way street that works best!

Preparedness

Aspies generally do not respond well to spontaneity or off-the-cuff situations. Don't surprise your Aspie. Don't touch them unexpectedly and certainly without permission – they generally do not like touch (the rare ones do but that is often when they have come to terms with it as an adult and have learnt to enjoy an intimate relationship or the rare Aspie child that has learned to enjoy healthy physical affection from a carer).

And don't change their routine without warning!

Your child or your student needs to know what is going to happen next, so that they can visualise and be prepared for it. And this is when they are not in obsessive focus on a specialist interest at that time! We need different strategies for that one!

If it's the end of the weekend and your child is going to school, or a weekend and they are going to stay the night at grandma, or your child is going somewhere familiar and routine to them, they still need to be prepared. Be prepared sometimes for a 40-minute quiz session as they go through all the questions. They need to visualise this whole process, from beginning to end (even if they have done this 50 times before). Neurotypicals don't need to do that – they just wing it within the very loose plan that we have.

If this preparation and warning time frustrates you or proverbially *drives you insane*, then that is actually your reaction and your problem. You want to help this child, right? You need to get past that frustration of yours.

The child needs to visualise a process from beginning to end. How much preparedness does your child need? The answer depends on where they are on the spectrum – the more Aspie they are, the more they need it. Fairly simple equation, I think. *Our end goal is to have a normal, well-functioning adult (this Aspie child who grows up) by the time we come off child-parenting duty.* Make the efforts now and you – and your child especially – will richly reap the benefits. If you don't give them time to prepare and process, you will have a highly strung, distressed and anxious child in all likelihood. Their fight or flight response is switched on and you simply have a miniature time bomb ticking away there. The other possible outcome is that they will just shut down and dissociate, like they are not there to all intents and purposes. It may make your supermarket shopping or teaching experience easier, but your child has learnt nothing (because they are shut down and in sheer survival mode with few of their cognitive executive functions working), except that life is increasingly distressing. This will have huge ramifications for them in their teenage years and late adult years.

> One seven-year-old girl needed to have good warning and preparedness. One thing she would do, in her efforts to get everything right, was to imagine the next morning and visualise getting ready for school and all the stages that were required. She would see herself wearing the red shirt – her favourite red shirt – and would plan her clothes and her routine. In the morning, she would get up and the red shirt (or whatever she had planned) might still have food spilt down the front and was lying in the bottom of the laundry basket. This so blew her plans out of the water that all she could do was weep deeply and become hugely distressed and anxious, especially if anybody tried to hurry her up. By the time, she was reasonable to approach, her eyes were swollen from crying, her nose blocked, and she was wild-eyed and stressed – and usually, this settling stage only started happening about two hours after school had started. She missed many days of school this way (unintentionally). Her mother has done a fabulous parenting job, and this girl can be good at being spontaneous and can cope with life's surprises – probably better than most people can, today as an adult.

If you are going to do something different and possibly even new, you will need to prepare this child much more than you will ever need to prepare a neurotypical child. Tell them you are planning a holiday and go through the description of where you are going to stay and all the details. Show them pictures. Make this a big conversation. The same process is there if you are changing their schooling or taking them to the dentist for the first time (a handy little tip – ask the dentist's receptionist to book you in for double the time as it will probably take that and in the end, everyone will be thankful that you did that).

> I was working with one Aspie child, and I agreed to accompany her for her first dental check-up. I thought I had thoroughly prepared. She was overwhelmed by the bright lights, by being backwards in the chair and this strange masked man sitting beside her, who kept talking to her in his muffled voice – even though we had prepared her for this. She screamed every time he bent forward, *the long spikey thing in his hand* terrifying her. As time went on and despite all his very best gentle attempts, he visibly broke into a sweat (he is a lovely dentist that I have known for a long time and has a very soft approach with children). She was becoming increasingly distressed. I whispered in her ear the rule we had made ("Remember if you open your

> mouth for the dentist for three minutes, you will get to go to McDonald's afterwards" – brazen bribery always works!). Her mouth popped open as she focussed on her favourite takeaway place that we had also visualised before, and he was able to do his quick inspection. She never had a problem at the dentist again – even when she needed to have her wisdom teeth removed as a young adult.

If your student is facing a piano exam or any new arrangement, walk through that process with them – step by step. If you are doing a field excursion to the beach, then prepare them. Break it down in detail into manageable bits. If you are a parent and are going to take them somewhere noisy and they don't like noise (maybe a street parade), give them earmuffs or earplugs. Guess what, you will get to stay for the whole parade, or the exam will go smoothly, or the beach trip will be safe because you don't have to be hyper-focused on one child losing the plot. Isn't this all that you want?

The wonderful plus is that when your child learns to handle this process, it will be a fixed picture and process in their mind, and you should never have a problem again. You will never need to deal with the neurotypical who chooses to forget the rules, or neurotypical nervousness and anxious fussing before a dental appointment or dance exam. They (your Aspies) know what they need to do, and they just follow the rules and get on with it.

Sometimes you may have a minor hiccup, so you might just have to add an addition to the rule. For example, that the examiner is different, or the trip might be in a bus instead of a car – and then you only need to go through the codicil. The clever carer needs to spot which part of the rule has changed and not get frustrated and say that this is exactly the same as last time – it is not for the Aspie. Again, if you do this successfully and with minimum fuss (from you especially), you will find that you will have also inadvertently taught them to be more flexible...and then you have worked a small miracle in their thinking and lives, which can help them immensely!

> They can also use rules in terms of relating to people. One girl, in her early teens, used to throw regular tantrums as she had her meltdowns. In these meltdowns, she was emotionally and verbally abusive to others in the family, to the extent that they withdrew from her because of the hurtful things that she had said. She then later complained and was confused as to

> why her siblings and her father were excluding her or being critical of her. Her mother explained to her that she had caused some deep emotional hurts within the family. The mother said that her daughter had also emotionally hurt her rather deeply. The daughter responded, with a complete lack of theory of mind but forcibly with her own rule and said, "No matter what I do, you have to love me. That's the rule. Because you are a mother! And that's what mothers have to do."

Their Need for Details

They need details. Details that you may think are irrelevant. You may want to snap at them and call them names in your frustration. You may demand that they keep quiet immediately and not ask so many questions. You may wonder later why you had such an unhappy day and why your child was so uncooperative when everyone else in the world – or so it seems – has cooperative children. Or you may want to give them details and save your sanity and theirs. So, you as the adult need to plan for this, to factorise it into your plans so that everything runs smoothly.

They need to know when, where, how, why, how long, how many, how much, will it cost, who will be there, what if costs more, will it be noisy and so on.

Similarly, they can give you details – lots of details (if they are either talkers, or you have encouraged them to talk), especially if they are talking about something in which they have a specific (and often obsessive) interest. They may not remember to eat their lunch at school, but they will remember obscure details about the sinking of the Titanic or astronomy or any other specific interest.

If they are distressed, you can then help them settle by getting them to talk about their specific interest. It is rather lovely when an Aspie finds an interest, but sadly, many are not exposed to enough life circumstances nor are encouraged to explore more, so they often never discover it (a special, absorbing interest and hence an outlet for them). This detailed specific interest is a tool that helps their self-soothing, serves as a distraction – and mostly, it just gives them emotional joy. With the difficulties, they have in finding a way to express emotion, then this joy is rather a wonderful release. But be prepared, timewise – if you ask them a question…!

And because they are not very good at reading expressions, they will not know you are bored or need to get away. You will have to very patiently teach them how to do this – by teaching them body language, or by teaching them to ask if they are boring you, or if they need stop talking yet. Make it a rule.

Another wonderful little hint, sometimes, just make time to let them tell you about their interest. In detail. They will just love you for it!

Naïve and Gullible

Your little Aspie is naïve and gullible. Mostly, it is quite cute – but it does not help them later in life to be naïve and gullible.

This is one of the reasons they often become the class joke, or even worse, bullied or even worse than worse, sexually assaulted in their teens and in young adulthood (especially females on the spectrum). They do not see the social build up, they do not see the posturing, they do not recognise the tormenting tones increasing, until it is often too late, and they have been humiliated or they have lost their delicious lunch that you have prepared for them to some obnoxious bully.

If you combine this trait with the other dominant trait of being literal, you can see that they daily enter a social mine-field, or even a *mind*-field. If you have developed a good relationship with your child when they are young, you will be their safe person. You can do this as a teacher or even a grandparent or a kindly neighbour, and obviously as first point of call – a caring parent. Encourage them to come and talk to their safe person. Gently teach them about the social hardship that life often is. Teach them to look out for danger but do it ever so gently so that they are not even more terrified of living their lives.

Stimming

Stimming is short for *self-stimulatory behaviour*. The experts in ASD consider stimming to be a self-soothing behaviour. In observing somebody who is stimming, they do appear externally to visibly calm down – and maybe to outsiders, it looks as though they have gone into a state of trance – as if they are no longer in the room. They appear dissociated from reality.

A stim is best described as an often-repeated behaviour familiar to the person or child in this case, each person having their own unique ritualised habit. It can present in many forms, and this is just a very short, incomplete list of ways stimming can manifest:

- Rocking
- Bouncing leg

- Tapping
- Rolling up in duvet (cocooning)
- Staring through a fish tank
- Finger clicking, or rubbing hands repeatedly over the fabric of their clothing
- Hand shaking/waving action
- Rocking
- Counting collections – e.g. buttons, coins
- Some may run out to a quiet place, often with their hands over their ears
- Watching favourite movies repeatedly
- Whisper to self repeatedly
- The need to touch material things, often a favourite object they keep close to them, but it may extend to include the need to physical touch a person, and so they may touch another child in the class (who may respond very unpleasantly)
- None of this is necessarily strange – except that it could happen in a public place, which then often opens up the child to comments and insults from external watchers. It may even open up bullying behaviour as the bully notices that the other is quite defenceless in this state.

(STIMMING)

I also notice that clients do this when overwhelmed with information, or emotionally or even sensorially, overloaded. It appears to be a distraction to allow them to process what is happening. Often after a period of stimming, the client seems more settled and seems to have sorted whatever was overwhelming them in their mind, sufficiently to process it or beginning discussing it if they have suitable language skills to do so.

My clients tell me that it is not a self-soothing technique. Most of them tell me or describe to me that it is a strategy to help them process a stressful situation but which leaves them extremely distressed if they are interrupted and the process cannot run its course. You can try teaching your child some techniques that may help.

> One young boy always keeps a special little Lego piece in his pocket of his school uniform or even his tracksuit that he can touch. No one else even notices him doing this. Sometimes, he will bring it out and put it on his desk and stare at it for a little while.

A really distressed child may often enjoy being held tight – although you would need to know the child and know that the child likes to almost be swaddled. An older child that likes to be comforted this way might like to roll up in their duvet – a common manner is to lie diagonally across a large double duvet, take a corner and roll up in it – like being inside a tube. They like the feeling of being comforted, wrapped, held close and also the barrier between light and the effect of having some noises muffled.

Of course, this teaching needs to be done at a gentle pace – at a quiet, safe and reflective time and with their full engagement. Later on, they will probably start collecting things, so let them have some time out with the bottle tops they have collected (or whatever else they enjoy).

If you are trying to calm a younger child down, it is handy to have a collection of odd buttons, for example, that they can sort into size or colour or whatever works for them. The repeated monotony is very soothing, as well as the singular focus on colour, shape, texture or feeling. Older children can rifle through a coin collection or any other collection. In fact, there is not much difference between this and mindfulness, which is currently extremely fashionable in the first world and has historically always been an important component in several religious communities. Who would have thought?

Hapa Aspies

Kathy Marshack, a clinical psychologist, author and mother of a daughter on the spectrum, has coined this phrase. *Hapa* is a word in Hawaiian, which means half. It describes children and people who have both an Aspie parent and a neurotypical parent or who show a combination of being both Aspie and neurotypical. Due to possible genes combined with their environment, these children can have traits of both. This makes it difficult for the parent or teacher, as the child falls through all the proverbial cracks. It is neither one nor the other and just misses diagnosis too so that any extra help cannot be brought in to play.

It has also been found that a neurotypical child born to and raised by an Aspie parent will show some Aspie traits, which they will have absorbed through their environment.

I believe that as time goes on and research continues, that we will be seeing more and more of this mid-group of children and adults.

Final Summary

- Factual thinking
- A lateral creativity around facts
- Difficulty around imagination
- Not limited by neurotypical limits
- Difficulty getting thoughts translated onto paper into written words
- Lack of theory of mind
- Overcoming unique hurdles
- Unknown limiting obstacles to ordinary learning
- Difficulty coping with change including holidays
- Children on the spectrum generally want to please you and do what you expect of them
- Multiple racing thoughts
- Difficulty in prioritising thoughts, intentions or instructions (similar to ADD in this one regard)
- Leads to stress and the beginnings of anxiety
- Absence of understanding idioms, or language nuances
- Keep to simple sentences with one focus and one verb

- Issues in executive functioning and cognitive processing, despite often high intelligence
- Cognitive rigidity
- Poor Reticular Formation
- Lack of empathy
- Can be taught cognitive empathy but may not manage emotional empathy
- Reaching overload with subsequent meltdowns
- They are very literal
- They often hide their social inadequacies by attempting to be the class clown
- Difficulty fitting into their social group (they will often have friends who are much older or much younger)
- Heightened multiple sensitivities
- Difficulties playing sport in a team
- Often have dyspraxia
- Difficulty in group work
- Poor eye contact
- Mirror cells not always connected, so poor at imitating facial expressions even if they make eye contact
- They like structure and order and thrive on it or in it
- They need to be prepared for changes, deeply prepared!
- They need details
- They love details
- They are often naïve and gullible
- They usually have at least one obsessive interest
- They *need* to STIM. Find appropriate STIMs for and with your child

Chapter 3
Neurodivergent/Autistic Females

Aspergic women from their late teens onwards are often very difficult to diagnose, and currently the male to female diagnosis is thought to stand at a 5:1 ratio, although some even say it's only 10:1. Regardless, I would say that in my experience, a substantial number of women – higher than the so-called statistical averages – have traits or are on the spectrum, as shocking as that statement may appear to be. This is not just a reflection of clients but also on the general population I have met. A colleague of mine once remarked that everyone is probably somewhere on the spectrum, with only degrees of difference.

Please let me remind you of my analogy again – a cold does not have a single symptom but a cluster of symptoms, which together can indicate a cold. Aspergers does not have one defining trait; it has a large cluster of traits that operate together.

Because the women on the spectrum often have a more neurotypical *male-brain*, meaning they are more literal, fact based, miss social cues and prefer to be more structured than neurotypical women – they will also often find it easier (socially) to get on with males. Aspergic women may have the same social difficulties as Aspergic men, but they are more likely to be aware that something is *wrong*, and they are unlikely to commit the many social faux pas that Aspergic men do. This means that they are not as obviously or noticeably as Aspergic as men are.

Women usually have a level of intuition to quite a large degree, and many Aspergic women typically are intuitive with a good sixth sense. Some Aspergic women are often very spiritually sensitive too (but not necessarily religious). If you combine this female Aspergic intuitiveness with a standard male brain, you get a very different kind of female thinking. For predominantly this reason, amongst others, many females are not easily picked up as Aspergic (because of their intuitive side). They can generally intuit when *something* relationally is not right but often cannot identify what that *something* is. Also, because of their interested observation, they are often great social mimics and can socially mimic their way through many situations – something that a male on the Aspergic (ASD) spectrum cannot do. Hence, they often come under the radar of diagnosis, and their diagnosis is then missed. They mimic neurotypical women and because of that, they mask their own traits of Aspergers syndrome or ASD.

> Some years ago, I met a hairdresser who could not cope with the female hairdressing environment, who became a mechanic and pursued her love of fixing up old cars. She is the only one who has ever managed my curls and waves perfectly. She was hugely detailed and I noticed she took twice as long as the other hairdressers, but she delivered an awesome job! I often saw her manager prowling around her, looking irritated and frustrated, reminding her that her other clients were waiting for her usually using an angry voice. I am not surprised that the poor woman left, but my goodness, do I miss her!

I have seen these lovely women working as pharmacists or working in pharmacies and being so sincere and knowledgeable. Because of their social and emotional detachment and their factual processing, it is easy to speak *medically* to them. They make good bank clerks, although sometimes their staff handling at management level may leave some emotionally hurt or disgruntled staff members at times. There are so many skilled Aspie women in the workplace!

Generally though, Aspie women do not enjoy working with the public or in public places, especially if they are introverted, which is more commonly the case. The exception is that they can work in a public place if they are in some way in control – as in, it is their own café for example. The other exception is working in a one-on-one situation, such as a doctor, bookkeeper, draftsman or as staff in a bank or pharmacy, as described above. They are great at jobs that require detail combined with work that does not involve too much contact, for example, town planners, hydrologists, linguists, engineers, architects, possibly maths and science teachers, veterinary nurses and laboratory technicians, and many of the trades.

Looking back many years ago – my maths teacher must have been on the spectrum! She always wore a tweed beret, and she had a small collection of these berets in varying shades and a few tartan ones that could have been tam-o-shanters and clothes that were fashionable in the Second World War (in which it was widely – and romantically, to us teenagers anyway, rumoured that her fiancé had died – she was still a tragic 60+ years old spinster in our eyes). She only had about four sets of clothes that she varied – mostly comprised of a wool or tweed skirt, check cotton shirt and wool waistcoat that usually matched the skirt. This ensemble was in varying shades of blue that brought out her own sharp, brilliant blue eyes. She would occasionally wear a scarf if it was cold and thermals under her shirt, and we would all talk about this change with schoolgirl interest. She had a grey shawl on the coldest days of winter.

We noticed that she rarely left her classroom, even at lunchtime. She did not seem to join the other teacher in the staff room. She always had a flask with her hot drink, or maybe a soup and some sandwiches and fruit. We knew what she had, as she had an open wicker basket, which she brought to school each day, and which sat under her desk. At times, when another teacher talked to her in a corridor or popped into the classroom during a lesson, we never noticed any tension between them, and the relationship was amicable, but again looking back, the conversation was always factual (what we overheard anyway).

She never made eye contact. She taught maths to the top students and top classes, and she was a brilliant teacher in that she really knew her subject and all her students did exceptionally well. On the first day of the year, she told us her rules. She didn't care what we did in her class as long as we did not leave our seat, talk or ask her any questions and if anyone broke that rule, she was totally fierce and hostile to that student for a few days. If a student asked her a maths question, she would simply ignore them, but we noticed that about two or three days later, she would answer that question which was worked into the maths for that day. She started talking exactly two minutes (she looked at her wristwatch all the time as we came into class) after the start-of-lesson-bell regardless whether students were settled or not, and she stopped talking exactly as the end-of-lesson-bell rang. Although she seemed to ignore us and be indifferent to us, when she needed to address us or relate about us to a parent, she would use our full name and simply make her point, looking directly but carefully at the top of our heads. If addressed, most of us looked backwards to see if another girl with the same name sat behind us because of her curious way of not looking directly at us.

She sometimes (quite often!) made me stay in for the lunch break (I think it was a punishment – how can an extroverted chatty 17-year-old not say a word for a whole hour?). Although she gave me chores to do, I thought at the time that she might have taken a liking to me, because she answered all my curious questions about her. She not only didn't growl at me for talking then but she did not respond like other teachers about her privacy. I knew she loved the theatre, looked after her elderly mother with whom she lived; she did have fiancé die in the Second World War, and she had several cats whom she adored (and when she talked about them, she would smile and her whole face would light up – it's the only time I saw her smile). She told me a lot about her cats, talking over my head while I did the chores. I learnt a lot about her in my final year of senior school (which it turned out later was also her final year in teaching – she retired at the end of the year!). And I became fond of her. Despite this seeming intimacy in our private time, she always ignored me in class. Another strange thing was on my last punishment; she gave me her personal home phone number and told me I could let her know how I got on with life. I phoned her for quite a few years, a few times a year. Somewhere in those years, her mother died. And then her phone didn't ring anymore – and that was the end of our relationship/friendship – or whatever it was.

Was she Aspergic or on the spectrum? My educated guess would be yes, much as professionally we do not armchair diagnose!

Aspie Women, Generally...

Defining Aspie women is as difficult as defining neurotypical women – as the range is individual and unique. Aspie women are more likely to be polarised in their behaviour though – more on the extreme outers than the neutral middles (unless they have worked very hard at mimicking a middle, more neurotypical, place and that of course would only present publicly). So I have made a long (very long) list of *general* statements that could make up a cluster of more typical female Aspergic traits. They are in no particular order:

- They often miss social cues. Social cues include body language, facial expressions and the tone of voice of a speaker (for example, they often miss sarcasm).
- They have limited, if any, theory of mind. This is alternatively known as mind-blindness. This is a difficulty or inability to imagine the perspective from which another person may be coming from. They generally cannot *see* (for example) that they are being manipulated or *see* the lead up to bullying and are sometimes left socially embarrassed at the very least.
- They are generally detail oriented – needing to get things absolutely, perfectly right but also taking in much more detail than neurotypicals do, in most given situations.

> One young woman I knew would do her assignments, often by hand – in a near perfect print. If she had a single error on her page, she would rewrite the whole page and tear up the incorrect page.

- They are very sensitive to visual, sound and other sensory details.

> My clients can hear the constant ticking of the clock in my office and struggle to concentrate and often ask to close the blinds as the outside is too visually distracting for them – despite my office facing a very quiet carpark and the walls are plain and non-stimulating, and the lights are low-lit (because the natural lighting is very good).

- They develop work routines, and they can become very distracted or upset if their routine is interrupted. Sometimes they cannot continue to function at work or stay on task if they are upset.

> One woman I knew worked in an administrative type of job. She had her stationery neatly lined up on her desk. Her colleagues would annoy her by (often deliberately) knocking her pens or stapler askew, and she would need to re-align them all before she could continue. She was very good at her job and could attend to careful detail in her work, except if the other staff rattled her for their own amusement. Once she was rattled, she would often seem to mentally freeze and be unable to proceed with her work.

- They have particular ways of doing things – like a set pattern (for example, the way the cutlery drawer is arranged), and they don't like that changed.

> A friend of mine has to re-arrange the cutlery at motels. "Who puts knives, spoons and forks in that order?" she will say. She just cannot settle if the basics in her environment are not *right* for her.

- Knowing that someone else has tampered with their set-up or will put things in a wrong place, can be very distressing or unsettling for them.
- They work best in a quiet, fairly predictable, structured environment. If they are unsettled, they find it difficult to function. They may try to resolve these issues themselves, but they may not be able to. This could be as simple as having a chatty colleague. They may bring earplugs to work to not hear that colleague. Then, neurotypicals being what they are, are likely to comment or even be critical about the earplugs. Some workplace non-acceptance and inappropriate responses can then escalate to an unpleasant level and the Aspie may have to resign due to the uncomfortable working environment.
- They also have difficulty if they are interrupted when speaking – mainly having difficulty in trying to gather their thoughts to proceed again. Sometimes they will start right at the beginning again. Somebody (and I can no longer remember who it was!) said that if you interrupt an Aspie, they often need to start at the beginning of the chapter again – meaning they will have to start again from the very beginning of their speech and repeat themselves to complete a discussion that is important to them. Females on the spectrum can be quiet while they appear to run through the conversation to where they got to again and then proceed. If I accidently interrupt an Aspie (I really try not to!), there is a significant pause while they gather their thoughts (especially if it is a different topic altogether).
- I may have given the impression that Aspie women are OCD (to suffer from Obsessive Compulsive Disorder) or that they are overly tidy. Some may be naturally and obsessively tidy, which you may well find on a neurotypical spectrum too. Some may have OCD. Others can be very untidy and disorganised.

- The more distracted and unable to function, the more likely an Aspie will not be able to simply complete a task. In their distress, they may often have a mounting disorder around them, particularly where there is also extreme external pressure. Neurotypicals can similarly not function when distressed in any way, but there is a major degree of difference between the non-coping of the two entities.

> I knew a young woman who was highly intelligent but couldn't get herself to study (because her clothes were not sorted) and twice removed herself from university. She moved back home with a roomful of boxes of clothes – a random assortment. She knew she need to purge and cull her wardrobe. Her anxiety about sorting and possibly parting with any items so hugely crippled her that she kept everything – despite still randomly purchasing more items (often op-shop buys), which went with the labels still intact into a box. The last time I talked to her, she thought that she had over two hundred pairs of shoes but could not part with one pair in case she had made a *wrong* decision. So she simply got more cardboard boxes for her expanding collection of clothes, while she had less and less space in her room. In the meantime, she kept wearing the same few items repeatedly, those that were not in the boxes.

- If they have a social circle, it is usually a very small circle and often with no, or only one, intimate friend in that circle. They are rarely extroverted.
- They often have difficulty making new friends.
- They can often have difficulty keeping friends and maintaining those relationships. They themselves make deeply true and faithful friends. The friendships are often lost because the Aspie does not appear to nurture it, or the *friends* do not understand or accept the Aspie. Despite these difficulties, Aspies themselves can make wonderful, warm, enduring friends.
- It is sometimes difficult to understand a relationship when one is in it with an Aspie woman, whether it is a friendship or a committed relationship. When they are with you, they appear to be fully engaged and connecting and then they will at another time seem coldly disinterested. Or they are fully engaged and then seem to drop the social ball, because they don't maintain the communication.

One lovely woman on the spectrum that I have known for a long time has worked out and fully acknowledges that she is a poor communicator. As she doesn't communicate with her friends and family, whether by phone or text, they assume that she is not interested in them and slowly separate themselves from the relationship.

Different Aspie/Neurotypical responses.

- Aspie relationships can also be confusing to read, as they will often, in their openness and honesty, enter a relationship very quickly, trustingly and deeply with a neurotypical and then seem to go cold. Whereas the Aspie has thought that she has been very social to someone that she wasn't interested in, and now that they don't need to be doing that, they don't follow up. Neurotypicals can misjudge the Aspie's apparent warmth; whereas the Aspie may simply be mimicking social behaviour as they think is expected at the time, as they see it.
- On the other hand, they will often have people responding angrily or at least dismissively, to them, as they may misinterpret the Aspie shyness or the consuming social anxiety, which will often present as a lack of response or indifference.

- They can often cross professional or social boundaries if someone is warm towards them and can mistake this for friendship or a more personal and intimate relationship.

> About 17 years ago, I had a client who was clearly on the spectrum (she was only officially diagnosed about a year ago). She also suffered from PTSD (Post Traumatic Stress Disorder) and had another mental health diagnosis, had been distressingly bullied at work, suffered from extreme anxiety and had such severe depression that she would, for some weeks, not get out of bed for days at a time. There were other issues happening for her too. She had no friends. She would leave a flower or note on my windscreen where I parked in the nearest carpark to my office. I referred her to an agency, with her agreement of course, that had external funding so that she no longer had the financial stress of counselling as that other agency could subsidise her. After that, she kept inviting me to have a coffee with her, which I declined – but about two years later, she had a birthday, and I agreed to meet her on that one occasion for that reason, for a coffee. I was aware that she was a lonely mental health client under the care of a mental health agency. I made it clear that there were several professional and personal boundaries, which she agreed to (including that this was a one-off coffee in respect of this important birthday – her 50th). At that forty-minute coffee meeting, she told me that she was so very glad for my friendship, and I had to explain to her that this was not a friendship at all, and it would not continue and develop into one. After that, there were no more visits despite her pleading to meet again, but she decided to then stalk me as she wanted to *just be near [me]* as she would tell me in the library or supermarket or wherever I bumped into her in our small community. She started sending texts which I read – knowing that for her they were expressing her dismay at not being able to meet with me – but to read the texts – they were completely abusive messages! I believe that she did not understand that they were abusive (because of her quite extreme mind-blindness). Initially, I simply replied asking her not to contact me again as we no longer had a professional, working relationship. Eventually, I had to block her completely. It was difficult for me to do this, as I knew of her extreme loneliness and that she had not had much kindness in her life and this final non-responsiveness from me was going to be very distressing for her.

- They often feel, and are aware to some degree, that they are a little different and this often leaves them feeling misunderstood and sometimes socially disadvantaged, even estranged. Like most human beings, Aspies deeply long for connection and community, but their own social condition prevents them from engaging in the one thing that they most want, which is social connection – mostly the females on the spectrum anyway and especially in their youth and young adulthood. From about their thirties onwards, most Aspie women stop even trying to socialise. Some do push through and join clubs like animal rescue charities or gardening clubs, in which they can safely meet like-minded women and work together constructively on a structured mutual purpose, with little social expectations on them to commit to the vagaries of female friendships.
- They can often be the butt of jokes of others, due to their naivete, their sometimes obvious quirks, or their misreading or misunderstanding of their social circumstance at the time.
- Unless fashion is a hobby for them, or they have a stylist, they can be quite indifferent to what they wear – as long as the items are comfortable. If clothes do become an interest or a hobby, they can be very adventurous, and sometimes, they think creatively out of the box. Mostly, they can pull off the most absurd idea and make it work. Others find a style that suits (like my history teacher that was mentioned earlier), and they simply remain with that…and why not?

> One very attractive young lady that I know took some dull grey fabric from which she cut out the front and back of a skirt. Instead of sewing the seams, she wore really giant safety pins on the outside, which held the skirt together. With a simply white top, she was stunning (she looked like a model anyway). She always pulled off the most unique and fun outfits, that all the neurotypicals admired and sometimes even envied her creativity! (Neurotypicals often do not realise how socially conforming they are.)

- They generally do not have accessories (except for the more extroverted Aspies who will often practise extreme fashion – they will be the ones who successfully pull off coordinated multiple bangles and necklaces), as they find these annoying or cumbersome. Some develop a set of rules for how to dress and will deliberately then set out to make the *full package* work.
- Usually, wearing makeup or false nails and eyelashes is an uncomfortable irritation for them unless one of their interests is fashion. I have noticed among my older Aspie clients that not many will even wear a watch. Younger female Aspies rely on their cell phones for the time.
- They usually work extremely hard and do not understand about breaks and are often unaware that they have missed one. In their head, they have to do a certain job and will just keep doing this without any self-awareness of fatigue, basic needs like hunger or a need to go to the bathroom! They often have significant stamina, but even then, some of these hard workers still, unsurprisingly, burn out.

I know of one professional Aspie female who resigned after burnout and was replaced by two professionals and four part-time assistants who undertook the same work!

- Their arguments and discussions are factually based, and often they will pick up a small detail and thrash that out, which is very confusing for a neurotypical who may respond emotionally.
- Neurotypicals often do not get the female Aspie logic. Many people in the field refer to the *Doctor Spock* logic, from the *Star Trek* television series.
- Generally, they do not like direct eye contract and have difficulty maintaining it (which does not help their social situation at all!). Many have told me that they force themselves to do it (make eye contact) because it is a rule…even if they don't like the rule. They can sometimes over-stare if they do force themselves to have eye contact, which is also very uncomfortable for neurotypicals. (Of course, neurotypicals are also hopelessly unaware of their own bias towards eye contact and their high need for that to happen socially).

> One Aspie professional told me that she had to make it a rule in her head that she had to do this (look people in the eye when she spoke to them and had deliberately trained herself.) She finds it such a relief in my office to be able to talk and focus on the blinds or the carpet or whatever makes her more comfortable as she speaks.

- They have huge difficulty reading between the lines, and they miss hints; social activity for an Aspie female is metaphorically like having a giant complex, people-communication puzzle that they have to solve under extreme multiple pressures…when they, to their great humiliation, do not always have the answers and certainly not at speed (because of their detailed processing)!
- Aspies, including and sometimes especially Aspie women – are very creative. Their creativity is unlimited as they have such lateral thinking and are so well able to work *outside the box*.
- They are often spiritually sensitive and quite intuitive.
- They often appear to lack initiative; for example, they may do their work but not necessarily notice that when they are finished that someone else can do with some help. Or they may simply wait for instruction.
- They often struggle with their self-identity and a low awareness of their own self. They often are quite clumsy and have a poor sense of space around them [proprioception]. In more technical terms, they often have gross-motor difficulties, which makes playing sport difficult to achieve. When they are very young, dance and swimming really helps to better develop this spatial and self-awareness.
- They have multiple thoughts running through their head continuously and have difficulty focusing on a priority thought. This impedes the cognitive switching in social situations too and makes it difficult for them.
- They often seem to talk *at* people rather than to or with them.
- They often forget to manage the pitch of their voices and can sometimes speak overly loudly and seem to have difficulty moderating their voices to suit social circumstances. They can often be overheard in the library or in a coffee shop, where people talk in more modulated tones.
- They often dread new situations – such as finding a train in strange city or

- especially meeting new people. This is probably because of difficulties imagining the situation in advance. (*Imagination and creativity are two very different things.*)
- From a young age, they can develop anxiety and may require lots of assuring.
- They often struggle with a form of insomnia, as adults. I suspect that this may have much to do with their anxiety and the adrenal after-effects from stressing. Learning to be more mindful in stressful situations will help ease this anxiety once they are in the middle of it. Also, a later processing, re-processing or debriefing of a situation is often a very helpful tool – whether they do this with another person or whether they learn to do this effectively on their own.
- They often appear controlling, as they want to stick to a routine that they are familiar with. Others (meaning neurotypicals mainly) would find this need for routine limiting and would perceive it resentfully as being controlled by the other person or sometimes by what only one person in a group may be wanting (or, more likely, needing). Some neurotypicals perceive this as a form of bullying.
- They can be quite inflexible. Change is often difficult. If change is coming, they need lots of warning to make a plan and cope. It is rare to find a spontaneous Aspie.
- They are incredibly kind, usually. They seem to have a lovely, genuine respect of other people. This is probably often because of their fondness towards animals, which may translate similarly to the way they treat *human*-animals. (One lady that I knew would refer to people with *hello human*, or *she is a nice human*, or *welcome humans*.) I suspect that they try to understand both in the same way and use the same attitude and skills to a large degree. It is often an Aspie female who will point out animal body language to me and explain what that body language means. [Does that make me neurotypically mind-blind to animal details?]
- They can be very gullible and suffer con artists without discerning danger.
- With their poor social reading skills, Aspie women are often caught in compromised situations, and many have experienced sexual molestation or have been pressured into a sexual act in which they do not want to

participate – and for which, they had later felt that they had not consented to.
- They are bluntly truthful. It is rare for them to lie (if they do become liars, they make it a specialised skill and become exceptionally good at it).
- They do not show a neurotypical range of facial or emotional expressions. If they do, the facial expression often does not match what they are saying. I have learned to focus on their words when I am with a typical Aspie woman. One also needs to focus on the actions of the Aspie woman too!
- Emotionally, they can be personally (meaning one-on-one) intense yet will often miss that other person's feelings (due to mind-blindness). Despite having very strong emotions, they struggle to show it overtly, or are unconscious that their emotions are often unreadable. Therefore, at many levels, communicating emotionally is very difficult.
- They can be very literal. Once they understand this, they can be quite funny at their own expense. They can then become very good comedians.
- They love rules and strict boundaries. They can be inflexible about rules, for example, playing a board game like Monopoly.
- They don't get variations in voice tones, such as rising annoyance, frustration, anger or sarcasm easily, so may miss social cues. They often don't read body language very well either, so they may miss cues that others have long picked up. If and when they realise this, they are often shocked and/or perplexed and confused and just can't get it. Once they are taught the rules of body language, they are absolutely brilliant. I have some books on body language that I lend to Aspies, or I teach them. One young lady has so well trained herself in these rules (*the secret human-communication code,* as she calls them) that she is brilliant and now picks up more than neurotypicals do!
- They have a wonderful sense of humour once they understand the rules of humour and will often maximise these. There is a lot of fun in listening to an Aspie making continuous puns, for example. Their humour is fabulous and is usually a play on words or *literalising* a situation for comedic effect.

- Despite often having average to very high intelligence, they are usually much slower than neurotypicals for processing social or emotional events. This is considered to be mainly because they do not remember events in a general manner like neurotypicals do (what I often refer to as lazy remembering), but they remember much more detail and specifics which they can often recall very accurately. It takes longer to file or process such detailed memories.
- They often have enviable, detailed memories long term and much better than any neurotypical, but short-term memory is often poor, or more faulty than neurotypicals.
- They tend to live a lot *in the moment* – even to the degree of appearing to not realise that something they previously were not interested in is now the main focus of their life. This often blindsides the neurotypical and leaves them scratching heads and questioning themselves – and may continue to do so for quite some years. This moment's reality is the Aspie main focus. Some can be quite extreme about this, and I have personally found this to be more likely in the extroverted Aspie women.

> One lady hated swimming in the sea but suddenly (as it appeared) decided to enrol in a deep-sea diving course, claiming that all her life she had wanted to do this. She had never alluded to this (now passionate) interest. Another decided impulsively to move to rural Australia because she believed that she always had wanted to do that. I had known her for about five years and had heard all her dreams and passions and she had never ever mentioned this or talked about it before. This same lady met a man and married him within a couple of weeks at a registry office, because she felt that she had always known him and it was always their plan to get married. Another who had an aversion (rare for Aspie females) for pets and animals suddenly bought a chinchilla with all the accessories!

When challenged on this mercurial flick, they can be completely, unwaveringly articulate and clear and patiently explain how this had always been in their head and how it was obviously the correct and only thing to do, and they leave no other option about this. Being neurotypical – well, we usually give people the benefit of the doubt, but when this happens repeatedly, it can be quite a struggle to understand it fully.

- It is not the desire to try new things that is the issue here. It is that it appears to be an instant decision but is usually explained as a deep-seated desire to always do that. This mercurial flick is not usually a trait in male Aspies.
- They can be quite black-and-white with few variations.

> An Aspie female client could not understand that a neurotypical person can have degrees of liking (or disliking) something – she said, "You do my head in! I am going to need a whole week to process that thought!" For her, it was a case of you either liked something or you didn't and there was nothing else in-between.

- They seem to retain a level of innocence and often appear a little naïve (which can lead to being gullible) at times. This is why they can often be easily manipulated and tricked.
- Their gullibility may originate because of their genuine belief that other people seem to be authentic, and they miss the cues and signals that would give better warning. Because they are often genuine, they seem to believe that others are too.
- They desperately want to please others.
- They often have a high level of anxiety, with a need to get things right. In an ordered and structured environment, their anxiety significantly decreases.
- They are often psychic, or at least spiritually or intuitively sensitive.
- The rules of religions that have quite a cultic nature can often appeal to them, especially if the cult appears to be very welcoming and seemingly homely.
- They are sadly often the victim of bullying.

> One teenage girl that I knew was particularly new to the neighbourhood and also exceptionally isolated. Her mother had had a stroke at a young age and couldn't care for her, and the father was absent from the picture. She desperately sought friendship for all of the normal teenage (and human) reasons. She was also clearly on the spectrum so she had difficulty communicating and connecting and would mostly giggle at whomever talked to her. She fell in with the *bad* crowd whom she thought were

> offering her friendship. They convinced her that she needed to throw rocks at one of the school cameras (while they were smoking in the background and invisible to the broken camera). Of course, she was recorded on the camera so was apprehended. She was stood down for a few days. On her return to school, they convinced her (with the promise of guaranteed membership of the group and their ongoing support) to egg a teacher's house that was nearby. They even gave her the eggs. She again was apprehended in the act, and of course, the girls disappeared and later denied any part in the deeds. Sadly, she was expelled from the school and had no further supports as it appeared that she never returned to school. So long-term, she missed an education as well as with her expulsion, she fell through the cracks of the education system.

- They do need lots of alone time, even if they are extroverted.
- They do not enjoy being hugged especially by someone not close to them and even then, will only just tolerate it. They can make rather awkward huggers. One young lady that I knew from childhood always came forward for a rather stiff hug the rare times that I saw her as an adult. One day, she told me how to hug her in greeting as she found my hug was too intense! I was utterly surprised but of course should not have been! I was grateful for her lovely honesty though, once I had got over my surprise.
- If they know facts (for example they are a scientist or a historian), they will process relevant information quickly and will respond quickly. Once they have data encoded in a way that suits them, they can assimilate and compare other related data very quickly – usually more quickly than neurotypicals who may have the same knowledge.
- Aspie women generally need more processing time than neurotypicals. They are poor at spontaneous decision making, feedback and responses, unless it is in their field of expertise.
- They struggle to make quick cognitive changes. Added to this is having weak cognitive coherence, alternatively known as weak cognitive shifting.
- Aspie women often find it hard to think through a future situation that is unpredictable – and this is considered a typical ASD cognitive difficulty in the area of imagination.

I remember spending nearly three hours with a young woman on the spectrum – or with at least many spectrum traits. She was leaving to go to another city, to university, and she was going to live in the academic halls with people whom she would not know. Her main concern was how to get to the correct lecture theatre without getting lost (she also had a particularly poor sense of direction). I explored with her the map of the campus and directed her. "But how do I you know you are right?" she would wail. "You have never been there!" We worked from two pieces of paper. One listed her timetable, with the lecture theatre room numbers on them. The other piece of paper had the campus layout. I would point out that a particular class was in AB16. This meant block A, section B (it had a star shaped type of layout), and room 16. Another was room F215. This meant this was on the second floor in block F, and the fifteenth classroom. She was distressed, crying and overwhelmed – both with the classification of the classrooms and the over-riding fear that I could be wrong. I pointed out that this was a common first world way of labelling apartments and offices in large buildings, which code was similarly used internationally, and explained earlier in her orientation guide. This settled her mind a little. We also made a plan that she would go earlier to campus and that she would follow my instructions and do a trial run of getting to the correct lecture theatres and check the timing of it from her new residence. Of course, it all worked out easily and accordingly. For me, the biggest thing was that this really intelligent girl took three hours to process this information, which to most NTs is common sense. Obviously as her fear escalated, her comprehension naturally declined, but it really was a struggle for her to get her head around this information and process it in a way that was useful to her. When my son went to university, I ran through the same information (because we come from a very small city) in under five minutes. He shrugged and seemed to think it was rather pointless that I needed to explain this to him as he had worked it out at first glance.

- Aspie women (and men of course) often lack facial expression. This is of course because of their mind-blindness for which there are many consequences, but one in particular is not giving facial feedback to others. Our faces – for neurotypicals anyway – express concern, amusement, frustration, interest and many other common expressions.

As neurotypicals talk with words, they are also reading others by their faces. Aspies cannot do this. This does not mean that they are not having emotions, or are not interested, they just can't show it. (This is a useful skill and advantage for playing poker at high stakes, but it is general not useful socially!) Combine this with their difficulty of keeping track of what is happening for others, one can see how a discussion can easily get out of control. There are two eventualities as a result of this:

I. The Aspie ends up saying something inappropriate and has to deal with the fallout of that, or they do not say the appropriate thing, which has a different fallout! (My goodness – aren't our social rules difficult to understand sometimes!)

II. Because there is so little variance in their expression, there is little warning when they suddenly become impatient/angry/annoyed or have a meltdown. The neurotypical would not have seen this coming at all because there would be no facial expression alerts or changes in body language and would be very taken aback. Unfortunately, the neurotypical will then usually blame the Aspie – in most cases – and the situation will escalate unpleasantly or unhappily.

> I often, in the nature of my work, have to deal with cases involving sexual assault and rape. On quite a few occasions, an Aspie has told me about what has happened to her, describing sometimes horrific details and has talked about this with a happy expression and a big smile. In situations of extreme distress, they may wear the mask of their best social expression. At no level can one say that they are happy, but in my work, I am alert to this incongruence and work with their obvious distress.

There is one other very sad tale that encompasses many aspects of these Aspie traits.

> A ladies' group organised a get-together and planned an evening over cheese and wine to celebrate and to display their original artworks they had painted. This particular lady brought along her own painting, carefully and painstakingly done and hung it up with the other paintings as instructed. As the women drifted in, they sauntered interestedly around the room viewing

> the artworks but eventually started to cluster around her painting, and soon there was much sniggering and hidden laughter. The lady initially never noticed this as she was helping in the kitchen but came out to see this happening around her painting. She quickly disappeared back into the kitchen to work out what was happening. When she later went out of the kitchen, she was aghast to find that her painting was missing. She went around the room, asking the various organisers and ladies if they had seen what had happened to it, and they denied any knowledge of having moved it, but she heard their gasped laughter and giggling when she walked away. She eventually found it, where it had been chucked up onto a high shelf. Then she overheard a conversation between two ladies outside, who were laughing at her painting and her apparent audacity to have submitted a paint-by-numbers piece of work. At that point, the woman realised that she had done something wrong and was mortified by their laughter and her misunderstanding. She then tried to leave in her panic but in her distress could not find the door and felt a panic attack coming on.

- Finally, one of the most difficult aspects of dealing with Aspie woman is her often mercurial nature. Something that she once appeared to love, she now seems to loathe – and will tell you how you missed a particular nuance and that's the difference. She is adamant that she has always hated that particular thing, and your memory otherwise is wrong. A lot of neurotypicals tell me that this switch *does [their] head in*. Arguments usually ensue, with both convinced that they are right. The Aspie usually wins those arguments because of her logic. Neurotypicals tend to generalise and so miss Aspie nuances and various sub-rules. You may have bought them flowers many times, but this time, you do it, and they are distressed, maybe crying, and they tell you that you should have known they don't like flowers. You may then get angry and defensive and miss that it is only daffodils that she doesn't like.

Aspie Overload in Women

Universally, all people are stressed, whether they live in extreme poverty or extreme opulence. Sadly, our stressful lives are referred to as living in the *rat race* or having *first world problems* – particularly in more urbanised societies.

The stresses can be vastly different in nature. This is a normal human condition – to stress about the rent, the children, work, family – the list could fill pages.

Add to this, the stress of having a neurological difference that makes it difficult to cope in social situations!

Add to this even more…having weak cognitive coherence, alternatively known as weak cognitive shifting!

Imagine doing everyday stresses but being hampered or having one's progress impeded to some degree, because one is unable to read the social environment with confidence!

Because this is what it is like for an Aspie woman!

One young woman said to me, "But if this is all I have ever known, then it is my normal. I do not know anything different." I replied that one can be born with a leg significantly shorter than the other. Both this person and another person can walk ten kilometres, but the one with the leg-difference will be more tired, will have exerted more effort and would have possibly exacerbated some hip and spinal damage – even though she can walk ten kilometres and the condition is her normal. I told her that I have a friend who is a tall woman. I am an exceptionally short woman. When we go for a walk together, she does a comfortable stride and I am semi-running to keep up. I do 1½ to 2 steps for every stride that she takes. It is not surprising that I am breathless long before she is and more tired afterwards. (I have done nearly twice the workout that she has!) But this is my normal – which makes it a bit more difficult when I am living or competing with the *normal* of the majority.

So, we hopefully have a small glimmer of understanding what it is like for an Aspie woman. By the time they are adults, most Aspie women have started sorting out what works for them, in terms of managing this daily stress and distress. Some learn a stim that they enjoy – which may be a favourite book genre or a movie, or a craft. They generally are not physical, so they do not stim with a sport like a neurotypical uses a sport to unwind. Stimming is not about unwinding. It is about processing and hence de-stressing, which can then result in the ability to unwind. Once de-stressed, they may well go for a swim or play badminton at the invitation of a friend. She might even be able to go and watch a noisy international rugby match – providing she is de-stressed and is ready for this planned event and has got her head around it.

> One young professional woman that I know is aware of her need to de-stress and is aware of her need to stim. She holds it together every day at work and plays her role perfectly – in fact, she is often promoted and given extra work. When she gets home, she needs silence. Her partner understands her, but he is also a very social young man – he has engaged in several sports after work so that he gets his social and sport fix, and she gets some alone quiet time. She is very aware that he is social, and she can certainly go out to social engagements together with him, but again, she has learnt to act her way through these so well, that she has generally learned to genuinely enjoy some of these events. They have never discussed with anyone that she has traits – the main reason being the social ignorance of the public and the fact that she doesn't want to be seen as being "mental" – or being treated in any inappropriate manner. This woman has also worked so hard at reading body language that she can read a room, her clients and her management team quite easily. This reading is not by osmosis but by a set of rules that she has learned about body language, which she applies with studious care.

Many Aspie women tell me that they can do the whole social dance – like an act. A camouflage of the real self. They can smile, listen with intense and rapt attention, pop in the odd sentence or two (more if they are extroverted) and completely act out social behaviours that they have observed and integrated over years. Then they get home and need complete silence, won't answer the phone and find a stim – which may last for hours, to recover from the social onslaught. A couple of teachers have talked to me about how they make a mad dash to their cars, to leave work as soon as possible, to meet the need to go home to recover. But not every Aspie woman has recognised the stressors in her life, nor has learned life skills to de-stress. The more out-of-control and overwhelmed they feel, the harder they try – until something in them snaps and they cannot do that anymore. Some people shut down, into a semi-conscious functioning state but in a withdrawn, dissociated manner. The next stage may well be a meltdown or a breakdown, which can go from devastating to quite psychotic looking to an observer, yet for the Aspie, it is a state of total breakdown in which they feel shards of their *self* are scattered like ash in the wind and they describe having lost any sense of personal coherence.

> One lady showed me a poem that she wrote about looking in the *looking glass* [a mirror], which breaks into shards and she cannot put herself together properly in the bits of mirror scattered around.

They tell me that they feel mindless, unable to extrapolate any useful thoughts or actions; some describing themselves as *just hitting a total blank*. Those who have experienced a few breakdowns and have had supportive counselling, have learned to catch the clues earlier and earlier and have a set of processes to allow an escape and a self-reconnection before a breakdown occurs. Those without support sometimes have to repeatedly face the humiliation and scorn of family and associates who react critically and unsupportively, and in extreme cases, the Aspie may end up part of the mental health or psychiatric system – usually with a misdiagnoses (commonly bi-polar or more rarely, border-line personality disorder).

Misdiagnosis of Women

This section is a discussion on misdiagnosed female ASD clients. It is intended to be a non-critical, non-judgemental and factual account of experiences.

The field of psychiatry is vast and complex, and the responsibility weighs heavily on a psychiatrist to make accurate, and often lifesaving, diagnosis. In an emergency, it may even be difficult to get any accurate mental health history. A diagnosis is often needed to justify or prescribe an anti-psychotic medication. The initial meeting of a patient and a psychiatrist is sometimes of extreme duress for the patient who may also have complex lifestyle situations which add to the stress of the patient. By nature of a first presentation at a psychiatric unit, there may be no psychiatric history or no measurable, physiological symptoms. Most hospitals and psychiatric units also run under very tight time schedules and pressures. So it is easy to then miss a diagnosis of Asperger syndrome in females within the meltdown presentation. It takes time to explore, measure and diagnose. Realistically, this can never happen in a time of an extreme episodic presentation.

Other clients have not had an emergency hospital presentation from a breakdown but have exhaustively sought help for their symptoms and traits. Many psychologists and counsellors completely miss the symptoms of

Aspergers, especially in women, and I have met these poor souls (the clients) who have wandered from psychologist to counsellor, back and forth, looking for support. Some clients felt that their counselling experience or experiences were negative as their counsellor or psychologist appeared to blame them for seeming to be uncooperative in therapy.

They frequently have an accepted belief that they are beyond help by this stage. Added to this is the difficulty of diagnosing females on the ASD spectrum. Because the women have (obviously) a largely female brain and because women can intuit better than men, these women have learned to wear invisible social masks and have also learned to camouflage themselves, so that they look neurotypical to a large degree. Women on the spectrum are notoriously difficult to diagnose, and it is known in academic circles that many are missed. I believe that there is an equal distribution of males and females on the spectrum, but this is anecdotal. Until we have better tools to diagnose women, we cannot accurately undertake these statistics.

> My friend and colleague, Dr Yvette Ahmad, a clinical psychologist, and I have long been working on a paper and a new pilot testing tool, to more accurately screen for Autism in women. This academic paper and test is at the end of the book, in the Appendix. You can also undertake this test online.

So in the light of all of the above, let us look at the experiences of some women on the ASD spectrum and issues with their diagnosis. Although only a few stories are captured in this book, they are the proverbial tip of the iceberg, as is well known in academic circles of so many other misdiagnoses of these women. I have included the following four stories, because they express far better any explanation that I can make.

When I have met Aspergic clients after they have been through the mental health system, mostly they are diagnosed most commonly as bipolar, borderline personality disorder where there is, or has been, self-harm, schizoid affective or a combination of these. Usually, they have the added co-morbidity of a depressive or anxiety disorder added on.

One client who is clearly a female Aspergic with PTSD (Post Traumatic Stress Disorder) has struggled within the mental health system for more than 30 or 40 years. A natural subsequent disorder that she developed as a result of her experiences growing up is a severe anxiety. Her childhood trauma was ignored altogether, and her final diagnosis was schizophrenia with schizoid affective disorder, as well as chronic anxiety. She was taken into a mental health unit as a result of an emotional breakdown. When she told me of her father, he probably walked out of a textbook on male Aspergers (metaphorically – for Aspie readers!), but back in the day the only diagnosis available to him was schizophrenia – bearing in mind that he had no schizophrenic episodes and his behaviour was consistent (if odd). This happened about 60 years ago. She grew up being told there was therefore schizophrenia in the family. She felt that as it was believed that her father was schizophrenic, then she was almost automatically given the same diagnosis. She has been on incredibly huge levels of medicinal cocktails over the last 30 to 35 years.

I would have met her originally about 25 years ago, and she was having what I would call a typical Aspie meltdown at the time that I met her. [It's important to be aware the diagnosis of Aspergers was just becoming current back then and I could see that, for several reasons, she was clearly on the spectrum. She also did not appear to have schizophrenic symptoms.] It is common for Aspies to cope through a system of rules and social rules. She had very strict religious rules and a constant sense that God was going to cut her off as the rest of the world had, because she didn't behave. So when I met her, she was in the middle of all of these challenging thoughts and self-imposed rules and feeling judged and out of control, and she was having a very understandable breakdown because of the many stresses in her life, none of which were her own doing (poverty being one of these stressors). She went to her district nurse who referred her to her GP, and she came to see me through her GP

Before we even met (she told me at a much later stage), the doctor had also alerted mental health, and she was picked up by the mental health unit. She was then raped in the psychiatric unit by an inmate – and that wasn't the first time. Of course, the event was dismissed as a figment of her imagination because she was schizophrenic. This lady is articulate; she is intelligent; she is clear, her memory is phenomenal, and you only had to listen to her to know how real, present and sane she is. Quite interestingly, at times of her breakdown, she would feel a noise in her ears, which could well have been stress and her blood pumping through her eardrums (as she described it). This was the only sign that the psychiatrist used to diagnose her schizophrenia, that she had audial delusions. She believed that God was going to destroy her because she broke his rules, but she never claimed to hear his voice, she didn't have any of the schizophrenic symptoms or any delusions or other possible bi-polar criteria. (I also never knew what religious rules she was supposed to have broken, but I came to understand that she was self-condemning.) Her belief was a very firm belief because of her history and because of her low sense of self-esteem and low sense of worth. But regardless, she was labelled as schizophrenic with schizoid affective disorder and severe anxiety and has been given no help except medication, proverbially – up to her eyeballs.

Over the years, I have watched her succumb to the various side effects of, at times, very high levels of antipsychotic medications and she has now been in and out of mental health care. I saw her on and off whenever she wanted to pop in. She felt that I was the only objective person with whom she could frankly discuss her difficulties. Sadly, I never discussed Aspergers with her because she was already distressed by all [her] labels and I just needed to bring her distress down. But she responded the way Aspies do to the distress management tools that I use. She had medication for her mental health conditions, which medications gave her tremors, so she had another medication for her tremors, which gave her nausea, so they gave her an anti-nausea, which made her sleepy and so on… Who can bear it?

That's one client story. Here is another…

Another client came in, having had an Aspie meltdown. This was an Aspie-serious-meltdown, a metaphorical level-9 on the Richter scale. A top-end type meltdown can look like a psychotic breakdown. She is a creative, lovely lady. She had children, lived with her husband in the family home, had a few university degrees, was well travelled and was a healthy functioning woman in her community. As Aspies are, she was easily overstretched by others demanding expectations. When she had an occasional meltdown, the family would roll their eyes and use the code that *mad Aunty Betty had come to town again*. On a few occasions, she was so irrational that her husband in distress and fearing for her safety [his perceptions], she was taken off to the local psychiatric/mental-health unit and put on very heavy tranquilizers and then sent home after a while again – but there was no real help outside of the medical mental-health framework (not even visits by a district psychiatric nurse). She was sent back home with a large bag of serious medication that would fix all her problems!

> At home, she would gradually wean herself off the tranquilisers. On tranquilisers and anti-psychotic medication as "[my] mental screen was blank and [I] had no emotions". They also added in a double dose of sleeping tablets each night, which left her lethargic, groggy, and unable to operate in a houseful of teenagers and her need to function as their mother. So when I met her, we talked about all of this last mental health experience.
>
> She was diagnosed by a psychiatrist as being bipolar with other comorbid mental health diagnoses. Her psychiatrist and GP were wanting to keep her on a heavy cocktail of medications. [Obviously as a counsellor, I have no influence over medications and am always clear about clients following medical advice. I cannot prescribe nor tell them whether to use their medication or not, and I don't.] Anyway, we had a few sessions and then I hadn't seen her for a while. Under extreme extended family pressures, I saw her again and she had just been discharged from hospital (the same psychiatric unit) again and wanted to come and process the last few days' events with me. She sat in my office and laughed at her latest, updated diagnosis, which was now: Bipolar (apart from fluctuating moods which are stress related, she has no other signs) with Borderline Personality Disorder (she has no signs of BPD) and an Object Attachment Disorder (which diagnosis actually does not exist in any psychiatric or other manual). I asked what that was about, and she said that when she was having her meltdown, the final straw was that couldn't find a particular nozzle for the vacuum hose – "and [I] needed to do a task and [I] couldn't find this part. And it was just the last straw for [me]." So the psychiatrist has given her a new, extra diagnosis on her medical file as having an *Object Attachment Disorder*.

Not so long ago I had a client come through the local medical system. Her doctor had referred her. She had been suicidal and had made a suicidal attempt. She had made a few attempts before, and she had been discharged from the local hospital but needed some further support.

At our first meeting, she clarified that her several other attempts had all been impulsive, and she used what was on hand – usually medication. This time she was under even further emotional strain. There was a separation in which her ex-husband had kept the children for whom she was grieving; she was new to our town; she was secretly polyamorous, which she didn't want to have exposed, her new boyfriend had dumped her by text, and she had had a breakdown and in an impulsive moment had swallowed all her prescribed medication for a sleep disorder. Someone found her; she was taken by ambulance to A&E (hospital Accidents and Emergencies department) and then on to the psychiatric unit. The psychiatrist there diagnosed her as borderline with bipolar disorder. She was again an Aspie straight out of the book – walked off the pages (not literally – if you are an Aspie reading this) in a classic breakdown or meltdown. She was completely overwhelmed by her circumstances and feeling out of control. She was very concerned because she was looking for work in a field that wanted mental health disclosures, which actually forbore that she could not do that work anymore, and here she was slapped with rather a heavy psychiatric diagnosis. She wanted to be employed in this social position and wanted to continue working and couldn't because of this health label. She gave me permission to call her psychiatrist who was actually a rather lovely man. I very gently explained the client's concerns but that I had known her for some time and she had not displayed any signs fitting the diagnosis. He did know me well, as I had worked with quite a few of his clients. I added that I believed that she was on the ASD spectrum, and I wondered if he would consider reassessing her and review the diagnosis. He firmly denied that there was anything Aspergic about her. Fortunately, he came back to me a few days later and said to me that he had reconsidered the matter and reviewed the files and thought that I was possibly correct, and he would have her reassessed. She was assessed by an external clinical psychologist and yes, she is diagnosed as Aspergic and no other mental health conditions were found. This went back to the psychiatrist. He accepted the diagnosis of Asperger syndrome but then refused to remove his own mental health diagnosis from her medical files.

Another client also had a complete breakdown and her doctor referred her to the psychiatric unit for assessment. She was not self-harming nor suicidal but extremely stressed and depressed. She was diagnosed as bipolar and was then sent to me so that she could learn to cope with this mental health disorder.

> Working with her, she was clearly Aspergic and there were no signs of bipolar behaviour, so we sent her off for a private assessment and yes, she was Aspergic. She contacted her psychiatrist to please have the mental health diagnosis removed off the file. She wanted to work in a field that involved children, and she was doing some training, but she probably couldn't professionally register in her chosen field one day once she had qualified because of her psychiatric diagnosis. The psychiatric department refused. They refused to reconsider or take any positive action. To this day, that mental health diagnosis is still on her file. In the eight or nine years that I have known her, she has never shown any signs of being bipolar. She has remained stable and is functioning well and relishing the understanding of her *Aspieness*.

Aspie Women in Relationships

There is a whole chapter on Aspie relationships, so this is simply a quick overview.

Aspie women are generally warm and intelligent and can be very entertaining. They have a great sense of humour. They are usually faithful and loyal and will give you all of themselves. Of course, you have to get to know them first.

The rare ones will be extroverted, but more commonly, they are quiet in social circles, as they *suss out the environment*. This means they have to work out what the social environment is and how they have to walk through the minefield of it. They will usually avoid loud places, like pubs and clubs, unless they are the rare extroverted Aspie female. You are more likely to meet one at work, or possibly online dating, or in an interest area, or more likely your friend's lovely sister, than in a noisy public venue.

The vast majority of people look for connection. For neurotypicals, it is primarily an emotional connection. For the Aspie female, it will be firstly an intellectual connection. She needs a compatibility connection, or a connection based on her rules and facts and will be more practical in nature. Aspie women can be very clear about their expectations for a relationship to happen. They are usually pragmatic about a relationship, not usually *gold-diggers* and are very accepting of the person that they have decided to be with – unless that person doesn't keep to their relationship rules – many of which may have been made by her. She needs someone who understands her, gives her space and lets her be herself, which might well be the comfy girl with no make-up snacking on nuts and wearing that ugly oversized mustard jumper that you don't like, when she is having downtime. (And about that jumper – apart from the fact that it was a bargain-buy – it is comfortable! It has no itchy labels or seams, the fabric feels just right for a snuggle and relax, and the colour is undemanding on the eye. Surely, those are all excellent reasons for wearing that jumper. If you want to be with her, you might need to get over yourself and ditch your concerns about the fashion-ability, or lack of it, of that jumper.) Usually, when she goes out with you, she tries to look her best, so let her be when she is *just chilling*.

If she is prepared, she is a great host or will be good company when going to a social function with you. But remember, she may need several days of quiet to get over that function. Don't surprise her with extra social activities (actually don't surprise her at all!). Don't go to your cousin's wedding and then invite a house-load of unexpected guests back home because you were having fun – unless you have expressly prepared her for this. She will probably disagree and not want the guests. Or if you surprise her, she may have a meltdown because her sensory and social mechanisms are way (way!) overextended and overloaded. She might agree to the extra intrusion, but then don't be upset if at some point she puts earplugs in and goes to bed in the most remote bedroom to avoid the noise or goes to her best friend's apartment instead (because the best friend is in Italy, and she has a key to the empty apartment).

Aspie women have systems in their home, and it is a good idea to keep them, for the sake of your relationship. When you make a coffee in the morning, please put the coffee canister back on the shelf, with the lid in and the picture showing outwards. And please put it between the milo and the tea canister, exactly where it always belongs. Why? Because it just looks and feels right there. You may have an issue that she often does not put it back herself. She has a system and a reason why, and it's floating around in her head to do it correctly when she can get to it. Does this strike you as terribly unfair? Then that's your problem. Perhaps you can rationally discuss this with her, at a good time and in anon-attacking manner. She will probably see reason and adapt to your system a bit. Otherwise, put up with it – it is a comparatively small thing. She is faithful, has your back covered, will support your idiosyncrasies down to the most minor details. It took me a whole paragraph to say – just put the cannister back correctly in its place. It's a small price to pay for the lovely woman who will always be there for you. (Remember – it is very rare for Aspie women to be unfaithful.)

Some relationships with an Aspie woman can be very difficult to understand. She may be attracted to you and want to be with you, so will concede to agree with you about all your interests and hobbies, as if hers are the same. In fact, she may nod and agree with you a lot, and you may have thought that you have found your dream partner. She is probably nodding and agreeing to appear friendly in her attempts to socially match you and does what you want because she is focussed on pleasing you. Some months (or maybe even a year or two later), she decides to stop maintaining that unmanageable façade that she has been carrying, and the walls come tumbling down dramatically. And you may then discover that what you thought about her was not correct. You are both broken at this stage and probably struggling to know how to redeem the relationship. She has not set out to deliberately deceive you, nor has she lied to you. She simply set out to please you and eventually couldn't count the cost of that strain anymore.

So you are surprised when she has a meltdown because you didn't see it coming? Aspie women are very patient and very accommodating, in fact extremely accommodating. She has put up with your dithering, your muttering, your unfair statements, your ubiquitous lateness, your grumpiness and high demands. She has shown little expression throughout all of this. She has had to process and process and reprocess all of those things that you have brought into her environment. And then she went into overload.

She is not very good at expressing herself, remember? She probably also has a few of the following additional issues to deal with, apart from your behaviours mentioned above:

Alexithymia: difficulty experiencing, expressing and describing emotional responses.

Misophonia: a hypersensitivity to certain sounds that are almost physically painful for her to hear.

Misokinesia: a hypersensitivity to certain movements that are almost physically painful for her too.

You have been pacing the room (misokinesia to her); a torn piece of curtain is flapping in the wind because you left the window open again (additional misokinesia); you have been munching crisps loudly (misophonia to her), and she has become increasingly distressed by your behaviour but can't explain it to you (her alexithymia). She has a raging meltdown and starts crying or says irrational things and then you walk out of the room, won't help her and tell her she's nuts *when it was all your fault to start with!* Well – maybe – but try to see her bigger picture.

You wouldn't put fuel (petrol) in a diesel car; you wouldn't drink sulphuric acid instead of water; you wouldn't put monopoly money in your bank account, so why do you keep putting rubbish into and onto her? She will be a wonderful woman in your life, so just look after her properly and care for her. The results will speak for themselves in a great long-term relationship or marriage, or you are facing a very short one if you don't.

On the other hand, she may just have had enough and it is not necessarily your fault. I have seen loving Aspie women apparently flick some sort of emotional switch and simply disengage from a relationship and leave that relationship. And you and your community are left stunned by what actually happened. She may try to stay friends; she may try to discuss this friendship with you. You may not understand her processing and be confused by her changing signals. She may even suggest some things like continuing a sexual relationship as a practical help, because in her logic you two will not need to engage sexually with a stranger who may carry STDs!

I have observed Aspie women in relationships, and sometimes, they do seem to suddenly end a relationship and walk away, for no apparent reason. But as I work through their separation with them, it seems that they had had a list of rules, to which the other was completely oblivious, that had been broken one time too many. The final rule was always around the thought that when this rule gets broken repeatedly, I will end the relationship. There were never any warnings. Neurotypicals on the other hand are devastated, sideswiped and confused. Neurotypicals often talk about Aspie females that they know, who treat others as *disposable objects*. I am guessing that the truth is somewhere in the middle!

Aspie Mothers

There is not much research on this topic, but a lot of reflective, anecdotal writings by Aspie women, such as Rudy Simone and Dr Lianne Holliday-Willey. I also have a load of Aspie mums with whom I have worked for many years.

This may seem shocking to neurotypicals, but Aspie mums don't often enjoy being mums, yet love their children. I hear this often. This sounds like a contradiction.

For neurotypicals, as mums, we get stressed, sleep deprived, develop that foggy *nappy-brain or baby-brain*, fret that our babies are not well, get exceptionally tired and drained, unsocial, and in high need of TLC (tender loving care), require support ourselves, and we definitely feel overwhelmed. For Aspie mums, they have the additional social skill issues and cognitive difficulties around focus. Some are hypersensitive in at least one area, have difficulty expressing how they feel, have limited theory-of-mind to interpret their baby and others around them, have delays in cognitive processing, and are super overwhelmed with often no respite to process and stim and chill out. Because Aspies often have relationship breakdowns, a large number of these mums are also solo mums.

Many Aspie women never become mums. Some because they do not want to. One told me that she could adopt if her husband really wanted children but that the thought of something growing inside her *like a parasite* completely nauseated her. Many are not driven by maternal feelings, longings or instincts. Many do not like the sex act itself, so procreation can be a bit of a problem in that too.

Yet some have taken to motherhood like a proverbial duck to water. Many of the older Aspies got married and had children *because that's what you do*. Because many have had relationship breakdowns, they have often ended up as solo mums, sometimes having two or three children from different dads. (This is of course, a refrain heard from neurotypical women at times too.) Those who have taken to mothering, do the parenting job a little differently to neurotypicals though.

As in all other life patterns, Aspie mums can be unconventional in how they parent. They will often talk to their children as if they are adults. They will miss social cues. They will have strict rules. And then at other times, they will roll around with the children like they are children too and will be the big child in a playgroup. Some of these Aspie mums are intuitively sensitive to their babies and children's needs, while others miss them to a large degree. This is all part of the fabric of the different mothering styles one will find in the material that makes up our society.

One of the questions that I am often asked is: "Is being an Aspie mum an automatic outcome therefore, that any children born will be on the spectrum?" There has been extensive genetic research on this, and the answer is still inconclusive. There does appear to be a genetic link sometimes, but the actual link (or gene) cannot be found yet. On the other hand, that link is also completely absent. An Aspergic mum may have three children with none on the spectrum, one or some on the spectrum, or all three on the spectrum. There are no accurate indicators or predictors. So still no answer to that question yet. Sorry!

As in the chapter on Aspergic fathers, the Aspergic mothers often have some mind-blindness – which is the understanding of how their child may be feeling emotionally or understanding a child's intentions. Also, because they are more likely to become overwhelmed than neurotypicals, Aspie mums can have some quite catastrophic meltdowns within their families. The children do not know what to do; if their father is around, he usually does not know what to do either. Once the rage and the irrational volley of attacking words are over, the children and the family walk on those proverbial eggshells around the mum for quite a while. And then she is bouncing back again, with some stimulating ideas and messy play!

Aspie mums are usually the ones who keep a record of school notices, make sure the lunches are packed, remember the sports gear, and get to school on time. On the other hand – and this is the other extreme – Aspie mums can be the scatty ones who are late for everything because they couldn't stay focussed nor on task. These are the more chaotic mums where the homework is lost, the kids are often late and lunches are forgotten. I am pretty sure that one of my daughter's school friend's extroverted mum was on the spectrum…from her obvious mind-blindness, talking *at* me, the way she jumped subjects and the lack of eye contact. I can assure you that list is not exhaustive.

> The girl was more of a classmate than a friend. My daughter was invited to her birthday party, a sleepover. I spoke with the mum who assured me that it was only her and her older sister…and of course the mum. The plan was for a movie, dinner and bed. My daughter phoned me at about 11 pm with our code word for not feeling safe so I went to pick her up. The house was in chaos, there was no children's party, the mum was drinking heavily, the sister and boyfriend were having loud sex in the room with no separation from the other two girls, all the lights were still on and the music was blaring loudly!
>
> One day, a short while after that episode, the little girl's mum phoned me and asked if her daughter could have a sleepover at our house. The mum explained that she had a new boyfriend and was going away overnight with him. After school, she brought her daughter over, with an overnight bag – which we later discovered had a set of summer pyjamas despite that the weather was getting cold as we were heading into winter. There was no toothbrush or hairbrush or fresh clothes. All of this we discovered, of course, after the mum had gone. The mum promised to pick up her daughter early the next morning. The mum stayed away for four nights! The daughter knew her mum's mobile phone number, but the mum never answered – the phone was turned off. The daughter thought this was all quite normal, although at age 11, she was starting to become aware of the oddity of the behaviour of her mum and was increasingly embarrassed as the days went on. I didn't know if the mother had had an accident, or if there were other safety issues. Regardless, she rolled up four days later to pick up her daughter, who went home in my daughter's clothes, with a new toothbrush and hairbrush and her few things washed and in her bag. The mum made no apologies, and off

> they went, seemingly quite happily. The little girl moved school soon after to another town and I never heard from them again.

Aspie mums, on the whole, are very good mums. So are neurotypical mums, in different ways. It is always the few, small in number, from both camps, that can let the whole side down though. We often hear negative stories, but the positive stories do exceed the negative!

Many Aspie women love having pets – by far the larger majority do. Many will have pets instead of children and are usually good, responsible pet owners. (A few are terrified of animals or pets and cannot bear their smell and other related furry animal issues – but among female Aspies, this is more rare than the norm.) An Aspie mum may have her child or children plus a menagerie of pets, which all combined become increasingly difficult to manage. Pets are more manageable than children because once the various duties of care are done, a pet can be returned to a cage or put out in the garden and the owner can go off duty for a while. Having children, a mum does not really ever go off-duty. Mind you, once the children are adults, there is usually a lot more downtime!

As grandmothers, they are more likely to crawl on the ground and play directly with their grandchildren and enjoy doing crafts and activities with them. They seem to easily get onto a child's wavelength and there are no adult expectations from children, just some good healthy engagement. Somebody – I can't remember who – said that Aspies can be childlike and they enjoy getting down on a child's play level. On the other extreme, they may be the withdrawn, embittered grandmothers who are not engaged with families – but that is also more rare and the result of other issues.

A few Aspie parents, particularly if they have a diagnosed child on the spectrum, will choose to home school their children and will often deliver a safe, secure learning environment in which they can school their children. This is often a more exhausting choice sometimes, but the mother, in other ways, benefits from not having the stress of school hours, external expectations and those conversations with the other mothers at the gate! They either do this because they feel that their children are receiving an insufficient education, they perceive their child is on the spectrum and may need some extra support, or the child may just need to be removed from some bullying in the school environment. Home-schooling helps the mother in many cases too, especially if there is support from the children's father and opportunities for extended family to be involved and to offer time out for everybody. The Aspie mums that I have met, who have and do home school, are very realistic about their limits and capacity. They are usually not emotionally hooked into the idea of home schooling and seem to be able to freely return their children to a classroom environment should the child require that.

Aspie mums who understand and accept their Aspie traits can make very good parents. For some, I have met their children, who are independent thinkers and have seemed well cared for. Independence is a word often used to describe the children of Aspie mothers. Aspie mothers are pragmatic parents and do not raise their children from and through an emotional filter.

Some adult children of Aspie mothers have written about attachment issues, in that they had difficulty attaching emotionally with their Aspie mothers, especially where the child was neurotypical. Some have gone on to describe their difficulties around their emotional validation and how to interact socially, as they had not learned this process by osmosis as neurotypical children of neurotypical parent often do. Most though, describe a parenting style that supported independence and have been very grateful for that.

Comorbidities

Aspie women can suffer all the usual comorbidities of people on the spectrum but with just a few more additions. The list includes:

- anxiety, both generalised and social
- they may be more prone to phobias
- they can suffer depression
- they can suffer low self esteem
- they can struggle with insomnia
- they appear to have a higher incidence of sexual abuse or rape experiences
- they may have issues with alcohol and drugs
- they have often experienced a lot of bullying
- they can be misdiagnosed – often as bipolar or sometimes borderline personality disorder
- they can have slightly higher likelihood of gender identity issues
- They can have a high likelihood of one or all of the following:

- Misokinesia
- Misophonia
- Alexithymia

Females with Asperger's Syndrome: An Unofficial List

This list is meant as a springboard for discussion and more awareness into the female experience with autism. (Used by direct permission from Samantha Craft) She has her own website as: www.myspectrumsuite.com and everydayaspergers@gmail.com. She also wrote the book, *Everyday Aspergers,* and has many other publications. This list is copied and pasted exactly as she has written it.

Section A: Deep Thinkers
- A deep thinker
- A prolific writer drawn to poetry
- Highly intelligent
- Sees things at multiple levels, including her own thinking processes
- Analyses existence, the meaning of life, and everything, continually
- Serious and matter-of-fact in nature
- Doesn't take things for granted
- Doesn't simplify
- Everything is complex
- Often gets lost in own thoughts and *checks out* (blank stare)

Section B: Innocent
- Naïve
- Honest
- Experiences trouble with lying
- Finds it difficult to understand manipulation and disloyalty
- Finds it difficult to understand vindictive behaviour and retaliation
- Easily fooled and conned
- Feelings of confusion and being overwhelmed
- Feelings of being misplaced and/or from another planet

- Feelings of isolation
- Abused or taken advantage of as a child but didn't think to tell anyone

Section C: Escape and Friendship
- Survives overwhelming emotions and senses by escaping in thought or action
- Escapes regularly through fixations, obsessions, and over-interest in subjects
- Escapes routinely through imagination, fantasy, and daydreaming
- Escapes through mental processing
- Escapes through the rhythm of words
- Philosophises, continually
- Had imaginary friends in youth
- Imitates people on television or in movies
- Treated friends as *pawns* in youth, e.g., friends were *students consumers members*
- Makes friends with older or younger females more so than friends her age (often in young adulthood)
- Imitates friends or peers in style, dress, attitude, interests, and manner (sometimes speech)
- Obsessively collects and organises objects
- Mastered imitation
- Escapes by playing the same music over and over
- Escapes through a relationship (imagined or real)
- Numbers bring ease (could be numbers associated with patterns, calculations, lists, time and/or personification)
- Escapes through counting, categorising, organising, rearranging
- Escapes into other rooms at parties
- Cannot relax or rest without many thoughts
- Everything has a purpose

Section D: Comorbid Attributes

- OCD (Obsessive Compulsive Disorder)
- Sensory Issues (sight, sound, texture, smells, taste) (might have Synaesthesia)
- Generalised Anxiety
- Sense of pending danger or doom
- Feelings of polar extremes (depressed/over-joyed; inconsiderate/over-sensitive)
- Poor muscle tone, double-jointed, and/or lack in coordination (may have Ehlers Danlos syndrome and/or Hypotonia and/or POTS syndrome)
- Eating disorders, food obsessions, and/or worry about what is eaten
- Irritable bowel and/or intestinal issues
- Chronic fatigue and/or immune challenges
- Misdiagnosed or diagnosed with a mental illness
- Experiences multiple physical symptoms, perhaps labelled *hypochondriac*
- Questions place in the world
- Often drops small objects
- Wonders who she is and what is expected of her
- Searches for right and wrong
- Since puberty has had bouts of depression (may have PMDD)
- Flicks/rubs fingernails, picks scalp/skin, flaps hands, rubs hands together, tucks hands under or between legs, keeps closed fists, paces in circles, and/or clears throat often

Section E: Social Interaction

- Friends have ended friendship suddenly (without female with AS understanding why) and/or difficult time making friends
- Tendency to overshare
- Spills intimate details to strangers
- Raised hand too much in class or didn't participate in class
- Little impulse control with speaking when younger
- Monopolises conversation at times

- Brings subject back to self
- Comes across at times as narcissistic and controlling (is not narcissistic)
- Shares in order to reach out
- Often sounds eager and over-zealous or apathetic and disinterested
- Holds a lot of thoughts, ideas, and feelings inside
- Feels as if she is attempting to communicate *correctly*
- Obsesses about the potentiality of a relationship with someone, particularly a love interest or feasible new friendship
- Confused by the rules of accurate eye contact, tone of voice, proximity of body, body stance, and posture in conversation
- Conversation are often exhausting
- Questions the actions and behaviours of self and others, continually
- Feels as if missing a conversation *gene* or thought-filter
- Trained self in social interactions through readings and studying of other people
- Visualises and practises how she will act around others
- Practises/rehearses in mind what she will say to another before entering the room
- Difficulty filtering out background noise when talking to others
- Has a continuous dialogue in mind that tells her what to say and how to act when in a social situation
- Sense of humour sometimes seems quirky, odd, inappropriate, or different from others
- As a child, it was hard to know when it was her turn to talk
- Finds norms of conversation confusing
- Finds unwritten and unspoken rules difficult to grasp, remember, and apply

Section F: Finds Refuge When Alone

- Feels extreme relief when she doesn't have to go anywhere, talk to anyone, answer calls, or leave the house but at the same time will often harbour guilt for *hibernating* and not doing *what everyone else is doing*
- One visitor at the home may be perceived as a threat (this can even be a familiar family member)
- Knowing logically a house visitor is not a threat, but that doesn't relieve the anxiety
- Feelings of dread about upcoming events and appointments on the calendar
- Knowing she has to leave the house causes anxiety from the moment she wakes up
- All the steps involved in leaving the house are overwhelming and exhausting to think about
- She prepares herself mentally for outings, excursions, meetings, and appointments, often days before a scheduled event
- OCD tendencies when it comes to concepts of time, being on time, tracking time, recording time, and managing time (could be carried over to money as well)
- Questions next steps and movements, continually
- Sometimes feels as if she is on stage being watched and/or a sense of always having to act out the *right* steps, even when she is home alone
- Telling self the *right* words and/or positive self-talk (CBT) doesn't typically alleviate anxiety. CBT may cause increased feelings of inadequacy.
- Knowing she is staying home all day brings great peace of mind
- Requires a large amount of down time or alone time
- Feels guilty after spending a lot of time on a special interest
- Uncomfortable in public locker rooms, bathrooms, and/or dressing rooms
- Dislikes being in a crowded mall, crowded gym, and/or crowded theatre

Section G: Sensitive

- Sensitive to sounds, textures, temperature, and/or smells when trying to sleep
- Adjusts bedclothes, bedding, and/or environment in an attempt to find comfort
- Dreams are anxiety-ridden, vivid, complex, and/or precognitive in nature
- Highly intuitive to others' feelings
- Highly empathetic, sometimes to the point of confusion
- Takes criticism to heart
- Longs to be seen, heard, and understood
- Questions if she is a *normal* person
- Highly susceptible to outsiders' viewpoints and opinions
- At times adapts her view of life or actions based on others' opinions or words
- Recognises own limitations in many areas daily, if not hourly
- Becomes hurt when others question or doubt her work
- Views many things as an extension of self
- Fears others' opinions, criticism, and judgment
- Dislikes words and events that hurt animals and people
- Collects or rescues animals (often in childhood)
- Huge compassion for suffering (sometimes for inanimate objects/personification)
- Sensitive to substances (environmental toxins, foods, alcohol, medication, hormones, etc.)
- Tries to help, offers unsolicited advice, or formalises plans of action
- Questions life purpose and how to be a *better* person
- Seeks to understand abilities, skills, and/or gifts

Section H: Sense of Self

- Feels trapped between wanting to be herself and wanting to fit in
- Imitates others without realising it
- Suppresses true wishes (often in young adulthood)
- Exhibits co-dependent behaviours (often in young adulthood)

- Adapts self in order to avoid ridicule
- Rejects social norms and/or questions social norms
- Feelings of extreme isolation
- Feeling good about self takes a lot of effort and work
- Switches preferences based on environment and other people
- Switches behaviour based on environment and other people
- Didn't care about her hygiene, clothes, and appearance before teenage years and/or before someone else pointed these out to her
- *Freaks out* but doesn't know why until later
- Young sounding voice
- Trouble recognising what she looks like and/or has occurrences of slight prosopagnosia (difficulty recognising or remembering faces)
- Feels significantly younger on the inside than on the outside (perpetually twelve)

Section I: Confusion
- Had a hard time learning that others are not always honest
- Feelings seem confusing, illogical, and unpredictable (self's and others')
- Confuses appointment times, numbers, and/or dates
- Expects that by acting a certain way certain results can be achieved but realises in dealing with emotions, those results don't always manifest
- Spoke frankly and literally in youth
- Jokes go over the head
- Confused when others ostracise, shun, belittle, trick, and betray
- Trouble identifying feelings unless they are extreme
- Trouble with emotions of hate and dislike
- Feels sorry for someone who has persecuted or hurt her
- Personal feelings of anger, outrage, deep love, fear, giddiness, and anticipation seem to be easier to identify than emotions of joy, satisfaction, calmness, and serenity

- Difficulty recognising how extreme emotions (outrage, deep love) will affect her and challenges transferring what has been learned about emotions from one situation to the next
- Situations and conversations sometimes perceived as black or white
- The middle spectrum of outcomes, events, and emotions is sometimes overlooked or misunderstood (all or nothing mentality)
- A small fight might signal the end of a relationship or collapse of world
- A small compliment might boost her into a state of bliss

Section J: Words, Numbers, and Patterns
- Likes to know word origins and/or origin of historical facts/root cause and foundation
- Confused when there is more than one meaning (or spelling) to a word
- High interest in songs and song lyrics
- Notices patterns frequently
- Remembers things in visual pictures
- Remembers exact details about someone's life
- Has a remarkable memory for certain details
- Writes or creates to relieve anxiety
- Has certain *feelings* or emotions towards words and/or numbers
- Words and/or numbers bring a sense of comfort and peace, akin to a friendship

(Optional) Executive Functioning and Motor Skills (This area isn't always as evident as other area)
- Simple tasks can cause extreme hardship
- Learning to drive a car or rounding the corner in a hallway can be troublesome
- New places offer their own set of challenges
- Anything that requires a reasonable amount of steps, dexterity, or know-how can rouse a sense of panic

- The thought of repairing, fixing, or locating something can cause anxiety
- Mundane tasks are avoided
- Cleaning self and home may seem insurmountable
- Many questions come to mind when setting about to do a task
- Might leave the house with mismatched socks, shirt buttoned incorrectly, and/or have dyslexia and/or dysgraphia
- A trip to the grocery store can be overwhelming
- Trouble copying dance steps, aerobic moves, or direction in a sports gym class
- Has a hard time finding certain objects in the house but remembers with exact clarity where other objects are; not being able to locate something or thinking about locating something can cause feelings of intense anxiety (object permanence challenges), even with something as simple as opening an envelope
- *This unofficial checklist can be copied for therapists, counsellors, psychiatrists, psychologists, professors, teachers, and relatives, if Samantha Craft's name and contact information remain on the printout. This list was created in 2012 and updated in May 2016.*

Final comment

Aspie females are wonderful, faithful friends and partners. They always try very hard to please. They are tender-hearted and gentle. Like most of humanity, they do the best that they can with what they have at the time. They are hardworking, creative and often highly intelligent. They are mostly utterly loyal. Like any relationship if you are in one with an Aspie woman, both parties need to be aware of their similarities and differences and use the magic of communication!

And…once you have had a relationship with an Aspie woman, you will never forget her!

Chapter 4
Neurodivergent/Autistic Males

Of course, males are different to females, and I am not sure why there is even a discussion about that. Males look different, think and behave differently. Social research and science makes great efforts to understand these differences in all the various ramifications of study on the subject. Those discussions can go on for a long time and can include influences like culture, the size and weight ratio, hormonal differences and a whole raft of other disposing factors. And of course, it is the same for Aspie males and Aspie females – they are different to each other in many ways.

In the introductory chapter, I talk about the work of Simon Baron-Cohen, who is currently a professor at the UK's University of Cambridge (there is also a Cambridge University in New Zealand!) and is also head of their Autism Research Centre – amongst his many other accreditations and achievements. His opinion, in his book *The Essential Difference*, was based on his studies of the neurological differences between males and females, and he opined (in my summation) that autism was a double male brain and not a disorder as such. This is also, by the way, in agreement with the observations made much earlier by Hans Asperger. So, in simple English, Aspergers is an extreme male brain: an autistic male will have a double male brain and an autistic female will have *male-thinking* influences on her female brain.

This opinion is very important. Many people, including experts, still see Aspergers as a disorder or a mental health issue, while I see it as a variation of a normal brain – with some negatives and lots of positives. To support the male-brain theory, there appears to be a clear link between Aspergers and testosterone, particular when the foetus (even a female foetus) is exposed to testosterone in the early stages of forming in the uterus. This hormonal influence in the early stages of foetal development supports the theory of a double male brain, which is formed at a very young age. Unfortunately, no one can explain fully why a pregnancy may experience a rush of testosterone in the early few weeks and why all foetuses are not affected by that unexplained testosterone exposure.

So, what does a male brain look like or perform? The male brain is singular focussed – meaning that males focus on one thing at a time, as well as looking at that one thing with intense focus. The male brain is spatially highly developed. The areas of the brain that focus on social and communication skills is less well developed than the female brain, which makes males poorer communicators when compared to females – and less socially adept. The male brain leans more towards STEM (Science, Technology, Engineering and Mathematics) skills and details related to those fields. So double those attributes and you can see, the *double male brain*. Of course, in a woman you would get a female who is wired neurologically like a male in some regards, although she may be quite feminine too. (Remember that we are talking about a statistically higher representation which makes a generalisation – which means not everyone fits within a statistical picture).

A General Picture of Male Aspies

Many people carry strange ideas in their heads about male Aspies, for example the characters of Dr Spock of *Star Trek*, or Sheldon Cooper of the sitcom, the *Big Bang Theory*. It perpetuates the thought that someone on the Aspergers spectrum is somehow a non-emotional alien who views humans rather indifferently and cynically.

The Aspie men I have worked with have struggled with huge emotions, often anxiety and depression but also sadness and loneliness. They are desperate, like most people on planet Earth, for companionship, friends, to be liked, to have a sense of identity and belonging in a group, to be loved and comforted within a relationship.

Sadly, as children, these men have often faced a lot of bullying and misunderstanding, and as adults are often manipulated and will sacrifice a great deal (and compromise themselves as uncomfortable as this can be for them), to remain in relationships. A few Aspie men that I have met, particularly religious men, have made authoritarian husbands and fathers – but this too is definitely in the minority.

All people have quirks and idiosyncrasies. A friend once commented to me that, "The more you get to know people, the weirder they become." That may not be completely accurate, but there is a level of truth in the fact that we all have quirks – one young woman calls them *foibles* – and the better we know a person, the more likely we are to be exposed by these usually harmless idiosyncrasies. Aspie men just have a few more idiosyncrasies and ways of living life.

Men who have Aspergic traits but are not necessarily fully on the spectrum, or are on the lower end of the spectrum, do have some threads of social awareness and they do, if often rather clumsily, make attempts at being social. This is easier if the other party has similar interests, even if it is not at an obsessive level – it still makes a common social ground. Some have a small group of belonging because they have stayed with a group of friends since kindergarten, so there is a lot of mutual acceptance, understanding and genuine fondness and support for each other. But few people are that fortunate. As they get older, because of social misunderstandings, most Aspie males become introverted and socially cautious, and it is very rare to see an adult extroverted male Aspie.

Unlike Aspie women, many of the males do not seem to notice that they are doing something wrong as in a social mistake, nor do they seem to have a developed sense of social appropriateness. They can continue blithely through their social mishaps without any insight or awareness.

Most of the Aspie men that I have met have tried to be polite, neatly dressed and socially conforming to the best of their abilities – even if it made them uncomfortable doing so. Just as we meet neurotypical oddballs, we can have Aspie oddballs too – the only difference is that the neurotypical is often making some sort of conscious social statement and the Aspie oddball is unaware of the degree he has become unusual. Some of the more unusual Aspie male clients I have worked with have had or done the following:

- I had one client who often stank of several body odours from not having washed and his long greasy hair fell over his eyes when he talked. He always wore the same grubby pair of jeans, which had developed an oily film over the surface, especially where he often wiped his hands after eating. He invariably came in with a pie, which he would eat very noisily in the early part of our session and then he would loudly, and satisfyingly for him, swallow down a coke. I learnt to book him into my last appointment of the day as it was so difficult to get the smell out of my office and some later clients in appointments were visibly uncomfortable coming into the smelly room.

- Another man never (ever!) wore shoes and would relax on the chair with one leg crossed loosely over the other so that he could play with his filthy toes. He would slowly scratch and pick between each toe and then eat whatever bits of skin, slime and detritus he found between his toes. He never noticed that I had to look the other way when his finger started moving towards his mouth. (I had a client who was a child who did this too.)
- Another had eczema on his face and arms and picked at the dried scabs, popping them into his mouth.
- Another suffered from hay fever, particularly being affected around his eyes, where little blobs of *sleep* would collect with regular frequency. He would pick at these and eat it.
- Some would sit rigidly still, awkwardly, as if they did not know how to organise their body in a counselling room, so they froze. One would sit very still, body tightly controlled and composed, trying to describe and talk about his attempts at romance. Suddenly, he would jerk and fling his head back for no reason and snort loudly, and then he would continue talking as if nothing happened, resuming the same rigid pose. I asked when he went out on dates, how he sat, and he said that he sat in the same manner as he did in my office. He was also totally unaware of this unusual significant tic that he had.
- Another had worked studiously at researching strategies for a potential relationship. He had worked out from hours of internet research that he had done, that women liked nice cars, a good physique and cleanliness in a man, and wanted a nice house (preferably with a swimming pool), which went with his nice job, and that women generally preferred Labradors (he called it the top ten things women look for in a relationship). These were his conclusions, and he worked and achieved all of this. But he had now reached midlife and still had no relationship, although he had two nice cars (one for *her*), the nice job, the nice house with a swimming pool, had worked on his physique in the gym and his grooming at a beauty parlour, and had the well-trained Labrador. We discussed relationships he had had and why they had ended. The majority of women all had a mole somewhere on their bodies, and he

could not abide moles. One woman had no moles that he knew of, and things went really well for several months, until summer came. When she bent over to attend to her daughter, her bikini bottom exposed a little more flesh, and he spotted a mole and had to leave her at once. We worked for about three sessions, and we seemed to be making some progress, as he worked out the irrationality of his fear of bodily moles. I talk a lot with my hands, and I was describing something when I saw him blanch, and he suddenly had to leave. My shirtfront had moved sideways and had exposed a small mole just below my collarbone. I never saw him again.

But these examples above are more on the severe end of the spectrum. The majority usually lack social skills and self-awareness – but not to the socially shocking level as described above. They have learned social rules over the years, and even if they make no sense, most of the social rules are upheld. Aspies work well with rules, so if an Aspie male is well coached in his youth, he can have an excellent set of social skills.

> A very intelligent, obviously Aspergic, male client lost his sight as a young man. With this, he lost his potential career and all of his dreams, and he understandably became severely depressed and expressed suicidal thoughts. He was given medication – but Aspergics and medications are a strange mixture, as they often do not respond as neurotypicals do (when they tell me about their seeming side effects). The medications offered no relief (despite unpleasant side effects) to him, so the medical team continued to increase the dose and add other anti-psychotic medications. This man became a walking (when he could walk), mumbling zombie, who either stared all the time at nothing or slept. I met him after he had had nearly 20 years of this treatment, was considered a mental health client at this stage but had deliberately weaned himself off all the medication. He talked. And talked. And talked. He was in extreme grief, suffering the loss of the last 20 years of his life of which he had absolutely no memory, which loss he blamed on the medications. And that had taken him back to feelings of depression again, but he dreaded going back on the medications. At that time, he developed severe pain in his abdomen and went up to the hospital emergency department. Because he was a mental health client, he was

> referred back to a mental health specialist, who put him back on his antidepressants and his previous drug-cocktail. He went back to the hospital in an ambulance on two subsequent occasions with severe stomach pain. No tests were ever undertaken for the stomach pain he told me. He no longer went back to the hospital but suffered the pain on his own despite my suggestion that he sought a second opinion on this intense pain. By the time the cancer in his pancreas was discovered, it was untreatable, had metastasized and he died within a few weeks. And in all that time, no one had diagnosed his Aspergers, nor had dealt with him in an appropriate way.

But many of these stories are exceptions rather than the rule. Let's take a deeper look at what are the more common traits of Aspergic males.

Lack of Theory of Mind

This same phrase repeatedly comes up whenever Aspergers is talked about. I will have repeated an explanation in other chapters (this repetition is for readers who like to dip into different parts of a book and often miss explanations). Theory of mind is the ability to interpret where the other person is coming from and how they are with the joint communication and whether they're responding appropriately and emotionally in a given situation. For a diagnosis of Aspergers (or being on the ASD spectrum), a necessary criteria is *lack of theory of mind*.

The ability to have theory of mind is lowered, if it is there at all, in someone on the spectrum. This means that they have difficulty engaging socially, especially in conversations and especially with a larger group of people. The ability to *read* the other person in a social situation is often impaired.

Aspie males can be taught the rules of courtesy and respect but will sometimes use them at inappropriate times and can leave the other party feeling a little uncomfortable and therefore creating a social awkwardness. Generally though, it is very difficult for an Aspie male not to seem rude, as they can be forthright and blunt, and it may be at a most inappropriate time. They also, more often than not, use the incorrect tone of voice when speaking. When called out because of their rudeness, they will often retaliate with an *I'm just being honest*, which may make a neurotypical want to grind their teeth with annoyance. Of course, the Aspie is also left utterly bewildered as to how his helpful and factual remark was offensive. These interactions of course are not great for relationship building!

> An Aspie father may be oblivious that his lumpy pot-belly is flopping out from his faded, holey t-shirt (from a music concert he had attended 20 or more years ago – when he was a scrawny young man – and has been his favourite t-shirt ever since) and be bewildered when his teenage daughter is humiliated that he still wears this in front of her – or even worse, her giggling friends. He probably also does not notice that she doesn't bring friends to the house anymore.

I have introduced this topic first, because lack-of-theory-of-mind imposes on nearly every social situation, whether one is an Aspie walking down the road or whether one is married for 30 years to an Aspie and has had children with their Aspie husband. Theory of mind is an awareness of context and social appropriateness.

> Another Aspie man (he was about 30 about that time) I know was attending a church service in which mention was made of a biblical quote. (Be aware that there are numerous different translations and prints and editions and fonts of the bible, and that most of the congregation would therefore have different size, shapes and numbers of pages in their bibles, in their hands.) He interrupted the sermon to ask what page he should be referring to, so that he could keep up. He told me that the church was very quiet at first, and then there was much laughter as if he were making a joke. The preacher asked for silence, ignored the question, and continued with his sermon. He said he tried again and did not speak but kept his hand help up high to get the preacher's attention. The preacher ignored him. The man then left the church in frustration. A neurotypical will usually realise that that is not the appropriate time to ask a question, or may ask a neighbour if he feels comfortable with that person. He would not interrupt a sermon nor keep waving his hand in the air to get attention in this situation.

Of course, as we explain about these situations and about the Aspie thinking, it all makes sense. But it never did for all those parties involved at the time.

Some TV series have been made around a main male character who is Aspergic [is diagnosed with Asperger syndrome] or on the ASD spectrum. Some of the shows are poor in quality and seem to be a little mocking of Aspies, as if *all Aspies are weirdoes* as one Aspie once said to me. Some actors try to portray the characters but often their eyes change or their automatic neurotypical body language in a scene betrays them. This leaves the media-watchers with a very distorted and often untrue portrayal of Aspies. Some shows that were successful in their portrayal of Aspie-type characters I believe, are *The Good Doctor, Doc Martin, Atypical, House* and *Boston Legal* (this last two I have only watched a few episodes, but I have also been told that some characters portray traits of ASD very well). Strangely, three all involve medicine as a theme – just a coincidence in this case. Some excellent movies include *Adam, Mozart and the Whale, My Name is Khan, The Rain Man,* (and hopefully this does not cause an outcry!) I see many ASD elements in *Forrest Gump.*

I read an article that Aspergers and traits of Aspergers can be found in up to 40% of surgeons, medical specialists, lawyers, engineers, maths and science teachers, and even more highly represented in systems and IT (Information Technology which in lay language means computer related). Active compassion did not rate highly in this group either. How the data was collected nor the accuracy of the testing, was not validated – but it proposes some interesting thoughts.

I read the following in a book on Aspergic males in relationship but I have also experienced this among my clients – Aspie males generally do not usually say *I love you* in relationships, something their neurotypical partners need to hear. Quite often their response, when challenged, runs along these lines – *I am still here. I said it once. I haven't changed my mind and if I do, I will let you know. I don't have to keep saying the same thing.*

Singular Focus (Often Obsessive too)

These men have distinctive interests (mostly). Some are unlucky enough not to have found one but most do. It could be old railway trains, clocks, astronomy, or genetics as applied to gardening or farming or breeding animals. In fact, the range of interests are enormous, but the interests are always avid and active – filled with pleasure and can provide a good source of stimming.

So, he might be interested in other planets and space. He doesn't hear you when you talk to him as he is off (mentally) exploring the possibility of other planets. He can remember all the planets from the sun outwards, and in order, right up to the 248th one, but he can't remember to pick up the milk on the way home or to put the rubbish out.

Our family knew a man who was obsessed with his health or imagined poor health, to the extent of having his own sphygmomanometer (an instrument for measuring blood pressure), which he would use three times a day, and he noted the results. Nobody dared to ask him any opening questions like the mundane *how are you?* greeting, or if he had been genuinely ill, we dared not ask him if he were feeling better. He would hook you into his conversation (one-way of course) for over an hour with comparisons of his tabulated blood pressure and data correlations from over the last couple of weeks. His hypochondria only complicated matters. At no point would he ask how his listener was. If the listener had been seriously ill, he would be entranced for two minutes by the key details and would then regale one with a complicated condition he had once had, or thought he had, which would take another forty minutes at least!

Aspies can be fascinated by new technology and inventions

On the other hand, that singular focus is sometimes just short of magical in terms of knowledge and application. They are the brilliant surgeons or scientists or detectives, in whatever field that they are interested in observing – providing that field is the basis of that singular focus.

> I knew an accountant whose office had wrestled for hours on a major, complex spreadsheet that they could not balance, and no matter how they calculated and reworked their data over several days, they could not resolve this. Eventually, they turned to their boss for help, who glanced over the spreadsheet and could immediately pick up the error and pointed to the one window on the spreadsheet in under ten seconds. He could see the number was wrong. They did not believe him, but when they went over the calculations again, he was correct.

When it comes to matters of the heart, their partners and spouses tell me that there is no experience, absolutely nothing like being under the gaze of Aspie male in those early days of interest and dating. They are totally interested in you, so their obsessive focus will be on you completely and unswervingly. They remember every detail that you have told them. You are totally the object of their singular focus. Of course, an old pre-existing obsession or interest can trump this focus, so he may have been looking lovingly in your eyes and recalling sweetly all the authors that you love reading, and your older brother drives up with his ancient Harley [Davidson – a popular old-school motorbike] that he is working on – and you discover that Harleys trump the new obsessive interest (you). On the bright side, at least he is not being unfaithful, and you do know what the obsession is.

Once they get into their focus subject (or obsession – as saturated, inundated family and friends will call it), they are completely locked in and can often continue through mealtimes or through the night if need be. Of course, that has multiple consequences socially and leads to often disgruntled partners and friends.

Need for Structure and Routine

Aspie males thrive best where there is a high level of structure and order. They thrive in environments where there are strong systems in place. McDonald's (takeaways) have wonderful systems, and you know at all times exactly what to do as an employee (except when dealing directly with the occasionally difficult customer). Everything is structured, timers are set and the staff duties perfectly outlined. If an Aspie man can cope with the noise and lights, such an organised structured environment would be a great place to work.

Of course, STEM (Science, Technology, Engineering, Mathematics) environments are usually highly predictable in their day-to-day work and structure. If he has used his STEM subject to go into teaching, he may find that teaching teenagers may be an additional stress. He may find it bewildering and frustrating that many of the students in his class do not share his interest and enthusiasm. They can make very good teachers on the whole, providing that they are not overwhelmed. They can be patient teachers (they know that the purpose of their job is to teach so will focus on teaching skills and strategies) but not emotionally engaged teachers.

Despite Aspies functioning best where there is structure and order, the Aspies themselves fall into two groups. As is usual with Aspergers, these male behaviours are usually found at either end of the spectrum. He can be highly organised to the most minute (almost irritating) detail. Don't move the pen on the desk please – it took him two minutes and 17 seconds to get it in just the correct position – and if his pen is moved, then he may have to go through that whole process again. Neurotypicals often think it is a joke to disrupt Aspies like this and laugh uproariously at the Aspie, but please don't consider doing this yourself because it is unkind and very stressful for the Aspie. To move his pen back into the correct position and be laughed at and observed at his distress is probably an unnecessary humiliation of a very good man, who is often one of the most hard-working staff members.

If he works in your office, he will most probably be diligent, and everything will be processed correctly. He will quickly spot errors, and senior staff will lean on him for his detailed knowledge. (Sometimes, they will also steal his ideas because he has little theory of mind and will not have realised that others can and will steal his ideas.) He will arrive at work exactly on time and will leave for his breaks and leave at the end of the day at exactly the same time. He will probably have exactly the same lunch every day, and he will probably have five identical sets of clothing. If you have a rushed job for him, well, give it to him early in the day, but don't expect him to stay late to do this task. He may stay to please you but will have such a distressed night that he may have to call in sick the next day. They are loyal, hard-working staff. Look after him (and put up with a few idiosyncrasies if he has them), as such staff are often irreplaceable. They will never fiddle the books nor cheat you.

Then again, some Aspies, despite loving order, live in chaos, almost all the time. In this way, Aspergers is a little like ADD or ADHD. It seems that all three have issues with poor reticular activation in the brain. Lorna Wing describes this process as being responsible for keeping the brain alert and organised [http://www.autism-help.org/points-lorna-jean-sensory.htm].

In simple English, it appears that the part of the brain that allows one to prioritise thinking and responses does not function fully – or sometimes not at all.

To me, this means that as all stimuli-demanding attention seems to be equal and that there is therefore difficulty prioritising one topic, for example, like staying on task in a job or a conversation without distraction or inattention. The ticking clock, the flutter of a piece of paper outside the window, the rumble of a truck passing, the flickering of the neon lighting, all fight equally for attention with your voice – so be patient when another stimuli grabs his attention while you are talking to him. He can't help it. It is a faulty short circuit in his brain. Gently redirect him to focus on you again if what you have to say is important.

I have a very bland, peaceful, unstimulating office, with only the basics and no pictures, posters, music, perfumes and so forth that could potentially distract an Aspie client. Yet my male Aspie clients still tell me they find my office overwhelming; they can hear the soft radio in the front foyer beyond the closed door, the light is too bright and flickering, the stripes of the slats of the blinds are distracting, the clock is too loud, the fabric of the seating and the cushions are distracting, their own clothing labels and seams are distracting – and my voice is only one of the many stimuli in the office demanding their attention. All the stimuli are equally demanding, and Aspies constantly have the battle of sifting what is the most important stimuli – usually our conversation in this instance. They have to fight against these enormous handicaps to stay focussed. Be patient with them, because generally they want to please you and are positively motivated.

An Aspie male, when I asked him to verbalise his flow of multiple thoughts, dictated a stream of consciousness that I could not keep up with, nor could I actually count the number of topics (with each having several *arms* or *branches*) that were running through his head simultaneously. I cannot even begin to imagine what that is like to have to live like this on a daily basis.

So, the opposite of the organised male Aspie as described on the previous page is the other type who lives in ramshackle chaos, always desiring both order and to be purposeful.

He will walk from the shed to fix the tap with his wrench in his hand, see a stone on the lawn, move the stone (so that it does not break the lawnmower blades later when he hopes to do the mowing) and then notice that the chickens have laid a couple of eggs, forget that he had put down his spanner on the lawn and has then become fascinated with the chickens scurrying around. The phone rings (he hates the phone), but he rushes to answer it. Once he hangs up, he looks for a pencil to make a note on the calendar for his appointment, but the drawer that he is looking in has the pressure cooker seal that he has been looking for, for the last three months. He goes out to the shed and has to move all the stuff he has dumped on the pressure cooker lid the last few months, and in the process… Well, you can see how this goes. At the end of the day, he has worked frantically, his house and yard are more chaotic than that morning and he has achieved little, if anything – and as he has not written down that appointment, he will probably forget it. Then he feels depressed because he has not achieved what he wanted; it's past midnight and the dripping tap is going to interfere with his sleep again, and he has no memory at all that the spanner is lying on the lawn at the spot from where he removed that stone. He longs for order so that he can complete his jobs (because he is actually very skilled at doing these).

A friend, whose husband is Aspergic, and I were talking one day. They had separated and he lived elsewhere, although she was always mindful and supportive of him. Her concern was his floundering in his constant striving to function, as some years later, he still had not got steady work nor had developed a self-care and daily living routine, so he would forget to cook and wouldn't eat and so forth. She opined that historically, in times gone by, society was a lot more structured (talking about the European/English culture). The role for men was often clearly defined, and the social boundaries really limited (divorce was not an option and employment was only within one's social hierarchy). There were distinct husband/wife roles and distinct social roles for example those of a serf or a merchant or a property holder. Often being in a marriage (no other arrangement was acceptable then) would allow life's normal routines to keep the Aspie going each day – for example, they would not forget to eat and his wife may have organised his clothes and so forth, so that he could get on with his business each day. With so many divorces these days and many of these single men being loose without the anchor of marriage or culture, we are seeing more and more lonely Aspie men with no family structures or home structures to support them – who often end up living chaotically.

> I met an Aspie man whose wife had left him. He was working as a respected chef. His counselling issue, apart from how to get his wife back, was that he could not eat. I explored the not eating – which was because he could not cook! This surprised me because he was a chef! Eventually, I understood that he could not cook because his routine was to have a wine with his wife in the kitchen, and she would talk to him while he was cooking as she sat at the bench (or breakfast bar) having her wine. Because these two essential elements to his routine (having a social wine and having his wife in the kitchen while he cooked) were now missing, he could not cook. The structure for cooking for him was not there and therefore he could not cook – he had no idea how to proceed and what the first step was! It took him a

> while to realise that he would have to adapt to cooking for one person and start a new routine. Once he understood that he was astounded that it was so simple and said, "Is that all?"

Lateral Thinkers and Creativity (Often Combined With Their Functional Literalness)

Aspies think literally and laterally. They do not think figuratively, metaphorically, or abstractedly.

In terms of literal – they cannot usually interpret sarcasm or even joking at times. They certainly miss voice-tones, innuendo and flirting. They do not realise that they are blunt, but if you are blunt and direct to them, they appreciate that immensely (as long as it is not hurtful of course). You will often hear them asking you to get to the point or exclaiming, "Is that all you wanted?" after a long explanation and lead-up. To stop them fretting, especially if you want to ask a favour and to stop them second-guessing and not listening while they are second-guessing, then simply speak out literally and directly. You will of course get a direct answer. If they can help, they will, if they can't, well, then you will know that quickly yourself too. It is much easier to communicate with an Aspie man if both parties are direct and clear about what needs to be talked about or done.

I heard of one man who went to see a therapist (who practised primarily as an art therapist). He was dealing with his grief – albeit about ten years later – because a parent had passed. She gave him a charcoal pencil, coloured crayons and a sheet of paper, so that he could perhaps draw how he *saw* the situation. She told him to draw what he saw. After waiting patiently for about ten minutes as he studiously drew, she eventually asked if she could have a look. He was trying to draw her with her bookshelves and her plant behind her!

Incidentally, Aspies appear to react in two ways to the death of a loved one. They appear to either be quite factual and accepting (seemingly cold), or appear to have no reaction but years later still cannot process that traumatic event. I have worked with a few older Aspie males who up to ten years later have not come to terms with the passing of a parent – especially if they had been long term in close contact with that parent.

Sometimes when a relationship has ended, the Aspie will often still stay attached to their partner. One Aspie male who was separated for more than 15 years, when hearing his ex was moving about 2000 km away for work, asked her to find him work and accommodation there for him too.

Aspies think laterally, which is a wonderful gift and can engender great creativity. People often assume that Aspies are not creative, but they are deeply creative when they need to be. This includes inventing things, such as a tool or machine, or adapting a part creatively. They are not limited by a lot of our neurotypical thinking, which will often stifle creativity as a neurotypical will disregard an idea, as it seems silly or not right or however not fitting their creative criteria. This lateral thinking is also a fabulous problem-solving skill and I am often amazed with the skills I have heard of and seen that have come through Aspies.

> I once happened to briefly have a conversation with an Aspie male. I was wanting a chair lift for my elderly parents for some steep stairs in my home but was not wanting to fork out over $20,000 or more at the time. Immediately, he drew on paper a quick and simple solution of a pulley belt and an old-fashioned lawn mower engine that would operate a chair up and down, and at minimal cost! Regardless, I never actually tried out the invention as I chose to sell the house instead. But the invention was perfect!

When they find their niche, they are incredibly creative and amazingly, wonderfully resourceful. They tend to think innovatively and ingeniously and can apply a resource that no one ever thought of using.

> One lovely man that I worked with had much joy in his upcoming nuptials but things were financially very hard. He went to the dump and computer-recycle yards faithfully, week after week, to find old discarded laptops. Through a chemical process, he slowly extracted the infinitesimally minute bits of gold out of the circuitry until he had enough to make (yes – he made them himself!) two beautifully crafted wedding bands. This was a man who had no training whatsoever in jewellery making. This was using lateral and literal thinking at its very best!

Often movies or TV shows that depict an Aspie-type male lead will focus on the resourcefulness of an Aspie. He will think laterally in a given situation and miraculously rescue the situation. These are the doctors, who, with a piece of tubing and a bottle of water can dramatically save a life in a new unorthodox manner, or the creative detective who can find ways to escape a so-called escape-proof trap, and so forth. This is of course entertainment, but surprisingly, Aspies are often this resourceful.

Male Aspies and Emotions

Aspie males are not very good at expressing emotions. Also, because they are not very good at showing emotion, they cannot express themselves in either way, and neurotypicals are often very surprised when the Aspie male appears to explode with anger for no apparent reason, or so it seems. Aspie anger is often the most common emotion that neurotypicals see, but it is usually an expression of overload that they do not know how to express in any other way.

It is hard for their everyday processing, as we talked about earlier, as lots of stimuli are happening simultaneously for them. If they are overwhelmed, or eventually having any extreme emotion, they can often appear angry, and they may well shout and wave their arms about as if they were very angry.

Because there is no or little theory-of-mind available to them, they are unaware that someone else may be distressed or intimidated by this huge anger which will often include a tirade of abuse shouted out aloud. It then makes a self-perpetuating cycle of people avoiding them because of their *anger* and the Aspie not being able to express themselves adequately. They try again, become overwhelmed, their voices are raised again, they are avoided, and the cycle continues.

> I had an Aspie man drop in on me socially, from time to time. In the beginning, he wanted to discuss his ex-wife. I did not want to do that but did not want to ask him to leave either as I thought that that was inhospitable on my part. Fortunately, he was easily distractible (more likely he headed off on his own tangents although if he didn't I would *help* him do that), and he would then head off at the distraction. The patterns were always the same: an interruption meant he would start at the beginning again (I call it *starting at the beginning of the chapter again*), and I do not like endless replays (often word for word identical). He would then become passionate about his pet peeve and that meant long discourses on his own (in theatre, they are called soliloquys!), and invariably, he would get louder and louder. He was completely unaware that I was not speaking (one couldn't get a word in edgewise anyway) but obviously because I was still in the room and looking at him (as one does respectfully when another is talking), he assumed that I was engaged. He had no idea of time or of overstaying his welcome or that I didn't even want him there. Hints that I had to feed, bathe and settle my children were not even acknowledged and then I had to ask him to leave – which he obligingly did. He seemed to enjoy the visit and it ticked the social box for him – despite that I was left quite drained and exhausted and that it was certainly not a pleasant social experience for me. (This was many years ago, when I was still quite new to the field of ASD.)

I understand from Aspies though that they have all the normal range of emotions but are often unable to express it. Sometimes they will tell me that they are very sad but have a huge smile that doesn't change, even as they describe their sadness. Their facial expressions do not vary much, and they also have a social face they *put on* when they are not at home. Unfortunately, they can neither vary nor fine-tune their social *mask*. When Aspies do express their emotions though, it is so intense that it is often overwhelming and parents and partners of Aspies withdraw or react because of that intensity. And the Aspie again is left without a means of processing those emotions.

Some early work by Temple Grandin and her research through MRI (brain scans) suggests that there are less connections to the parts of the brain that relate to socialising and to the processing of emotions. I explain this to my clients by using the following metaphor. I suggest that all their emotions are trapped in a giant dam, but the only way to deal with them is by letting them drain the dam through a straw. I then work very hard with them, to teach them how to recognise, name and process emotions effectively and to make the *straw* bigger and stronger – and the flow and management of emotions more workable.

Feeling stressed is a thought process which results in an emotion of feeling stressed and then distressed. All mankind, and animals it seems, suffer from stress from time to time. On the whole, Aspies appear more stressed than neurotypicals. This could be the overly analytical thought, the inability to prioritise a single thought and remain with it, or the difficulty processing emotions, combined with a very stressful life of growing up in an Aspie-unfriendly world. Stressed Aspies either have loud, angry unhelpful displays when they are overwhelmed, or they completely shut down – often to the extreme of dissociating. Their body is in the room with you, but they are no longer there – often to the extent of not or hardly responding. I have seen two men become almost catatonic at this time of emotional stress (with no other signs of the mental health condition known as Catatonia).

Aspie Males, Relationships and Sex

So why would you stay in a relationship with him? Well, Aspies are usually faithful and loyal and devoted, once they become attached to you. They generally do not lie, nor do they play mind games. They are sincere and truthful (sometimes a little bluntly and occasionally unintentionally brutal). They are predictable. They are usually gentle and non-violent. And they will genuinely try to please you, even if you insist on being told that they love you every two hours (they will set an alarm to do so if need be).

Aspies do not get speech nuances, tones of voice or inferences – All of which help understanding known as theory of mind. This man did not get the obvious rebuttal from his partner.

He will not understand your flippant comments, your snide remarks or sarcasm. He will (possibly annoyingly to you) repeatedly take you literally.

Aspies generally are very faithful and loyal, and if they are in a relationship, then are more likely to be monogamous than neurotypicals. I know of very few exceptions of unfaithful Aspie males. Part of their relationship steadfastness is because you are their main commitment and they maintain that literally. Another part is that they sometimes miss the cues that others are flirting with them, so do not engage in that social game which can often lead to affairs. They also miss the social cues to start a relationship too and their lack of response is taken as non-interest. They are of course, often not socially inclined anyway, so their social field in terms of being unfaithful has a small range.

They can also be faithful, if somewhat dutiful when visiting friends or family, which they often seem to do from a sense of obligation (which neurotypicals often do too). Regardless, some have a unique style. Their time management can be somewhat unusual as Aspies are often clock-watchers. One Aspie man who visits his extended family and has done for years, sets himself a time limit. He is polite and social for exactly one hour. He brings a snack to share, converses on his favourite subjects and checks his wristwatch regularly. At exactly one hour after his arrival, he says cheerfully that it is time to go and that he doesn't want to overstay his welcome, and then heads off happy that he achieved this social exchange so well, in his mind. He was faithful to his relationship and to his relationship with his extended family.

One particular and rather odd exception around the issue of being faithful occurred.

> I met a man who could not stop himself having sex with anyone who was willing – male or female (which included a long list of sex-workers, his builder working on his house, the plumber) and included some bestiality, despite this man being married to a woman and despite being a deeply religious church-goer. He had no guilt or shame about the matter and could not understand his wife's distress (even though he was a highly intelligent academic). His wife had discovered him in *flagrante delicto* on several occasions with men and women of different ages, blatantly in and around their home, none of to whom he was attached so he did not see himself as unfaithful. In fact, I thought his obsessive interest was sex, which to him differed from a relationship. Needless to say, he is a divorced man now.

There is a separate chapter on relationships which follows at a later stage.

Aspies have relationships with neurotypicals and with other Aspies. On the whole though, Aspies are drawn to neurotypical partners. Like all relationships, these have their own level of complexities, with some unique elements related to and influenced by Aspergers.

Aspie Males, Children and Fatherhood

As with many Aspie topics, I have noticed the extreme ends of the spectrum in terms of behaviours of adult Aspie males to children. On the one hand, I have noticed that Aspie males can relate very well to children, and probably because of their lack of self-awareness, they can easily work at a child's level and become engrossed at that level. For some children, they are the favourite uncle who buys great gifts or who treats them as if they were grown-ups. I have seen some very patient Aspie male teachers. For the few Aspie fathers I know who have passionately fought for custody of their children, they have been diligent and attentive parents, despite the limits of emotional engagement. (Most Aspie men, sadly, will not fight for their rights, nor are they confident enough with their children to demand more time with them after a separation – these relationships often drift apart quite easily.)

On the other hand, most Aspie males seem to have difficulty connecting to children, as they seem to have difficulties connecting to all people. At this point, they mostly avoid contact with children, and I have seen quite a few Aspie males shudder with distaste at the thought of being around children. These Aspie males can be rude, dismissive, disinterested, and unkind – but again, it is more rare to find this behaviour. A similar range can be found in neurotypical men, although neurotypical men will have a more even spread across the range of like and dislike of children and less extreme than Aspie males. A big plus again is that it is less likely that an Aspie man (compared proportionately to neurotypical men) will be violent or an abuser of children.

Generally, they are awkward and uncomfortable around babies, toddlers and young children and avoid interacting. They also avoid intimacy with their offspring (or don't need or know how to have intimacy). They may functionally feed a baby or change a toddler, but the intimacy of the act will be missing. I have often seen partners of Aspie males instruct them as to what to do with the children; for example, "Play Lego with Billy and teach him how to make a house", or "You have to spend some time with the children so tomorrow morning you will take them kayaking." Their engagement with children is often mechanical, dutiful and directive – especially if they are not the full-time active parent (which they usually are not).

> One separated Aspie father had delusions of what a good father he was – despite rarely attempting to see his children who were freely available for unlimited access. Because he felt that he was a good and interested father, he believed that he was. With no (categorically in this case) theory of mind, he never realised that the main ingredients in a relationship were clearly missing and that he was an estranged and distant father who rarely saw his children more than twice a year. When he did meet, he had a movie script (it seemed) in his head, which he would act out. In this *script*, he was the warm and loving father, who would try to embrace children he seldom saw, and he would have a strange type of indulgent conversation with them. At a certain point, the lone single acting would wear thin and he would depart (usually huffily), until the *curtains opened again* at another access visit he chose to undertake maybe six months later, when he would simply appear as if he had never been away.

As parents, they can be distant, distracted, and non-involved. They will often treat the children as little adults. Their children are later often able to manipulate their adult Aspie parents quite well emotionally, especially if the children are not on the spectrum. A small group of Aspie males, often those in various religious circles, can *fulfil* their roles as fathers and can often be hard, sharp and critical. Affection generally does not come naturally to them. Fulfilling is a role with many rules, and these fathers can apply the rules, sometimes down to the smallest *dot and tittle*, using a religious term.

Adult children with an Aspie father often have a distant, clinical relationship with that parent. Their social engagement, if any, follows a standard course that worked well at some time and has since become the normative pattern. The Aspie parent of adult children will meet them, buy lunch, talk about their current interest, pay for lunch and go home. Later they may find out from elsewhere that the adult child has moved to a new house or changed jobs and so forth, because there was never an opportunity to bring that up and discuss it. The Aspie parent of course would have missed that their adult child may want to explore an important subject with their father.

On the whole, Aspie males are often, or try to be, very good providers for their family. They will work hard, even in jobs that they cannot bear, to keep on providing. They will often be more focussed on providing the income rather than focussing on their family, often considering that their employment was their part of the family contribution and commitment – even more so as they struggle with mind-blindness and alexithymia. They are also often resourceful providers. Then again, on the other end of the spectrum – the intention is there, but they often do not seem to *get it together* to carry out their best intentions of providing for their family.

Aspie Males and Finances

Again, like any other topical discussion on Aspie males, there is often not a middle ground. Finances are usually managed on the extreme ends of financial management scale, which is either disastrous and haphazard, or scrupulous down to the smallest detail.

Some Aspie men will know their bank balance to the last cent – in fact, they may have a minor (or even a major) obsession with their finances. They may get drawn into investments and know actuary tables and formulas for the financial stock market and the particular shares in which they like to trade. If they are investors, then they usually have little emotion about it; they will evaluate statistical risks and be intellectually calculated about their investments. There is not a feel-good or emotional element about it. They also do not generally have anxiety about these calculated risks either. Unfortunately, they can be gullible to a stock-market shark or shabby investment crook, as they cannot read the social cues to be wary of the manipulations of others – especially if they do not understand the market or are inexperienced investors.

On the whole though, they are sensible and sound investors, if this is their specialist interest and hobby and they usually have good, if tight, money management skills. Many Aspies have good jobs, the better paid jobs being in STEM subject areas. I have met Aspies who are beautiful craftsmen with pride in their work. I have also met Aspie men who are tradies (tradesmen), who have a deep pride in their jobs. I have met lawyers, accountants, surgeons, teachers, a hairdresser, electricians, engineers, white-wear technicians and in many other vocations. They are good, solid, knowledgeable, dependable, reliable tradesmen. They all generally do have some social difficulties, but they manage to work around that.

On the other hand (or the other extreme), as long as they have a few dollars in their pocket, they can be quite happy. They often live in crisis mode as they forget about bills or have spent the money in their pocket thoughtlessly (maybe on an awesome expensive pen that costs 200 times more than any other pen because it can write on a ceiling – like a space or anti-gravity pen!). These Aspies are usually quite happy when in a relationship to allow the other partner to manage the finances. This can be good where there is teamwork but that's another story! It is not easy to be on an Aspie team – they are not generally team players. These people also tend to be extremely generous and are often easily manipulated financially. As dads, they are easily coerced by clever little children, who easily run rings (socially and manipulatively – but literally too if they are little) around this kind of dad.

If the expenses exceed the income, the pressure on these Aspie males is enormous. They then become overwhelmed and stressed, with all the issues that will result from that stress reaction. In most cultures, males are raised to be family providers, and when they cannot fulfil that role, they can become very distressed. It is an important cultural rule that they are breaking. As it appears, more Aspie males (proportionately) than neurotypical males are unemployed (one UK statistic recently showed that only 16% of males on the ASD spectrum were employed full time), and there are then a great deal of men struggling with this issue. In overwhelm mode, they can then be relationally destructive, being verbally abusive and appearing to be continuously angry and reactive out of that anger.

Aspie men who attend a simple bookkeeping or budgeting course, or a course on money-management or similar, and who engage in the programme, can be taught the *rules* of simple financial strategies. This is of course, like anyone, only where they are willing. These would include an account for bills that wages go into, an account for saving or upcoming bills (like annual expenses such as rates or insurance) and having an account for day-to-day expenses for that coffee at the train station, and if applied, they can eventually manage their money far better. They are generally not rule breakers (even if they seem to follow their own drummer sometimes), and as long as all goes well, they can stay on a fairly even keel. Trying to get them to appreciate a separate account (where this is financially viable) for unexpected expenses, such as a car mechanical repair that is costly, is a little more difficult. They are not very good at projecting, nor have mindful consideration of a future event that could be financially devastating. In this way, they are caught short again and struggle to recover.

Comorbidities

A comorbidity is usually another major problem that exists along with a main first issue or may even be a result of the first issue. The depressed Aspie man who resorts to alcohol or drugs to cope may eventually develop an addiction. They may develop a severe depression. It is reasonably common to have Aspie men suffering from depression or anxiety, which means that they are often unable to hold down a job, so they lose their job, and so this kind of cycle continues.

For many Aspie males, a difficulty that they struggle with is cognitive coherence. There are gaps in their cognitive processing. Some are very good and organised. Others, probably a greater majority of Aspie males, because of these gaps do not function well within society. As described in a little snippet earlier, they can be very disorganised because of this lack of cognitive cohesion. A family friend kept missing his hospital appointments for the treatment of his cancer and in the end passed as the cancer had spread too much. It is not even known if he managed his medication. So some Aspies need to be organised and have a type of secretary! Many of the younger generation coming through make use of their mobile phones for appointments and reminders and are faring better because they have an electronic secretary.

> I know of one man who had issues around (misunderstood) Aspergers, was adopted, was abused physically and emotionally by his adoptive parents and therefore suffered trauma, was an alcoholic and a regular marijuana user. For his family, it was a very fractured, difficult relationship, with his wife trying to shield and protect the children as much as possible. None of his many children ever seemed to develop a close and intimate relationship with their father, yet he appeared to long for that kind of closeness.

As children, the vast majority of adult males were misunderstood – by parents, family, teachers and peers. From each source, he would have grown up with their negative attitudes towards him. He would also very commonly be bullied. I have not yet met an Aspie male who was not bullied in the school playground as a child. These experiences, at the very least, would leave anyone with low self-esteem and a poor and damaged sense of self-worth.

Out of their childhood experiences and usually with an awareness that they *just don't fit in with normal society*, most adult males suffer from either depression or anxiety, but more commonly from both. The road to recovery is usually long and very difficult for Aspie males who struggle with these conditions and any other co-morbidities.

Quite often, they will dissociate, which means that their processing, as well as their relationships, are very damaged and are increasingly so. This then results in extreme loneliness. This may seem strange, as Aspergers or ASD is a social development disorder, and often, Aspies do prefer to be alone yet I have never met one who wants to be completely isolated. They never want to be socially active on a big extroverted scale, but they all long for a friendship or a relationship – which they may seldom experience consistently.

If they are in employment and struggle with comorbidities, they will find the work, concentration and possible work social environment even more difficult to manage. They will become isolated from peers and may often have to endure their critical attitudes and comments as well.

The more comorbidities that people struggle with, the more likely they are to be unemployed and often isolated and without external supporting structures. They often will then live in a state of poverty, which further exacerbates their distress.

It also seems that many Aspie males struggle with a sense of personal identity, including a gender identity or sexual orientation. A proportionately large number of people who are transgender for example, often seem to be on the spectrum as well. Again, not ALL people, just a *proportionately* larger number of Aspie men are represented.

Summary

- Lack of theory-of-mind or mind-blindness
- An obsessive singular focus
- Heightened sensitivity to noise, light, distraction, with multiple thoughts
- In social situations, they have poor reticular activity (their filters don't work too well)
- More likely to have STEMM (Science, Technology, Engineering, Maths, Medicine) skills and are likely to be uncoordinated and not sporty
- Literal thinkers
- Lateral thinkers (they can be very good at problem solving, finding creative solutions that neurotypicals are less likely to think of)
- Loyal and faithful, with no guile
- Enjoy structure and routine
- Have difficulty expressing emotions, and this combined with lack of theory-of-mind, can make them appear quite wooden and unresponsive socially
- Have difficulty finding and maintaining employment the higher up on the spectrum they appear

- Often have a comorbidity, if not more than one
- Like most of the human population, they can be either very good or very poor at handling their finances, but Aspies are often found at the extreme ends
- Often have difficulty working with and understanding children
- As friends or partners, in long-term relationships, they are faithful and try very hard to please others – trying very hard to be good providers while having some lovely old-school values
- They are resourceful and enterprising
- They are usually not materialistic
- They are generally good, honest people

The following is included, with full permission of the author, Maxine Aston.

This is a list of tips for men with AS, who have asked for ideas to make their partner happy in and with their relationship.

- Smile when you greet her.
- Compliment her on her looks, clothes or something she has done.
- Buy her flowers/chocolates/fruit/gifts.
- Buy and write a nice card to go with your gift.
- On special occasions, always write a special message which includes telling her that you love her.
- Tell her you love her at least once a day.
- If she is crying or upset, give her a hug without necessarily saying anything.
- Never presume a hug means sex.
- When you hug or kiss her, try not to think of anything else but her.
- Try not to interrupt her while she is talking to you.
- Try not to correct her if she mispronounces a word or uses the wrong word.
- Try not to correct her if she exaggerates in company.
- Explain beforehand that you may at times have to be alone or leave the room.
- Find another way to express feelings if words are difficult for you to find.
- If you feel overloaded, leave the situation and resist becoming reactive.
- Do not presume she is being critical; ask her first before assuming.
- If she asks for your opinion on something sensitive, suggests she asks a friend.
- Agree to a compromise on how much quality time you spend together.
- Limit the time you spend on internet or with your special interest.

- Do not even begin to explore porn on the internet; you may soon be drawn in and displease her.
- Do not expect her to participate in your particular routines.
- Do not force your need for structure and inflexible plans on her or your family.
- If you collect things, then agree to a limit on the space you can use for those things.
- Encourage her to spend time with friends and family, as it is a form of social and emotional food for her.
- Ask her to write down any errands or tasks she wants you to do.
- Do not be tempted to fix her problems unless she asks for your help.
- Sometimes she will just want you to listen and not try to solve anything.
- Give her your time and attention, making her feel close to you.
- Tell her you love her when you make love.
- If you have children, remember that they are the responsibility of both of you.
- Come to an agreement on how chores and childcare can be divided between you.
- Try to have fun with the family and laugh with them.
- Check with her how your child is doing in respect of their ability to perform certain tasks or their mental processes.
- Do not alienate yourself from the family; find something you can share with them.
- Agree a time that you can share with the children, doing things together or sharing an interest.
- Believe and trust that she loves you; accept and thank her for being in your life.

(Pg 198–200) from her book, What Men with Asperger Syndrome Want to Know About Women, Dating and Relationships.

Chapter 5
Autism/Neurodivergence in Study and Work

This subject has been touched on in small sections in different places of the book, but it is good to have all the information together in one chapter too. In case you are *dipping* into different parts of the book and have skipped the often *boring* bits (lots of people skip the introduction, for example!); there needs to be a quick refresher as to what Aspergers is. Then we will look at how schooling and work is affected by Aspergers syndrome.

Aspergers Syndrome, Autism Spectrum Disorder (ASD)

I have made a fairly comprehensive list of traits of Aspergers and possible (more neuro-typical-like) responses that would be helpful to the person on the spectrum. Remember, it is healthy to have a mutually supportive relationship in the workplace, whether you are the employee, employer or a colleague of the person on the spectrum.

Lack of Theory of mind, or Mind-blindness

Be direct and specific. Hints are not understood. Say what you are feeling and thinking if it is relevant to give another person your context. Aspies cannot always work out your context (that *context* is what is often referred to as a *subscript* that neurotypicals seem to just *know* and which is absent often in Aspergers). *Spell* out your responses in a clear and non-judgemental, non-emotional manner.

Lack of, or Minimal, Eye Contact

Understand that your Aspie student or work colleague is listening to you. Once they are comfortable with you, they may glance at you briefly or watch you peripherally.

Note to both Aspies and Neurotypicals. Mostly Aspies don't like eye contact. Neurotypicals do like eye contact. So Aspies and neurotypicals are uncomfortable with eye contact, in different ways. When neurotypicals don't make eye contact with other neurotypicals, they put *meaning* into it (remember the secret code of neurotypicals?). Well, lack of eye contact to a neurotypical means that the other person is either angry with them or lying or being dodgy in some way. This then makes the neurotypical guarded and possibly angry, and they then act out of this emotion. When I have told Aspies this, they are often astonished, to put it mildly! They cannot comprehend all this meaning around something so uncomfortable to them.

Aspies are uncomfortable with direct eye contact and then uncomfortable with breaking the rule of the expected making eye contact. All the time. In every social interaction. They know, know, know, you want eye contact (well, usually).

John Elder Robison, who writes and speaks internationally, and is himself on the spectrum, on several occasions has remarked (in one way or the other) on the oddity of having to stare at eyeballs to be acceptable.

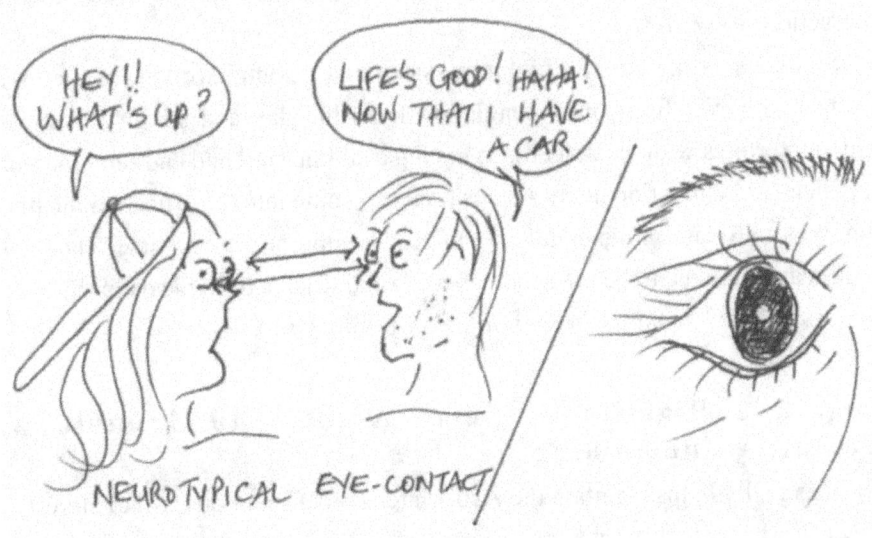

Autism Is a Social Development Disorder

Unless you have an extroverted Aspie talking *at* you, most Aspies do not seem to have the social, gregarious, herding instinct that neurotypicals have. Having a social development disorder means that *social* communication is particularly difficult for someone with Aspergers. Social communication includes reading social cues such as body language and eye movements, recognising different tones of voice, recognising when sarcasm is being used, or even when a rhetorical question may have been asked. Expect your Aspie colleague to have missed some of your cues and then go on with your tasks pragmatically. This also means that the Aspie will probably also not get office or school ground politics and may also miss unconscious social hierarchies. You can teach them office etiquette but not political nuances.

Aspies Often Struggle With Sensory Overload

This includes lights, noise, movement, smells, and other distractions. Where possible, allow them a workspace in which they can reduce the lighting and please let them use noise-cancelling headphones. It will also help to reduce other sensations, like smells of food or perfumes and scents – and to limit small constant movement like fans and flags. Keep the work environment as unstimulating as possible. Their own busy minds, with often multiple thoughts running in a speeded-up stream of consciousness, does not need external distractions as well.

Some also struggle with nighttime sleep and insomnia (often they are still trying to recover from over-stimulation from the day and sensory overload, which interferes with their sleep), so having a sliding start and end time for work may help. You may find many Aspies prefer to come into the office at lunchtime and work until late at night – all circumstances appropriate of course. There will be less distractions in the afternoon as well (and tired neurotypicals in the office are less talkative towards the end of their working day!).

Cognitive Rigidity in Some Areas, and Trouble with Executive Functioning

This really helps maintain the Aspie intense focus and obsessive interest, as they are not easily distracted once on task – especially in the right environment with few distractions and their noise-cancelling headphones on. On the negative side, when interrupted they struggle to connect with what you are trying to say to them or if the topics keep shifting, they may struggle to follow the conversation and may only pick out the odd fact without context. Also, if you give them a lot of information at once, they will be unable to process it immediately, especially if you have interrupted them. Give them time to process and respond, otherwise expect a random answer which will probably be slightly on task but will be totally out of context with your current conversation.

There is also the difficulty of finding and framing the right words for Aspies – beyond the difficulties of mind-blindness and lack of facial/emotional recognition in another. One descriptive metaphor is that the busy Aspie mind can sometimes be like a massive shed in which everything is dumped and is then hard to find or access. They often know what they want to say but cannot find a verbal way to accurately represent their thinking. It is definitely there – but accessing this may need a little time and processing. They will then probably respond at an inappropriate time and fully out of context once they have processed. Neurotypicals can sometimes find this quite attacking because of the delayed response and what then looks to them like a calculated comeback.

An important note here about cognitive rigidity. You know your campus has a brilliant mathematics professor who is absentminded (this *rigidity* may explain the absentmindedness). This professor keeps forgetting meetings because they were announced at short notice or was mentioned lightly at the end of the meeting when the focus of the professor was elsewhere. So email that information to your professor well in advance. Help staff diarise it with a reminder and an agenda. If the department has a secretary to organise this kind of administrative task, then train that person up in Aspie-understanding skills, so that the professor can manage. It is not unusual for brilliant minds to need a bit of micro managing in their daily lives! As someone once commented, "They can list all the stars in the universe to over the three hundredth one and all lined up in the westerly direction, but they forget to eat or put the rubbish out!"

Two advantages that neurotypicals have are that their *brain wiring has both central coherence and a high executive function* (put simplistically – juggling multiple tasks at once). What does this mean? *Aspies are known to have poor executive function*, but this can be improved with reminders, apps and a timeline chart for example.

Imagine that a company is launching a new product, and the CEO's (chief executive officer's) function is to coordinate that. The CEO has to make all the managerial decisions such as who will be working on the product, who the product is aimed at, who will supervise the teams, how many teams will be needed for the different areas of this product, what is the order of this product, while also ensuring the dateline for the launch is met.

This is obviously a highly detailed plan that needs to be actioned and followed through. This is a really detailed plan that needs to be done – that means completed. If there is a hitch in the plan, the CEO can switch the order around or change some of the details to get it back on track again – which is the function of the executives.

The central coherence sees the bigger plan or the big picture, while the executive functioning carries it out. The executive functioning is the breakdown of the big picture into doable parts, so that there is a structure and an order. Cognitive flexibility is the last, little important piece that makes the system work. If something breaks down in the plan or in a part of the executive functioning, then the cognitive flexibility of the brain is the tool that takes over and finds another solution, feeds it into the executive functioning, from where the process continues again after a short hiccup or glitch in the system.

Aspies are generally not good at seeing the overall picture. This is called weak central cognitive coherence of the brain. Without central coherence in the brain, the executive functioning part of the brain cannot work properly. Aspies often have cognitive rigidity (an inability to adapt or substitute an alternate plan or action); they have a poor executive functioning (which means that they cannot re-order a project without enormous difficulty and break it down into manageable parts), and they have poor cognitive coherence overall, which manages this whole process.

As we go on to explore Aspies in the workplace, these three brain functions, or lack of them, can significantly influence employment and functioning in the workplace.

Autism Syndrome and Study (Such as School or University)

If you are neurotypical, imagine this scene below, with all the elements imperatively and individually monitored but combined in one scenario:

- Overhead lights flashing
- Being in an overly bright room
- You have to notice all the posters on the wall in detail
- There is a lot of clutter and books around on shelves and tables, and you notice each detail specifically
- A lot of people talking at once
- Some voices are high pitched, some are scratchy and hoarse
- Laughter but you don't know the cause of the laughter
- Strong smells, like body odour and bad breath, unpleasant perfume and cheap deodorant spray in the air
- Vague interruptive clattering
- There is a stream of traffic noises outside
- Nearby someone is bouncing a basketball and throwing hoops and cheering with somebody else
- Your shirt is an original scratchy itchy hair shirt
- The people around you speak your language, but their culture is so weird you just cannot keep up with what they expect from you
- Lots of different movement around you: up, down, backwards, forwards
- One adult person speaks to you in a steady but animated voice and waits for an answer

So what did that person ask you?

This is a very mild introduction to the oft Aspie world if you are neurotypical. If you are Aspie – well, yes, I know, I left a lot of stuff out!

On the other hand, not all Aspies suffer the same set of symptoms and may not have sensory overload but may have other issues.

> I have met Aspies who are oblivious to heat or cold. One young schoolgirl came into a meeting mid-winter. She was wearing her school skirt, which was very short, a short sleeved open neck white cotton t-shirt. It would have been about 4°C outside. She was Caucasian. Her blue veins stood out. Her skin was goose-fleshed and extremely white. Despite her body clearly reacting to the cold, she was oblivious of it when I questioned her. Another young woman came in on a hot and humid summer's day wearing a long sleeved t-shirt and a thick heavy hoodie (with the hood up), jeans, shoes and socks – and showed no signs at all of the effect of the weather. Her body didn't even respond.

Being Aspergic is, as mentioned often before, a spectrum issue. For some, the sensory issues are not as bad as described, yet for others it is far worse. What is surprising is how many Aspies do succeed and make it through the school system, and then go on to other training in a relative field – despite all the hurdles in their path that they have needed to overcome along the way. They are champions!

Aspie children struggle with all the usual sensory issues, as described in the chapter on children. These sensory sensitivities come with them to school as well, with the cognitive inflexibility issues, the multifarious social issues including mind-blindness and difficulty with reading social situations, the obsessive tendencies and the massive downloads of data in a school classroom. Added to that is the loneliness of living like an outsider in one's community; with the longing for a best friend; with a desire to please and learn and reach expectations; with the longing for peace and solitude; with the *internal* and external pressure to perform socially to an unreadable code; and with the anxiety and distress each day of having to face that struggle again. Because of their youth, they also have not yet understood nor become aware of, nor learned, strategies to manage their condition.

Let's look at how we can do things differently for Aspie children, and then loosely cross-apply that to adult learning institutions too.

- **In an ideal world – if that exists:**
  - Enhancing a sense of social safety
  - Carpeted floors and sound insulation in walls and ceiling
  - Comfortable lighting or let them wear their Irlen lenses

- Small classes
- Minimal distraction on walls which are a muted colour
- Longer lessons, e.g. a half day of maths and then a break. In high school, one might have a day of maths or science or English (or key subjects) with good breaks for processing. Short lessons means lots of interruptions and needing to change mentally.
- Places to process
- Introduction to other skills sets (sport e.g. badminton and swimming, other languages, woodwork or cooking, art, and so forth)
- A mid-term day for specialist interest activities
- Extra one-on-one staff where needed
- Introduction to busier classrooms (e.g. a computer class or engineering and design) and gradually extending their time in these environments as they become more familiar with it
- Coaching into teamwork and cooperation with others
- Coaching in social skills
- As they get older, increasing integration with support into mainstream, with a well-coached mutual understanding between mainstream and Aspies
- As the integration continues, Aspies are supported when overwhelmed or needing time out

Isn't this just the loveliest dream?

But this is not practical; there are funding issues, staffing issues, balancing other students in the school, preventing the Aspie classes from becoming a stigmatised group and issues assisting Aspie group immersion with all kinds of people. Another significant issue is that a lot of Aspies haven't been diagnosed and the females on the spectrum are even more likely to fall through the proverbial safety nets. Even children are rarely diagnosed, often not until adulthood sometimes. This dream is just not a reality and dreams also have plenty of flaws, which raise complex issues. But surely, we can rescue some elements?

CLASS CAREER SPEECHES

Surely, teacher trainees can have more education regarding recognising and teaching Aspergic students – and similarly with lecturers? Surely, we can make some conditional time-out safe spaces for Aspies? Subjects, curriculums, teaching methodology and ideology, school timetables are all based on the needs of neurotypicals, who have shorter attention spans and different social ways of interacting and learning.

I have thought that in larger schools, there could be a neurotypical class and a *silent* adjoining class, in which anyone could go to watch the same teaching via a screen with no distractions. Or small labs for Aspies who could cocoon (like google staff cocoon rooms) alone if need be and watch the lesson online whilst still on school grounds. There are so many options if we are creative about it.

I so admire the many Aspies I have met who have endured school. Each day was an endurance. They tell me they *just knew* it was a rule to go to school and follow all the rules, and so they endured each day. And succeeded. And generally did well at school. And went on to become doctors and lawyers. Some even went on to become maths and science teachers themselves.

Looking back, I had a maths teacher and a history teacher, who today I *armchair reflect* as probably both having been on the spectrum. Interestingly, they both demanded certain things (when I look back now). They:

- Never had the lights on except on the darkest winter days
- They both demanded absolute silence in the class
- They never interacted one-on-one or personally with their students
- They had rigid ways of teaching
- They spoke *at* us and never made direct eye contact
- They made rules which were always kept on a side white/blackboard like:

    - There will be two tests per term
    - All homework must be…(and several instructions followed)
    - And rules of the classroom like no talking in class, no rubbish left behind
    - That students were expected to make their own notes – no notes were handed out, but as the teachers talked, they made notes on the blackboard or whiteboard, which we were meant to copy.
    - They wrote clearly and would not accept any teasing at all from students pretending they could not read the writing.
    - They wore the same clothes with little variety, over the five years that I was in high school.
    - Their comments on our school reports were simply a list of our scores and a factual comment around that. There were never personal comments such as the other teachers made, for example: "Janey is a kind girl who willingly helps other students" or "Mark daydreams and shows lack of attention in class".
    - Because of their strange interactions, we were all mildly scared of them. Yet they were never abusive, nor did they shout or display any intimidating behaviour. Their classes were all delightfully quiet, with just the scratching of our pens on our pages (we didn't have laptops then!).

- I remember our maths teacher would give us *three minutes*, for example, to do an exercise. She would stand and look at her watch (not the class), and when the time was up, she simply continued teaching.
- They were brilliant teachers if you were willing to learn (and not draw or play other silent games in these classes), and I achieved excellently in both these classes. On the whole, their classes generally achieved higher than other classes. (Before we even went to high school, we were warned about these teachers and to hope that we never got them in senior school! I was terrified the first day in their classes, but later, I actually was fascinated by them as I couldn't place how they were so different. Also, I thought it was a privilege to be in those classes, as we knew that the students in their classes usually did well!).
- When not teaching, they seemed to be alone (we were very good at working out which teachers became friends and hung out at school together).

When I tell Aspies that I loved school, especially my five years at high school (or college in the USA), they are usually astounded! I tell them how I joined in as many activities as possible before and after school as well – they are amazed that anyone could think or behave like that. Looking back, I can still say that I truly enjoyed school and even more so in my teenage *high school years*.

Sadly, I have also worked with Aspies who cannot manage school, who have developed anxiety early in life about classrooms, who are often ill before school, or simply often ill, and who by high school are struggling with anxiety and depression. I have worked with smart students who are failing because they cannot concentrate due to all their sensory issues – but who do brilliant homework if they are able to manage class at all. Some are so depressed and unfocussed; they start skipping school. Some endure with broken souls and spirits and enter adulthood that way. Those who get a *reader-writer* and a separate quiet room during examination and test times, fare far better in this situation. It is not that Aspies cannot read or write (in fact, they are often better than neurotypicals in this regard), it is that they cannot focus for all the many sensory issues affecting them.

And often, they become unemployed adults. An article headed *86 Percent of Adults with Autism are Unemployed* (Taylor Simmons · CBC News · Posted: Apr 09, 2019 4:00 AM ET) led into the article about Spectrum Works Autism Job Fair. This is a shocking number of unemployed Aspies in Canada – but worldwide, the stats are pretty similar. Of course, like neurotypicals, there is a wide range of abilities and skills, and the article does not define these.

We have a vast resource of potentially skilled people that we are not engaging with or embracing within our society. I see that as a sad waste at every level. We need to change this situation, right from school level!

- **In reality – Aspies at school and what we can do.**
  - Parents – do all you can. Read all you can. Join an autism support network or group nearby.
  - Consciously support your child. Give your child time to stim and process.
  - Teach them good boundaries, both personally and socially.
  - Love the person. See the person and not the condition.
  - Have an unstimulating support area for your child to do their homework. Switch off the TV and limit and manage external noises. Maybe they can do their homework nearby while you make dinner and are available emotionally and physically to help.
  - Talk to your children's teachers and school about how you can all make this more manageable for your spectrum child.
  - Maybe co-ordinate a speaker on Aspergers and/or autism for the teacher's professional development slots.
  - Get involved on your child's school board so that you can help present options for all children and make decisions.
  - Western society has worked hard at inclusion for all school children, regardless of race, gender, religion and so forth. Ensure that inclusion of Aspergers and autism are also noted and managed. Despite the idea of inclusion, many Aspies and the needs of Aspies are generally not included.
  - Teachers – maybe allow your Aspergic, autism spectrum, or even ADHD children some noise reducing headphones. Allow them a quiet library nook where they can withdraw if they need to.

> "In a noisy place I can't understand speech because I cannot screen out the background noise."
> Temple Grandin

- I have heard that some people are using sound-reversing earphones, so that instead of increasing selective sounds, it decreases it. Musicians use this, and one can often see the earpiece (or professional music ear plug) removed (dangling behind them) after they have finished a piece of music. Different filters can also be used, depending which decibel range you may want to filter. Talk to your audiologist. This may be cheaper than noise reducing headphones and also less obvious. And your child will not be so self-conscious and overtly *different* when trying to cope with a noise sensitivity.
- Buddy them up with a healthy caring neurotypical who can look after them on the playfield. Teach your classes some inclusive social skills. Encourage their strengths – sometimes publicly if need be.
- Know their stim! And help them to use it appropriately!

> "When I did stim, such as dribbling sand through my fingers, it calmed me down. When I stimmed, sounds that hurt my ears stopped. Most kids with autism do these repetitive behaviours because it feels good in some way. It may counteract an overwhelming sensory environment…"
> Temple Grandin

- Parents and teachers – teach your spectrum children to speak up and ask for help. Give them words, or even a signal, they can use when they need help but cannot verbalise what they need. Or give them a signal or agreed quiet touch when you need to get their attention.
- Very important: both parents and teachers – keep to a predictable routine for schoolwork and homework and if there is a change, then warn the Aspie child well in advance.
- Parents can work with teachers or the school to ensure that a friend or buddy is encouraged at home and at school. Make sure that this buddy enjoys the friendship and benefits from it too of course.

- Often Aspies are not very co-ordinated. Focus on sports that can help develop these strengths. Swimming is good. Maybe table-tennis. Dance is also very good for balance, muscular strength and confidence.
- Don't single out your Aspie and focus attention on them negatively.
- If there is a new instruction that will help the Aspie, try to make it optional that the whole group has to follow. An example could be that all children could write the draft of their ideas in pencil first (knowing that the Aspie may get angry with an ink draft that is incorrect and will freeze at that point and be unable to proceed.) [This is a socially acceptable strategy as all Aspies have to generally follow expectations for neurotypicals, so an occasional change is not an issue].
- Remember that our job as adults is to show leadership that is kind, healthy and appropriate to all children. Remember *that your Aspie is a child* even if they seem quite adult at times.
- Your Aspie will sometimes either parrot words or say something (it may even be cruel) that they don't seem to comprehend the meaning of – or not comprehend that it was inappropriate. Try to remember that they are Aspie, have cognitive rigidity, and if there is an issue, work it out in private at an appropriate time.

> I remember one mother and teacher being very distressed when their eleven-year-old Aspie laughed long and loudly at another student who fell and was both badly injured and bleeding. He (the Aspie child) explained to me that he was very sad for this child in pain but the picture of blood on the knee and elbow was so incongruous that the picture itself was funny. He even chuckled when he remembered the scene, but then covered his mouth because he knew he could not laugh. And yet, he expressed his sorrow and compassion for the boy. The teacher said that he was also the most helpful of all the students as the injured student recovered.

- Be very explicit with clear, unambiguous instructions.
- Assign the groups in your class where teamwork is required. Often Aspies are either included because they will do most of the work or

will be excluded, e.g. from a sport as they often may not be as coordinated as the neurotypicals.

> My son went to university and registered to do a software engineering course, on which we both expected to see many Aspies – in fact, he made a lovely long-term Aspie friend there. On the last lecture of the day, the first day of the course, the (new to teaching) lecturer said that he was available for any kind of course related questions. He did his intro and at the end of the lecture, opened up the floor to questions. They were still asking questions two hours later – my son noting that the questions were often repeated with only the slightest variations (Aspies need absolute fixed details) and seemed to come from predominantly the Aspie quarter. They all missed their dinner in the halls that night, as the kitchens were closed by the time they were dismissed. My son had to find a takeaway outlet for dinner. He noted that the lecturer never made that kind of open invitation again and was very pedantic about the boundaries of question time. (Note to readers: many students acknowledged they were on the spectrum – we were not *armchair diagnosing*.)

- As teachers, and parents, keep in mind that the combination of cognitive rigidity and mind-blindness can mean that your child or student will have difficulty seeing things from another person's viewpoint and consequently cannot change their mind or adapt the strategy of another. Help them to learn how to sift information. They need this kind of *sifting* conversation with you.
- If your Aspie is not looking at you, they are probably still listening to you and giving you their full attention. Try not to get too hung up about this. As a parent, you may one day, at a very good time however that looks for you and your Aspie, take an opportunity to explain to them that some groups of people need eye contact, and give them a few helpful tips in this regard.
- Remember that they are wonderful learners generally and very eager students. With encouragement and support, most children and people can reach their potential.

Autism and Job Interviews

Before you even get to an interview, make sure that your CV (curriculum vitae) or resume is up to date and accurate, including copies of your qualifications and references relating to your experience. If you are going to a job that requires some creativity, then prepare a small portfolio of your work, whether you include originals or substitute originals with photographs or short descriptions of what you have done. You could go to a professional CV writer and ask them to put a CV together for you. You can make a copy and send it in to the company or recruitment officer who is working with you. If you are making one yourself, keep it short, accurate and inclusive of your relevant qualifications and/or experience.

Each job that you apply for should not have a standard covering letter, although your CV can be a standard one that you send with all your applications. Write a brief but unique covering letter for each application that you are submitting. Make it relevant to the job description. One job advertisement may be looking or people who are honest and can work well by themselves, and another may be seeking someone who is specifically accurate, for example, although they might both be the same type of work (for example, an accountant). Maybe ask someone you respect, like a friend, a family member, or a social worker if you have one, to look through all your paperwork before you submit it. Then send it off and hope for the best (like everyone else who has applied for the same position).

- Prepare a succinct, informative CV
- Send an individualised covering letter for each job that you are applying for.

If you are the Aspie being interviewed as a potential candidate for a job

Most interviews are framed around the dominant neurotypical way of doing things. One rather alarming interview statistic that I read was that the interviewer unconsciously decides in the first eight seconds whether they are likely to employ the interviewee or not.

Neurotypicals very quickly judge each other by physical presentation, which includes dress, social responsiveness and emotional confidence. One of the clues of *confidence* is eye contact. Again – a neurotypical will assume that no eye contact also means no confidence (meaning an eye-contact-avoiding Aspie) in which there is already an obvious power imbalance. The interviewer holds almost all the power in this situation – so an awareness of the imbalance of power is not only important but it is also essential that the interviewee is able to manage imbalance and awareness in a healthy way too.

Before you even apply for a position, read up about that position if you have not had that particular type of work before. Think about that job-related work environment. Can you manage that environment? Can you do that job in that particular environment? When you were at school, how did you manage different environments? Maybe talk this through with someone who understands your Aspergers and gather all the information you can, then sift through it and see if that job can work for you. You may not like working where there are a lot of people but that McDonalds' job (that you saw advertised) in the kitchen out the back may suit you perfectly as everything is ordered and systemised and you know exactly what you have to do – and you do not need to deal with customers directly. Submit your application in time! Do not submit a late application! Then wait and see if you are going to be called in for an interview.

If you are intimidated by the interviewing process, then do some research. Go online and search for the key questions that interviewers will ask. In the peace of your own home, consider the question and prepare an appropriate answer. Write down the questions and answers and practise them where you need to.

Maybe a good friend, or a social coach, or even a professional person like a counsellor or psychologist, can practise going through these with you. Perhaps treat it as a game with its own rules and patterns. Recognise the patterns of this interviewing-social-game.

Be prepared at the interview when you feel stumped to say things like: "Please give me a moment to think about that", or "please could you repeat that question", or "I am sorry, but I must have not put that document in – could I please scan it to you when I get home?" ...Of course, this all depends on the type of question that you may be asked. Try to go over something like YouTube clips (including the fails!) and see what you can learn. Do some research on what you think the job is worth and whether you can manage the hours required. Also, if you have anything important happening in the near future, for example, your grandfather's 90th birthday and a giant combined family reunion happening overseas and for which you have already booked your flights and accommodation, be prepared to mention it and negotiate that your contract allows you to be released from work for that time. Unfortunately, you cannot usually expect your new employer to pay you fully for that holiday early in the new employment, but if the employer has been warned in advanced and has given approval, then you can still probably get to go.

Practise sitting upright, making *eye contact* (aiming just above the bridge on someone's nose if you cannot do direct eye contact), practise walking in a steady, confident manner with shoulders upright and not slouching and with your feet not dragging. Go through your wardrobe and ask someone to help you clean and lay out a set of appropriate clothing, relevant to the nature of work that you are looking at. If the firm has uniforms, then dress smart-casual. If the firm requires black pants (for example, many judicial courts expect all staff to have a black suit – black pants and a black jacket for all staff), then wear a pair of black pants to the interview. If you are looking for tradie work (as a trades-person, for example a hairdresser, a technician, a builder), then again, dress smart-casual.

Then once you have made it to the interview room or waiting room, wait patiently unless a notice on a desk or a door advises you otherwise.

I once had an Aspergic male client for a follow-up appointment. He was early, and I was finishing off with another client. This Aspergic man was obviously very anxious when he came in and looked around the front waiting room nervously. He was a large man and clearly very agitated – which could have looked threatening to someone else observing him. I have a glass office door, so I could see his arrival, and I can see into the waiting room. He paced about frantically – did not take in the meaning of the large bright yellow (with *black* ink) notice to take a seat and that I would attend to clients as soon as possible – walked out of the building, walked in again and then stood helplessly frozen in place for about thirty seconds. He then walked up to the reception desk (which was unattended at that time) and started banging furiously on the desk and stared at me through the glass partition. I was worried, as he may have had a health issue, so excused myself from my client and went out to see him. He then told me that all he wanted was for me to know he had arrived and then visibly relaxed. (If he were coming in for a job interview, his behaviour would already have excluded him from the position, before he even had the interview, if the interviewer did not understand Aspergers.)

Way before your interview, prepare your paperwork. You will have sent in your copies in your CV, but perhaps have a small zipped, plastic file (so that you can close it and not lose documents, so that documents are not crushed or damaged and also if it rains so that your documents will not get wet), with some originals or some further examples of your work. If your work is an app or programme, be sure that you have a copy with you on your phone if need be.

Before your interview, make sure that you are showered and clean. Give yourself plenty of time to get ready. Perhaps have a light snack. Then pick up your documents and get yourself to the interview in time. Monitor your breathing so that you are steady and constant (not holding your breath nor hyperventilating). If someone can go to the building of your interview with you, then you may find that helpful and supportive, and it will probably keep you on time and focussed, then even better. It is best generally if you do not take a support person into the waiting room with you – and in the vast majority of cases, especially not into the interview room.

Remember that most initial interviews are reasonably brief. If you are called back, it means that they may have short-listed you and may be even more interested in your work and you personally, as a potential candidate for the advertised position. This interview may be a little longer. You may even have more than two interviews, especially if you are going for a more senior position in that firm.

There are two very important things to remember in the context of the above:

I. Try not to be daunted or overloaded by all of the above. If you go back and read through it again, you will see that it is an ordered, systemised, stage-by-stage process that I have written down for you. Applying for a job is a process, which you do step-by-step, like a recipe, or building an app, or even building a house. You cannot build all of the house at once. Break this down into manageable steps for yourself as I have done, and then do the process step by step.

II. Awareness and understanding of Aspergers and the ASD spectrum is growing steadily, and I hope that in the near future, more and more interviewing staff will be enlightened and will adapt around you. Until then, you may have to sadly *fake-it-till-you-make-it* in a neurotypical way and feel sorry for those many neurotypicals who may not get all your strengths.

Do you tell them about your Aspergers/Autism diagnosis or not?

There is no rule about this and probably no correct answer. The closest to correct answer is that this depends on circumstances. If your Asperger syndrome diagnosis is understood by the company or the recruitment officer and the company is looking for your skills, then you may discuss your diagnosis briefly. Be sure to bring out how Aspergers works for you and your specific strengths, which will benefit your employer.

Sadly, society does not on the whole understand Aspergers yet. As I said a few paragraphs ago though (and in the example in the following section a few pages away), there is hope as more and more people are coming on board with understanding and have an interest in Aspergers. This is not only in the Western culture but also within the Eastern and Asian cultures – and some academic papers on the subject are steadily coming out of South Korea and China for example. If you think that they are not prepared for someone on the spectrum, then it may be a good idea to simply discuss your strengths without referring to your Aspergers.

Autism and Working in a Neurotypical Environment

> *A very short story used as an illustration:*
> You live on the island of Ranji-bucky. Most people there have a livelihood working as vlasykin. They speak the language of Grashti mainly, but where needed, they introduce Bonishtibickri – which is their secret wordless code, culturally learned from birth and *talking* subtly with various parts of the body, especially the face and tonally with the voice, which replaces large chunks of language. Bonishtibickri has some complicated social manoeuvres, which you need to get perfectly correct to even get a job, let alone get any sort of comradery, and possibly some promotion, and has to be used naturally, as fakes are very quickly spotted! Although you got top marks training as a vlasykin and you speak Grashti fluently, you are not from Ranji-bucky nor have you acquired much Bonishtibickri and it is probably unlikely that you will ever get this fully correct. How are you going to manage your job interview tomorrow and if you do get the job, how will you proceed?

Did that seem like *gobble-dee-gook* or *Double-Dutch* to you? That level of expectation and unreadable social demands are everyday difficulties for an Aspie.

Okay – the above scenario is a bit weird, but I think if you are neurotypical, that you get the picture of some of the difficulties of fitting in and surviving the proverbial rat-race – and that's before you have even started working! And if you are an Aspie, I sympathise with your difficulties. It is hard enough as a neurotypical fitting into a new neurotypical workspace with whom one spends the best part of each day and even when you communicate in their pattern already!

Autism in the Office or at Work

I love this quote from Temple Grandin, one of my favourite authors and researchers on the ASD spectrum:

> "What would happen if the autism gene was eliminated from the gene pool? You would have a bunch of people standing around in a cave, chatting and socializing and not getting anything done."
> Temple Grandin

There are Aspies in most workplaces. It is sometimes lightly joked that 40% of lawyers, accountants, surgeons and engineers are on the spectrum. Aspies thrive where there are tight rules and systems. Sadly, many are unemployed or underemployed and often may have several degrees and yet are still struggling in lower paid jobs. I know a medical doctor who works in a fish and chip shop, a woman – with a master's in social work – who works on checkout in a supermarket, and a software engineer who does the produce in a grocery store. All good honest jobs but not the jobs that they were trained to do. The best hairdresser I ever had, left to work on vintage cars that she repaired, because she could not fit into that very neurotypical environment.

In a recent internet news article (CBC News dated 9th April 2019), a quote was made that in the US, 66% of people on the ASD spectrum were unemployed, whereas the national unemployment rate went up to 4% overall in the US, as of January 2019.

An article in the New Zealand Herald dated 16th July 2017 reflects that those on the spectrum in fulltime employment in New Zealand is estimated at around 10%, with possibly another 10% in part time employment. The national manager (at that time) of Altogether Autism (New Zealand), Catherine Trezona, estimated that in New Zealand there were about 80,000 ASD unemployed. Considering that the estimated population of New Zealand in 2018 is 4.8 million, this is a lot of adults underemployed or unemployed and often living in poverty. That's a lot of families affected in multiple ways, in such a small country! In most first world countries that have larger populations, the statistics must be hugely significant!

> I worked with a lovely Aspie man, who knew me reasonably well and appeared to feel safe with me, who desired a career as a life coach. He was very inspiring and had some great skills; he also had studied extensively at university – and had come to see me as to what else he may need to do this work. Sadly, his social skills were very poor. He made no eye contact; he was off-topic more than on-topic; he asked a question and then talked about something else before I could answer or even as I started speaking; he had many pet peeves and would go off at a heated rant about these unrelated peeves; when I could get a word in – he immediately interrupted; he seemed to not take on board what I said and also seemed to forget it immediately; his body language was cowed as if he were intimidated; and he would wander off at tangents about his interests and obsessions – and this was in an office and with someone who was Aspie-friendly! Yet, as peculiar as his social communications were, he was genuinely interested in life coaching! (He also repeatedly came back because our work had been so helpful to him and wanted to learn more.) A major concern of his was how to convince neurotypicals to accept him. I suggested that we stop and reassess and explore some workable facts first. I then asked *Professor Google* what the world population was that day, which amounted to 7.7 billion people. We then divided that by 67 (representing the very conservative estimate and ratio of 1:67, being ASD to neurotypical), which came out at 115 million people at the very least – because of our conservative estimate. Because he could do his life coaching online in various types of face-to-face apps, I suggested that he improve his own skills, which he could then teach to others on the spectrum. He was very excited because he saw how huge his potential market (targeted at those on the ASD spectrum) was.

An article in the Chicago Tribune (written by Nara Scheonberg on June 12th, 2019) briefly explores some employment issues for those on the *spectrum*. One man, who had a degree in applied statistics, could not find a job for five years and had often worked as a kitchen aide (which was not his training). In those five years, he mentions that he had *328 applications, 135 rejection letters and 14 interviews*. Another man speaks of waiting six years for a tech job, after working restaurants and retail to get by.

An online article from Chicago Tribune this year (2019) runs a clip on Walgreen's Distribution Centre and their initiative to employ people with disabilities, and the article claims that 80% of people with disabilities do not have employment. An autistic woman, *Julie Riley,* got a job in a Walgreen's distribution centre in the US, in an initiative to employ staff on the spectrum. There is an interesting back-story to this: the enterprise was begun as the directors were believing that those on the spectrum would cope better with routine work, are less likely to go off sick, would make more faithful long-term employees (staff retention is better) and were better at noting specific but relevant details. This initiative arose as the chief supply officer (CSO), Randy Lewis, had an autistic son and started realising that those on the ASD spectrum or those who had disabilities had potential to make very good employees – where they were able to cope with the environment. His company then boldly and confidently hired 1000 staff who was on the spectrum or who had disabilities. They worked alongside everybody else, under the same employment conditions and for the same remuneration. The first distribution centre in which this initiative occurred apparently recorded the most productive levels in all the history of the company – which was first established in the early 1900s – and that inspired the company to expand their initiative to other sites! Going back to Julie Riley, she is autistic and has a learning disability plus hearing loss. Later, in 2008, she married a young man she had met at her work. It's always nice to hear happy stories!

In Canada, in 2017, an annual event has started in Toronto, Richmond and Montreal. It is called the Spectrum Works Autism Job Fair and the aim is to bring together potential employers and potential adult employees on the ASD spectrum. It was estimated that about 500 people on the spectrum attended. Potential employers included banks and IT companies, amongst other large companies. Apparently last year (2018), 10% of autism spectrum attendees gained full time employment through this. A 2012 Canadian survey found that only 14.3% of ASD adults nationally were employed.

Several large companies are all looking for a range of staff, which they refer to as being *neuro-diverse*. Although they value their neurotypical staff, these companies are looking for neuro-Atypical staff, and in this particular case, people on the ASD spectrum or who have ASD traits. In regards having staff on the ASD, the international world has come a long way and yet we are still horribly short of the mark, as there are still so many specifically ASD people unemployed. Sadly, little is possibly little hope of being employed as things currently stand in the first world economic marketplace.

SAP (Systems, Applications and Products) and *auticon* in Germany are two IT companies that welcome people on the ASD spectrum as staff. In fact, they almost exclusively prefer ASD spectrum staff in some departments. Fortune Magazine, in an article (by Dinah Eng dated 24th June, 2018), states that in October 2017, Ford Motor, DXC Technology, EY (Ernest & Young), Microsoft, JPMorgan Chase, and SAP – formed the Autism at Work Employer Roundtable to share best hiring and workplace practices and to help other companies see the return on investment in hiring autistic employees.

I have observed (through internet) the work of one international company, *auticon*, because of their specific interests in employing staff who are on the spectrum. Some of the background and details are below. The company is noted for its significant work in this area and have achieved international respect and acclaim for it.

auticon [sic] was started up in 2013 because Dirk Müller-Remus has an autistic son. He realised that those on the spectrum would be unlikely to find paid work in their careers unless the employment market *environment* was changed, so he set out to do exactly that. As of 2nd January 2019, the firm employed 150 employees in several countries in Europe, many of them on the spectrum. One article said that *auticon exclusively employs analysts and technologists with autism spectrum disorder*. I remember a few years ago seeing an advertisement for employees for a Dutch firm (which I now suspect was *auticon*) expanding into Holland (or the Netherlands) and being delighted that *only* people considered autistic need apply. What wonderful reverse discrimination and a great opportunity for potential ASD staff! In the US, *auticon* and Mindspark merged in about June 2018, as they had the same agendas and directions. Gray Benoist of Mindspark apparently has two autistic sons who also work in their father's company. These two international companies supply IT staff to some of the biggest companies in the world like BMW, Siemens, GlaxoSmithKline and Allianz, amongst many other big names.

They comment regards their Aspergers staff that in particular performs highly in certain areas, namely:

- Their skill in seeing patterns and recognising them, in the midst of enormous quantities of data.
- That the standard of Aspies doesn't drop – they can consistently manage a high standard.
- They state facts with candid honesty; there are no mind games nor politicisation of issues. It simply is what it is, for an Aspie.

> I have met an accountant employed in a senior position by a very large organisation. He told me of several occasions in which he spotted an error in a massive spreadsheet. His staff argued in disagreement, saying that they had gone over the spreadsheets several times already. But he can literally pinpoint the incorrect block on the spreadsheet. He tells me he *cannot say why* they are incorrect, but on looking at it, it simply stands out obviously – and this error spotting has always been unfailingly accurate. He says it is simply a feeling that he has. This particular feeling seems to be infallible, as is often the case with these kinds of data/error-spotting Aspie traits. Ironically, a few days after seeing him, I happened to be at our domestic airport and was standing right by the main exit. This man was returning from a trip and walked towards me, looked directly at me – then he walked right past me and completely failed to recognise me. I left him, as I did not wish to upset the apparent *headspace* that he was in. Regardless, a few days later, he was telling me about this flight, and I told him about the airport incident. He was very embarrassed and had no memory at all of seeing me. So he can miss a human being he knows, a familiar person who was also practically blocking his exit and yet can spot one small incorrect number in the middle of a spreadsheet containing thousands of numbers and figures! Incredible!

Many of these larger American companies (and the German companies, SAP and *auticon*) show great support for their staff. Apart from their Aspie staff having all the entitlements of neurotypical staff, they are also allowed headphones and tools to support them in the work environment, as well as communication coaches! (I assume that the coaches are probably all neurotypical.) The job of these coaches is multi-faceted:

- They brief neurotypicals about Aspie wiring.
- They brief Aspies about neurotypical wiring.
- They can be an intermediary between a business (a company client) and the Aspie staff member doing the work, so that both sides are clearly understanding each other.
- They support the early stages of settling into the job, including even helping the new employees with bus/train timetables and organising their day to get to work and establish a routine around work
- They help them to understand office politics to some degree and also office hierarchies and how to manage these.
- They create frameworks around setting outcomes or goals, including setting boundaries and time limits.

- They help the Aspie staff member to assess a situation and work through it.
- They coach and train the Aspie staff member to be self-aware and to institute strategies, for example, regular breaks to help with processing and to prevent being overwhelmed.
- Coaching may also include some things that neurotypicals take for-granted – such as noticing the speed at which a person is talking or their tone of voice, whether the other person is waiting for your feedback and even how an Aspie may use their body in a given environment (for example, to be aware of not standing too close to another person). [*Proprioception* is a common issue for Aspies, in that they often cannot tell internally how their body is using and filling the external space – socially and environmentally – around them.]
- Coaches also help with any misunderstandings and help resolve them.
- And they supply any other coaching that may be needed.

The More Common Reality: Making Changes

Life is hard.
Life is hard for neurotypicals.
Life is much much harder for those on the spectrum.

The reality is that the majority of the population, and hence the majority of the employers and staff, are neurotypical. They will need to see good reason to change their ways. On the other hand, the Aspie has grown up in this environment and accepts it and will struggle on valiantly in this neurotypical environment.

Change happens through incentive and awareness – both of which stem from education or knowledge, or reliable and dependable information. We (mainly neurotypicals) also, as the dominant hegemony, need to be aware of our unconscious biases or prejudice. We have beliefs about others that immediately discount other people and may influence our decisions about them.

As mentioned earlier, if within a few seconds we have made no eye contact with the other person, we neurotypicals have already dismissed and discounted them. As Marie Antoinette reputedly said when told that the poor had no bread, "Let them eat cake" – which seemed an obvious solution from the perspective of a twenty-four-year-old woman who had been indulged since birth. She spoke from her perspective only. Sadly, and not surprisingly, she literally lost her head about four years later – for multiple reasons, but one significant factor being an unwillingness to change and adapt to the desperate needs of others in her community.

As neurotypicals, we are usually so very unaware of our biases and how very damaging these are to others despite ironically priding ourselves on being understanding of others and compassionate and connected human beings. Most neurotypicals lump the whole broad range of ASD into one very biased stigmatic picture. I often wonder how the majority of neurotypicals would like it if we were all viewed as the same! We would resist that fiercely and point put our differences, our strengths, and maybe note our weaknesses.

Randy Lewis, chief executive of Walgreens as mentioned earlier, made a great statement. He says their company, when employing disabled people, people with physical health conditions or people on the spectrum, uses the ATP principle. ATP stands for *Ask The Person*. Ask The Person who has lived with a barrier all their life, how they cope with their barrier, and how they intend to overcome this barrier in regards their potential employment. He refers to *Harrison*, a young man on the spectrum who was looking for employment. Harrison said that he could pack ten boxes a minute. Randy asked Harrison how many that would total in an hour, as they worked in *hour blocks*. Harrison could not answer and did not know. The company standard was four hundred boxes an hour. Harrison said he could do ten boxes a minute and did not know that that totalled six hundred boxes an hour, despite being a reasonably intelligent young man. At that point, most employers would have shown him the door [*shown him the door* for Aspies reading this, means that he would have asked him to leave the interview and the building], because he could not do abstract arithmetic. Well, Randy gave Harrison a chance. And... Well, Harrison did what he said he could do. He packed six hundred boxes an hour, day after day, week after week, routinely – two hundred boxes per hour over the limit without fail! For over three years apparently, Harrison has worked at a hundred and fifty percent consistently and whichever area he has worked in!

What is particularly impressive here is that Walgreens is a large company. I understand that it is the largest pharmaceutical distribution centre in the USA. A Walgreens fact statement from their own website states that as of August 2018, they employed more than 240,000 staff. They are not a charity. They are not looking for a tax release via charity work. This is a fully, market-driven, commercial company who are basically interested in their profit margins, as does any business. All staff is employed on the same terms. This is a successful commercial model.

> In my work as a counsellor, I often need to use the WHODAS scale test. This is a test for a medical related insurance company that is used with much other data, to see how much a person is affected by their disability – in my work usually my clients are reflecting their wellbeing in regards dealing with their Post-Traumatic Stress Disorder. WHODAS stands for World Health Organisation Disability Assessment Scale. There are two questions towards the end of the test that really throws my clients. They are:
>
> - How much of a problem did you have because of barriers or hindrances around you?
> - How much of a problem did you have living with dignity because of the actions and attitudes of others?

This questionnaire always makes me think of my Aspergic clients and the ASD people that I know. Every day of their lives, they have to deal with the prejudices and biases of neurotypicals, and the dismissive attitudes that come with that, which is a very real social hindrance to Aspies. And how does one live with dignity because of the attitudes of others, especially when it is often a subconscious bias? How does one even begin to challenge that? It is therefore not surprising that over 80% of Aspies are unemployed. These are good hard working people. Recently, a support group of spouses-and-partners-of-ASD-relationships met for coffee. At this particular meeting, it turned out to be all female, as no males had arrived that day to join the support group. One woman pointed out that the job skills of their Aspie partners were significant; there was a maths teacher, three accountants, two engineers, a couple of IT specialists, and an electrician, amongst other skills. (These men were, of course, in the 10–20% of Aspies employed.)

Some difficulties that Aspies need to learn to manage or overcome include:

- Aspies can experience bullying excessively: find resources to deal with this such as knowing what bullying looks like, what the company policy on bullying is, and dealing with the correct people in regards a complaint.
- Aspies have difficulty with boundaries: know your boundaries clearly, look at what the boundaries of others are, know your job description so that you do not keep ending up with work that is not yours, get help if you or others are having difficulty with employment boundaries, or social and environmental boundaries in the workplace.
- Aspies are not always good with faces: so make a hierarchy picture of the staff. Note the managers, supervisors, your peers or colleagues, your juniors and then the kind of people who will come to you for your skills, services or whatever your work is. The marketplace people are your clients, vendors, providers, suppliers or customers.
- Aspies have difficulty knowing when and who to ask for permission for what is needed: such as time away to deal with a family crisis, using noise-reducing headphones at work, permission to close the curtains or blinds or dim the lights. Know who does the HR work in your area and ask them when needed.
- Aspies and tools: Aspies like their tools available and are usually quite ordered. It is important to keep desk stationery and your working tools together in one place. If they are your privately owned tools, then label them clearly and keep them in one place.
- Aspies sometimes have difficulty understanding jokes or comments that have made other people laugh. A comment, after some praise, like *that hoody is going to be small for your head now*, may need interpreting from a good safe work colleague or for a trusted friend after work.
- Perhaps find a way to ask your HR (human resources) person at work for some professional development around the ASD spectrum, so that they understand you. After all, you have been trying to understand neurotypicals for years!

> One professional person had an overflowing toilet in his apartment, and the waste from other apartments kept flowing through his bathroom. There was some difficulty getting hold of a plumber, as this sewage problem occurred on a weekend. When they did get a plumber, he was unable to finish the task, as he needed more hardware and the stores were shut, which meant that he had to postpone to Monday. The employee had a very uncomfortable relationship with his supervisors and manager and had no idea what to do, as he couldn't go into work (he had to be available to the plumber and make financial decisions around the job that needed doing). He sat in his dark apartment, getting more and more miserable, and unable to take any action, he literally froze on his couch. Fortunately, a friend contacted him. The friend first convinced him to come out and have a shower, and then the friend cooked dinner for them both (as the man had not eaten in his state of despair). After a shower and a meal and because of the safe environment, he began to try to process his concerns with his friend. He then tried to resolve the issue about being unable to go to work. Should he lie and say that he was sick – knowing that he wasn't very good at lying? He explored lots of options, all of which scenarios became eventually ridiculous. The friend advised him to simply contact his manager by email (as it was the weekend) and tell him the truth about why he couldn't come to work the next day. The man was astounded that it was so simple.

- Aspies need to learn to read body language if their jobs take them consistently into a social environment. It does have its own set of rules. There are plenty of books on the subject and plenty of courses and seminars from time to time.
- Aspies need to clarify the expectations of others, such as managers and colleagues. To Aspies, some of the communication is unclear. Be specific.

My argument is that that there are a wide range of skilled people out there, who will probably be faithful and hard-working, minimal absenteeism (in the right environment) and will have both good detailed focus and data retention. Who wouldn't want that in an employee?

So neurotypicals need to change too and also be less exclusive. Significantly. Even as Aspies try to do their part.

The Results of Employing Autistic People under Neurotypical Standards.

Let's look at some shocking things that I have heard:

- Aspies are seen as difficult
- Aspies break the rules
- Aspies are rude
- Aspies are unpredictable
- Aspies are disrespectful
- Aspies have meltdowns
- Aspies get stuck on trivia
- Aspies get obsessed
- Aspies can't join in socially or are socially inappropriate
- Aspies are not good conversationalists.
- Aspies have a lot of absenteeism
- Aspies don't do their homework (for schoolchildren) or complete assignments.
- The attacks then become more personal – such as the food they eat, the clothes they wear, their lack of facial expression, their lack of social activities, their cleanliness/lack of cleanliness and the list goes on and on exhaustively.

A significant point that I need to express here – is that I have seen all of the same behaviours and more, from neurotypicals. They just do these behaviours in neurotypicalese, so that are not noticed as much!

My goodness – this could be an exhaustive and exhausting study on prejudice and ignorance.

> Steven Covey, a motivational speaker, said something along the following lines:
> "Seek first to understand, to be understood."

It reminds me of an experience that I had had when I was over in Africa.

> My very good friend, Ivy Ngcobo, a Zulu woman, had told me that Zulu hospitality was culturally very important and that Zulus were very generous. If a Zulu offered you something, say they had opened a full bag of oranges to offer this to you, that it was very rude (quite offensive) in fact to take only one. Perhaps one ought to take half the bag; this would be considered polite and appropriate (as uncomfortable as it would be for me to do as this is not a usual European or Caucasian custom). Only taking one is a rude rejection of their hospitality and person. Later the same day, I spoke to a White, English speaking South African male who was incensed. He had offered his Zulu workman *a* cigarette, and the workman had taken half the packet, much to his astonishment! He finished off saying that he would never offer this workman a cigarette or anything again with a disgusting racist comment, concluding with *give them an inch and they take a mile.*

Yes, that story is shocking. And the relevance is that *ignorance of others* keeps us in a state of prejudice. And our outcomes could be so much better, with very few simple adaptions required.

I often hear neurotypicals complain and groan that they are the ones that have to do all the changing and the adapting and *what makes the Aspie so special that the neurotypicals have to put in all the hard work*! Some things to remember here:

a) Aspies live in the dominant hegemony made up mainly of neurotypicals.
b) Aspies have been adapting all their lives, often with great difficulty.
c) Even when they are working with you, they are having to adapt to your neurotypical demands which have been drilled into them since they were very little such as: "Look at the person talking to you! Don't be rude!" (And they have to filter how to do this while talking to you).
d) They also have to decipher your language and your idioms and saying such as: "We'll cross that bridge when we get there."

> One Aspie, a young new trainee, who asked a colleague a question, was hugely distressed by the answer. He asked the colleague if he wanted to do their filing. The colleague replied with, "I'd rather shoot myself in the head." And the poor Aspie man has been trying to save his colleague from any filing since (or at least, until I explained that his colleague simply meant that he really hated doing filing.)

e) They are adapting all the time to you too, their familiar habit. This is not a new thing for an Aspie, but for neurotypicals, it is a new discovery – this need for adjustment on their part – and they very quickly seem to tire of it and get frustrated. Be compassionate and understanding – this is how Aspies have lived with you most of their lives.

f) Some Aspies work very hard and many achieve way over expectation and generally give 150% or more. If one day they come in tired and frustrated and only manage 25%, don't become hard on them or angry. Give them space and quiet and in no time, they will be back at superspeed again.

g) And this consistent eye contact issue. I have said enough about it…

So I have to say, neurotypicals in the workforce, get over yourselves this once. You have a faithful meticulous colleague delivering some great work even if socially the two of you are not a comfortable match. It is not about you but about the job that needs to be done. If you can get past your discomfort, then you will both probably relax and produce better work. Even better, if you communicate often by some sort of writing method (text, email) that works for both of you, you should both get by more effectively in your work. Much simpler!

And for both the neurotypicals and the Aspie, remember that you are both genuinely trying to do your best here (one of the reasons why you are actually reading this book!). Like a simple cottage pie has a recipe, so there is a great recipe here for both the neurotypicals and the Aspie once you learn it. Neurotypicals be aware of the Aspie make up, but Aspies be aware of the neurotypical make up. Neurotypicals like it when you greet them with a simple *Good morning* or whatever appropriate greeting where relevant. Sometimes ask them how they are, or if you know of a special event, you could say something like, "How did that birthday party on the weekend for your ten-year-old go?", or "How did your golf game go yesterday?" For Aspies, it only needs to be the shortest chat, and then politely excuse yourself and get back to work. Neurotypicals – please answer briefly and succinctly and don't wander off on tangents and multiple other side stories and issues. If both sides do try and do their best, this can and does work admirably!

The relevance is that neurotypicals need to work on their biases and prejudices which result in statements such as the list on the previous pages. Let's look at the list of items one by one and see how that particular *prejudice came about*:

1. *Aspies are seen as difficult:* The main issue here is usually miscommunication. In electronics, we know that items connected in series only works if all the items work: if one element does not work, the whole electronic pathway stops working. According to Dr Kathy Marshack, neurotypicals use at least ten different centres in the brain for communication. A simple conversation or communication has all these parts of the brain lighting up. She uses the example of the old type of Christmas tree lights that are connected in series; when one light bulb stops working, every little light bulb has to be checked, and the faulty one replaced before they can all work again. Similarly, the ten or so centres in the brain need to all work, for the communication to flow freely. In Aspies, one or several of these centres do not work or are faulty, hence the miscommunication and the block in flow. (BTW – modern Christmas tree lights are wired with LEDs differently so that the problem as described above no longer occurs.) The social fix – stay on topic and discuss one issue at the time and go through a process smoothly and sequentially. This may seem tedious for a neurotypical, but it is good for neurotypicals to clarify their thinking this way too. It is a helpful skill both ways.
2. *Aspies break the rules:* Aspies can be quite horrified to find out that they have broken a rule or instruction. But if they do not understand the rules (usually social in nature), they can't be accused of wrongdoing. Most Aspies break rules in their striving to find creative solutions to a problem. That is why so many Aspies are inventors and artists and

creators of new programs. But it does look like they do things their way and their way only.

> There is a delightful scene in the TV series *The Good Doctor*. Dr Shaun Murphy [Freddie Highmore] is a brilliant, autistic, surgeon-in-training but his people skills are sometimes found wanting. In one episode, the chief of surgery bans him from speaking to a particular patient as he has managed to highly distress this patient. On the other hand, Dr Murphy desperately needs information to solve the medical issue, and only the patient may have this information. As he reconsiders the rule he has been given, that he is not to speak to the patient again, he finds a solution. He goes back into the patient's private hospital room, ignores the patient on the bed (who is aghast at his presence again), and cross-questions the patient's sister instead. He is then consequentially surprised and disconcerted later as the chief admonishes him and threatens him with suspension from his job, that he was not supposed to have taken this action either.

3. *Aspies are rude*: They are direct, factual and often blunt. Remember that there is a form of mind-blindness or lack of theory of mind. I suggest that if you work with someone like this, that you perhaps gently tell them that you were hurt by their comment and explain why. The vast majority of Aspies that I have met are very kind-hearted and will be happy to learn from you so that they do not repeat a behaviour that offended someone. They of course don't understand *neurotypicalese*, in turn.
4. *Aspies are unpredictable*: They are usually wonderfully creative lateral thinkers, which is very useful when trying to find solutions. They are not *always* unpredictable, but they (like everyone else of course) have moments of unpredictability, which I find quite endearing. Enjoy their solution focussed, problem solving way of responding.
5. *Aspies are disrespectful*: the answers are the same as [3] above, with the addition that Aspies do not always understand social hierarchies and may greet their manager the same as they greet a friend or the same as they greet the janitor or office cleaner. No social games with Aspies – a greeting is simply a greeting.

6. *Aspies don't stay on task*: in the right environment, they are very on-task, more so quite often than neurotypicals. They can often produce greater volumes of work too.

> One medical person that I know, when she resigned from burnout after working part-time, was replaced by one full time professional and two assistants!

On the other hand, it is good to be mindful of potential distractions if they are not on task and to see how those distractions can be limited regarding their interference.

1. *Aspies have meltdowns*: Yes, they can and do – but rarely and usually if they are overloaded. Most save their stress and overloadedness for home, and they stim in ways to resolve this so that they can come back the next day. One young man said on autistic blog page that I read some time ago, that his meltdowns were necessary. If he could have a meltdown on a Richter scale of 3, he was not only doing well but preventing a build up to a meltdown at a level 8 on the same Richter scale. Ideally, in the right environment, these meltdowns will not be happening.
2. *Aspies get stuck on trivia*: *Trivia* of course is in the eye of the beholder. One's person's trivia may be a major issue for another. Aspies do like generally to have everything going just smoothly and do notice details that are incorrect. That's why they are such valued team members.
3. *Aspies get obsessed*: With the correct coaching, Aspies will realise that most of their obsessions cannot have a place at work. If they do, then it is either useful (as in IT and they work in IT), or they are in the wrong job.
4. *Aspies can't join in socially or are socially inappropriate*: The majority are introverted, so often will not join for that reason. By adulthood, they have also faced much criticism, so they can be quite shy socially and emotionally guarded. The crux of Aspergers is that it is a social development disorder. And with good support, most Aspies like to be included.
5. *Aspies are not good conversationalists*: Sometimes they are not too good at the give and take of conversation. And they can at times override

others and go into great details about their own special interest. This is mostly adults we are talking about, who have limited their obsessive interests in conversation, but if they repeatedly go on more than one can manage it, just gently say that that is as much as you can manage in one day. They can also be coached or befriended and simply quietly nudged if they go too far, as a little sign and reminder to them. Have that conversation with them – but do it in a kindly manner. My son and his friend have agreed to, and coined the word *Sperg*, and the word is a reminder of a Sperg, or Aspergic, moment. The friend then stops the inappropriate behaviour.

6. *Aspies have a lot of absenteeism*: It is very unusual for Aspies to stay away from their jobs or to be absent. Aspies are usually noted for their retentiveness – they usually stay a long time in their jobs (and as in separately from their often phenomenal data retentiveness) and rarely miss work. They are faithful and hard working and will usually stay. They will generally not be absent because they are on the spectrum. If they are repeatedly absent because of the environment of employment, then do some research to see if anything can change. If not, the Aspie might have to find a better environment in which to work – just as neurotypicals have to when they are in a work environment that doesn't suit them.

7. *Aspies don't do their homework*: Generally, they get all their tasks done. Those who haven't are either overloaded and exhausted, distracted by an unsuitable environment or are unsuited to the particular work that they are doing. Generally, they are very good at meeting deadlines or will work voluntarily in their own time, where possible, to complete their tasks.

8. The attacks become more negative and criticising Aspies then becomes irrelevantly more personal and usually increasingly petty (for which they would not usually criticise a neurotypical) – such as the food they eat, the clothes they wear, their lack of facial expression, their lack of social activities, their cleanliness/lack of cleanliness and the list goes on and on exhaustively. So why become personal? People, mainly neurotypicals, do this when they don't understand a (often frustrating) situation, so they attack the other human being with whom they have associated these irritations. People are unthinkingly cruel this way. A

dignitary may be addressing a function on an important matter and members of the audience may be criticising what the dignitary is wearing – which has no relevance usually.

9. I could add that neurotypicals are often (but for different reasons):

- seen as difficult
- break the rules
- rude
- unpredictable
- disrespectful
- having meltdowns
- getting stuck on trivia
- obsessed
- socially inappropriate
- not always good conversationalists
- often have a lot of absenteeism
- don't do their homework (for schoolchildren) or assignments.
- The attacks on others then become more personal – such as the food they eat, the clothes they wear, their conscious and deliberate lack of facial expression at times, their lack of social activities, their cleanliness/lack of cleanliness and the list goes on and on exhaustively.

This is for different reasons though and will appear more fully in the chapter on neurotypicals.

So, please remind me, why are we picking on Aspies for the same issues?

Autistic Strengths in the Workplace

(especially when they are the job that is a right *fit*)

- They thrive on routine and repetition
- They are orderly and methodical
- They are conscientious and consistent
- They are rarely absent

- They generally are truthful
- They are direct and factual
- They like detail and data
- They are excellent at sorting data and information and later recalling these facts
- They have excellent pattern recognition
- They generally like repetitive predictable work
- Their loyalty makes them very valued staff members
- They are good at lateral thinking, which means that they are often good at solving problems
- They are usually extremely knowledgeable in their area of skill and their areas of interest – which are often combined in their jobs.

Solution Focussed Approach

Most larger first world businesses and companies, or Aspie-friendly businesses, have policies to look after their staff. These policies include time out, a period of short leave, or possibly other job options in another department. There are some issues with this:

- Not all businesses have other departments, nor may they have the ability to operate a business with a staff member having time out.
- Even if the business is very Aspie-friendly, the senior staff there do not always understand the best environment and support for their Aspie staff member – despite their very best intentions.
- Sometimes they get frustrated with the way an Aspie may do their job. A simple rule of thumb – work with the strengths that you have instead of attacking the parts that you have issue with.

I had a client that I worked with, who was diagnosed on the spectrum with Aspergers, who had had a breakdown because of work stress. He is a good man, faithful, guileless and hard working. He trained as a tradesman and worked for a good-sized company who considered themselves very Aspie-friendly, and they thought they had been both supportive and inclusive. They were also very supportive of him during his breakdown. My client would get a list of call-outs that he had to attend to each day, like any other of the tradesman. Each tradesman also had their *own* vehicle supplied by the company, although most of the tradies came customarily with their own tools. The background to my client is that he had an exceptionally understanding and supportive wife and a big family, and he was also studying for a final set of exams for another aspect of his trade. He felt under enormous pressure from work and although he reportedly had the most *perfect* work (in terms of how well he did the job), the company found him too slow (possibly because of his thoroughness). The other issue is that if he got stuck on a problem, he (a) could not proceed and (b) did not ask for help, so would stay in a mental tangle for a long time in the same place where the job was. From his side, he had several pressures, but the most pressing work one was his time management on jobs. He had come to a brilliant solution, which was to create a perfectly fitted and ordered van – and everything was very ordered (often more ordered than the storeman's depot!). Unfortunately because of this efficiency, his workmates would *borrow* items and either not replace them or would not put them back in the same place (simply a spur-of-the-moment thoughtlessness on their part and not intended to distress him). He would go to a job, find what he needed missing, and freeze – unable to know how to proceed. He could not get from Step 1 to Step 2 if something was missing. He said it could take him up to two hours a day to sort out his van and supplies again. He and his wife saw me for a letter to explain his Aspergers to his boss, and he also got some sick leave and a brilliant letter from his GP. Some strategies were adapted by his work. I also agreed to come to a work staff meeting to explain Aspergers, but that never eventuated through the workplace. Unfortunately, nothing changed for him at work, and it was simply that they *just do not get it* as his wife aptly summed it up, although he had some more *tools* from me to manage his situation. He remains a highly valued employee still.

(Below I have included the two letters that were written if this is useful for anybody to give a framework. Personal details have obviously been altered or deleted. The letters are used with the full permission of the client and were deliberately donated so that others could possibly be helped.)

Letter 1: from his counsellor

I have recently met with Peter *(not his real name)* and his wife. As you know, Peter has been diagnosed with Aspergers. I have known Peter for many years, prior to his even beginning his studies and apprenticeship as an [trade]. I have worked in the field of autism for over twenty years.

Talking about his recent crisis, it would seem that a) Peter is overwhelmed and overloaded, and b) that perhaps his employers do not fully understand his Aspergers and c) what is the best road forward. There is no criticism of his employers at all from him or any perception of criticism – he deeply values that staff and management have genuinely tried to work around his autism; he is also significantly grateful for the work and the support. Peter wants to work and appears to enjoy his work. He also wants to finish his final papers. It seems like he is having difficulty doing both together.

In Aspergers, the brain is *wired* differently. There are a lot of technical connections, so to speak, and less connections around communication and socialising, and cognitive processing of data. This simply means that he would be poor at communicating his needs, and when overloaded mentally will simply *shutdown*. Shutdowns are rare and not dangerous – it is as if the brain needs to catch up with its filing and processing. Processing in ASD is a lot more complicated than for us non-ASD folk (most of the population), because we do not process every bit of data which he does; we simply generalise, minimise and skim for the most important information.

A simple analogy is as follows: we walk through the forest and see trees, lots of trees, but we skim over ninety percent of the details. Someone on the ASD spectrum see trees and branches and individual detailed leaves and stones and flowers and birds, and their brain tries to file all of that with all the related miniscule details.

Two difficulties in Aspergers are: cognitive rigidity and mind-blindness. Cognitive rigidity means that his brain does not flexibly or easily move from one subject to another. He needs to stay in one area until that is complete. Having his work laid out for him in an ordered fashion (as it mostly is) works very well for him. He moves from one job to another and that works well. So distracting him is unhelpful (as it is for most people except that he may take a little longer to recover). It also means that his imagination is limited; for example, he cannot *imagine* challenging or changing a situation if he is stuck – he will simply keep wrestling the same problem over and over again. He also cannot *imagine* that someone would be able to help him if he communicated that he was stuck – in fact, he cannot *imagine* asking for help. Mind-blindness is an inability or limited ability, in *reading* other people and their social cues, so he may not get that others are irritated or frustrated with him, or that someone is maybe manipulating him, or that they are even waiting for him to communicate with him.

His strengths are: attention to detail, being meticulous, following learned procedures, incredible honesty, no deviousness or guile; he is reliable and predictable and very faithful and loyal.

I have suggested the following may work for him:

- Reducing his hours to 30 per week.
- Working full time Monday, Tuesday and Wednesday
- On Thursday, he has a shorter day and makes up the thirty hours.
- On Friday, he works on collating the data he has collected for his various unit studies to hopefully complete his next qualification by the end of the year.

People with Aspergers thrive on routine and order. This will give him a fixed routine with the aim of completing his papers. The early day on Thursday allows him to then spend his own time, at least two hours, organising his van and tools. If his tools are not organised, he has great difficulty functioning and will be very distracted by that (something that generally does not affect us non-Aspergers-wired people too much). With organised tools, and some relief around his studies, he should be able to show up for work on Mondays in an organised, ready, unstressed manner. Having weekends off from his cognitive turmoil will also give him better focus.

This is by no means a permanent solution. Once Peter is finished his next exam, he can possibly resume his full time responsibilities.

This is a suggestion, a possible way forward, which may work for Peter but not necessarily for the company. All things are open to discussion once there is understanding on both sides.

Letter:2 – *from his doctor.*

I am writing on behalf of Peter and Peter's current work situation.

Peter has been diagnosed with Asperger's syndrome, and it has been having a cumulative effect on Peter's work. Peter is currently having a week off work due to the cumulationsic [sic] of stress and the anxiety relating to this.

There are some aspects to this syndrome, which are often intangible. We usually expect to see that technical skills are normal, but the main issues surround communication, language and processing. People with Aspergers often need to have things done in a particular way, or it can cause a great deal of stress and anxiety. Peter's work and Peter's set up would be a good example of this.

Communication that most people take for granted often involving huge volumes of subtext require considerable concentration to execute. Even with this, there are assumptions with language that are missed, leading to communication breakdowns.

Putting all this together, simple day-to-day functioning requires a lot of extra mental effort. Despite this, Peter is doing his usual work duties, helping care for his family, his home, and his mother's homecare.

With this in mind, I feel that the best thing to do for Peter and his work situation moving forward, I think in the first instance, trialling a thirty-hour week would be best.

Some Ideas for Employment That Can Work for Those on the Austism Spectrum.

Aspies do best, like all people, in environments that suit them and their strengths best. Generally, because of their sensitivities and their anxieties, which lead to lower stress tolerance, they do best not working in highly social environments like busy department stores or working in stressful public related fields. They also do best not working under pressure where they have to remember vast numbers of changing details such as being a bartender or a gaming (casino) dealer.

Please note:

- In some of these jobs, there may be some minimal level of social contact or contact with the public. In the right environment, this is doable for those with Aspergers, as long as they are only dealing with one person at a time such as an optometrist or a bank teller, apart from those in teaching and lecturing professions.
- The environment will need to be suitable for the person on the ASD spectrum and their sensitivities are minimalised. They may also need the motor skills to do certain jobs, for example becoming a carpenter when the person has gross motor difficulties would simply endanger the person and maybe others working with them.
- If needed, try to have a more neurotypical person doing the public liaison, and let the Aspie do their skill; for example as an electrician, it would be best if someone else dealt with the public and the electrician worked on the electrical issue, where possible.
- And be practical; do a job within your strengths and abilities and be aware of your limitations. If you are less than 1.5 m tall and weigh in at 45 kg, it is unlikely that you will be either an air steward or a police officer – you will simply be a risk to the team and the public (and possibly to yourself) and not realistically employable in that area.

The list below is my list of potential jobs (it is a list I keep and add to as I think of another). It is not comprehensive by any means and was never intended to be so, but I hope it is wide ranging enough to give you hope that you will probably find jobs for most people on the spectrum.

Professions: Accountants, auditors, lawyers, surgeons, medical specialists, mathematicians, physicists, biologists, pharmacists, engineers (civil, chemical electrical, mechanical), mathematics/physics/biology/computer teachers, librarians, actuary, magnetic resonance imaging (MRI) technologist, all areas of computer technology, analysts and systems analysts including logistics, historians, anthropologists, linguists, wind or solar energy engineers, scientists, researchers (for example, legal, medical, psychological, social), vintners, botanists, zoologists, journalists, cartographers, immunologists, sound engineers, hydrologists, optometrists, specialist military or policing jobs, journalist, surveyors, animal veterinarian, architect (land or naval), statistician, pathologists, areas of police force, nanotechnology engineering, nuclear specialists, archaeologist, meteorologist, geologist, security analyst, animator, forensic scientist, town planner, economist, prosthetist, property valuer, computer data base architects, geneticist, astronomers, phonetician.

Trades: arborist, mechanic, electrician, hairdresser, plumber, builder, butchers, farmers, carpenter, furniture craftsman, tailor, graphics designer, typesetters, newspaper design and layout, computer repairman, deep sea rescue diver, boat builder, munitions expert, jeweller, glassblower, make/repair/tune musical instruments, baker, television repairman, perfumer, radiation (X-ray) technicians for people or industrial, aerial installer, washing machine or fridge technician, carpet layer, house painter, radiation technologist, copy writer, commercial artist and layout designer for magazines and newspapers, locksmith, draftsman, printing press operators, forensic technician, equipment designer, panel operator, dental laboratory technician, optical lens technician (or ophthalmic laboratory technicians), upholsterers, military radar and sonar technicians, engravers, waste treatment plant operators, sawyer, embalmers, robotics technicians, solar engineering technicians, glazier, plasterer, tiler, stonemason, cytogenetic technologists, safe repairer.

Other: banking (like a teller or other behind the scenes type banking but not working directly with the public), postman, delivery person, working in factory lines and distribution centres, handling grocery stock and re-shelving stock, gardeners, working in an orchard, shepherd, cattle-hand, farm-hand, seamstress, clerical (non-social contact) such as working for Inland Revenue or government agencies, caddy, administration doing paperwork or figure work with minimal social contact, postal service mail sorters, groundsmen, preparing brochures and books for print, zoo-keepers, cleaners and janitors, window-cleaners, ceramics artists, court stenographer, digger drivers, working traffic lollipop jobs, fencer, garage door installer, working in a museum or record-keeping role, niche artists and artisans, kitchen-hand, laundromats (but not directly with public), a veterinary nurse, an animal trainer, a translator, inventory control, stage and costume designer, school-crossing attendant or lollipop person (although intense at times, it is a brief time on duty which makes it more manageable), warehouse jobs, wood carving, bone carving, recycle-plant doing sorting, translator (if they have language skills), wild life rescue worker, watch repairers, laboratory worker, security (such as watching video, etc. but not working with public necessarily), florist, payroll clerks, graders and sorters, working on an assembly line (providing you can cope with possible noise), long distance train driver/engineer, if a good driver and not easily distracted when driving – then a long haul truck driver or even a taxi driver or tow-truck driver, an accident assessor and investigator, fire-fighters, fish and game wardens, forest fire inspectors and prevention specialists, data entry keyers, mechanical door installers, meter readers, payroll clerks, pest control workers, bicycle repairers, fraud investigators, online merchants, air conditioner or heating mechanics or installers, web administrators or designers, video game designers, archivist, art or museum curator, working in a plant nursery, bee-keeper, animal or pet breeder, working in a storage facility, tattooist, copywriter.

Temple Grandin has written extensively on Aspergers and autism. The article below is one of hers, which she has given me permission to include.

Choosing the Right Job for People with Autism or Asperger's Syndrome

Temple Grandin, Ph.D.
Assistant Professor
Colorado State University Fort
Collins, CO80523, USA
(November 1999)

Jobs need to be chosen that make use of the strengths of people with autism or Asperger's syndrome. Both high and low functioning people have very poor short-term working memory, but they often have a better long-term memory than most normal people. I have great difficulty with tasks that put high demands on short-term working memory. I cannot handle multiple tasks at the same time. Table 1 is a list of BAD jobs that I would have great difficulty doing. Table 2 is a list of easy jobs for a visual thinker like me. I have difficulty doing abstract math such as algebra and most of the jobs on Table 2 do not require complex math. Many of the visual thinking jobs would also be good for people with dyslexia.

The visual thinking jobs on Table 2 put very little demand on fast processing of information in short-term working memory. They would fully utilize my visual thinking and large long-term memory. Table 3 is a list of jobs that non-visual thinkers who are good with numbers, facts and music could do easily. They also put low demands on short-term working memory and utilize an excellent long-term memory. Table 4 shows jobs that lower functioning people with autism could do well. For all types of autism and Asperger's syndrome, demands on short-term working memory must be kept low. If I were a computer, I would have a huge hard drive that could hold 10 times as much information as an ordinary computer, but my processor chip would be small. To use 1999 computer terminology, I have a 1000-gigabyte hard drive and a little 286 processor. Normal people may have only 10 gigabytes of disc space on their hard drive and a Pentium for a processor. I cannot do two or three things at once.

Some job tips for people with autism or Asperger's syndrome:

- Jobs should have a well-defined goal or endpoint.
- Sell your work, not your personality. Make a portfolio of your work.
- The boss must recognize your social limitations.

It is important that high functioning autistics and Asperger's syndrome people pick a college major in an area where they can get jobs. Computer science is a good choice because it is very likely that many of the best programmers have either Asperger's syndrome or some of its traits. Other good majors are: accounting, engineering, library science, and art with an emphasis on commercial art and drafting. Majors in history, political science, business,

English or pure math should be avoided. However, one could major in library science with a minor in history, but the library science degree makes it easier to get a good job.

Some individuals while they are still in high school should be encouraged to take courses at a local college in drafting, computer programming or commercial art. This will help keep them motivated and serve as a refuge from teasing. Families with low income may be wondering how they can afford computers for their child to learn programming or computer aided drafting. Used computers can often be obtained for free or at a very low cost when a business or an engineering company upgrades their equipment. Many people do not realize that there are many usable older computers sitting in storerooms at schools, banks, factories and other businesses. It will not be the latest new thing, but it is more than adequate for a student to learn on.

In conclusion: a person with Asperger's syndrome or autism has to compensate for poor social skills by making themselves so good in a specialised field that people will be willing to *buy* their skill even though social skills are poor. This is why making a portfolio of your work is so important. You need to learn a few social survival skills, but you will make friends at work by sharing your shared interest with the other people who work in your specialty. My social life is almost all work related. I am friends with people I do interesting work with.

Table 1

Bad Jobs for People with High Functioning Autism or Asperger's Syndrome: Jobs that require high demands on short-term working memory

- Cashier – making change quickly puts too much demand on short-term working memory
- Short order cook – Have to keep track of many orders and cook many different things at the same time
- Waitress – Especially difficult if have to keep track of many different tables
- Casino dealer – Too many things to keep track of
- Taxi dispatcher – Too many things to keep track of
- Taking oral dictation – Difficult due to auditory processing problems

- Airline ticket agent – Deal with angry people when flights are cancelled
- Future market trader – Totally impossible
- Air traffic controller – Information overload and stress
- Receptionist and telephone operator – Would have problems when the switch board got busy

Table 2

Good Jobs for Visual Thinkers

- Computer programming – Wide-open field with many jobs available especially
- in industrial automation, software design, business computers, communications and network systems
- Drafting – Engineering drawings and computer aided drafting. This job can offer many opportunities. Drafting is an excellent portal of entry for many interesting technical jobs. I know people who started out at a company doing drafting and then moved into designing and laying out entire factories. To become really skilled at drafting, one needs to learn how to draw by hand first. I have observed that most of the people who draw beautiful drawings on a computer learned to draw by hand first. People who never learn to draw by hand first tend to leave important details out of their drawings.
- Commercial art – Advertising and magazine layout can be done as freelance work
- Photography – Still and video, TV cameraman can be done as freelance work
- Equipment designing – Many industries, often a person starts as a draftsman and then moves into designing factory equipment
- Animal trainer or veterinary technician – Dog obedience trainer, behaviour problem consultant
- Automobile mechanic – Can visualize how the entire car works
- Computer-trouble-shooter and repair – Can visualise problems in computers and networks

- Small appliance and lawnmower repair – Can make a nice local business
- Handcrafts of many different types such as woodcarving, jewellery making, ceramics, etc.
- Laboratory technician – Who modifies and builds specialized lab equipment
- Web page design – Find a good niche market can be done as freelance work
- Building trades – Carpenter or welder. These jobs make good use of visual skills, but some people will not be able to do them well due to motor and coordination problems.
- Video game designer – Stay out of this field. Jobs are scarce and the field is overcrowded. There are many more jobs in industrial, communications business and software design computer programming. Another bad thing about this job is exposure to violent images.
- Computer animation – Visual thinkers would be very good at this field, but there is more competition in this field than in business or industrial computer programming. Businesses are recruiting immigrants from overseas because there is a shortage of good programmers in business and industrial fields.
- Building maintenance – Fixes broken pipes, windows and other things in an apartment complex, hotel or office building
- Factory maintenance – Repairs and fixes factory equipment

Table 3

Good Jobs for Non-Visual Thinkers: Those who are good at math, music or facts

- Accounting – Get very good in a specialized field such as income taxes
- Library science – reference librarian. Help people find information in the library or on the Internet.
- Computer programming – Less visual types can be done as freelance work

- Engineering – Electrical, electronic and chemical engineering
- Journalist – Very accurate facts, can be done as freelance
- Copy editor – Corrects manuscripts. Many people freelance for larger publishers
- Taxi driver – Knows where every street is
- Inventory control – Keeps track of merchandise stocked in a store
- Tuning pianos and other musical instruments, can be done as freelance work
- Laboratory technician – Running laboratory equipment
- Bank Teller – Very accurate money counting, much less demand on short-term working memory than a busy cashier who mostly makes change quickly
- Clerk and filing jobs – knows where every file is
- Telemarketing – Get to repeat the same thing over and over, selling on the telephone. Noisy environment may be a problem. Telephone sales avoids many social problems.
- Statistician – Work in many different fields such as research, census bureau, industrial quality control, U.S. Dept. of Agriculture, etc.
- Physicist or mathematician – There are very few jobs in these fields. Only the
- very brilliant can get and keep jobs. Jobs are much more plentiful in computer programming and accounting.

Table 4

Jobs for Nonverbal People with Autism or People with Poor Verbal Skills

- Re-shelving library books – Can memorize the entire numbering system and shelf locations
- Factory assembly work – Especially if the environment is quiet
- Copy shop – Running photocopies. Printing jobs should be lined up by somebody else
- Janitor jobs – Cleaning floors, toilets, windows and offices
- Restocking shelves – In many types of stores
- Recycling plant – Sorting jobs

- Warehouse – Loading trucks, stacking boxes
- Lawn and garden work – Mowing lawns and landscaping work
- Data entry – If the person has fine motor problems, this would be a bad job
- Fast food restaurant – Cleaning and cooking jobs with little demand on short-term memory
- Plant care – Water plants in a large office building

Her final email to me in August 2019, reads as follows:

Dear Dee – You have permission to use my lists. For the visual thinkers like me, the high skilled trades are often a good choice. Some examples are auto mechanic, plumber, electrician, or welder. There is a huge shortage of the skilled trades. These are good jobs and they will NOT be replaced by computers.

Temple Grandin

Chapter 6
Neurodivergent Parents and Older Autistic People

I have grouped these subjects together, mainly because there is not much clinical research on them. There is very little in research specifically on Aspies as parents and even less on older and elderly Aspies and how their lives have panned out. Aspergers and ASD are a fairly new diagnosis, which came and went in the last twenty years, so the long-term picture is not clinically clear yet.

A Quick Overview of Aging

It is a fairly universal understanding that after age 35, one enters *midlife*, and after about 65, one enters the varying stages of *old age*, depending on which human development theorist you adhere to, where in the world you live and what cultural beliefs are intrinsic to you. The beauty and the tragedy of having pets is that mostly they have short life span, and we get to see the whole life journey mirrored through their aging stages – from very young to mid-life to being elderly. Human beings though, despite having the physical example of pets, still seem surprised by their aging and often are not prepared for the changes that come with these multiple stages of life in the second half of our life spans.

By middle age, we are becoming more self-accepting, and by old age, there is a realistic self-acceptance and mostly, a letting go of the negative experiences that we have had. Mind you, a few hold on to these old offences and we have all experienced this kind of older person who will harbour an old historic grudge, with resounding dollops of bitterness. Some people start reconnecting with their roots, their families, their genealogies and their life experiences – oh, yes! There is lots and lots of reminiscing...did I forget to mention that? Most become more altruistic and community minded, as our bulging demographic of retired volunteers in our communities usually demonstrate and what a welcome active group of difference makers they often are! A small group will hold on to their acerbic tendencies, disappointments and resentments and will withdraw socially even more. Again, this seems universal, regardless of whether one is on the spectrum or not. It's the nature of aging.

Winston Churchill once said:

> "When you're 20
> you care what everybody thinks.
> When you're 40
> you stop caring what everybody thinks.
> When you're 60
> you realise no one was ever
> thinking about you
> in the first place."

The Dalai Lama said, "Live a good, honourable life. Then when you get older and look back, you'll be able to enjoy it a second time."

In this age group, it is reasonably universal to look back at one's youth and early adult years and make comparisons to how today's youth look at life and live life. It is a very critical, often opinionated, rather self-righteous look at the *youth of today*. In every generation, the older members have mostly looked at the younger with despair, and they fear that the youth are destroying the world. The youth (unless they are at war) bring in new fashions (often shocking to the older generation), new music, new dancing, new adventures, new art, new technology, new discoveries and consistently challenge age-old traditions. The old but familiar musical, *Fiddler on the Roof*, deeply explores these challenges, and Tevye's five daughters in different ways challenge his age-old traditions and customs. There is also in this age group, a sense of grieving for loss of youth, particularly their optimism, naiveite and pure physical energy, and a particularly negative concern for the current youth of their time!

Amongst this older generation of 150 years ago, the sensuous paintings of the Raphaelites had raised much comment. The first engines on train tracks were considered to travel very fast at 8 mph (miles per hour) and *will probably set all the farmers' fields alight and cause a famine* (as is often quoted). Meanwhile,

Henry Ford's cars were considered very dangerous and *would be the cause of death of many* (as is often quoted too!), and – rapidly moving forward in history – there were the shocking *pelvic gyrations* of Elvis Presley, which was often considered lewd and disgusting; the Beatles' haircuts and their *terrible music* was certainly *not going to last*; and my own father snapped my LP (long playing) vinyl record of *Aqualung* by the group *Jethro Tull* over his knee as I watched in horror at the age of 14, as he thought the lyrics were so irreverent and disgusting! Universal aging, I believe, seems to have a necessary journey of assessment and criticism of the upcoming next generation who are breaking the traditions that were previously established. In their own youth and maturing developing process, they had broken down their parents' customs, who because of the two world wars and social history broke their parents' customs and so forth. Once the criticism is completed, the older generation resignedly let go of any last controls. The older generation traditionally looks on with horror or at very least, concern, at the younger generation. Maybe we need to change that, and how we do this generational handing over – but that is another separate book!

A quote attributed to Socrates (470–399 BC) reads (in translation): "… boys and girls are dressing alike. They love luxury, have bad manners, show contempt for authority, show disrespect to their elders and prefer to chatter than to exercise. Children are now tyrants and not the servants of their households. They no longer show respect when their elders enter a room, they contradict their parents, chatter over the top of their elders, gobble their food at the table, cross their legs and tyrannise their teachers." (This was written approximately 2500 years ago!)

In the older years, from mid-life onwards, people often begin to seek out their spiritual roots, or their spirituality along with the retrospective exploring of their genealogical roots. The number of years one has lived does not bring about maturity, but certainly, the life experiences of those years can contribute towards a greater maturity in understanding oneself – often resulting in reaching out altruistically to understand and help others. It is common developmentally that most philanthropies begin in mid-life and peak in the fifties. Cultural stories, understandings and faiths are often gathered and reconciled into their own aging development again but from more mature perspectives.

Aspies seem no different in terms of adapting to their later years. They realise their limits and keep to safe social environments, or retreat to home. They are more likely to be introverted and accept that they enjoy their own space. They realise that they do not have to fit in someone else's *box* of social rules. Their social needs are fairly low. They accept that their adult children may roll their eyes at their quirks, that the family find them a little *odd* and that they do not have to enjoy socialising. They have learnt that on most social occasions, to follow the social rules – and after an exhausting evening, event or week – they can hide away in their own home to process and recover, knowing that they made it work. They accept their routines and lifestyle. They too begin to live in a manner that suits them (within permissible boundaries) and while their adaption may seem odd sometimes to neurotypical observers, importantly, it works for them.

Some may become involved in organisations that suit them. Garden clubs are quite popular, and a lot of collector organisations have a significant demographic in this age group, for e.g., avid model train collections to retiring and restoring old locomotives. I once read of a retired elderly professor who spent most of his life collecting milk cans from various countries and has the largest milk can collection in the world (about 250 cans from 19 different countries). One Aspie said to me that she thought most of the membership of her gardening club were on the spectrum. Of course, that does not mean that they all are, nor that all gardening clubs are full of Aspie members. But even if they are, there in overwhelming numbers, between them, they would have the most detailed knowledge and to sit under their collected teaching would be very fruitful (excuse the pun!).

Summary

- The fact of life is that we are born; we develop throughout life, until we die
- From 35 onwards, there are many more development phases to come – some examples include:
    - ☐ Becoming grandparents
    - ☐ More senior positions at work, or an established business
    - ☐ Eyesight and hearing reduced
    - ☐ Physical abilities reduced
    - ☐ Better at problem solving than younger people
    - ☐ More prone to diseases of getting older: e.g. diabetes, lung disease, hypertension, arthritis
    - ☐ More set in their ways

- Hair becomes grey and eventually white – some become bald
- Long term memory is often stronger than short term memory as they move into the geriatric years
- More knowledgeable about life in general
- More cautious mainly because of learned life experiences
- More critical of the next generation
- More altruistic, community minded and less focussed on self (except for the rare few who are still holding on to old issues)
- Emotional network becomes smaller and has a very limited number of emotionally close relationships if any
- Often become more spiritual especially in their later years

Autistic Parents

Do Aspies make *good* (however that is defined) parents? Just like neurotypicals, some are great parents and others are not. In many ways though, the parenting style appears to be a little different between the groups. And with the vast difference between males and females on the spectrum, there is also a vast difference between male and female parenting in neurotypicals and Aspies. If Aspies are actively and healthily involved parents, they enable and encourage their chicks out of their nest and enjoy the rest from full-on parenting. If they still have children in the house, they will either be chaotic but present parents, or they will be micromanaging their child's needs and will be continuously anxious that expectations (often from outsiders) need to be followed. This will include things like: *they must have music lessons*, or *they have to play one sport a week,* or often doing their children's science projects to *help* them get good marks. Generally, once the fledglings fly, Aspie parents that I have talked to don't hanker for those parenting days, which often neurotypical parents will do – particularly the high nurturing neurotypicals (and I admit I was one of them!).

A few of the things that stand out in the research and writings quite consistently is that children of Aspie parents are often very independent, are logical thinkers but have emotional difficulties – particularly if they are neurotypical children.

A few years ago, I heard that there had been a small study of adult children who had at least one active, involved parent on the spectrum. (I can no longer remember who wrote this!) One of the chief traits that were noticed in this next generation was that they were very independent and self-sufficient, and the author noted that the style of Aspie parenting was more practical, task-focussed and not emotionally biased (as neurotypical parents often are).

> Some years ago, I was working on communication between a couple, especially around their children's needs. Their young child had been found wandering on a part of the highway that went through town. The child was picked up by the police and delivered to a child agency for safety and subsequent investigation. The agency tracked the parents who had become aware that their very active toddler was missing (or had done a runner as is not uncommon with autistic children). The other older child in the family home was then also uplifted, the social agency alleging issues around care of the child and their safety. The agency claimed that the parents had mental health issues, the father suffering from dysthymia (long term depression) and the mother being described as a mental health client with additional anxiety issues and were therefore unfit to have main care of their children (in the opinion of the agency's social worker). When I met them, they both appeared to be on the spectrum, though I simply dealt with the symptoms before me. They both suffered from depression and anxiety too. I remained with the issues that I had been directed to work on, mainly some parenting awareness and effective adult communication. What was very interesting about the case was that the agency was pressing the court to permanently place the children in foster care with supervised access with the parents because of their apparent mental health conditions. A psychologist's assessment on the children, parent and the children's school raised no undue alarms. I loved the judge's final decision, which was: No, on the grounds that in our country we do not do social engineering of people and that in all regards, the children would be better off in the care of their parents who in most aspects were decent people doing their best.

Spectrum Issues that Could Affect Parenting

There are a few issues around being autistic that could present as parenting issues.

- **Theory of Mind, or with Autism, Lack of It:**

The first of these issues is, of course, around *theory of mind*, which has been explained quite a few times in this book already. The inability to *read* another person, whether adult or child, can make relating to that person difficult – and in effect, difficult both ways. There is not enough imagination to begin to interpret the motivations, intentions and emotions of another person. This lack of Theory of Mind (often referred to as ToM) can lead to misunderstandings, incorrect assumptions and reactive behaviour – instead of more considered behaviour that is inclusive of understanding the other person, which would be the ideal outcome. This is sometimes also referred to as a state of *mind-blindness*, or to the person being mind-blind.

I have over the years heard some very (what I thought were inappropriately) harsh beratings of a few of the ASD parents, towards their children. These times that I am referring to were inappropriate to the situation and in every case that I have heard – based on incorrect assumptions on the part of the parent.

Another issue around mind-blindness or ToM is that a parent does not know when they are being manipulated and a clever child can be very manipulative of these parents – without being spotted and will often *get away with murder* (as the expression goes – for Aspie readers, it is not meant literally!). For these children, they avoid natural consequences and their siblings who may not have the same manipulative abilities will feel that favouritism exists in the family, which becomes the main reason why that particular child appears to get away with a lot of behaviours that would be found unacceptable if that behaviour was displayed by their other sibling/s. One of the consequences of this is that it could lead to jealousy among siblings.

- **Changing From One Cognitive State to Another:**

This ability to flick from one subject to another has nothing to do with intelligence. An Aspie who is highly and brilliantly intelligent will still find small talk (chatting lightly about this and that) and changing from one topic to another, very difficult and very frustrating. An example of this would be a light conversation demonstrated as follows, where the topics will often be in short sentences and will quickly move from one subject to the other:

> How is Uncle Billy, is he still in hospital? (followed by short answer)
> - Did you hear about that plan crash over Singapore? (followed by short answer)
> - Oh rats! I forgot my grocery list! (This doesn't warrant much of a reply)
> - Are your children going to the school disco? (followed by short answer)
> - Talk about school, when are the holidays? (followed by short answer)
> - I didn't sleep last night. The cat brought a rat in and was chasing it around.
> - Got to rush – got a dentist appointment! Nice seeing you!

When people struggle to switch subjects (changing from one cognitive state to another), it is referred to as *weak cognitive coherence,* or *weak cognitive shifting,* and several other similar terms. They all mean the same really, with subtle variations. On the whole, Aspies do not easily shift from one brain compartment or circuit to another. If an Aspie is talking about their favourite author and you switch the subject to asking about their cousin who was ill, the gears often seem to change slowly and the Aspie may temporarily appear confused. They have also been interrupted and possibly from their favourite interest, so the shift is often doubly difficult.

> One Aspie father was very focussed on something that he wanted to do. His child, a toddler, had just fallen down some steps, as the father was passing. He continued to walk past the bleeding and crying toddler, completely oblivious to that scene as his mind was singularly focussed on his purpose.

This is of course, excluding any other influences such as noisy children, overly bright lighting, multiple perfumes, odours and so forth. The conclusion here is that if a parent is intensely focussed on balancing their accounts over the internet and a child is about to fall off a precariously high ladder balanced against the guttering outside, then the internet could probably win in this case. This is not because it is the internet but because it is where the main attention is focussed.

> One man, who is a lawyer, was asked by his wife to watch their baby for a few minutes. The baby was placed on the couch next to him. The man agreed, glanced at the baby, then continued to read the documents he had previously been perusing. Naturally, the baby rolled over and then fell off the couch. The baby was crying loudly while he sat frozen on the couch not knowing what to do or how the baby got to be on the floor and crying, and then had to face a furious wife. By the time the baby was six months old, his wife could no longer trust her husband to mind their baby fully unless she was around to (discreetly) supervise the husband (who thought he was supervising the care of the baby). This next story relates to a family friend. The couple had shifted to their new home that day, with their 20-month-old son. The house had a fenced swimming pool. It was decided that she would go and grab takeaways from nearby for their dinner, as he didn't want to go out. He agreed to mind the child. She made him focus on her completely, and she clearly demanded that her husband was not to go in the pool area, nor to inspect the pool pump, until she came back. She knew he had been fascinated by the pump and was keen to go and inspect it. He looked her fully in the face, gave her his absolute attention and agreed that he would wait. Of course, you can guess how the story ended. The toddler was playing, and the father of the toddler slipped away. He removed the pump cover down at the pool and started fiddling with the pool pump, utterly absorbed. He did not even register the splash in the water nearby. It was purely luck that caused him to look up to find their toddler floating face down in the water. He (the father) had actually been trained as a lifeguard earlier in his life, so he dived in and rescued the child from the deep end, flinging the child outside of the pool (and cutting the child's lip open in the process as the child hit the concrete surrounding the pool, face down). The wife arrived home with her hands full of hot food, to find the house empty. Around the corner was the sopping wet father and (thankfully – alive!) son, with blood still dripping from the child's cut lip. She also noticed that the father was not holding the child to comfort him (the father was abstractedly searching around for a towel it turned out) but was walking beside him to take

> him into the house. She also noticed that the pool gate was still open as the father and son were returning to the house!

- **Sensitivities:**

Some sensitivities can inhibit children of an Aspie parent. This may mean that they cannot make a noise, or play with paints as the parent may not like the smell, or engage in any children's playtime activity that may upset a parent.

- o Aspies can have many issues around babies. Many Aspie males refuse to change diapers, mainly because of extreme sensory issues. Neurotypical women with Aspie partners or spouses are usually left to do all the parenting and childcare when the children are babies and toddlers and report not having breaks and feeling very lonely as if they were a single parent.
- o One Aspie mum proudly told me her baby son's first word was *wo-wee* [sorry]
- o Also because of sensory issues, neurotypicals often feel that once they are looking after the children, that there is a lot of walking on eggshells around the other Aspie parent because of that parent's sensitivities

> As a child, one neurotypical woman was told by her father not to sing as her singing upset people. Later, she joined a children's choir. One day, the choir mistress stopped and tested each singer alone in front of the room as she had heard that someone was badly off-key. This woman had been mortified as she thought that it was her singing, but it was poor little *Glennis* instead. Regardless, she stopped singing altogether except when alone. She loved singing. Many years later, she married an undiagnosed (at that stage) Aspie man. He came home unexpectedly one day and told her he didn't want her to keep singing as it really caused him pain. Mortified, she never sang again except when she was absolutely alone. She sang once when she was about 40 for a dying friend, and the friend encouraged her to sing publicly, but again, she couldn't. One day, when she was nearly 60, another friend overheard her singing and encouraged her. She has found her voice and now sings happily. She realised it was not her singing that was execrable but that

> both Aspies were too overwhelmed and couldn't bear *any* singing. As a child, she was influenced by her demanding father, and as a child, she heard a different message which affected her for the next 45 years.

- **Interaction with Children:**

Aspies, and particularly Aspie men, may not understand the emotional and developmental needs of their children.

- o Some Aspies do not know how to play with little children especially neurotypical children. It helps if they let the child take the lead in these games, or a neurotypical spouse or partner coaches them through the child's needs.
- o Because of their often poor communication skills, Aspie fathers appear to often have poor emotional connection with their children. They may often be annoyed because of their sensitivities and need for alone time, especially after work, and so may be very irritable and very hard to please. Praise, like apologies, is very rare in Aspie fathers.

> One neurotypical daughter whose father had very high expectations of her came home as a 16-year-old with very exciting news, which she knew would please her father and might actually this time give her the recognition she craved from him. He came home after work, took off his shoes and as usual, went into the family lounge in his socks, picked up the newspaper and began to read. No one was actually allowed into the lounge during this time, but she ventured in, hoping to catch some alone one-on-one time with him. She addressed the open newspaper that he held up as a barrier and as he read, she told him that out of 240 students, she had come top of maths at school and had gained a 100% pass. He didn't even move the newspaper, but said, "Get 110% next time then." She responded that one couldn't actually do that in maths, but he did not reply. She said that that was the moment when she realised at last that there was nothing wrong with her but something very definitely wrong with him.

- On the other hand and at the other extreme, Aspies, especially females, can get down to a child's level really easily and can engage like a child for hours with any child and not tire of it. Aspies are removed from the *herd* mentality of neurotypicals, which can sometimes inhibit free play, whereas Aspies can be quite free in their play with their children.
- Aspie games with children are often not emotional such as playing with dolls and various pretend games but may still be interactive but constructive. This may involve building the Tower of London from cardboard boxes or playing board games.
- Other Aspies, particularly Aspie mums, are developmentally very engaged, particularly if they and their child share an interest. Aspie mums cope well with new ideas, so they are often very supportive of their children who often go on to achieve very highly.
- Aspie mums can be amazing mums, as they often are not cluttered with a lot of neurotypical expectations and limits
- Aspie parents will often work with their children as if the children are adults and will mostly engage in adult language and expectations. This can be a hardship for a young child, but it also brings about a healthy independence in a child at a younger age than children from neurotypical parents.

> One sad story that I heard was of a rigid Aspie father who came home late from work and found that his two children had not finished their chores before they went to bed. He then woke them up just before midnight, and insisted that they do it then and there, and after the chores were completed, he sent them back to bed.

- Aspies usually make very responsible parents (and pet keepers!)
- Occasionally, some neurotypical children of Aspie parents can grow up very depressed and feel unloved and uncared for, with a resultant depression or other similar mental health conditions later in life. Others sometimes feel disconnected, as if there is no one to love or look after them, so they develop resources to look after themselves. For both though, the longing to be connected and cared for by a parent doesn't seem to go away. Aspies often cannot make these

early bonding and emotional connections, especially with their neurotypical children.
- Where parents are one neurotypical and one Aspie, it seems that the neurotypical parent shoulders most of the emotional and childcare in the family. They often feel very alone in this and do become emotionally worn out themselves. Some of these neurotypical parents will often develop depression themselves or become anxious within this lonely task that they feel that they have.

One Aspie father had accepted a wonderful promotion 2000 km across the country. He instructed his wife not to tell their very social, neurotypical child as *the child will tell everyone [our] business*, as her mother told her in later years when she questioned her about this move. On the day that the movers were to pack up the house, he took his daughter to school, and as she got out of the car, he told her *to say goodbye to all your friends because when you come home we are catching a train to [the new city] and never coming back*. And he drove off. She was ten years old and stunned and recalled the incident as an adult, with tears in her eyes. She felt that she was so shocked, she was unable to say goodbye to her friends and walked around in a daze all day. The teacher apparently knew and did a little farewell speech, but that was also part of the blur of the day. The two-day train journey also happened in her daze. When they arrived, he took her straight to her new school. There was no discussion about leaving nor preparing for the new school. As an adult, she can no longer bear saying goodbye when travelling far away, as she becomes traumatically overwhelmed by this old unresolved grief, or even when someone else is going far away. (As an adult, she tried to find out what the secret was, but apparently, everyone else knew except her, so why her father felt she would have spilled a confidentiality still leaves her puzzled – there was no reason for that statement from him.)

Voices against Autistic Parenting

There are some (a rare few, thank goodness) psychologists and lawyers, particularly in situations in which the parents may have separated, in which one parent has sole care of a child or children for period, who are adamant that a parent on the spectrum should not have unsupervised care of their children. This is usually raised in custody or childcare battles. Their thinking is that a parent who has sensory overload issues, poor recognition of emotional needs, combined with poor insight into the motivations and intentions of others are not fit parents! As the children get older, the parents may also depend increasingly on their children – for example, asking the children to help them socially. Examples include the need to have their children deal with most of the social issues, or to have the children tell their parents when they (the parent) are speaking inappropriately, or if the Aspie parent is overwhelmed and therefore lost in a shopping mall, they may depend on their child to help them back to their parked car.

> Dr Liane Holliday Willey, who on the ASD spectrum, quotes from her own autobiographical book as follows:
> "We cannot help but tell people what we think the moment we think it. I never for instance leave my kids to wonder what I am thinking and I routinely vocalize my thought processes, often to their dismay…things are often skewed in our family, turned so that Mom ends up relying on the kids for their judgment and guidance…& I look to them as confidants and best friends…& I ask them to help me find my way out of malls & to hold my hand when my anxiety mounts, to tell me if I am saying things that no one wants to hear." (Holliday Willey 1999)

One USA family lawyer wrote ardently (and I thought quite scathingly) on a site that has since deleted the article, against the fitness of diagnosed autistic people being sole parents and that they should not be allowed custody in separations. He writes witheringly in the same article, with some surprise, that the *Law* in all its various forms has not made efforts to stop Aspies having sole care of their children – a statement that I find utterly ridiculous!

I personally find three glaring flaws in his argument:

i. There are no documented cases and evidence particularly focussed on Aspie parenting, so his argument is based on his assumption of his seemingly limited understanding of Aspergers and his assumption of the impact of Aspergic parenting on children.
ii. He cannot seem to see any positives of Aspergic parenting.

iii. He does not consider that neurotypicals are very flawed too, or their often-poor parenting that also can occur. His piece of writing was inflammatory (I thought) and used scaremongering tactics of extreme examples. He does not do this with extreme examples of poor neurotypical parenting.

If his argument is correct, then the same argument of *poor parenting* can be used that all neurotypicals should not be raising children.

There are many writers and bloggers who explore the Aspie trait of heightened sensitivity or sensitivities, overload, angry outbursts, blunt speech and lack of empathy. The effects of these are discussed – the effects on their children in particular. Some children have been left anxious or angry because of their parents' outbursts and blunt criticism; they have been left depressed because of the lack of empathy and emotional support, and they have been left deeply scarred and socially embarrassed by their Aspie parents.

Some of these negative comments about Aspie parents are valid experiences, particularly for children of an Aspie parent or parents. There are adults who were children to Aspie parents, who recall the many embarrassments of their parent or parents. These included the way they talked socially, the way they dressed, their many needs that needed to be met, their oft time's chaotic living, or alternatively, the controlled micromanaging parents. There are times I joke that Freud was right – we are as we are, and we can therefore lay all the blame on our parents. Of course, these are examples tacked together and are not at all a general reflection of Aspie parenting.

Nobody has written a counter argument on the many neurotypical failings as parents though and that bothers me. These and similar articles seem to also be based on the assumption that the majority, the vast hegemony of neurotypicals, are correct in their parenting strategies and skills and that this is an appropriate standard for comparison. A lot of political, racial and ethnic hate policies are based on the majority consensus for thousands of years but that does not make them acceptable or correct – and the majority in society have always been neurotypicals.

I have found the majority of Aspie parents that I have worked with, love their children deeply and are fiercely committed to doing their best for their children – just like any other neurotypical parent. Unlike many neurotypical parents, I have found the Aspie attention to detail quite amazing and, they can often work out by a gesture or a flick of the head how their child is feeling (having literally analysed details of their child since birth so that they can understand this child). I have found that because many Aspies – especially the females – are so intuitive they know when something is wrong, even if they can't necessarily read body language fluently. I have found Aspie parents deeply understanding to others, including neurotypicals, when it comes to talking about the frustrations of parenting. But mostly, I have found that their children have good school lunches, that they have good clothes that are clean, that their children have done their homework, that their children are glad to see them after school, and that they cuddle their children and manage through all the minefield of their own sensitivities to be the best parents possible.

In working with parents who have separated, I have met with Aspie mothers who have gained fully custody, Aspie fathers who have gained full custody, and separated Aspie parents who have shared care arrangements around their children. I worked with one Aspie father who was passionate about care of his children as their neurotypical mother was emotionally, mentally and physically an unfit mother to their children. She was distraught to lose her children, but the parents settled to an arrangement that he would have them four days a week and she would have the other days with possible extension (he was very open and generous to her as a long term parent), providing she attended some child-parenting courses and engaged with a counsellor who would help her further develop the parenting skills needed. She eventually was stable enough for them to have shared care on alternate weeks, as well as extensions of care for a good reason from time to time. They amicably work together in their children's best interest, although they have both moved on to other relationships.

I believe that if you take the range of neurotypical parenting, and the range of AS parenting, that the ranges will be very similar – *good* parents and *bad* parents. The only variations will be the differences of the two types of parenting styles, as they will have differing strengths and weaknesses.

- ☐ There are good parents and others with poor parenting skills and the range would be similar for Aspies and neurotypicals.
- ☐ Aspies and neurotypicals often raise children slightly differently but maintain most cultural expectations.
- ☐ Aspies raise independent thinking children, with good problem-solving skills.

- Most Aspies and neurotypicals appear to love their children.
- Aspergers issues can affect parenting, such as overload from noise and other external stimuli, sensitivities, difficulties shifting cognitively, and mind-blindness.

Most research is critical of Aspie parenting from a neurotypical viewpoint, but I have not seen the opposite criticism of neurotypicals by Aspies – and I am sure that there is much to be critical about!

Aging Aspies

In 1994, Aspergers was first recognised as a diagnosis and since then the focus has primarily been on children, on which there is extensive research. In fact, that first group of children are now in their early years of adulthood, and as adult Aspies will be the first of the recognised and supported generation of Aspies – hopefully, they will have the availability of a lifetime of support. This is a new and different generation of Aspies. The older generation of Aspies of this chapter have not had that support or understanding and often not even a diagnosis until well into their older years.

Of course, with the publication of the American Psychiatric Diagnostic Manual in May 2013, Aspergers as a diagnosis was removed and included as part of the Autism Spectrum Disorders (ASD). Using the quote from Juliet in *Romeo and Juliet*, Shakespeare's classic play, of "a rose by any other name will smell as sweet" – I would boldly say that Aspergers by any other name would still manifest similarly, regardless of what it is called.

Most of the parents who are on the spectrum, or older Aspies, have usually only deduced their own diagnosis because a child or grandchild was diagnosed and follow-up checks were done themselves. Some have been formerly diagnosed in later adult years, whereas others are really self-diagnosed as they recognise the signs and are happy with that self-assessment. As there are currently few benefits from a full diagnosis in this age group, most are content with a self-diagnosis. A few on the spectrum have sought a diagnosis because they absolutely want to know and don't like getting by on hunches and suppositions. Those in this age group that I have met, who have received a formal diagnosis, have unilaterally declared their relief to be diagnosed as they have a satisfactory explanation for many things, for example, sensory overload, which have consistently troubled them all their lives.

When we talk about elderly Aspies, I have expanded the margins generously around *elderly* and am looking at those aged 45 and over. For those that are offended at being labelled *elderly* when you are in your forties, please understand that it is only for the purpose of this chapter. Most Aspies over 25 are currently still not diagnosed and especially so the female Aspies – and I am writing here about the mostly undiagnosed Aspies who have lived on the spectrum for at least 40 years. I am talking about Aspies who have long been aware that they were different in some regards from the majority of their peers and their family who are predominantly neurotypical.

In terms of academic research on this age group – to date, there is very little. There are a few opinions by Professor Temple Grandin, Professor Tony Attwood, Professor Simon Baron-Cohen, Professor Liane Holliday Willey, and a few specialists in the area. Temple Grandin herself is on the ASD spectrum, of course, and is famous for her work in the area. She is – at the time of writing – in her early 70s – and is a fine example of someone with ASD who has made her condition work for her in a most successful way – and a lot of her journey has also been in the public eye. She has also contributed significantly to the field in terms of knowledge and research and has often been a *human guinea pig* for research. For the sake of science (in the field of neurology), she – as a healthy woman – has had more MRIs (brain scans) than probably any other healthy person ever! Professor Liane Holliday Willey is also on the spectrum with many books and much work in the field credited to her, while Tony Attwood has a middle-aged son on the spectrum.

Aspies Getting Older

Never Being Understood and the Consequences

Imagine spending 35 years or more, never or seldom being understood, rarely being able to express emotion appropriately, making endless social gaffes and being humiliated by others repeatedly. Imagine also having to live life with multiple sensitivities, having experienced bullying when young and perhaps still so at work, being called names, being emotionally abused repeatedly in relationships and always being told to *just behave like a normal person*. A lifetime of social and emotional torture is experienced by most Aspies in this age group.

> One lady I know had three independent growing children, all adolescents, living in an unfinished home. The framework and some walls were there but a lot was unfinished. For years, she tried to follow all the rules of being a good mum, constantly suppressing her own overload. Eventually, things would come to a head and she would be so overloaded that she would have a breakdown, which looks like a psychotic meltdown to any observers. The family code was – mad Aunty Betty has arrived – when this breaking point happened for her. She would occasionally be put in a psychiatric ward if they thought she was unsafe (to herself) or when her husband could no longer cope. After a few days of heavy tranquillisers in the ward, she would be released. She then lived in an absent but *indestructible mode* (her words), unable to have any feelings and moving in a hypnotised dazed manner. She would then work harder to be a *better mother and wife* and not collapse with overload while she weaned herself from her psychiatric cocktail of meds, but of course that point would come again, and the cycle continued. At one stage, she was on a heavy cocktail of anti-psychotic medication, which was supposed to act as a preventative to her apparent insane phases and to work as an emotional inhibitor. She weaned herself from them because she could not bear who she was on them. Interestingly, from the time she self-diagnosed her Aspergers (having seen it in her younger son and having done research on the subject), she has never had been a patient in the psychiatric ward again. She also has had to learn to manage her overloads and meltdowns, then to learn to manage her circumstances so that she did not get to the point of meltdown again. So many years of suffering and being alone in it, without any resources to help! Her husband and family are learning supportive skills too (with varying degrees of success), to the best of their ability, to understand her, as she has given all her adult life to understanding them.

Because most Aspies have not been diagnosed for their entire lives until this point, their issues and meltdowns often exists simultaneously with depression and anxiety, and have sometimes left them stranded on psychiatric wards. You see, an Aspie meltdown can look like a psychotic episode, with the Aspie yelling and crying, acting irrationally, is distraught and possibly even aggressive. They will often at this point be suicidal or at risk of self-harm, or they can be so dissociated and shut down that they appear frozen, almost catatonic and also may then too be a suicidal risk.

Both states are triggered by the amygdala – the brain's survival mode – which is also known as the freeze, flight-or-fight centre (often referred more loosely as the fight-or-flight centre). When the Aspie *freezes over*, there is absolutely no connecting to them or with them. They are simply *not there* in the purest form of dissociation. When someone presents in this state at a psychiatric unit, there are no other signs and the presenting symptoms of course are, and need to be, treated just as one would treat any other psychotic patient displaying the same symptoms. There often is no time or understanding in a pressured psychiatric ward to take long histories as the professional staff have to deal with the immediate symptoms in front of them. It is difficult to tell the difference, even a psychiatrist who is a specialist in this regard. Just as panic attacks can look and feel like a heart attack (so I am told), so too can an Aspie meltdown look like a psychotic episode.

My assumption, which may be entirely incorrect (but this assumption is agreed on academically) – is that many Aspie statistics are tied up in mental health statistics. There is no way to go back and separate these statistics simply because the diagnosis has been made late in life. We know that Aspies are more likely to suffer from anxiety or depression, or more commonly both at the same time, over and above dealing with their own unique Aspie traits. We also know that the statistics for mental health clients (whether they are on the spectrum or not) to either have suicidal ideation, or to have completed a suicide, is higher than the general population. Can we infer then from historical data that suicidal ideation and the risk of suicide is higher is Aspies? That would be an unsafe, hugely dangerous, insensitive assumption and diagnostic jump, with little science and accurate data to back it – but it is good to be mindful and have that awareness of the possibilities. Again, I need to emphasise there is scarce data at this stage, for this age-group of Aspie clients who may have no comorbidities and even less for those who are on the spectrum and have comorbidities. (A reminder here that a *comorbidity* in this book refers to a significant mental health condition alongside Aspergers.)

Of course, we do know (statistically) that depression and especially long-term depression combined with difficult circumstances can sometimes lead to suicidal thinking and may occasionally lead to such an attempt. We also know that statistically, the risk of suicidal thinking is higher with clients who have mental health issues. Added to that we also know that the risk of suicide can be there when one is under severe stress. Many of my older Aspie clients have wanted the suffering to end but not their lives. Quite a few have discussed this [suicidal-ideation type] thinking with me and have been frightened of their thoughts. In the academic journal, *Molecular Autism*, an article was published in 2018 in which the research shows that those adults (although one age group is not specifically targeted) with autism and mental health problems have shown a higher risk of suicidal thinking. The main underlying reasons were the hardships of fitting in (often academically referred to as *camouflaging their autism*) and the lack of active support for Aspergers and other AS conditions. The other three core reasons were the same as the general population who suffered mental health issues and suicidal ideation.

The article also did not state some further clarifying details of the clients being assessed with autism and a mental health condition. We do not know if they were all in this older age group. We also do not know if they were autistic in its purest sense, Aspergic, or any of the other varied diagnosis of people on the Autism Spectrum Disorder (ASD).

> Professor Simon Baron-Cohen at the University of Cambridge, in August 2018, in an article in Medical Press, commented: "It is totally unacceptable that autistic people are born into our society as happy individuals and that by the time they reach adolescence or adulthood many of them have felt so battered by society that they no longer see any point in living. It is not for autistic people to change: it is for society to change, to become more welcoming to people who are neurologically different, neurologically more sensitive, and who struggle with disabilities related to socialising, communication, and coping with unexpected change. This urgent change has to start from preschool onwards. A single death by suicide of an autistic person is a tragedy and is one too many."

Relationships in the Older Years

Some Aspies are still married (to the same original spouse). Some have never married but have a long history of being financially or sexually taken advantage of or exploited in some way (I remember meeting one particular woman who needed an old house renovated. She got into a relationship with an Aspie builder

– or certainly a man with many traits – and ditched him when the house was completed. He never saw it coming.)

Some have had brief relationships. Some have remained single. To my knowledge, there are no accurate statistics on these long-term adult (*elderly* in the case of this particular chapter) Aspies. One writer (whom I won't mention by name as I found her comments so offensive) threw out a claim that there was an 80% divorce rate where one partner is on the spectrum – which is totally spurious (meaning wrong and insulting and a probable fabrication!), as she had absolutely no data to support this. Perhaps her client base is only separated Aspies – in which case her data is mathematically and statistically so extremely skewed that again, it is not worth looking at. (I would say these statistics are not worth the paper that they are written on! Internet googlers beware!)

I have met many male and female Aspies in long-term relationships, almost always with neurotypical partners or spouses. By the time they have reached middle age or middle-adulthood (approximately 40–65 years of age), they mostly have adult children and the relationship has reached a level of mutual acceptance of quirks and foibles in both parties. They also seemed to have stopped trying to change each other. Neurotypicals will often work hard to change their Aspie partner. After a long relationship, both parties simply start accepting each other.

> "If I could snap my fingers and be non-autistic, I would not. Autism is part of what I am." Temple Grandin

With the awareness of Aspergers, many have come forward to ask for help for their relationships. For myself as a counsellor in these situations, I become a *translator*, meaning that I translate their behaviours and even their spoken words to each other – very much as if they are from two different cultures and language groups. Slowly, they gain insight and work together in a more supportive way.

These long-term couple or family relationships have patterns that may be peculiar to outsiders but are well accepted as a family culture, and it often seems that all the parties work around the Aspie, or Aspies, if there are more than one in the family. These are well-tread, familiar emotional and social walks!

Couples in this age group have become stuck in their recurring inadequate habits of coping and are often glad to break these usually very destructive cycles. It's also good to understand each other better too. Sadly, some use their history and knowledge of each other destructively, and it can make for a very unhappy relationship.

> I have met one neurotypical lady, who has probably been married to her Aspie husband for good 40-plus years. He is a terrible driver as he misses details and drives as if he is the only driver on the road, yet he is deeply offended if she infers that she prefers to drive. She may do the two-hour drive on the national freeway with him to the next big city but then has to find tactful ways to let him allow her to be the main driver in the city traffic. Unfortunately, he has no sense of direction and is extremely poor at taking any instruction, for example, after the next lights, turn left. He begins

> yelling and panics and inevitably misses the turn off, meanwhile endangering anyone else on the road and even a pedestrian at times. His last driving debacle had broken her, and she could no longer face driving anywhere with him. Even as a passenger, he is obnoxious in a vehicle, but this last episode was heightened as he was once again leaving a job because of relationship breakdowns with other staff, so the whole driving situation carried even more stress and tension than usual.

Many Aspies (in this age group) in relationships are married or have made a formal commitment publicly, at the very least. This is because *it was expected* as a social norm when they were younger. Some Aspies were married very young and were still in a first-and-only relationship. A lot of Aspies tell me they *just did what was expected* and went through all the social protocols. Others are on their second long-term relationships – often having vowed to never get into another relationship yet met someone with whom they cliqued. The vast majority of the relationships that are described in academic texts are heterosexual. In this age group, there are gay relationships and other gender variations of relationships, but they are a minority. I would put this rarity down to several factors. The first is that they (non-heterosexual relationships) are still a minority group in the general population, and secondly, when this middle age or older group of people were younger and getting into relationships, there was still a fairly worldwide cultural taboo or strong disapproval of non-heterosexual relationships. (Remember we are talking about older Aspies in this chapter, and this is the context in which these relationships are being described.)

Some Aspies have an active sex life in their relationships, others rarely have sex, and some have forgone sex permanently – again, as common as across a broad spectrum of most neurotypical relationships. Generally, these relationships, particularly the Aspies, are very faithful, and infidelity is rare.

Most Aspies have a relationship with neurotypical partners, although a few have ended up with partners on the spectrum too. Just like any other couples, they have disagreements and resolve them in ways unique to that couple. Both partners look for love and want to be loved.

The relationships are usually non-demonstrative, nor are there public displays of affection (colloquially often referred to as PDAs). If a couple hold hands or stand closer together, it is usually initiated by the neurotypical partner. There also seems to be little eye contact along with the lack of overt affection.

The conversation is usually factual. Then again, in this age group, I have observed a similar range of behaviours in older neurotypical relationships. My thinking is that this may be due in part to the mirroring and role modelling of the relationships of the two generations prior to theirs.

This is of course, all compared *to neurotypical relationships*. It seems that we generally have little else to compare to, and as happens usually, the majority dictates the normal. Therefore, if a couple do not behave in relationship in a neurotypical way, we deem that there is a flaw or fault in their relationship. Is it fair to compare relationships this way? Absolutely not, but it is what we have done and still do, and we need to change! Just because a quarter, a third, or even a tiny minority of the population operates differently, they still often operate in valid ways that works for them. We, as relationship counsellors and as a society, must change the way we do things and stop forcing all relationships into a stereotypical, neurotypically based mould.

> One woman I know decided she could no longer cope with her husband's behaviour. He was rude and distant, over-reacted to situations, could not handle change, ruined an extended three-month, long-looked-forward-to overseas trip as he appeared to control everything. She was also with him continuously on a daily basis in their home life, as he was self-employed and worked from home. Using the holiday example, she meant that she could not have a coffee when she felt like it, could not on a whimsy pop into a shop and so forth. He micromanaged every part of that historical trip. Another trip was looming, with dread by her, and she had reached the end of her tether. The joy of this future holiday had already lost all its pleasure as she projected that his behaviour would once again rob the joy of it. After we discussed options, including her researching the AS spectrum (he was clearly on the spectrum), she went out and had a good think about the positives that her husband brought into the relationship and there were many! She came back and decided not to leave him (he was, of course, oblivious of the emotional difficulties she was having), and she was going to creatively make this relationship work for her. She decided that she would go back to work (despite their not needing the extra income) as she needed to not be isolated with him all day – in this way, she could meet many of her neurotypical needs. She found that if she gave him fair warning, he would consider change. She also realised that she could disagree with him. In the past, any

> disagreement from her would leave him agitated and seemingly angry, so she avoided disagreeing with him. Before the upcoming holiday, she had a discussion with him and agreed to some of his agenda, but she not only included her wants, she also outlined that she was going to do some things she enjoyed from time to time. She acknowledged that this was impulsive on her part from his perspective, but she also assured him that their relationship was important to her, and she would respect his needs. I was in the main town library the other day and she approached me, telling me in glowing terms how she had made the marriage and situation work for her, that she still used the tools that I had given her and spoke glowingly about their recent holiday and renewed relationship. A great example of how it should work!

A big resentment by neurotypicals, I find, when I am working on long-term relationships is that the neurotypicals generally *feel* that they do *all* the changing and adapting, and they are deeply aggrieved when they think any more change and adaption is required from them. I know that in the story above, it was the neurotypical above who took the steps, but she had sought individual counselling for herself and had not brought him in for couple counselling. And the tools worked for her. Aspies also have to change in areas that are difficult for them to change. Teaching AS people takes a little time, but Aspies often are usually so very willing to make their partners happy and change where they need to in most cases – just as neurotypicals are. Maybe the Aspie approaches change a little more rigidly, but their willingness usually is worth many gold stars!

Both parties need to change. The older Aspie needs to learn a little theory of mind (like a list of rules rather than instinctively *know* as neurotypicals do). Meanwhile, the neurotypical partners need to stop walking on eggshells fearing outbursts from their partners and be more direct about their needs and expectations (but not demanding – there is a fine line between the two). If it is an older Aspie-Aspie relationship, they both need to learn to communicate, instead of doing things that result in dramas in the relationship. And if it is a neurotypical-neurotypical relationship you are wondering about, then you are reading the wrong book at the moment!

In relationships in this middle-age and older group, there is generally an acceptance, due to their developmental stage in life, and they both have started accepting what they perceived each other's idiosyncrasies to be – and they bear it, sometimes with humour, sometimes begrudgingly. They seem to just shrug, sometimes bicker and argue, and then move on. This is more in relationships where both parties expect the relationship to continue. Once the Aspie has processed an upset or situation (which can sometimes take days), they are usually back on board again.

The issues are different in a relationship in which at least one party is on the spectrum – or at least has multiple spectrum traits. The issues are usually about poor communication by at least one party, the need for structure and routine by at least one person, the difficulties staying focussed, the lack of theory of mind, the neurotypical way of jumping subjects in conversations and avoiding Aspie obsession or focus-interests – and the neurotypical criticalness and rejection of those who don't fit the subtle social rules and models. The same issues that are there for the Aspie are the same issues that present in the relationship. And then, like any relationships, there could be other external pressures such as different cultures or faiths, family cultures, parenting styles, financial issues, external family pressures and that list can continue and be very lengthy.

It needs to be said that most of these few studies have been done on heterosexual relationships and are anecdotal in nature. Because of the nature of Aspergers, the expectation is that relationships are affected by Aspergers, by personality, by culture, by finances and by many other very important factors. The section here is to highlight that Aspergers affects other people too and can affect relationships.

Anecdotally, and from what I have read on some blogs and websites, it seems that Aspie men in relationships do get grumpier and angrier (or at least more intolerant) as they age while at the same time seemingly increasing dependent on their spouse (older people still generally have more traditional relationships) or partner to resolve issues. Unfortunately, this spouse or partner also bears the brunt of the Aspie's moods and sometimes that can be extremely unpleasant.

Aspergers on its own, as is being a neurotypical too, has its own up and downs, strengths and weaknesses. Being Aspergers or neurotypical in a relationship always involves two people, and both parties need to work at it, with understanding, communication, compassion and laughter.

Summary

- In relationships that have survived, both parties are more self-accepting and accepting of each other as they age together.
- A relationship takes two people who are committed to working on it and endeavour to maintain a health reciprocity.
- Aspies can often appear to be controlling as their need for predictability, order and safety makes them a trifle tetchy about change, whereas neurotypicals tend to walk on proverbial eggshells around Aspie expectations and demands.
- Relationships with Aspies often lack spontaneity.
- Aspies in relationships can be grumpier as they get older, especially the males.
- They may have higher expectations of the NT's partners/spouses and are more co-dependent as they age.
- Comorbidities, like anxiety, depression and substance abuse, are common and can detrimentally affect the relationships.
- Where the Aspie partner is skilled and brings in the finances that the couple are dependent on, the relationship often shows the positive effects of financial stability.
- There is more faithfulness from the Aspies in these long-term relationships.

Elderly, Aging Aspies

Most aspects of functioning are affected by the aging process. One of the many areas affected by aging is cognitive functioning. This means that that as one ages, new learning and short-term memory recall is not always as good as it was in youth – and concentration is reduced. Solution-focussed thinking that is enhanced by a lifetime of experience has given them a greater worldview and understanding, so older people are good at solving problems. A lot of long-standing social connections – a supportive auntie or grandparent – will have passed away, or at best, are frail and in care and less available. Friends have moved on, sometimes to live with their grown children or to retire in some long-hoped-for setting. And sadly, the body begins to age too, so mobility and agility is affected. For some, a form of disease has set in. Anything from arthritis, heart disease or kidney dysfunction, to being coeliac or developing glaucoma. Maintaining a large home and garden are no longer possible, managing the stairs in houses or apartment living becomes an ordeal. Often work opportunities and finances are increasingly limited. Adult children may have their own financial struggles and will need grandparents to mind their grandchildren, so that both parents can go out and work. Vacuuming and cleaning up after young children becomes increasingly arduous and physically painful. Some of their adult children have their own adult children.

Aspergers itself does not *age*. Just like neurotypicals, it is a form of wiring we are born with and die with. Some symptoms may decrease and some may increase. Neurotypicals may become less impulsive. Older Aspies are less likely to have repeated, restrictive movements like the need to flap their hands or the need to physically express stimming behaviours. They can also delay the need to stim and wait until they have some level of privacy to do that. Not all Aspies stim, of course.

Similarly, most people, whether on the spectrum or not, have also become more self-accepting. They are more likely to speak out bluntly with little or no attempts at moderation, and they are more likely to be fussy about their home or about where they will go when leaving home. An Aspie may not go to a wedding of a niece because it will be too crowded or noisy, yet when they were younger would have gone and perhaps endured and struggled to cope, as they would have felt pressured to socially conform. I think at this stage of life, Aspies have unconsciously, intuitively or even consciously, stopped aspiring to be neurotypicals. They are often overtly irritable and grumpy and may often ask you to leave if they have reached their social endurance limit.

In older people, some AS symptoms from childhood return, particularly inappropriate social skills. This illustration below is an actual experience that I had except the older man in the conversation was not a relative.

Victor Meldrum, the lead character in the television sitcom *One Foot in the Grave* is a bit of a classic Aspie-type in my opinion. Many older Aspies become absorbed by their hobbies, such as working on old trains, or even digging out their model trains and filling an old room. Isolated tasks are more enjoyed – like sewing a new top for every day for a year, focussing on growing one particular flower, tree, bush or vegetables. They appear to be even less conversational and are more likely to engage in monologues (one-way conversations) and will not necessarily be interested in answers or responses and may even walk away (especially when overwhelmed).

Dr Liane Holliday Willey, in her books and interviews, speaks very fondly about her father, whom she believes as much on the spectrum as she is. She writes that she has gratitude for him, as he role-modelled to her how to live well with the same conditions that she struggled with. For her, it was her diagnosed autism/Aspergers, which diagnosis she only received once she was well into adulthood in her mid-30s. For him, it was never officially diagnosed – but they both struggled with the same wiring. One thing she did note was that as he got older, he continued to live alone independently and generally managed quite well. Yet if he were upset about something – perhaps an upcoming age-related assessment by a social worker, or an incident in his day that went wrong – he would resort more to his monologues on trains (his stim and favourite subject) and many of his previous stress-coping strategies no longer worked.

It is known that depression in older adults has some links for developing problems in thinking processes and it affects memory – particularly short-term memory. It is also fairly well documented in research that adults on the spectrum are a third more likely to develop depression than neurotypicals. At one point, Temple Grandin talks about her depression and she appears to believe that it is part of her particular wiring. After many trials and trying to go without medication, trying to use alternative methods to combat her depression – which she sees as a mild or low level of depression – she believes that her depression is an organic part of her Aspergers. She has found taking a maintenance dose of the lowest level of a prescribed anti-depressant daily, helps her significantly. She has less of her lows and feels that she remains more level in mood generally. If a third of Aspies struggle with depression, then we need to be monitoring this situation for them very carefully, as it is a small thing to offer a medical solution, but that makes a big difference for them. And even more so as they become older and elderly.

In this later stage in life, many will have developed comorbidities. Common ones are severe anxiety or a deep depression. Their ability to enjoy life is significantly decreased, if it was there at all, once comorbidities develop. Some (a small group) may have become alcoholics over the years and are just quietly drinking themselves to death, despite dire warnings from their doctors. They are utterly miserable and feel their isolation and aloneness, but the comorbidities prevent them from socialising effectively too. So, a cycle develops and simply takes over, increasingly estranging them and in a continued cycle, from knowing mental and emotional wellness.

I have worked with a few older (from mid-40s onwards) Aspies who have struggled and were having an ongoing struggle with suicidal thinking. Those who struggle with chronic depression and feelings of hopelessness may have made some sort of plan, so this removes them from just thinking about not wanting to continue life as it is at present. Most do not want to continue living but do not have a plan as such. This state is one that professionals often refer to as suicidal ideation, and it means they are thinking about it but do not yet have a plan. Some tell me they have worked out a very careful and detailed plan just in case they *need it one day*. Unfortunately, because most days are difficult for them (with social and sensitivity issues) and they often need to meet specialists in overly brightly lit hospitals, with the noises of people walking and talking or making noises, as well as dealing with the difficulties of old age – they often refrain from seeking the help that they need (unless they have developed hypochondria). Their stress levels are quite high. They then move to their now almost automatic thought of wanting to *end all of this*, which takes them to their suicidal thinking in one way or the other. Again, this is not present in all Aspies but in my experience is not uncommon either.

When we repeat a thought very often (like learning a song or our timetables in primary school), we usually, unintentionally or intentionally, memorise it. This memorisation is the result of a track that we have built in our brain (called a cognitive pathway). Repeating the pathway makes it stronger. (I remember an interview many years ago, of Donny Osmond who performed the lead role in Broadway, of Joseph, in the show, *Joseph and the Amazing Technicolour Dream Coat*. He had since, and excluding rehearsals, performed it over 2000 times! The interviewer asked him if he forgot his words, and there was a stunned silence for a few seconds before she received a gracious reply.)

Imagine repeating a pathway thousands of times, but with the addition of factoring in strong emotions – like depression! I have to work with my clients to tell them that that pathway, in a sense, now owns them. It is often their first thought but not necessarily their only option. We have to work very hard at times to break those old and dangerous pathways and help them develop other more helpful, constructive pathways. In this type of depression, medication and therapy work very well together.

The poorer their theory of mind throughout their youth and mid-years, the worse it becomes as Aspies become older again – well, so it seems. So they might be the older woman who cannot bear to have a renter living next door to her, or the elderly neighbour who yells at the boys jumping his fence and stealing his peaches. Again, the lower the theory of mind or the more impaired their mind-blindness, the more isolated they become too – which often means the grumpier they become socially.

Sometime ago, I sold my house and temporarily rented an apartment with a garden while my new house was being built. I had an old cat who slept indoors all day, and an old, very placid, people-friendly dog (looks like Lassie except she is a tri-colour rough-haired collie – for those who remember that series), who for many years had been my therapy dog. She (my dog) came to work with me just about every day for nearly six years as a therapy dog and later she just retired to my office.

The day I moved in, I heard a high-pitched, shrill voice over the fence, saying, "Get out! We don't want you here." I thought that I had misheard or misunderstood these words. Between my house and the next house was an access lane, through to another road and the two schools nearby.

I moved in on a Saturday. I walked the dog on the Sunday, and she yelled at me then to get rid of that dog! I observed her – especially after the incident recorded below – and saw that she had no visitors, seemed at odds with most of the neighbours who looked the opposite way when they walked passed her garden, that she made no eye contact, yelled at my son for parking his car legally on the road (and not near her garden), and she sat in a glassed-in veranda watching all the neighbours. Every day in that first week as I came home from work, she would yell at me to get rid of my dog, and by the Thursday, I had had enough.

On the Thursday afternoon, she did the same thing – obviously by now watching and waiting for me to walk past and then yelling at me again. I decided to go and settle the matter with her, face to face. I still had my dog on her lead, with me, and the dog sat quietly as she was instructed. I introduced myself politely by name. I introduced my dog and told her my name. She neither acknowledged my name nor gave hers. Instead, she said she did not want me in the neighbourhood (we had never met before, and she had no idea who I was). She talked to the top of my fringe and never made eye contact. After that, this is how the conversation went (with her still shouting in that high-pitched shrill voice):

Her: The whole neighbourhood wants you and your dog to go. She barks all day when you are not there, and everyone is terrified of her.

Me: When did she bark all day? (I was most surprised by this outrageous comment.)

Her: Today. All the time. The whole day today. I am sick of it! No one can come near your fence.

Me: She was at work with me all day, so that's not possible.

Her: Well, yesterday then.

Me: She was at work with me all day then too.

Her: Definitively, Tuesday then.

Me: Actually, I took her to a dog day-care all day – for a change for her to mix with other dogs. I have a receipt on me, with her arrival and departure time. Would you like to see it?

Her: Well – Monday. I know it was this week.

Me: She was at work with me on Monday all day. We saw six clients together. Do you want me to phone them and you can ask them yourself if she was there?

Her: No! (neck muscles straining with anger) We just don't want her here. Everyone is terrified of her. In the mornings, the primary school kids can't use the lane to school anymore because they are so scared of that dog.

[Take into account that I had only moved in the weekend previously and had hardly been home the weekend and not the weekdays when I was working – and the dog slept in a locked-in porch area]

Me: And what time do the children come through? [I knew the school started at 9 am].

Her: From 8.30–9! They are terrified she will attack them. They have to walk the long way around the block to school now. If you don't do something about that dog, I will!

Me: I walk to work every morning. I leave at 7.30. She comes to work with me every day, so she is not here when the primary school children walk past.

Her: It's the high school children then – every afternoon! They scream [she was screaming now]! They are so scared of her!

Me: And what time do the high school children come out? [I knew they finished 3.20]

Her: About 3.30!

Me: Oh, okay. I walk home from work. I only leave work at 4.30 and get home just before 5. This is not my dog we are talking about because she is always with me.

Her: Get out of our neighbourhood! [shouting now] Nobody wants you here. People like you just bring down the neighbourhood! You renters come here with all your problems!

> I turned and walked away (with my dog who had sat placidly throughout the whole show), noticing the twitching of several curtains in some of the other apartments and little houses at the end of this cul-de-sac.
>
> As unbelievable as the above is – it really happened. I was so fascinated by this exchange that I went indoors and immediately wrote the whole conversation down!

A lot of elderly Aspies appear to be single and where they can afford to, prefer and deliberately choose to live alone. In one way, this gives them relief from having to have any social interaction and communication. But in another way, they lose any social structure, and generally, Aspies thrive on structure. Living with a spouse, partner or even an older sibling helps to maintain a daily structure and some semblance of social skills. There is an old academic saying about social skills – *if you don't use them, you lose them*, and that is profoundly and sadly true. So, as seen in the story above, this elderly lady had few social skills, and even her talking with me was not a conversation but talking *at* me. She never greeted me back, nor ceased her high-pitched shriek; she never considered my responses; she remained focussed on her own beliefs (in this case about my therapy dog and about *renters*) despite all her beliefs in this case being obviously wrong. She had no *normal* conversation in any manner.

As they get older, their previous obsessions return. One of my neighbours was so obsessed with weeds that she weeded in the manner below in the illustration – and for hours every day! She worked square by square, with a magnifying glass and a kitchen fork. The pair of scissors was for cutting the grass! Her flowerbeds were immaculate, and there was never a dead leaf, flower and certainly not a dead plant to be seen.

As their health declines, Aspies, like many neurotypical elderly, will often not like to admit or acknowledge their declining health. Already they are aware that their mobility, independence and freedom is impacted and increasingly limited. The fear of being forcibly moved into care or losing their independence and autonomy is as strong as it is for most people – especially in our western culture, which generally no longer has families absorbing their elderly into their home. Dr Tony Attwood, in an interview on YouTube, commented that Aspies seem to have less difficulties after childhood, but after middle adulthood, they seem to slip back into difficulties that are strongly typical of ASD, so any form of community living for elderly and geriatric Aspies becomes a social nightmare and hence an anathema for them.

> In another story of lack of ToM, an Aspie grandfather had a granddaughter who had a year prior struggled with body image and anorexia. She made a huge effort to travel a long distance to visit him, and the first remark that he made to her was that she had gained weight!

The following was taken down directly from a posting on internet. References to the writer and site are clearly made, with respect to their ownership of the posting.

<u>Danish Conference</u>: Even though this conference happened six years ago, we still have not made much progress, despite the outcomes!

A conference organised by Rehabilitation Forum, Denmark May 21, 2014 referred to the theme of autism and aging. A presentation from the Danish National Social Agency's representative called *Current best knowledge about autism and aging* is enlightening. Highlights from the topic are available online and can be read here too:

http://www.rehabiliteringsforum.dk/fileadmin/filer/Konference_Socialstyrelsen/kl._13.00_-_WS4_-_Charlotte_H._Kaumanas.pdf

Some important points to mention include:

- The great majority of the older population with Asperger's/ASD have never been diagnosed
- Persons with autism spectrum disorder may lack the capacity to recognise and respond to signs of disease
- Elderly people with High Functioning Autism (often referred to as HFA) may have reduced ability to sustain attention, reduced working memory and oral skills, while other cognitive areas are intact. (HFA and Aspergers are probably almost interchangeable terminology)
- Alternatively, autistic symptoms may diminish with age in line with the physiological aging process and better coping strategies
- A serious problem is the lack of knowledge of Asperger's/ASD by professionals and employees in elder care

There is very little research/literature on aging and autism. Autism Spectrum Disorder affects all aspects of life – of the person with ASD, of the family members, relatives and society.

The Autism Diagnostic Research Centre in South Hampton noted a few years ago that their early research shows that the *severity of symptoms increase with age* when referring to aging Aspies. They find that the increase is noticeable more in social situations. There are cognitive difficulties with what is known as *flexible thinking*, which means that there are difficulties coping with new ideas, coping with any change but especially cognitive change (the ability to move from one subject to another) – and that communication difficulties with any form of communication increases.

My own comment here is that it is important to note that all of the above signs are part of the general aging population, and the difference is that it is more noticeable in the Aspie population. The degree to which this is more noticeable has not been qualified and I expect that with all Aspie versus neurotypical comparisons, there are degrees of difference – and for most, the degrees of difference can vary greatly but can also be very small at other times.

Tony Attwood, in one of his online interviews on *YouTube*, affirms that aging Aspies can be more offensive or their social offending can and often does become worse. A neurotypical woman notes that this is so too, but she struggles as there is no help for her or them in the community, as she has to contend with her increasingly (socially and relationtionally difficult) husband. Aspies appear to care less (or maybe they are just less aware than even before) as they get older about who or how they are offending – and about how they socially offend (for example talking loudly in a library, wearing unwashed clothing). They are also not careful with their word choices and can be rude and insulting. Doc Martin of the show with the same name is well past middle age, and he remarks callously to his neighbour's six-year-old child that her violin playing is *execrable* – and directly informed the child's mother that she should cease playing immediately as she has no talent!

It needs to be emphasised that the better the cognitive processing and the higher the intelligence of an Aspie, the more likely they are to have insight, and if spoken to clearly (as in not spoken to obliquely or ambiguously) and frankly, are more likely to try to change their behaviours. I have noticed that Aspies in their 50s and 60s can still learn and make the changes that would make their social lives and marriages easier while also working very hard at it when they choose to (and of course if it is important to them). The few that I have met aged 65 upwards, did not look like they would ever change and their social behaviour did seem to decline even more as they got older.

People (usually neurotypicals) in a relationship with older Aspies find it increasingly difficult to cajole their aging Aspie spouses, partners, or parent, out of their increasing grumpy moods and consequent anger. Sometimes the Aspie family member may refuse to even cease stimming. Again, referring to Dr Liane Holliday Willey, her father would stim on his train-hobby if he became upset in any way. He would not respond to his carers but instead spoke unceasingly about his trains at them and directly over their conversation or questions. Any distress, no matter how minor, would trigger this talking without a break about his trains – more so if he felt disturbed by a change. She found it increasingly difficult to pull him back out of this stim so that she could talk to him and find out what it was that was distressing him – and hopefully fix it for him or help him through it.

> Another man seldom worked at his electronics bits and pieces and tools, which all lay in an untouched, dusty cluttered mess on a long workbench which was in his lounge, probably for many months, if not for a couple of years. He had a caregiver who came in regularly, of whom he was quite fond and tolerant as they had worked together for quite a few years. While he was napping one day she decided to tackle this bench which he had once, in their early working relationship, asked her not to touch, and for years, nobody had touched or tidied this bench. She sorted all the similar bits together and cleaned and tidied up that table, and gave him a good working surface (she thought). He was so distressed that he actually called the agency to whom she was contracted and had her permanently removed from caring for him. She was, of course, moved to another client and he got a new caregiver – which in turn distressed him further. He was also angry with the world in general for months after that because he couldn't find anything – it's all been lost! And this, despite the fact that the caregiver had thrown nothing out at all – not even the broken little light bulbs and the obviously frayed, unusable bits of wires.

It is important to remember that what is important to an Aspie is usually not important to a neurotypical – and similarly the other way around. So as a neurotypical, we may not even notice what has subtly changed that has upset an Aspie. This aspect of AS does increase in older years. Of course, the Aspie does not usually notice that to us neurotypicals; we are fragile about social communication and can easily take offence if it (the social communication) is just slightly wrong or odd. Aspies can also become increasingly obsessive as they age.

Unfortunately, it seems that a large number of Aspies do remain single, even if they have had a relationship or relationships, earlier in life – particularly so for men on the spectrum. This idea is often expressed in various ways in research, although there is little documented evidence, and most researchers note this anecdotally. For myself and my colleagues, when we have discussed this, we anecdotally have the same impression. Realistically, ASD is a social development disorder – this means having difficulty getting on with or being amongst people, hence a long-term permanent relationship is more difficult to attain than for neurotypicals, who can quickly read the signals and play the dating and romance game, sometimes again and again.

It therefore makes sense that more Aspie older people are single than non-Aspies. In my experience, this is so but I do not have data or research evidence to back this up. Research that I have read is that, on average statistically, less than a third of Aspies are in a relationship and even less are married. There is little research on this subject and the data does not seem reliable.

In the aging years, many more people are single as partners and spouses pass. I assume it would be proportionately the same for Aspies who have lost partners and spouses. The differences are that the Aspies generally do not have a social circle to support them when this happens. If a spouse passes, the Aspie is often lost, especially if there are no other social structures in place – and often there is not.

Older Aspies in Summary

- Have all the normal physical and mental signs of aging as the general population, although their Aspie-ness becomes exacerbated by this same aging process
- Seem to return to some of the childhood Aspergic social and communication tendencies

- Higher risk factors for developing depression
- With developing depression, there are more problems in memory and cognition – as it is generically for all elderly people with depression
- Most older people like to stick to a routine, Aspies even more so
- Younger Aspies have obvious Aspie tendencies settle more during adulthood, but in late adulthood onwards, it appears that the symptoms come back with vigour, and basically, the older they get (generally), the more Aspie they become again
- In their older years, their sensitivities are much higher
- Their social skills and communication decrease again, as they age – for multiple reasons
- They begin to increasingly have monologues again or *talk at people*
- They are definitely more capricious and curmudgeonly as they get older, particularly the males (although the female in my story could not have been described as anything other the same as these males!)

Chapter 7
Neurotypicals

(Disclaimer and confession: I am neurotypical!)
I am what I am – Dee

From an Aspie point of view, neurotypicals (NTs) are irrational, often illogical and highly emotional. Neurotypicals apparently also say things that they don't mean, they don't follow through on commitments, and are highly dependent on their emotional filters for decision making and responding.

A neurotypical will often buy a house, a car, or a pair of shoes because it *feels* right. They may have done some prior research, but they will perhaps incorporate that or override that, through their *feeling* filter.

These kinds of statements may make neurotypicals fire up in anger (an emotional response, of course!). Such statements in a vast hall of neurotypicals will cause pandemonium with: "That's not true!", "How dare you!" and "We are not all the same!" We would feel the injustice of being labelled as a whole group and dismissed in such negative terms!

Yet this approach to labelling and diagnosing an exceptionally large group of people is exactly what has been done to Aspies for more than the last 20 years! Using different websites for statistical data, we find the ratio of Aspies to neurotypicals stands at 1:59. Another reliable website claims a statistic of 1:38, which we will ignore for this moment and just go with the even more conservative approach of the first ratio overly simplistically as a statistical model of the population being either neurotypical or autistic. The world population is 7.7 billion (August 2019). This means that approximately 130,000,000 (one hundred and thirty million) Aspies all go into one box – all the same…branded, labelled, stereotyped, but it is not okay to put all non-Aspies in one box too? Can we say that all seven billion, 570 million neurotypicals are all the same too? Of course not! But let's explore the world of neurotypicals in similar format used to describe Aspies.

Definition

A simple, clinical definition of neurotypicals is that they are not neurodivergent, nor autistic nor Aspergic nor any variation of these identifiers.

That still doesn't tell one very much about neurotypicals. It is like saying a defibrillator or an isthmus is not a *cup* for example, but it still doesn't tell you what either a defibrillator or an isthmus is. Saying that a defibrillator is an external cardioverter, or an isthmus is a land strait still doesn't help describe what either noun actually is – even if we can find the best synonyms.

If we try to break the word neurotypical down from its Greek roots, it translates roughly to *having an impression related to nerves*. So that doesn't help either. Saying that neurotypical means typical of 7.57 billion people also fails to give a suitable explanation. *Neuro* means being part of the nervous system, and in particular, relative to humans, specifically in this discussion. The Central Nervous System includes the brain. So, to oversimplify – neurotypical means wired or configured neurologically (in the nervous system and the brain) like the vast majority of people on this planet.

People, particularly Aspies, have tried to clarify this further to be more specific and have sought a few other words to replace *neurotypical* and have created some of these words. These words include *allistic* and *nypical*. *Auto* in autism means self, or alone, from its Greek roots. *Allos* is from the Greek word, meaning *other*, so the idea of being non-aspergic or non-autistic is summarised in the word allistic. Nypical was another word used in an attempt to explain the opposite of being autistic, and it tries to take the original meaning of neurotypical with an added emphasis on not having developmental delays – and not being neuro-divergent in any way. Regardless, the words allistic and nypical to describe the common population majority group has not taken off or become popular.

Autism is considered a developmental disorder. Again, over-simplified, a developmental disorder is a disorder in which the standard neurotypical pattern of the *normal growth (or developmental) pattern* from birth to adulthood and possibly throughout adulthood too is not followed. A developmental disorder typically begins in early childhood and usually persists, albeit sometimes in a milder form, up to the age of about 22 but can continue throughout the adult life span. By the way, we are neurotypical from birth, which is also a developmental process as we grow and move through all the milestones developmentally – and appropriately as per the majority of the population.

The word *normal* is usually used to explain the huge population of neurotypicals. The word itself has a major philosophical variance in meaning and creates offence in some areas when used as a comparative description. I tend to see and refer to neurotypicals as the majority group, which they literally are – and whatever the majority looks like, is the *normal* or the *norm*. It may not be okay, but it is the norm. We may look back on history at some of the atrocities that have occurred, which was the *norm* for that period. It doesn't mean that we approve of the atrocities or that they were okay in any way, but it was the *norm* for that time.

Most academic bodies and autistic organisations highly recommend remaining with the word *neurotypical* to describe this main human group that is not on the ASD spectrum.

This can be shortened to NT for a neurotypical or NTs in plural.

So that takes us to the next part of the discussion. The argument above and the terminology (which has caused some offence to different people at *times*) suggests that the diagnosis is an either-or situation. One is either in one camp or in the other, and of course, that is rarely the true picture.

The reality is that whether one is neurotypical or diagnosed with ASD, the diagnoses are both on very broad spectrums. And somewhere the two spectrums cross over, or overlap, so that we have Aspies with neurotypical traits and neurotypicals with Aspie traits in a middle core. And a spectrum suggests different intensities of different aspects as one moves along that spectrum – so there are no absolutes. As one colleague of mine put it, "We are actually all on a spectrum somewhere, and to some degree we are all on the Aspie spectrum." Alternatively, I could also say that we are all somewhere on the neurotypical spectrum!

And then if we throw in the work of Simon Baron-Cohen regarding male and female brain wiring, the matter becomes more complex. He says that "the female brain is predominantly hard-wired for empathy. The male brain is predominantly hard-wired for understanding and building systems." This adds another layer to the intensity or dullness of certain factors along that spectrum line (and is also the reason so many women on the ASD spectrum are missed!) and how each person may be affected.

And talking about diagnosis, the irony is that there is no diagnosis for being neurotypical! It is a default position if one is not on the ASD spectrum. This of course is a rather odd way of defining something – by something it is not. But that is what it is at present – right now.

Another term has also been coined, which is *Neurodiverse*, the intention being that all people are neurodiverse and are somewhere on a human spectrum - being neurotypical or neurodivergent. Originally, it meant not neurotypical: having a diverse type *of* neurology that is not typical. In itself, the word is popular with a small group of people and can be a word used by some employers, in that they employ people whatever their neurodiversity is. If you are not neurodivergent, then you are probably neurotypical. There is some valid academic and philosophical argument that neurotypical is also a neurodiversity.

Spectrum

Neurotypicals are on a vast spectrum too. Neurotypicals can be high functioning to low functioning. The majority of neurotypicals are in the mid-spectrum, meaning that they function appropriately or *normally*. A well-functioning neurotypical will have multiple social connections, is more likely to be, or have been in, at least one long term committed relationship as an adult, is most likely to be earning an income whether self-employed or in paid employment and will be of average or above average intelligence. Even introverted neurotypicals are most likely to be found behaving as a functioning neurotypical, although they will probably seek more alone time than the average neurotypical or will have a smaller number of relationships, and may require longer timeout.

A non-functioning neurotypical may be:

- possibly low intelligence and requiring some caregiving, and may live dependently or semi-dependently
- physically disabled, although many are often still high functioning in other ways as a neurotypical (a common description here is not being *able-bodied*)

- *drama-queens* (meaning that this group of people is particularly ego-centric, and all issues are relative to them and them only) with, usually deliberate, attention-seeking behaviours (this kind of behaviour is often on a spectrum too)
- highly needy, especially emotionally
- they may have mental health issues
- or they may be socially dysfunctional often due to abuse, which may result in social isolating, narcissistic, psychopathic or criminal functioning.
- Furthermore, if we combine the neurotypical spectrum and the Aspie spectrum, there is an area in which the two overlap significantly. This is where the studies on the male and female brain is useful.

Male and Female Brain

There has been a lot of research on the difference between brains of males and females. There are strong indicators that there are some significant differences. A lot of this work has been done by Professor Simon Baron-Cohen, and he presented it in his book *The Essential Difference*. The studies of various researches on male and female brains has been well collated with much understandable application in several books by Barbara and Allan Pease. One of their books, a classic, is *The Definitive Book of Body Language*, which I have loaned out to clients until the book has been worn out and I have had to purchase another! They have other really interesting books such as: *Why Men Want Sex and Women Need Love, Why Men Lie and Women Cry, Why Men Don't Listen and Women Can't Read Maps*. In the last few years, Jordan Peterson has also picked up some of these studies and used them relevant to his field. All the above people regularly do the public speaking and teaching seminars around the world on the subject of male/female differences.

The essence of these writings is the difference between the way men and women operate. These differences are generalised to 83–87% of the population. Simon Baron-Cohen very urgently and strongly warns that it is the science that they are exploring. Science does not stereotype. Science statistics explore various kinds of mathematical averages. Furthermore, the research is also based on neurological data, not human attitudes and cultural frameworks. Regardless of race or culture, science still stands.

The statements below are based on this research. Please keep reading them in this context.

Very over-simplified, women are more emotionally and socially wired, men are wired to problem solve and develop systems. Is this true for all men and women? Absolutely not! But it is for the majority, for more than three quarters of the population. It appears that most baby girls from as young as ten days old start making eye contact and relating to people by looking at their faces, whereas boys only begin start doing this at about six weeks of age. In the meantime, boys are extremely interested in objects and seem to be already making sense of their world, while girls are generally less object focussed.

Women have a strong sense of empathy, and of course, so do many neurotypical men. Predominantly in social interactions though, women are the key players when it comes to empathy.

> "Empathy is our ability to identify what someone else is thinking or feeling and to respond to their thought or feelings with an appropriate emotion. Empathy makes the other person feel valued, enabling them to feel that their thoughts and feelings have been heard."
>
> Professor Simon Baron-Cohen

If women have a problem, they hint. Let's take the following scenario…a woman is peeling vegetables for dinner. There is another person reading a newspaper at the dining table nearby. She says, "I am so tired." If the other person is a man, he will respond (if he hears her!) by saying that she ought to go to bed early. Later he wonders why she is very silent and not making eye contact with him! If there were a woman reading nearby, she would usually get the hint and jump up and either begin helping with the dinner preparation or at the very least, offer to help. (For Aspie readers, neurotypical women often go silent when they are angry.)

Men have an amazingly singular focus, which is essential for understanding systems and problem solving. I once took my car in to a mechanic as something was clearly wrong with its performance. He opened the bonnet and listened for a few seconds to the running engine. "Can you hear that noise? That's the problem!" he cried out enthusiastically. I could hear the road traffic, the conversation the receptionist was having on the phone, another mechanic talking to a customer and my two little children arguing in the car. I could not hear *the noise* that I needed to. I obviously do not have singular focus!

While men are good at a singular focus, women are generally good at multi-tasking.

> This is a story very similar to one told earlier – but our family experience. Many years ago, when our eldest son was only 20 months old, my husband and I moved into our new home, which also had a large swimming pool. On moving day, with our child getting hungry and the food not yet unpacked, I offered to get some takeaways for dinner (it was before the days of home deliveries!). I clearly asked my husband to a) not take his eyes off our son at all and b) to stay away from the swimming pool and the pump (in which he was very interested), until I came home again. I arrived home about 20 minutes later. Both my son and my husband were sopping wet, their lips were blue and their teeth were chattering (it was winter), the pool gate was open, the pump cover was lifted off, my son's lip was bleeding and he already had the beginnings of a bruise on his chin and my husband was wildly tipping boxes looking for a towel! It was obvious that my husband was looking at the pool pump and looked up (he later told me with much angst) to see our son floating face down in the deep end of the pool. Fortunately, our son was alive but things could obviously had become a lot worse if he had stayed focussed on the pool pump for even another couple of minutes.

Women can multi-task well. They can work and look after children simultaneously. They can work and have a conversation. I generally do not enjoy TV so if I want to see a show, I will usually read a book at the same time or balance my bank accounts or do some chores in the TV area. Research shows that multi-taskers are not as fast or as thorough on each task as compared to doing each task singly with focussed concentration, but multi-taskers do get many tasks done at the same time and do it pretty well.

Men focus on one thing at a time, particularly when they are problem solving. My husband hated being interrupted when he was intensely focussed on something and would often lose his train of thought and want to start all over again. This makes men dominant in the engineering fields, the trades and in many skills that require problem solving, such as medicine or technology. I think it was Barbara Pease who said that if you were angry with the man in your life, talk to him while he is hammering something or shaving!

> I often use this example when I have taught on this subject. Men need to fix things, and they are generally very willing. So a man may say that he lost his wallet. A woman will say that she had gone to town with her friend Sarah; they had had a coffee; she had bought groceries and picked up some library books; she had gone into the office to do some paperwork and since then could not find her purse. By this stage, the man does not know what he is supposed to focus on, and he may comment on any part of the conversation. Or he may interrupt the conversation with helpful comments (or he thinks it's helpful) about Sarah's talkativeness, when she bought groceries did she pick up the item he needed and will probably miss her increasing stress, and at the end may deliver a short lecture on her oft-times carelessness with her purse and that she should be more systematic about where she put it when using it. As women, and I am certainly a key example of that, we tell the whole context because our conversation is an emotionally connecting one. We want to share the whole emotional distress about all the places we had been, what our day was like after that with multiple clues we are processing (but usually no solution), and the impossible task of finding our purse because of the multiple layers of events.

Women need to socially talk in depth about an issue and share opinions as the situation is examined from all ends. We are of course usually looking for emotional answers. We are not usually out to fix a situation or that solution may be the indirect goal.

Body language and tone of voice are both very important to women. If a friend stops talking to you and does not make eye contact, she is probably upset with you and maybe angry, or maybe she is making it clear that she is offended by you or even no longer likes you. And you would need to ask her what the problem is. There is then a little back and forth [which I call emotional negotiating] before you may eventually get the issue out. Then there is the complex issue of resolving the issue, as we try to maintain the steps of the emotional dance at the same time.

Men do not notice body language and tones of voice as much. They usually do not notice if a woman is flirting with them if their focus is elsewhere. Men are also generally comfortable with silence. They are then surprised when their silent female partner withdraws, usually angrily. They (men) like silence from chatter when they are problem solving – they do not want the back and forth of conversation. Ironically, I find it fascinating that my sons could study with their music blaring and not hear the music as their focus was elsewhere, whereas I have enormous difficulty in concentrating and focussing when there is a lot happening around me.

> On one occasion, my husband came home from work. I think there were about 22 children playing in and around the house. The neighbourhood kids had all dropped in and were having great fun with my children. I was completely bewildered when he asked what the noise was, as I could not single out any particular noise!

> Many years ago when my friend was a rural GP at a Mission hospital in a remote part of Africa, I had gone to spend some time with her. She had a few tasks to deal with while I was there, and on one beautiful day, we traipsed a few hills in a low mountain range to reach a particular Zulu tribal settlement where she had some work to do. (On that walk, I nearly got bitten by a night-adder which I had not seen but that is another exciting story!) She had explained that there was a major problem happening for this tribe. I can no longer remember the issue. The women were sitting in a semi-circle, legs apart with the back of her neighbour towards her, checking each other for head lice and seeming to all talk at once. Despite the glorious sweltering day, the men had lit a fire and were sitting in silence around the fire, obviously concerned and looking distraught and stressed but not speaking at all!

Generally speaking, because of this trait of being systems-focussed, men will not ask for help unless the other person is an expert or considered knowledgeable. They will not, for example, ask a random stranger for direction if they are lost.

For women, we will generally collect five carrot cake recipes from different people and not be fussed whether they have ever been an expert cake-maker. We may even accept our friend's auntie's recipe even if our friend had never tested the recipe herself.

So a reminder again, this is not a sexist or culturally biased discussion. This is the way the majority of people are wired. We are increasingly seeing more male nurses and male kindergarten teachers, and more women in engineering and doing trades. In fact, it is rather lovely that all people can now do what they are good at rather than having culturally defined roles and limits within many societies.

It is therefore on the basis of these studies, that Simon Baron-Cohen came up with his findings regards ASD. He concluded from his intense research that there is a double-male brain in ASD males. Males who have a double male wiring become more male, and females with a male brain become more male-like neurologically (not physically). Both of these aptly describe the Aspie male which is more obvious than the Aspie female. Aspergers or ASD is far more obvious in males, as these males miss more of the social cues and are fixated on systems. Female Aspies have their female neurology overlaid with a male neurology, which means that they get some social cues but are more wired on systems and fixing things than typical neurological females. A female Aspie will not necessarily know what she said wrong but will notice by the reactions of other females that she made a social error. A male Aspie will often not even be aware of the reactions of others around him.

It is therefore easy to see:

- That there is a blurred line between Aspies and neurotypicals, in that there is a large area of crossover that has strong elements of both
- How difficult it is to diagnose females on the spectrum when they still have quite a few neurotypical traits.

But back to neurotypicals behaviours as stated below.

So Neurotypicals are

(the following is not a discussion but simply a very long list, in no particular order, of neurotypical traits, as perceived by either or both, neurotypicals and Aspies)

- Neurotypicals consist of at least two thirds, probably closer to four-fifths at the very least, of the world's population. (This depends on which statistics are read on the proportion of Aspies in that community, so the overall statistics vary hugely.)
- The neurotypical brain wiring is considered to be the standard, or the norm, against which others who are not neurotypical are measured. This is because they are the majority universal population group.
- Neurotypicals are primarily socially wired, with a quite strong herd mentality or instinct. They generally like to meet with other people and will often seek out company. Even shy neurotypicals or introverted neurotypicals long for and enjoy company, but on a much smaller scale than the extroverted neurotypical.
- There is a keen sense of group mentality which includes patterns of
  - stay with the pack,
  - don't jump ship, and
  - enormous pressure to retain conformity to and within the group.

- All pack or herd animals are similar within the pack, having rules, protocols and hierarchies, which others in the pack respect or occasionally challenge. An animal that does not follow the rules of the pack will generally not survive very long. Neurotypicals have an elaborate and vast set of social rules and hierarchies, and sub-groups that we could call *cultures*. One can belong to many cultures, such as being middle income, studying with university groups, belonging to a dance studio, within a family subgroup and so forth (they may even change how they use language within these different sub-groups such as swearing a lot in one and abstaining in another!). I personally think that all these rules have never been written out, and if they were, the volumes would take up many library shelves. No wonder Aspies find it so difficult! Strangely, most neurotypicals just *know* the appropriate rules,

or closest ones – as if they are learned mainly through a type of social osmosis.
- ☐ Neurotypicals have *Theory of Mind (ToM)*, mostly to a very complex and high level.
- ☐ ToM or Theory of Mind is the ability to *read* the conversation as it's happening for other people as well as ourselves, in more than just the words that are communicated. Theory of mind is very dependent on body language and facial expressions, in which there is a section much later in the chapter.
  - It is sometimes said in Communication Theory that only ten percent of our conversations actually consists of the actual words spoken. The remaining 90 percent of a conversation uses another language, which Aspies often refer to as the secret code of neurotypicals. This language is usually referred to as body language.
  - Some of these *codes* are easy to identify, such as military epaulets, nametags with the wearer's status on it and position cards at a business meeting denoting rank.

> Did you know that some organisations like the Freemasons have developed their own secret codes and signals, which is increasingly taught as one goes further up the Freemason hierarchy? These very discrete codes are used in public as identification symbols between members.

  - The remainder of the communication code between neurotypicals is made up of body language, facial expressions, the language of eye contact and tone of voice, the expression of the mouth...most of which Aspies miss, as they often have face-blindness (prosopagnosia) or do not use their eyes to *read* what is being said in the faces of others who are talking to them, simply because they are avoiding eye (or face-to-face) contact.
  - *Body language* is important to us neurotypicals. Crossed arms mean *cutting off the other person*, but it could also mean that a person is cold, although we can usually tell the difference. A body position can be relaxed or have an insouciance about it which suggests arrogance and power and can be threatening – and we know the difference there too. We understand pleading body language,

thankful body language, the timid body language and the menacing-meaning-to-be-intimidating body language.

- Neurotypicals find looking into people's eyes a very important communication tool. There is a level of intimacy *spoken* in that way, and if someone does not make that eye contact, there are huge messages being said which will be missed. Exceptions are the unwritten rules within a social hierarchy, like a cast system or a military hierarchy for example – when inferiors do not look their superiors in the eye. Such behaviour of looking a superior directly in the eye is considered a challenge and is usually punishable within that system. It is considered insubordination.

- Love poetry has been written extensively on the eyes or the lips of the person that is the centre of attraction, for thousands of years, in nearly every language and in most major cultures.

> "I love your lips when they're wet with wine
> And red with a wild desire;
> I love your eyes when the lovelight lies
> Lit with a passionate fire"
> Ella Wheeler Wilcox (written approximately 1883)
>
> "My mistress' eyes are nothing like the sun;
> Coral is far more red than her lips' red;"
> William Shakespeare (written 1609 approximately)

- In the song, *Lyin' Eyes* by the Eagles, the rich old man with whom she is in a relationship, knows that she is unfaithful from her body language. It continues with the conclusion that she can't hide the truth when her eyes are lying, and that she has the smile of a liar. It has a very clever set of lyrics!

- In another well-known and quaint old country-music song, *The Gambler* by *Don Schltz* and famously sung by *Kenny Rogers*, the gambler notices his train companion's eyes. The old gambler observes that the young man is down and out so he proceeds to tell him how to succeed at the whole body language of professional gamblers. He tries to give the younger man a quick lesson to success in that cultural lifestyle.

(COUNTRY-MUSIC SINGER)

- There are hundreds of adjectives to describe the expressions of eyes. Some eyes can be haughty, shy, kind, scheming or cunning, sad or loving, as just a very few examples. Eyes can be described as *glassy*, meaning that that person may have a fever, may be in shock, in milder form the person is bored or extremely tired, or they may be using or abusing substances. A lengthy list of adjectives that go on describing the emotions expressed in eyes can go on and on. Unfortunately, to see these emotions in someone's eyes – one has to look into another's eyes. Neurotypicals just know this and do it and understand the processes quite well and can usually interpret eye-meanings.
- Neurotypicals read mouths and the expressions that our mouths portray. Mouths describe many emotions: a smile, laughter, a sneer. A person can be thin-lipped, which usually denotes anger or

- contempt, or another can force their lips out, which is emotionally described as a pout or sulking.
- Neurotypicals also automatically look at the muscles around the eye or mouth, which tells us whether an expression is genuine or fake.

Leonardo da Vinci's famous painting, the *Mona Lisa*, has fascinated people for over 500 years. Her smile is described as enigmatic. People have studied her eyes and her mouth, to see what emotion the artist was painting. It is thought that her smile is mysterious, particularly when looking at the eyes. The two combined expressions in her eyes and mouth suggests that she has a secret. Regardless of the interpretation, it is her facial expressions that have drawn discussion over the years.

- ☐ Neurotypicals also have selective obsessions, hobbies, and specialised interests but do not use these to stim. They also can manage to stop a conversation if the other person is bored or not interested. I don't particularly enjoy or care for rugby, so most fans only give me the briefest information when they know this.
- ☐ Interestingly enough, neurotypicals are often subject to fashion statements – whether in clothing, music, vehicles, and an extensive list of acquisitions.
  - There is an enormous pressure is many social groups to have the *right* music, or clothing or status symbols. Ironically, conformity is expected particularly in Western cultures that often values eccentricity and non-conformity, which probably results in our fashions changing so often.
  - To be individual and to resist the status quo in fashion amongst peers is usually an immediate demotion socially – until conformity is reached again.

Imagine a social gathering of 16 to 25-year-olds, all dressed in fashionable, very expensive label brand denim fabric, all torn in the same pattern at the knees (which was the height of fashion). The denim is all in varying shades of mid blue to black and the torn slits in the jeans are all horizontal at the knee but in different shapes and sizes (to create some individuality?). What happens to the boy who arrives in bottle green corduroy pants, neatly pressed and with no holes? The group will clearly indicate socially that this clothing is unacceptable, through pointing, sniggering and avoiding contact with that person.

- ☐ Neurotypicals generally enjoy crowds and will willingly go to crowded places, such as fairgrounds, various types of circuses, rallies, music concerts and rugby or soccer matches. They are gregarious by nature. They are fond of clichés like: *there is safety in numbers.*
  - In the herd mentality mindset, they are prone to copying each other, as in all dancing similarly, or responding the same at a rally, and even developing crowd hysteria as they are swept along by the same feelings and emotions.
  - Some will go to these sort of events regularly, such as discos or nightclubs, every weekend where possible in their similar age groups.
- ☐ Surprisingly, neurotypicals do get obsessed by current fashions, politics, music and various social arenas of this type. Yet this obsession is not exclusive as in Aspies obsession. Also, neurotypicals know when someone is not interested and will not overshare or bore another person.
- ☐ Neurotypicals often need to have some physicality, such as touch. The men will often shake hands, or if they know each other well, will lightly slap another man's shoulder or back. Women will often hug and may kiss each other as well. In many social situations, men and women will hug and kiss each other, as a social greeting.
  - There are a vast number of complicated rules about who touches whom and how and why, whether touching is an appropriate greeting, who then kisses whom and how. These rules are all instinctively known, and faux pas are rare and usually followed by embarrassed apologies and forgotten.
  - On occasion, these rules are taught to children, such as *kiss and hug grandma when you first meet with her*, and usually, this is then a rule no matter what the circumstances.
  - This is a normal pattern at social events, particularly where people either know each other, no matter how vaguely, or know of each other distantly (they may never even have actually met before). I have been hugged by strangers at a meeting because they had heard

of me or thought fondly of me! [For the record, I would not consider myself *a hugger*.]
- This physical contact is carried out at many social events, such as business meetings, weddings, regular church events, and even family greetings on a daily basis.
- I have even experienced total strangers touching my pregnant belly in a supermarket, because they were *feeling the baby* in the fondness of their thinking.

☐ Most group social behaviour patterns are instinctive but are within a sub-code of the greater group culture. These sub-codes may be organised around religion for example, so that men are fed the best morsels of dinner before the women may eat their food (separately to the men); or a gang culture where a gang member cannot hug someone from another rival gang even if that other person is a family member; or in some situations public displays of affection are not socially permitted for some reason. Of course, all neurotypicals usually know the rules instinctively, but non-neurotypicals are completely lost. If neurotypicals are confused about the appropriate behaviour, they will either observe others discretely or will withhold such behaviour until they know what is appropriate, expected or permitted.

☐ Neurotypicals can visit and change cultures and can by a type of visual osmosis appear to very quickly absorb the unwritten rules of the other culture that they have recently entered. Once again, faux pars are rare, quickly dealt with and not repeated.

☐ Wearing the incorrect clothing at a social event, regardless of how minor the event (it may just be the gathering of four or five friends casually) will result in immediate critical judgement and the wearer may be labelled as *weird* or *abnormal*.
- A sub rule is that when one is alone in their own house, they can dress however they wish. Some people though, fear unexpected visitors and potential scorn that that may bring if they are caught in inappropriate clothes and will therefore dress appropriate to the group in which they sense they belong so that they are always conforming – even in the physical absence of other group members.
- It is not uncommon for a rally leader, speaker or prominent person to be monitored or even criticised not for their speaking or their

facts, but by what they are wearing and how they carry out the correct status greeting styles. Common examples are political party leaders, royalty like Her Majesty, Queen Elizabeth II, and quite often female leaders in a male dominated arena.

- How neurotypicals behave is decided by the word *protocol*, which covers the rules, customs, and descriptions for an almost infinite number of variations of social activity – again, mostly known and understood by neurotypicals instinctively. Even in a foreign situation in which they do not know the customs fully, most neurotypicals will know that there is a custom or protocol procedure and will therefore endeavour to find out the details beforehand.

- It is very important for neurotypicals to know beforehand as to how to conform to a group that they are prospectively meeting.

- Neurotypicals understand social hierarchies. They know how, when or whether to address those senior to them or below them in the hierarchy. Hierarchies are very important to neurotypicals, and a lot of an initial small chat will be made to ascertain where one is upon that hierarchy. They also know how to initiate conversations in friendships and in peer circles.

> I once called a local psychiatrist on behalf of a client, to pass on a message only. She was amiable enough for the first minute of the conversation but then asked me my profession and qualifications, which really was not relevant nor necessary. Regardless, I answered politely. She responded that she did not talk to lesser qualified people about clients and hung up on me – never waiting to hear what the client required from her! (For Aspies reading this – it was totally inappropriate for the psychiatrist to behave like that, even though she may have had a belief that she was academically and socially superior.)

- In some situations, it is considered inappropriate for a lower rung person to talk to a higher rung person, within a particular hierarchy. So, a janitor may not approach his company's CEO, and a CEO might deign to approach a janitor but will usually have subordinates to do that.

- In the military (and within the royalty and peerage classes), there are particularly strong social divides between ranks, and cross rank fraternising on a regular, unscheduled basis is extremely frowned upon. At a school or workplace level, this may be acted out as the *cool* group and the *not cool* members.

☐ Neurotypicals know that hierarchies are exclusive. The excluded ones usually have a deep desire to be included, and some will try to find conscious ways to deliberately do so.

☐ Neurotypicals find it hugely flattering to be seen socially with someone above their hierarchy. They might be very excited (an emotional response) to book a room in a hotel and then find that they will be sleeping in the same bed that a famous person had slept in seven years beforehand.

☐ After which statement, it is easy to segue into – neurotypicals are considered to be irrational.

☐ Neurotypicals are considered to be emotional and to filter facts through emotions, which usually can result in an irrational response. What they feel about a person or a situation is significant in its influence. They have to work very hard to exclude emotions and only focus on facts, when needed – especially female neurotypicals!

- Some neurotypicals will know cognitively that they are being irrational – but will still not be able to deal with an issue because their feelings are so very strong.
- Neurotypicals can often have immediate responses and opinions. One Aspie remarked that these quicker responses are not often thought through, yet they are usually intuitively correct! Despite the *feeling-filter*, neurotypicals can process information and circumstances quickly and make decisions on the spot and without hesitation generally. An example of this can be that they will instantly make and go along with a new set of plans, at very short notice and with very little detail and discussion (unlike Aspies).
- *High functioning* and *low functioning* are the descriptive divisions mostly used for Aspies. The functioning part relates to how closely Aspies cope in neurotypical society, whether they can live independently or need support, and how much they mirror neurotypical behaviours – which, if one looks at that analytically, is a simplified description of the measure of an Aspie's sociability amongst neurotypicals. Neurotypicals have a broad separation too. A low-functioning neurotypical of a normal intelligence range is often considered a lower being socially. They are more broadly divided into *good* and *bad* types of human beings.
  - A high-functioning neurotypical is kind, caring, loving, patient, thoughtful, time/financially/emotionally generous, praises people, is helpful and encouraging, is gracious, respectful, courteous, naturally humble, is socially adept, honest, intuitive, is careful, obeys most rules and laws, understands social rules and is quite diplomatic, is trustworthy, feels safe to be with, is protective, open-minded, non-judgemental and can work collaboratively and mostly they live independently and contribute positively to their culture and society. (Note how many of the adjectives describe emotions and/or sociability!)
  - A low functioning neurotypical, on the whole, is the opposite or a contrast of the above. A *bad* neurotypical can also have criminal and deviant attributes or behaviours. These neurotypicals can be cruel, deliberately and consciously manipulative, hypocritical, opinionated; they are spiteful and can be malicious; they appear to like playing mind-games and are very self-serving, self-centred and

egotistically egocentric. They are often bullying and can also get involved in criminal or gang-related activities. The very manipulative ones, especially those that have narcissistic or psychopathic tendencies often become cult leaders and can be considered socially quite dangerous.
- o Some low functioning neurotypicals are so because they may have intellectual or physical disabilities and are dependent on carers.

☐ It is rare for neurotypicals to isolate and totally avoid socialising, in which they may often choose to live like hermits. A few introverts may withdraw socially and have extended time alone but will usually appear from time to time and fill up their social tank. These neurotypicals who mostly avoid socialising may have mental health issues such as depression or forms of anxiety like agoraphobia or social phobias; they may harbour deep bitterness, resentment or emotional hurt, which has usually been caused socially; they may suffer from shame – another socially caused condition usually; or they may be hiding criminal activities. The emphasis here is that this is relatively rare. There are other reasons for withdrawing but are not usually for reasons of choice to avoid people. Such conditions may be severe pain or terminal illness and are not usually of a neurotypical's own choice to socially withdraw. The withdrawal socially in this case is related to pain and health issues.
- Even very introverted neurotypicals like some form of company, and of course, they always behave like neurotypicals in company.

☐ Neurotypicals have degrees of likes and dislikes. This means that they may like some people more than others and dislike others on a spectrum of their own personal dislikes. They may say something like, "I don't like her; I really don't like him; I hate him; I really really hate her." Another neurotypical will understand those degrees. Aspies are usually a lot more black and white about their likes and dislikes. One Aspie, when I described these *degrees of liking or disliking* told me that the thought and explanation *did [her] head in for weeks* as she tried to understand this way of coping and thinking socially.

☐ Neurotypicals are considered good at the social graces and at being diplomatic and the better that they know the rules of diplomacy, the better their social graces. The better their social graces, the more they are looked up to by other neurotypicals. The better their communication skills, the better their social skills. And it is a marvellous cycle that continues to go around and round!

- One Aspie noticed that neurotypicals can talk in groups and be part of several conversations, and they seem to manage to follow all these conversations simultaneously. It is a particular neurotypical skill at times.
- Neurotypicals often stand close together and don't seem to mind – such as in malls and queues and concerts. Neurotypical children even seem to require less space than neurotypical adults.
- Neurotypicals are experts at using – what some of my Aspies have called – the hidden codes of communication. These include tone of voice, body language and the use of eye contact. All of these have communication meanings attributed to them.
  - Eye contact: Neurotypicals love, need and use eye contact extensively. Eye contact allows one to *read* the other person really quickly. Eye expressions can tell neurotypicals a huge range of emotions: like and dislike, emotional warmth and coldness, happiness and grief, longing, romantic love, depression, anxiety, tenderness, hope, excitement, hatred and anger, interest or disinterest, respect or disrespect and can sometimes express selfish desires. Wide eyes suggest innocence. Large wide eyes suggest innocence and surprise. And these are only a few examples. The eyes can express a vast cavern of emotions and intentions. If you are feeling romantically attracted to someone, for example, your pupils will probably dilate when you look at them. (Of course, there are also lots of other reasons why pupils dilate too!)
    - Eye contact can also tell you if someone else is drunk or stoned (on drugs or mind-altering substances).
    - A lack of eye contact, for neurotypicals, means that the avoider is hiding something. This suggests that the [hider] is being dishonest, devious, cunning or something else unpleasant. It immediately means that the looker is distrustful of the other and will try to avoid them.
  - Tone of voice: This is also very important to neurotypicals. A brisk tone suggests annoyance. A loud brisk tone suggests urgency. A

raised voice suggests stress or anger. A clipped voice suggests that someone is trying to be polite, but they no longer feel polite and is slowly losing their patience. A soft voice suggests shyness, kindness or patience. A soothing tone suggests caring. There are not only tones of voice, but there are also pitches within those tones. It is said that men generally only hear three pitches within those tones, whereas women apparently hear five different pitches. Neurotypicals depend very heavily on the tones and pitches of the speaker.

When a woman is flirting, her tone goes up a pitch. In this scene, the man may be talking to her but not be interested in a relationship beyond the conversation. The man does not notice the tone of voice but observes that someone is talking intensely to him, so he answers back, often enjoying the attention. The woman then continues that tone of voice along with lots of flirting facial features and may even lightly touch the man. If the man has a wife, she will be furious with him for engaging in and encouraging the flirting. He will be astounded and will respond that he was only talking to her – and he is most times probably correct (unless he is a natural philanderer)! He generally cannot hear the flirty tone. He will deny flirting – and sometimes vehemently so! He sometimes genuinely will not have noticed the flirting too, especially if he were only being polite and the flirting were very subtle. Obviously if the flirting went to a further stage, he would notice – and then he would have to choose his next decision and action, depending on his circumstances.

- <u>Facial expressions</u>: Neurotypicals are very interested in expressions – the flared nostrils, the raised eyebrows or brow, the gentle smile, the pursed lips, what the mouth is doing, whether there are frowns lines or not, old lines of bitterness around the mouth, the upturned nose, pointing with the nose, laughter lines, the balance of a tender expression, the mocking glance, the cynical glance, the secretive look, the begging look, the sneer, the haunted look of fear – and there is a huge list that goes on and on – thousands of novels are filled with this kind of information for the reader.

- Body language: this is another very important one to neurotypicals. Crossed arms suggests being emotionally closed off and self-protective, or alternatively being cold if they are rubbing their arms too. Not standing up suggest they are a peer (a social equal) or are more senior on the hierarchy than another, or it could be a sign of disrespect or contempt. If they are standing talking to you in conversation, and they are genuinely engaged, then they will face you with their feet towards you. If they don't want to engage, they will turn their body away from you and look at you side-on. If they are interested but, in a hurry, they may be faced towards you, but their shoes are pointing towards the door. If they are fidgeting, they are usually uncomfortable. If their thumbs are looped casually in the belt loops of their pants, they are relaxed or trying to look cool, or their hauteur could be one of arrogance. The same thumbs in the trouser belt loops, with shoulders hunched forward and an angry expression suggests aggression or superiority, and the more so as the voice gets louder. The salesman who sees that his sale is imminent will lean forward a little intimately and hold – usually fake – a large eyed guile-less expression. A hunched body and furtive expression combined suggests guilt or suggests a devious ulterior motive being acted out.
- Neurotypicals also use their hands a great deal, as they are talking, making explanations and *conversational* additions with their hand movements.

It is said that when neurotypicals are speaking that (depending on which study you read) only about ten percent of the communication is words, the remainder (about 90 percent of it) of the communication is made up of messages around eye contact, facial expression, tone of voice and body language.

- No wonder Aspies find us so difficult to understand, as they do not like eye contact (our number-one-go-to-place when communicating!); they are poor at remembering people's faces; they are poor at reading expressions and body language and usually are in such sensory overload that do not notice the change in tones of voice.

☐ Developmentally in neurotypicals, the social rules of communication are surprisingly mainly learned by osmosis by neurotypical children! It is said that little girls at ten *days* old are already making eye contact and making emotional connections!

> I always remember an amazing thing that a female client said to me many years ago. She was officially deaf and depended very much on lip reading. She said to me, "Why do people not realise that they are still talking long after they stop voicing?" I think that I will probably never forget that.

☐ It is said that neurotypicals are not dependent on words only to communicate, which is why they often do not take sufficient care with the words that they use. To Aspies, words, when communicating, are the essence of the communication.

☐ Because Neurotypicals are not fully reliant on words, they often do not realise how much their words can hurt others.
- Neurotypicals seem to get offended when their words are corrected. They also get offended when their words are used against them in an argument. The offensive is usually around so much meaning being lost when one is looking only at the literal speech content (which Aspies often do).

☐ Neurotypicals have lots of rules – such as dress codes, rankings of the acceptability of others socially, and about how they communicate. Surprisingly, most neurotypicals seem to *just know* the unwritten code and seldom need to be reminded of it (especially their social rank – and this even in a supposedly classless society as in USA, Canada, New Zealand and Australia!).

☐ Neurotypicals are considered by many Aspies to be judgemental, with very strong opinions which may ignore or override facts and firm beliefs that their views are correct. The judgements are fairly instant and are made on race, gender, sexual orientation, culture, hobbies and interests, religious beliefs, politics, career choices, parenting abilities, qualifications or lack thereof, skills or lack thereof, and even everyday things like diet, clothing choices, house-decorating styles, and the music another may listen to and enjoy, or even movie or book genres!

- Aspies note that neurotypicals often take a long time to say goodbye and may often start a new conversation as they are leaving and then move onto several sub-conversations. To an Aspie, it looks like the neurotypical is not actually leaving! It seems that an abrupt farewell greeting is considered rather rude by neurotypicals. Goodbyes are protracted and slow unless there is a good excuse or reason, such as running late for a medical appointment for example (and the hasty departure is then explained and an apology for this apparent abrupt rudeness is made).
- Aspies have also observed that neurotypicals seem to constantly need company, and that in company, they talk incessantly – especially neurotypical women.
- Neurotypicals engage in what is known as *small talk*. Small talk is an essential screening mechanism. No major or critical discussions occur during the small talk period. In *small talk*, people will mention the weather, the time of year, that they are busy/quiet at work *(small talk prefers that work is busy* – it implies that a busy person is important and successful), maybe that the family is all well, that it is good to be on this course, that grocery shopping is a chore (if the small talk is happening at the supermarket), or a light overview of the day ahead. Anything meaningful is not discussed until the small-talk ritual is completed. Small talk can happen at a brief chance meeting, waiting for your children to finish soccer practice, just before a wedding ceremony starts, at a funeral, before a meeting or a break during meetings, before a concert starts, with a stranger one meets on a train or at an airport, as just a few examples.
- Small talk is of course, for neurotypicals, a screening process. The uppermost questions in the mind are:

    o are you interesting to talk to?
    o do you like me?
    o do I like you?
    o what are our comparative social rankings?
    o do you feel the same about this event as me?
    o are we on the same page? And so forth.

It can be a social bonding process. Of course, this is all a minefield if you are not socially wired. Some cultures have a deliberate conscious ritual for this small talk, and nothing can be said until the ritual is complete.

> My Zulu friend taught me her greeting in her culture. It is a long process of:
> - How is your father?
> - My father is fine. How is your father?
> - My father is well/not well.
> - How is your mother?
> - And so on through both of the families. The full greeting and *catch up* can last for about ten or 15 minutes. It is considered very rude to barge into possibly important messages before the ritual is completed (short of an emergency or a crisis).

> Living in New Zealand, there are processes that are quite formal too, when introducing oneself, whether privately or appropriately at a meeting. If you are Maori, a formal greeting includes affiliations such as your mountain, river, sea or lake; your *waka* (the boat/canoe that your ancestor first arrived in New Zealand on), then the naming of your original family ancestor in New Zealand, followed by tribal and sub-tribal affiliations, followed by your Marae (base of the tribal meeting house). Then the introduction continues to say where one is from followed by an acknowledgement of one's parents and the full name of one's parents, and then one's own name. Maori are a spiritual people who seek connection with others and do so through their genealogical roots, their home roots and family roots, which are clearly honoured, before we come into the direct family and lastly one's own name, which becomes an important insertion into the context of the above. The background introduction is a deliberate record of their roots as New Zealand First Nation peoples.

In Western culture, this process is often less formalised and devolves into small talk as we often have to *fish* for the identity of the other person and to see if we have any common ground.

- Of course, neurotypicals like to chatter as well, to connect and to fill time. This is also considered *small talk*. Aspies are often appalled at how much working time is wasted by neurotypical's small talk and are sometimes irritated by it too.

> "What would happen if the autism gene was eliminated from the gene pool?"
> "You would have a bunch of people standing around in a cave, chatting and socializing and not getting anything done."
> Temple Grandin

- I read somewhere of one Aspie who tried to follow the rounds of small talk before a meeting and was rather astonished to find that similar conversations were being repeated around the room. Of course, the Aspie was analysing the words and the speech contents and was not realising that for neurotypicals the words were only less than ten percent of the communication.
- What was even more surprising was that the neurotypicals still managed to complete their large volume of daily work despite this small talk, and it appeared that short bouts of small talk or chatter seemed to enhance work processes.

☐ Sometimes at conferences or meetings or social events, it is difficult to *read* people's reactions to that event. I have been surprised to see people almost snoring at conferences, oblivious of what has been said, to later say loudly and often cheerfully how much they have enjoyed a conference. I have heard other people say how much their minds had wandered (and I admit at times so has mine) during the conference and they couldn't remember very much. For others, they have enjoyed their conference as the delivery has simply suited them in every way. Others may pretend to enjoy the conference. So if neurotypicals often don't cope reading each other, then how are Aspies supposed to?

☐ Ironically, neurotypicals who are so very socially driven (very gregarious mostly) – initially wear what are called social masks. It is called the polite face, which shows a mildly interested expression. This does not mean that the person is feeling polite or is interested. The social mask is to hide what they are feeling and thinking, which is why everybody does the *small talk* thing – to break through the mask. A person may also have a social mask if they are forced to relate to someone that they do not like or approve of, for example somebody who may have historically offended them or even their boss. They need their boss for their job, so they wear the social mask to pretend that all is right in the world, when it isn't so for them. The old English word for this act of wearing a social mask is called *dissembling*. (I love that word!)

- A person who does not let down their social mask during small talk is usually left alone and later avoided.

☐ The whole process of social connecting includes social masks and bonding rituals and includes talking trivia or making small talk.

One of my favourite books is the rather old transactional analysis book called *What do you say after you say Hello* by Dr Eric Berne. In essence, the next thing we or the other speaker says after the greeting is the start of the small-talk sifting process in which the identifying of several issues and boundaries are explored, before going on to the next stage. The next stage may be a development of a theme, or it may be a dismissal of the theme or the person. This ritual appears to happen whether people know each other well or not, and it simply varies in content when there is some familiarity involved.

☐ Conversely to the social mask, neurotypicals can sometimes proverbially wear their heart on their sleeve.

> I sometimes watch the neurotypical social steps that I see as an emotional dance, around a pre-meeting group, and I can't help thinking that it is very similar to dogs sniffing each other's tails and bottoms, as they relate to each other. Rather a crude picture I know but quite funny. Of course, I hide that thought behind my own polite veneer!...

- The actual talk of neurotypicals can also be difficult to understand. The words of course are not the most essential tips. Neurotypicals can *read* when someone is not listening or is annoyed by:
    - The order of the words
    - The tone of voice
    - Watching each other's eyes
    - Body language
    - All of which is of course totally lost on Aspies, who for a start are often avoiding eye contact.
- Women codes are a bit more difficult to interpret. When neurotypical women are quiet, they are often angry. They may be asked if anything is wrong, to which they will usually respond that nothing is the matter. This doubly means that the woman is probably angry and may even be escalating to furious.
- When neurotypical women avoid eye contact in a friendly environment, it means that they do not want to be friendly with the person whose eye contact they are avoiding.
- An Aspie may speak their mind truthfully and in genuine kindness but will say something like, "You can go now. I don't want to talk anymore." A neurotypical will find that abrasively and shockingly rude and will not want to meet with that person or talk to them again. The Aspie has broken the neurotypical bonding or departure code by being rudely spoken, as considered by the neurotypical and has therefore seemingly wrecked the social bond.
- When neurotypicals use words, they do not necessarily explain their statement fully or clearly. They speak in abbreviations or hints or allusions, without necessarily clearly outlining each thought and sentence. This is a mutually understood code, and it is referred to as speaking in subtexts – which really means the hidden message within or behind the message.

> A brief example of this could be a 60-year-old woman with the haircut, clothing, piercings and styling of a 16-year-old. Two others looking across the room at her, may murmur *mutton* to each other and smile amusedly, catching the mutual joke. They are referring to the disparaging idiom of *mutton dressed up as lamb*, with reference to that first woman, and are both in agreement that her façade of youthfulness can be blatantly seen through. They are then amused at the other woman's pretensions and are also mutually amused that they are both in agreement and have both seen through the mask of the first woman's presentation. So, in this example, *mutton* was a subtext with a large meaning yet needed no further explanation.

- The presentation above of the neurotypical socialising rituals is not to imply that neurotypicals are necessarily shallow. Many are thoughtful, insightful, altruistic human beings and who think about their fellow man often with goodwill. They may care about the environment, volunteer for St Johns ambulance, donate to worthy causes generously and be actively involved in their community. These are deeper layers of the neurotypical, which they will express once the social rituals are completed or the situation is appropriate to do so.
  - Neurotypicals may often work voluntary out of goodwill for the social aspect of the community work, whereas Aspies may do so with passion and drive and often out of a special interest.
- Yet neurotypicals can be – sometimes easily – offended if all social rules and etiquette are not followed. They can be generous if someone is not of the same culture or is still learning the culture (like a child or a foreigner) but will become impatient and annoyed otherwise. The older the neurotypical, the more likely they will be wanting everybody to conform to, and respect, their social rules.
- My father becomes incensed by boys wearing caps, especially as these young men break multiple old-school social rules!

  - The cap should only be worn as a sunshield and protection
  - The cap should never be worn backwards (this one really gets his blood boiling!)
  - A cap should never be worn indoors, and

- Should always be taken off as a sign of respect to anyone older or an important social person (like the local priest, doctor, police officer, teacher) or a dignitary (like the prime minister). (And you thought Aspies had a lot of rules!)

Any breach of these rules is taken as a deep and personal offence!

- ☐ All people have beliefs. Beliefs are complex thought structures around important ideas that have meaning for the person. Some of these beliefs are really deep, such as religious beliefs or political ideologies, or even around the individuals' own self-worth and self-esteem, and are often difficult to challenge or shift. Other beliefs can be quite strong but changeable, such as those beliefs formed around fashion and parenting styles. Many of the beliefs are in *grey areas* (a subtext for us neurotypicals!), which means that they are not necessarily as firmly fixed as the believer might think. Aspies have fairly straightforward black and white thinking, which is usually quite fixed. Hence, they find that neurotypicals can be quite fluid in their beliefs, meaning that they see that neurotypicals can change many of their beliefs quite easily and oft times – very conveniently. Aspies feel that neurotypicals flip-flop around many beliefs and are confused by the lack of pattern or logical thought around this flip-flop. An Aspie will often argue with a *but you said...*, and the neurotypical will answer *yes, but that's not what I meant...* At which point, they both gradually become increasingly and mutually upset or angry.
- ☐ Many of these beliefs are viewed through the emotional filter of *feeling right* for neurotypicals. Aspies find this difficult to understand as there is sometimes no real, deep logic behind this and because it is often based on a feeling. Then the feeling changes, the beliefs change, and the Aspie is left bewildered and confused. (Sometimes neurotypicals are too, but it is more temporary, and they also quickly and more likely accept the change as a fairly normal happening.)
- ☐ Aspies have voiced that they sometimes find neurotypicals inauthentic. Neurotypicals can often take on different personalities in different environments. They can *roughhouse with the boys* one moment, and then speak in the correct saintly language when they see their pastor walk by,

and then fall back into the same crude behaviour with the boys again. A woman can be furious at her partner and be shouting vitriol at him, and then answer the phone sweetly to a caller. One woman can whisper something cutting and menacing to another woman and drip charm and flirt with another colleague (whom they were previously criticising) immediately. They may appear to support a person of a higher status or someone that they are attracted to, or someone that they look up to in some other way, and then may appear to agree with all that other person's opinions even when they go against their own personal beliefs. They may hold strong beliefs about treating all people the same but may appear to enjoy somebody else's racist joke to appear to be on the same footing as that person and to keep their approval, or as the cliché states – *to stay in their good books*. This is largely due to that social herding instinct, gaining social points and self-preservation that was talked about earlier, but Aspies find this manipulating and deceptive and simply – just phoney.

- Neurotypicals do not like continued talk about something that they are not passionate about, so they will silence others, talk across them or try to stop them talking. This confuses Aspies, as it appeared originally that the person may have enjoyed that topic before in a different setting.
- Some Aspies have noted that neurotypicals can be quite mercenary about friends. Neurotypicals may proclaim and act as if they have a genuinely deep friendship with someone, but they may change their allegiance to another social subgroup and may drop their friends, seemingly instantly. In fact, few people have long-term friendships from school days so may stress this in social circles, as it is an exception.
- Aspies have noticed that neurotypicals will often cut off another person, or speak over that person, to express their own opinion. The rules about when this is and isn't appropriate, or acceptable, are quite blurred. When Aspies do this, they are not tolerated for very long in a neurotypical group and are then reprimanded or excluded, sometimes even ostracised. Unfortunately, the social rules for this vary from group to group.
- Neurotypicals will often judge another person's value in the group and will either choose them to be included, or will choose to exclude them. This can also be in games and in sports. This can also vary from situation to situation.

> I have seen Aspies excluded from groups because they may not be good at sports. Neurotypicals who enjoy the feeling of winning very much and are often competitive, may be blatantly unkind about any possible inclusion that will detrimentally affect their outcomes – even if they believe that they are *inclusive* thinkers. So they may have excluded someone from a group for a sports event but later in the day may suddenly appear friendly and chummy up to that same excluded person, and then include that person in another group, for example a trivia competition group, in which the newly included member may excel.

- Neurotypicals in their egocentricity and in self-absorbed moments will often have no idea about how their words have hurt others, despite being socially minded – because they do not always focus on only the words that they are using. At other times, they deliberately use words to inflict emotional pain.
- Neurotypicals are often flattered when invited and allowed higher up in another rung of their social hierarchy (and again, this book is based on an apparently classless society, but there are still internal rules about one's place in any community).

> The media made long-term and an unprecedented fuss about Megan Markle joining the ranks of British royalty, with her relationship and later marriage to Prince Harry. Megan was a commoner [not royalty], of a different nationality [American not British], and of a different race [African American and not British Caucasian], amongst many other social and hierarchical differences, all of which was cause for great private and public discussion amongst mainly neurotypicals.

- Neurotypicals can also be extremely jealous about an *equal* who is permitted up the social hierarchical rung, when they are excluded or when the *equal* does not bring them into that new inner circle. A jealousy by the unincluded neurotypicals can then take root, something that Aspies do not always understand.
  - I remember Temple Grandin stating in an article that she had no concept for jealousy and did not understand that emotion.

- Some of my ASD clients are polyamorous and cannot understand why some people are jealous, when they have several simultaneous relationships and want an exclusive relationship instead.
☐ Neurotypical adults generally can understand their emotions, control their emotions and recognise emotions in others. Of course, they also filter most situations through their emotions and are often controlled by these emotions. A common neurotypical expression in an important situation when decisions for the greater good have to be made is to put *your emotions aside*. Aspies would rarely have to be told to do this.
☐ Neurotypicals understand a play on words and jokes or even sarcasm. When Aspies get clever with puns repeatedly, neurotypicals seem to get annoyed. Neurotypicals have an indefinable fine line about when jokes stop and start.

- Aspies find that neurotypicals seem to make a lot of noise, especially at social gatherings. They talk a lot; they chatter; they clatter cutlery; they play music loudly; they eat loudly.
- Aspies say that neurotypical senses are often dulled – they do not have the same sensory issues that Aspies seem to struggle with.
- Neurotypicals seem to seek approval and validation from other neurotypicals, especially from peers, teachers and managers. There seems to be a need to be publicly acknowledged as having some level of importance. They may also seek this approval from parents or from their children particularly if those children are adults. They may even have a measure for this approval, for example, that their son in a cross-country race came 15th out of 267 runners – the subtext being how well that son did in comparison to the majority.
- Neurotypicals are usually very good at recognising faces and will often remember that person's name, sometimes their full name, or at the very least, the context of where they last saw that person. They can also easily differentiate faces in a group.
- Neurotypicals are not very literal and are always looking for subtexts. This is probably why they enjoy jokes so much, as there are often at least two versions, one being a play on the literal and the other in the subtext. Double entendres often elicit much mutual pleasure.

> Every morning at sunrise, I walked my old dog. For a short while, sunrise happened to be the same time that my neighbour left for work, so every morning for a few weeks we met and greeted each other. One morning, he said, eyes twinkling, that we should stop meeting this way. For Aspies who may not understand what's funny about this, it is an old joke and the innuendo suggests that the meeting, where no one else is about and looks coincidental, is actually a secret rendezvous! After a short while, sunrise was earlier and earlier as we went into spring, and my neighbour and I eventually stopped passing each other.

- Neurotypicals generally cope well with job interviews and try to bring to the fore what the prospective employer is looking for. The majority of neurotypicals get through the interviews and usually eventually land themselves a job – and the majority of neurotypicals are in employment.

Most neurotypicals can get through job interviews because they are naturally sociable; they understand the protocol around hierarchy and social roles, and they have a level of polite social diplomacy. Proportionately, significantly more neurotypicals are in paid employment than Aspies.

- ☐ Neurotypicals can obsess about trivia and meaningless information, like a celebrity relationship, or a cliffhanger TV series, or what jewellery a celebrity wears and their clothing. People in the public eye are conscious of potential criticism around their clothing and also dress code flops and the consequent embarrassment due to mass media criticism.

> I heard of one famous rockstar who was fronting an event for a charity for the impoverished and homeless community. That he gave his time, finances, talents and efforts at his own expense to the fundraiser, was not even noticed or remarked upon – but his critics loudly criticised him for wearing an expensive Rolex watch!

- ☐ Neurotypicals are often considered to be small-minded at times.
- ☐ They are described as often having an underdeveloped sense of loyalty and will change brands or even political stands, saying that they had changed their minds. Many of these changes are done for emotional reasons, and Aspies are quite quick to point out that the facts in this situation are often not considered.
- ☐ Aspies say that they find it difficult to understand neurotypicals as they often:
  - Say what they don't mean (as in *I am fine thanks*, when they are not), or in this case, do not tell the truth.
  - They also say what they don't mean, just to avoid emotional conflict or to not hurt someone's feelings, so they may say that one is welcome to stay when clearly they want you to leave. The mixed messages are confusing for Aspies particularly and embarrassing to other neurotypicals as they try to decipher the actual meaning.
  - They can appear to agree with someone and then backstab that same person, sometimes publicly, a little while later.
  - They will also in the moment say that they will support somebody but then often fade away into the background when their support is

actually needed. It takes enormous courage to come out into the public and support someone. And in private, they may say that they will support someone whose loved one has died, but within a few weeks, very few people are still showing support.
- If they are angry, they pretend they are not and stay polite.
- They play mind games – which is extremely manipulative.
- Their language is often ambiguous. If it is deliberately ambiguous, they are playing mind games. If it is not consciously and deliberately ambiguous, it is because they are vague and haven't thought the matter through properly and often lack details.

☐ Clothes have a meaning and importance to many neurotypicals. They are an expression of status and fashion consciousness, which is often very important to neurotypicals – especially the women. There is an old idiom that *to feel good, one most look good* – only a neurotypical would have first coined that phrase! People all want to dress like individuals, but when you look at a group of neurotypicals, they mostly wear the same sort of current styles – more so around their own particular sub-cultural group. They are very influenced by their peers and the social media, a fact used very cunningly by fashion houses who use models and role models and draw in the media for full exposure.

> Some years ago, I was going out with my daughters and daughter-in-law to an international theatre company show performing *The Phantom of the Opera*. We, who all love that musical, of course bought tickets to see the performance. The girls were excited and were getting all dressed up in their finery, with their hair done, make-up done, lashings of perfume and jewellery. I chose to wear a simple black pants and a suitable top, with no makeup or fashion bits. My girls were horrified and tried to persuade me otherwise, but I realised that night that all that effort to sit in the dark to watch a show was really an unnecessary stress. Several thousand people were attending, with their perfumes cloying into one giant vaporous fug, who would later fill several bags of make-up-remover towels. I decided that it was ridiculous. They tried to very carefully re-educate me that that was part of the *fun* of going out to a show. The noise, the press of people, the perfumes, the lighting, the many smells did not bother me, but for a

> wee moment, I had a sense of our ridiculous social rituals and went a little bit against the norm.

- ☐ Neurotypicals can have rituals for no purpose. They do things because *that's the way we always did it*. The smaller and more closed the community or family group, the more likely there will be this comfort of doing things the traditional way – but it is an unconscious process, again just learned on journey through life.

> There is an old joke from years ago. In it, a young woman is found making her first roast dinner for friends who are coming over. She had a leg of lamb, which she careful sawed in half and then put this in a crushed L-shape into her roasting pan. Her friend asked her why she did it that way, and she said that her mother prepared and cooked it like that. She then checked with her mother, who said her mother had done it that same way, which is what she had copied. She then checked with her *grandma*, who said she did it that way, because when she first got married as a very young woman, she only had a tiny roasting dish, and that was the only way in which she could fit her leg of lamb into the dish!

> In a separate incident, I was watching my mother make a salad one day. I need to add that this is a story for illustration, from my experience, and no disrespect to any family members is intended! I was an adult with children of my own at that point. She suddenly did a strange thing with the cucumber, which I had remembered her doing when I was a child. She cut off the end bit, and then grabbing both bits firmly, she rubbed and rubbed it across the top of the cucumber, until a delicate froth was formed. She then threw away the end bit. I asked her why she did that – and she was surprised, and probably dismayed, at my ignorance! She told me that that was the way it was done on both sides of the family, through several generations. Again, when I pressed her as to why that needed to be done, she thought about it, and then sagely told me that her grandmother had told her it was a trick to draw out the bitterness of the cucumbers, and that was why her cucumber was never bitter in a salad!

- Aspies tell me that arguments and discussions with neurotypicals are often emotionally based and not based on logic and facts. In such a situation, both parties get very upset and frustrated.
- Neurotypicals often have a strange idea of what consists *fun*. I see a lot of young adults play the *peg game*. In this game, one discreetly clips a clothing peg to another person's clothing, in such a way that the person is not aware of it. There may be lots of giggling and sly smiles, until the person *twigs*. Sometimes they don't and the game is to see how long your friend manages to go through the day without discovering it. Once discovered, the peg wearer feels embarrassed and then is only emotionally satisfied if they attach the peg to another suspect.
- Neurotypicals are often considered gullible and easily fall into the trap of salespeople who use body language effectively while stroking the potential buyer's ego and working hard at making them feel good and empowered during the process of the sale. The salesperson, who can feel the sale pending, closes the deal with a few discounts. The customer, who now feels victorious and having *pulled the wool over the salesperson's eyes*, submits a wily offer. The salesperson adds to the drama by hesitating but grabs the offer, with the buyer not realising that they still offered way too much. This sales concept has an idiom to go with it – *to tickle the trout* (a great image).
- Aspies notice that neurotypicals can feign laughter. They do not know how to respond to that.
- Unkind neurotypicals will make fun of people who are different.
- In social research experiments, it is known and shown that there is an inverse relationship between altruism and the size of the population group observing. The more people around, the less likely somebody will step forward and intervene to defend a vulnerable person. On the whole though, most neurotypicals are kind-hearted and have a decent level of compassion.
- Neurotypicals can be more impressed and often influenced by celebrities than by facts. I find it amazing that when people become celebrities, they suddenly have opinions that people want to listen to, such as how to raise children and what consists of a healthy diet – despite that they may never have trained in nutrition and may only have one young child themselves (if any!) with no prior training in the theory of parenting! Their opinions

are widely written up in regular magazines, which people read and are influenced often by these articles.

> In the song, *If I were a rich man*, from the musical, *Fiddler on the Roof*, Tevye imagines that if he were wealthy, then people would defer to him and consider him wise – which does not happen now as he is a poor milkman

- ☐ Neurotypicals are usually quite spontaneous. They can usually change their plans quite easily, even if they have very little detail. They often do not need to ask many questions to understand things. They can also speak spontaneously, without appearing to think a matter through beforehand. They appear to be able to process and speak simultaneously, unless the facts are extremely complex, in which case they may simply speak a little slower. Generally though, neurotypicals can think and respond on the spot, and change plans spontaneously. They will not fill in many details of a changed plan but will usually just *make it work* as they go along.
- ☐ Neurotypicals – to avoid hurting people's feelings, may hint at something, rather than speak directly. Aspies find this difficult, as they need to be spoken to directly. Neurotypicals may hint that they will be too busy to attend an event, without refusing directly. Or instead of hinting, they may be vague if asked directly what they might be doing at a particular time of day, if they do not want to go to that event. Another neurotypical will realise what the story is (or the subtext), but an Aspie will probably not. The Aspie then will not drop the matter as they have not gotten the hint, until the neurotypical either resentfully or brutally responds or walks away. Sometimes it is a very convoluted world that we live in.
- ☐ Neurotypicals will often speak figuratively; they will say that the main wage earner brings home *the bread* or *the bacon*. Aspies need conversations that are more literal in nature.
- ☐ Neurotypicals usually have an excellent short-term memory and do not need to process or stim to recall, some preceding events. On the other hand, they do not take notice of huge volumes of detail, so once the Aspie has stimmed and processed, the Aspie will usually have a far better long-term memory than the neurotypical. The long-term

memories of neurotypicals are usually not as detailed or as precise and accurate as Aspies.

- Neurotypicals are fortunate in that they are able to tolerate, or even block out multiple stimuli. Multiple stimuli – like loud music, smells and odours, bright light and lots of activity do not generally distract the focus of a neurotypical who can often stay on task and oblivious throughout.
- Neurotypicals usually have good physical coordination, and the vast majority of sportspeople are usually neurotypical. It is also probably why they have so many social rules around sports games, sports events and sportsmanship. And the post-game or match celebration is also a very important part of this cultural group.
- Neurotypicals are usually aware of and can explain when they are physically, mentally and emotionally tired, or even exhausted. They also know how the difference between these feel for them. These feelings are also visibly expressed in their face, body language, tone of voice, their eyes and their expression.
- Like the peg game mentioned earlier, neurotypicals have another common social game. Out of fondness for another person, they can teasingly be critical or even unkind, if one were only listening to the words. They will all laugh. Sometimes this game will go too far and end up in tears or anger, and the culprit will apologise and say that they were just joking and that they didn't mean it. The apology will be accepted, the new rule limit unconsciously noted, and the game may continue. This is considered a kind of banter, providing the tone and body language are lined up positively. Sometimes really ugly things can be said, but no offence will be taken. This really confuses Aspies, who miss all the other cues. Usually, the neurotypicals are completely unaware of how much their rules upset Aspies, and in particular, stress them deeply – to the extent of shutting an Aspie down completely. They totally cannot follow this kind of social *game*.

- ☐ Neurotypicals are more likely to cheat (not all neurotypicals!)
    - About money and finances
    - On taxes
    - On relationships
    - In exams.

Sadly, if they are successful with this kind of cheating, meaning that they are not caught out or apprehended, they might, in certain closed circles, make a boast of it – with seemingly no guilt or shame. They may often treat this as a joke. And they are usually likely to repeat the behaviour at another time.

- ☐ Neurotypicals will support a team, usually a sports team, but it could be a model or an actress or a singer, not because they are good but because of local fervour or a sense of nationalism – even if the team or the person comparative to others is not strong enough in the field. Facts are ignored and patriotism or emotional zest and zeal kick in. Neurotypicals often get very excited and very emotional particularly about a sport that they are strongly interested in.

- ☐ One of my Aspie clients was very frustrated by people she considered friends making suggestions like, "Let's catch up for a coffee this week." The Aspie would wait expectantly and be prepared to go out for this coffee when the invite happened, but inevitably, the invite didn't come. This became a very difficult thing for her to process, and she vacillated between "they are liars" and "what's wrong with me that they didn't follow through?" I had to explain to her that there was probably a different truth acting out here. In the moment, when neurotypicals say "Let's have a coffee and a catch-up this week", they usually genuinely mean it at the time. They then usually forget or get too busy to be able to do it and don't let the other person know that is the case and are sometimes embarrassed when reminded. So they had probably forgotten. A corollary to this rule is: if they just say, "Let's have a coffee", or "Let's have a coffee sometime" – then they are generally not going to follow-through.

- Aspies often say that neurotypicals will exaggerate – the ubiquitous exaggeration about the size of the fish they caught being one example. But they will also say things like "my ice cream serving was huge/monstrous/ginormous/gigantic", or "What's for dinner – I'm starving!"
- Neurotypicals do not handle facts about themselves very well if the facts are not flattering. Telling a neurotypical that "You are getting a little pudgy since I saw you last! Eating too many bikkies, eh?", will probably result in a response – at best – with weak smile and cold eyes, and a

quick departure, and probably no future contact. At worst, you may face some hostility and anger, and a clear message to mind your own business!

- ☐ Neurotypicals will usually only get into deep or intense personal conversation in a setting in which they trust the other person deeply, or in a setting made for deep conversations like a philosophy class.
- ☐ Neurotypicals can be easily embarrassed and will often go to great pains to avoid being embarrassed. They will lie easily, as a preference to avoid being embarrassed.
- ☐ Neurotypicals can endure social occasions for a long time. They can literally party all night. It is inevitably the neurotypicals who are last to leave the social gathering – and usually the most sociable neurotypical of the bunch will be the last to make their departure.
- ☐ Neurotypicals usually know when it is time to talk and when to enter a conversation, or when someone has finished talking. It is usually body language and a change in pitch that indicates this. Neurotypicals can keep conversations flowing.
- ☐ Neurotypicals can generally read the intentions of others, whether those are positive or negative – and can respond appropriately. If one enters a supermarket at closing time, the glare of the security guard either discourages one from entering or encourages one to get the required item in under three minutes!
- ☐ Intentions and understanding them are usually very important to neurotypicals, who often have the patience to wait for explanations which would make these intentions clearer.

A friend of mine lived far out of town. She is a generous, thoughtful, kind person. She had recently had a serious operation and could neither stand nor walk for a few minutes and tired easily. She was not allowed to drive. She asked me to come over and give her some company and break the monotonous daily tedium for her. It would have taken me about fifty minutes' drive to get to her. I managed to change some work hours and intended to go out for a few hours (as appropriate) one afternoon, as arranged with her. The night before going out, she phoned me to cancel our visit. A young mum and neighbour of my friend had to have treatment for her cancer and had absolutely no one to support her. Despite the

> arduous trip, my friend decided to accompany this person to her treatment and stay at the hospital with her for the day's treatment.
>
> A simple cancellation after all the effort I went through and planned to go through for the visit could have caused some annoyance at the very least. Her explanation plus my understanding of the necessity for my friend's sacrifice to help her neighbour gave me sufficient insight, and I was okay with the situation (in fact, I had an unexpected free afternoon!).

☐ In conclusion, Steven Covey (the author of *The Seven Habits of Highly Successful People*) once said at an interview, "We judge ourselves by our intentions, and others by their actions." I have also heard another version (that might have been misquoted!) that says, "We judge ourselves by our motivations and others by their behaviours." It is probably a very good description of neurotypicals.

Comorbidities:
Neurotypicals are more likely to develop most comorbidities such as:

- Addictions – gambling, alcohol and drugs
- Family breakdowns
- Arguments
- Unfaithfulness
- Stealing
- Lying
- Criminal and deviant behaviour
- Racism
- Sexism
- Fighting within and against other societies and cultures that make up mankind
- And a large majority of the negative behaviours that we see in our society

(Sorry, neurotypicals, but it's true!)

Social Communities

A short essay of the influence of Neurotypicals on our world

Without neurotypicals, we would not have had thousands of years of society and organised groups with structured social systems to hold them together.

From the earliest caveman drawings, we have seen societies depicted in groups and at work together. They have hunted and planted, domesticated animals, minded and raised children, set up pastures and villages and later built small walled cities. They have created little kingdoms, with kings and the king's retinues. They have formed hierarchies, societies and dynasties. For survival and safety, people have generally clustered together in groups to look after their own. (Not much different to most fish, birds and mammals really, which theory could be described as a biological belief.)

Small groups formed larger groups. Larger groups dominated and took over smaller groups, taking their food and animals, and often making slaves of the yielded group. World history is full of ancient civilisations, medieval ones, moving through to our own current world communities. The various civilisations and communities have tried to understand life, forming religions and beliefs as they searched for meaning. Some of the wisdom was collected as writing developed, and the thoughts, musings and often emotions of many wise elders and later philosophers became recorded – a different stage to insular oral histories. There were also always the travellers and explorers, the adventurers, or the sheer necessity that forced people to leave the social nest and the human drive to push further outwards.

Some cultures became patriarchal, some matriarchal. Some developed a contempt for the weak or poor, some created a philanthropic support network for the underprivileged. In some societies, girls were disposable, and in some others, they were highly valued (on the whole though – females have had a pretty poor handout throughout history!). Most cultures, right up to current times, were undergirded by religious concepts and many complex rules. I wonder what our cultures will look like in a few hundred years. What will remain? What prized beliefs that we have today will be the object of enormous scorn and be upheld for its sheer lunacy and ludicrousness in the future?

> Generally, western and middle-eastern cultures were patriarchal, and the more far-east nationalities were more matriarchal, within the home. In the vast majority of cultures, men were the leaders of the nations, with a few exceptions. The role fell to men probably because they were physically bigger and stronger and therefore dominant, and therefore better defenders (except for the Greek mythical Amazon women!). In most cultures though, men were often allowed multiple wives (polygamy) and yet females were generally not allowed multiple husbands. Polyandry (in which one woman has two or more co-existing husbands) is very rare and only found in a few cultures, notably in rural Tibet.

A couple of classic and famously satirical novels have explored this theme of how a social construct in a group of people is formed: *Lord of the Flies* and *Animal Farm*. (Of course, there are thousands of other novels that explore social themes – from Geoffrey Chaucer to Thomas Hardy, Charles Dickens and Jane Austen, Solzhenitsyn to Leonard Pitt.) *Lord of the Flies* explores how a group of boys abandoned on an island create their functioning but changing society. Similarly, *Animal Farm* through the technique of personifying farm animals examines how they too form a society and the interplay of the dynamics between the protagonists. Initially, all the positive social strengths of neurotypicals come to the fore. They are cooperative, consider others, help the weak; they protect each other, share what they have and what they need to do; they discuss issues and work together as a team to solve these, and there is kindness and general altruism – all of these forming a collective hope and happiness. Then the negative side of neurotypicals slowly seeps in. The self-indulgent and greedy, the selfish behaviour combined with laziness (I like the old English word for this – slothfulness!), the need to be noticed and the rising egoism, the flexing of power, the bullying, and a hierarchy around leadership (usually the bully emerging *victoriously* as the leader), and those on the new lower rungs of the hierarchy facing the brunt of the abuse, work and minimal rewards. All of these forming a collective feeling of hopelessness, despair and unhappiness. One of my favourite quotes from *Animal Farm* is, "All animals are created equal." As the dynamics and the social infrastructure change later in the book, the new leaders declare: "All animals are equal, but some animals are more equal than others." The second statement completely disabuses the first.

The social destruction is caused in both novels by emotions and driven thoughts. By that I mean the need to be superior and dominant, the need to feel respected and honoured, the need for social approval, the need to only feel good when one has total control – and when this combination is satisfied, there comes one of the deepest emotions of all...pride. There is of course a healthy appropriate pride, and then the unhealthy pride which leads to arrogance and often abuse of others. Most philosophies and religious discourses on humanity focus on pride as a major issue and encourage humility – with the under story suggesting that it is only in mutual humility that societies can succeed. This belief has engendered many a cult, which has often started out with the best intentions. Unfortunately, the best beliefs and churches and charitable organisations are often fabulous in principle, until human beings get involved!

Very few people succeed at this trait of genuine humility. Most of those who do, of course do not get public attention as humility of itself does not seek such reward.

> I once met a man aged about 30, who in total and genuine self-belief in his sincerity told me that he *was the most humble person [he] knew*!

Regardless, few have been noticed, but most of us, if we think about it, can warmly remember the few humble people that we have met. These people are usually sincere, genuine, modest, unassuming, cooperative, not self-seeking, unpretentious, forgiving and often caring people. Some people revere Mother Theresa and Mahatma Gandhi as extreme examples of living humbly, but it's important to point out that humility and a vow of poverty are not related. Nelson Mandela was considered a very humble man, but he did not live in poverty after his transcended jump as head of state not too long after his release from prison.

Pride is an example of one of the *many emotions and drivers* that can get out of hand. Another strong example of an emotion and driver is the need to have social approval. It is such a strong drive amongst neurotypicals and is often a main social driver, yet it is almost completely absent in younger Aspies. Neurotypicals seek attention, praise and affirmation, and if they cannot get it, they will often yield to feelings of worthlessness and subsequent depression, or feelings of anxiety in their striving in one way or the other *to make it* or may even go to devious means to attain this.

> A story that I have read some years ago, of this behaviour (being devious to get emotional and social credit and standing), is set in the book of *Acts*, in the Christian bible. The early disciples of Jesus meet together (after his final departure) and combine their resources and support each other. Some people who have owned a piece of land seem to have sold this to contribute to the community funding. One couple, apparent newcomers, see this and decided to sell their land and contribute it but agree to pretend that they have handed all the money over whilst secretly withholding a substantial portion. They perceive a social standing that such an act may give them, and this perceived approval becomes a great emotional reward and incentive. They are both separately exposed in this deceit with dire consequences. The ridiculous thing is that no one asked or expected them to do this, nor was it any sort of requirement. As the leader, Peter, of the new community says – it was their property to with as they wanted – there was no need to have put on this saintly farce. Yet people are so very driven to social recognition, however it looks.

But this public deviousness and public manipulation is such a quintessential neurotypical behaviour and Aspies cannot understand it at all and often are victims of the use of these neurotypical tools.

> Another example of this deviousness to gain something at the cost of another is the true but financially shocking story of *Sixto Rodriguez*, a simply brilliant American musician, who is blindly robbed and exploited of his royalties, and he is eventually found living in dire poverty. He was the victim of a completely abusive financial process in which he was manipulated out of his deserved earnings. He never got those significant earnings back.

Neurotypicals can be wonderful kind and caring, supporting the elderly, their families, working faithfully and quietly for many within their communities. The ones who do get the attention are either self-seeking or notorious. Neurotypicals are also more likely to be the ones who murder, violently abuse children, commit elder abuse, commit atrocious acts, perform torture, are bullying and are definitely the leaders in most inter and intra-human socially deviant and horrifying behaviours. Horror stories abound. American and European fathers who kidnap their daughters and have children by them through continuous acts of rape, gruesome murders, crimes of hatred and jealousy, the infamous Inquisition, burning people alive or crucifixions, people abused horrendously due to religious laws or cultural beliefs, anti-Semitism and many other -isms, and wars possibly beyond count.

Despite the sickening acts described in the paragraph before, we need to remember that mostly it is only performed by a small minority, even if that minority appears to be mainly neurotypical. Millions of neurotypicals are quietly raising good wholesome children, maintain warm and wonderful friendships, have regular gatherings with extended family and care for the people in the world around them. A neurotypical who is struggling but has a good circle of friends will always have someone checking up on them – whether a phone call or a visit. Many of the elderly are looked after lovingly by family. My second cousin and his wife cared for his parents until they passed, and then he nursed his wife who became terminally ill. My in-laws cared for both of their respective mothers. An ill neurotypical will usually have a bevy of concerned friends visit them in hospital and at home. One man I know has volunteered as a soccer coach for the littlies for over 20 years. Another elderly couple volunteered their Sundays for years (well into their eighties!), to watch travellers' vehicles in a tourist spot notorious for car break-ins. Many are involved with meals-on-wheels or volunteer for St John's. One client, who is very unwell long term, has had nephews and nieces dropping in on her weekly. Thousands of wonderful, noble deeds in every little town and city. Unnoticed mostly, unrecognised often – but beautiful social acts by mostly neurotypicals.

Socially, human beings have both a great record and a very shameful one, but these records are mainly through neurotypicals.

When I meet my many Aspies who aspire to become fully neurotypical, I sometimes have to ask them: *why?*. I sometimes quietly tell them that being neurotypical is not always the best that they can aspire to. But neurotypicals, because of their social behaviours, form our societies – and we almost all want to belong somewhere.

The neurology of neurotypicals shows advanced and complex brain structures that support socialising. This is the gift of neurotypicals.

How they choose to use this gift is another matter.

> "The world needs all types of minds"
> Temple Grandin

Chapter 8
Relationships

There are multiple relationships that are part of living: parenting, friendships, couples, collegial, with senior or junior staff in the workplace, with services such as the tax department or bank staff, neighbourly, family (including extended family and possibly in-laws), social and even briefly with strangers at times.

This chapter focuses primarily on couple and more intimate relationships but will because of the way relationships cross over with other relationships – give some helpful clues regarding relationships generally.

This chapter on relationships covers those relationships that have at least one party on the spectrum. If you are new to the book and have not yet read the other chapters, *on the spectrum* means that at least one party in the relationship is diagnosed as having Aspergers or Asperger syndrome (AS), has Autism, Pervasive Developmental Disorder – Not Otherwise Specified (PDD-NOS) or a very closely related diagnosis linked to Autism, or as all are currently now known generically, Autism Spectrum Disorder (ASD). Those that are referred to as Aspergers or High Functioning Autism, I often refer to as *Aspie* – as is commonly used. The term, *Aspie*, is used fondly as per many internet blogs and colloquially. It is used with respect. It denotes a person with a form of ASD who is functioning independently within society and makes some social connections – however that may look and vary.

Healthy Relationships

Most people search for a healthy relationship. Most adults want to be part of a warm and intimate couple relationship. Yet it can be so very difficult to find such a relationship. There are a huge number of apps that try to serve this purpose, and a phenomenal number of dating agencies trying to do effective matchmaking. Today, we can shop to find a relationship, and many people have had shopping success, with whatever app they have used.

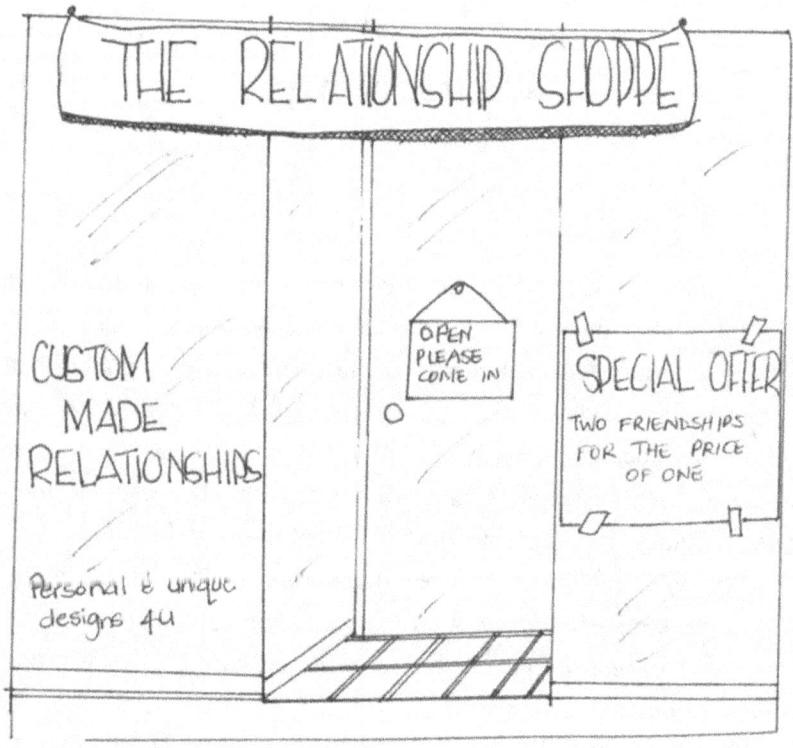

Healthy relationships share similar patterns. These patterns are based on mutual respect, adapting around each other, making major decisions jointly and clearly understanding each other's limits and boundaries. In some relationships, there may be a dominant partner. In some specific areas within a relationship, one partner may dominate as they may have a greater knowledge in that area. In New Zealand, Maori often uphold three key principles in regards tribal and other relationships – where possible, these principles of consultation, collaboration and cooperation are primary. In relationships, regardless of differences, the same principles will prove invaluable.

In most relationships, the two people are often very different in many ways. It is very rare to have two similar people with identical interests and work, childhoods and living patterns, habits and lifestyles to be together. More generally, there are lots of variations and differences, and we have the cliché that *opposites attract* in our English language for good reason! People learn to adapt around each other, and they make their own unique relationship work for them. When a relationship has ended and the parties go on and form a different relationship in time with another person, that relationship will be unique too, as these two people adapt around each other.

Some people come into relationships having different religions, or their origins being of a different country, culture or ethnic group. This also brings its own strengths and difficulties and many people have very contented, successful relationships as they work around these. One can also understand how these differences can bring contention within a relationship. And yet, neither party can be faulted – it is simply points of difference.

It is the same with an Aspie-Neurotypical relationship. It is not that either party is wrong, weaker than the other or any other negative attribute. It is that the two people bring in significant points of difference into the relationship. With many cross-cultural relationships, the points of difference are often obvious such as having a different accent, a different skin colour or differences in the hair type and eyes and noses, or wearing clothing or ornaments relevant to a particular religious group.

Unfortunately, Aspies and neurotypicals do not come with external and obvious points of difference. It is a difference in how their brain wiring (neurology) works. Over time, these differences become obvious. It is not the Aspie that is wrong. It is not the neurotypical that is wrong. Those who have worked around these differences have gone on successfully and had good, long-term relationships. With misunderstandings and blame, the breakdown of the relationship can quickly follow.

A lot of the chapter attempts to look at examples of these differences and how the misunderstandings both ways have made things work or not work.

A Very Brief Overview of ASD

This has been covered extensively in the first chapter and continually throughout, which allows readers to dip around the book. For the reader-dippers, here is a brief overview of the chief areas of ASD that affect relationships.

Developmental Disorder

- This means that a person is born this way and that it becomes apparent from early childhood. The traits and signs are usually there throughout adulthood, although – like most of humanity, there is a maturing and self-understanding that often happens, that ameliorates or softens the signs. Also, as people all mature, they often become aware of their strengths and weaknesses, and develop skills and strategies around both. Some people may need help, and in terms of personal development and relationship skills, a highly skilled practitioner in understanding ASD and its various, multiple manifestations, can make a profound and significant difference. It can be a very satisfying and emotionally rewarding field in which to work in – both for the client and the therapist.
- For clients on the ASD spectrum, some also use the term *neuro-diverse*. This means that they are neurologically different to the mainstream population group. This in turn means that the brain wiring is different in ASD as it is to neurotypicals. Some areas that are strong in neurotypicals (e.g. communication and social interaction) are far weaker in Aspies, but processing of data and facts, for example, comes more quickly and easily to Aspies than neurotypicals.
- Aspies are often developmentally immature. They seem to be two to three years at least behind the average development life-span milestones and developmental stages. This social immaturity can leave them quite naïve and vulnerable to social manipulation by manipulative people or even predators.

TOM: Lack of Theory of Mind, or Mind-blindness

- Lack of Theory of Mind, or mind-blindness, simply means that the person with lack of ToM cannot walk in your shoes, or moccasins as the American Indian's proverb says. For Aspies reading this expression about walking a day in another's moccasins to begin to understand how that person walks through life is of course not literally meant. It means that you have difficulty understanding how other people work mentally, emotionally and socially when you are mind-blind or have a lack of Theory of Mind.

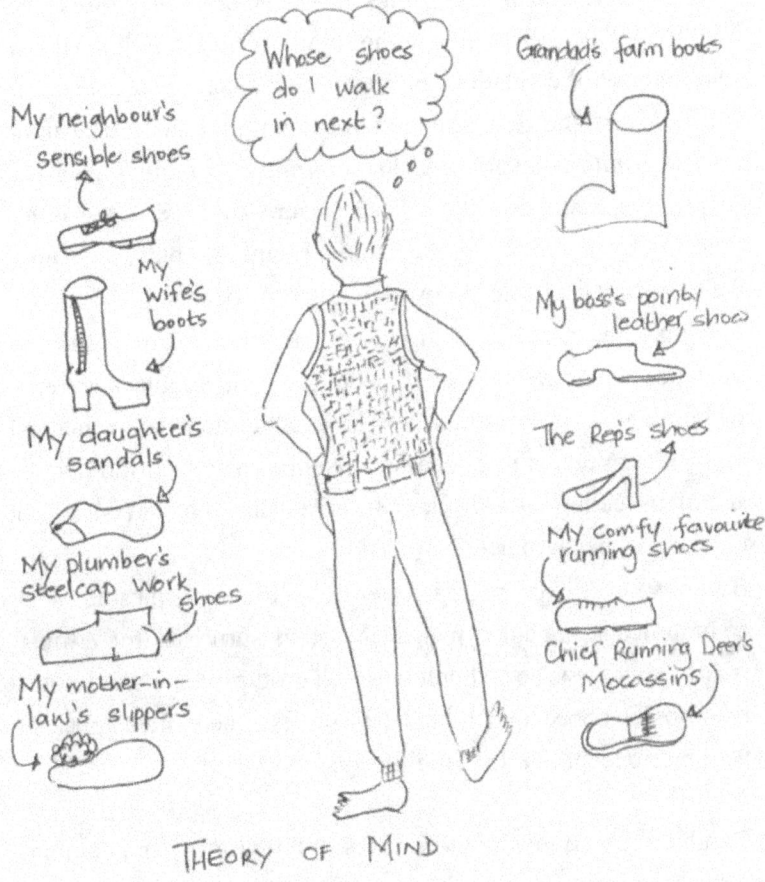

THEORY OF MIND

- This simply means that the person on the ASD spectrum just does not *get* you sometimes, often despite being brilliant intellectuals and maybe even a psychologist or someone passionate about the lives and rights of *human beings* (as Aspies may often refer to people socially).
- You and the ASD person struggle to connect, increasingly as you get to know each other better.
- To cope socially, Aspies will often initially play out a social role that they may have seen in real life or on TV – or some sort of screen (TV is a great Aspie tool for learning about *humans* and the functioning of *humans*). This social mask or veneer can drop very slowly and only if the Aspie feels safe to do so. If they don't feel safe in the relationship, they simply abandon the relationship attempt. Females on the spectrum

will initially play a role that they think is appropriate socially. Unfortunately, the neurotypical (non-Aspie or not neuro-divergent) will initially accept the Aspie and the role as if this were the natural person and often as the relationship develops or comes to an end are quite confused and shocked. A common catch phrase that I hear in my work is: *this is not the person that I met initially – I thought we were on the same page*. Categorically, I need to state that the Aspie is not being deceitful by any means in their initial social role-play; it is simply often the only way they often know how to cope socially.

- This may be a shocking thing to say, but with lack of ToM, Aspies can treat people sometimes as if people are disposable and replaceable, without any awareness that they have either done so, or understanding the ramifications of this behaviour. Neurotypicals are left hurt, confused and often reeling with shock or surprise when they have been subject to this kind of behaviour.

- Because facial expression is often limited, and Aspies are not good at communicating, neurotypicals are often surprised by Aspies' either sudden outbursts or shutdowns. Neurotypicals also do not see a relationship break-up coming from Aspies – there often appears to be no warnings except overload meltdowns.

Some authors extend this mind-blindness a little further and combine it with the poor executive function often found in Aspies, the result being referred to as *context blindness*. In simple English, this can be summed up by saying that Aspies say things inappropriately to their physical circumstances or environment; they may talk loudly at length in a library; they may end a relationship while their partner or spouse is recovering from surgery or has just been made redundant and other very inappropriate social timings. One woman unexpectedly separated from her husband, leaving him with a massive mortgage, which was financed on both incomes; she then declined to pay maintenance (he had the children) as it would affect her mortgage on the new house she had purchased! There was no consideration of her previous financial commitment nor the needs of the family she had left behind.

CONTEXT BLINDNESS

Communication

- Communication in relationships is completely managed by the ways our brains processes information, within each social and communication task.
- Where Aspies are involved, there is a lot of academic terminology that comes through in this relationship context. This terminology includes *poor executive function, cognitive rigidity, limbic and cognitive empathy differences,* and *egocentric; these* are just a few examples of neurological differences in Aspies to the majority of people.
- Poor executive function: This is in the part of the brain that does forecasts, makes plans, and carries those plans out. In communications, there are at least ten (if not many more at times when highly complex thinking and cognitive processing is required) parts of the thinking

(cognitive) brain that work together, but they are all linked. If there are links missing, pathways of thought can just reach a blockage and sometimes not even return to the main thought.

> A friend lived in an apartment block, who after purchase discovered he had some building issues. One of these central issues was around the stopcocks for the plumbing. The first four flats had individual stopcocks, but thereafter the remaining 17 apartments were linked in series to one stopcock. Every time a toilet blocked or there were drainage problems, it affected all the other linked apartments. The stopcock for those 17 apartments had to be turned off every time a plumber was called and because of the poor initial workmanship, that turned out to happen quite frequently and distressingly.

- Cognitive rigidity: It is as if the executive functioning is not flexible. It can be quite rigid at times. The ability to follow the flow of social adaptions is very limited. Those Aspies who can manage (or survive!) the social give-and-takes common to life are usually exhausted afterward each episode and need quiet time or a block of stimming.

> In the TV series, *The Good Doctor*, the autistic surgeon, Dr Shaun Murphy, becomes overwhelmed. At such a time, he freezes physically except for his hands stiffly held in front of him, which hands are then rhythmically shaken by him. In a monotonous tone he repeatedly wails, *No! No!*, and cannot proceed with what he was meant to be doing. In the series, he is diagnosed as having autism.

> When I told a long-term family friend that I was possibly moving to a new house to take up work about 2200 km away, he responded lightly with a false cheer but left almost immediately, shaking, and visibly distressed. It took him many weeks to process it, and he could only endure short conversations with me, until he had processed the emotional shock of my moving away.

- Aspies can appear to be very blunt and direct, and this is sometimes offensive, especially to neurotypicals. They are even more so when overwhelmed or overloaded.

- Egocentricity: Lack of theory of mind automatically seems to predispose one to egocentricity. Little children are usually always egocentric.

EGOCENTRICITY

Differences in Limbic and Cognitive Empathy:

The limbic system in the brain is where our feelings happen – it is the emotional headquarters in the brain. We can have emotional sympathy which is where we feel the pain or distress of the other, and we can have cognitive sympathy in which we imagine the pain the other could be going through. So we could imagine that it must have been terrible for the office lady's best friend's mother to have passed, but we do not fully feel emotional empathy, as we neither know, nor are with, that person (the best friend in this example). But if a neurotypical were beside that person, the neurotypical would feel an emotional empathy too, as they relate to that person directly (the person who has lost their mother), even if we are not close to that person. Neurotypical and/or healthy empathy involves both kinds of empathy, simultaneously. Because Aspies have poor emotional expression and awareness, plus a lack of theory of mind, they can only respond with cognitive empathy, which is like intellectual sympathy. Even in this, they may also be socially awkward and inappropriate.

- Despite often being very caring and very moral, Aspies often lack emotional empathy. At most, you may get cognitive empathy. The sense of being empathetically connected is often not there.
- They are, in my words, detail-centric. They can be fastidious, meticulous and pedantic about details but will often miss the main point of a discussion as they get stuck in the hamster-wheel of details.
- They interpret situations literally.
- Aspies can easily become overloaded. This could be mentally or emotionally. If they do get to this state, they shut down and will withdraw or stim if they are not in a public place.

> I can't remember where I heard or read this, but one Aspie said that his brain felt like his laptop – when too many windows were open and running at once, then the laptop either ran more slowly or froze (or *crashed*).

- Aspies have huge emotions but have difficulty both processing them and expressing them. I sometimes use a metaphor of a dam being full but only having a straw to drain it.

Sensitivities

- Aspies have sensory issues. They may be sensitive to one or many or all the issues that affect the senses: visual such as light or movement, auditory, olfactory (smell), taste, texture and touch.
- A sensitivity issue can hugely affect a relationship.
- Light can be too bright, the mohair jumper is too itchy, there might be too much noise in the room – and the list is a significantly long one!

Common Aspie Comorbidities: (Neurotypicals also have comorbidities)

- They may have social issues and anxieties
- They may be struggling with depression
- They may have an eating disorder
- They may be coping (or self-medicating) with the use of illegal drugs, marijuana, or alcohol abuse
- They may be struggling because of a history of bullying in social circles, which memory still invades every potential relationship
- The comorbidities are quite extensive. Although many neurotypicals also have comorbidities, Aspies seem to a have a higher risk of having comorbid issues.

Male and Female Aspies are Different

- Although there are many similarities, for example ToM, communication issues, sensitivity and cognitive issues, and obsessive interests, male Aspies appear to have more of a double male brain as compared to neurotypical males generally, and females seem to have a more of a male brain than neurotypical females. Female Aspies appear to be more intuitive than male Aspies who appear to have the minimal intuition that goes with a double male brain.
- Male Aspies can commit a major social faux pas and be oblivious of it; female Aspies may do the same but then become aware that something is wrong. Sometimes the females can work it out and sort it out. Males don't generally try as they are unaware. When the males are confronted about this, they may shut down and respond in flight or fight mode, and they may be a bit aggressive with it (aggression in males in fight or flight mode is not unusual once that mode is switched on in the brain).
- Female Aspies can camouflage or mask their ASD to some degree when in social circles. They are also good at mimicking neurotypical females. When Aspie females drop the camouflage or mask, or stop mimicking, the other partner is often left very confused and sometimes angry, with a sense of either being deceived or used (which of course was unlikely to ever be the Aspies' intention).
- Aspie females who are socially confused, or when the mask comes down, often act in classic passive-aggressive ways. This can be

extremely difficult to live with. It is also unpredictable when another passive-aggressive series of confrontations will occur.

Couple Relationships: Background

It is important to note that all relationships are affected by both parties and what they bring into the relationship. When we are talking about what the Aspie brings into the relationship, there is no intention in this writing that exonerates the other party, whether neurotypical or not, from what they contribute positively and negatively to the relationship. The focus on this chapter is exclusively though on the Aspie strengths and difficulties and how they could and have affected their relationships.

Most research on couple relationships in which there is at least one partner who is on the spectrum is based on heterosexual relationships. The vast majority of relationships are heterosexual, as most societies are significantly dominated by heterosexual behaviour. A minority of Aspie relationships are same-sex, although this is statistically slightly higher than same-sex neurotypical relationships. Regardless of the gender or sexual orientation of the relationship, the issues remain the same in many ways, in terms of how ASD affects the relationships. Heterosexual or gay relationships are both affected by ToM (mind-blindness), communication issues, sensory issues, obsessive interests and behaviours of the Aspie partner (or both if both partners are on the spectrum) and the typical comorbidities of the Aspie partner.

Aspies on the whole are warm, caring, kind partners. They are usually intelligent and have a quirky but funny sense of humour. They often are hard-workers and are positively motivated. They thrive on routines and rituals. They love order and structure (even if they can't make it happen themselves), and predictability. They thrive on being told exactly who is coming over, why and for how long the visitor will stay. They then focus quite often on hospitality and are generous in their hospitality. And if they are well in themselves and feel safe and can trust who they are with, they can even put up with those times of crazy social timetables, loud eating and neurotypical habits of sometimes breaking the rules (assuming of course the Aspie has a neurotypical partner) when socialising with a group of neurotypicals.

They won't:

- Support you unless you tell them how to, in detail!
- Intuitively pick up on what you are feeling – tell them!
- Know they are offending you – explain how they are and tell them what you would prefer!
- They probably won't be spontaneous! There is the rare Aspie that is impulsive and extroverted but that is relatively atypical.
- They probably will not join the conversation much when all your friends come over – enjoy your friends and let your Aspie have some space.

The magic that makes a relationship work is thrice –
Communication, communication, communication. Forget abracadabra!

Communication is about:
Words
Listening
The right timing and space
Staying focussed on the important subject
Listening more
Thinking
Explaining again
Listening more
Respect
Not jumping to conclusions
No accusations
Reflective listening
No character annihilations
Taking turns
Listening even more
Not assuming
A positive attitude that never shifts
Laughing
Trying again
Until you get it right
Then remember the pattern that worked and use it again

If it were two neurotypicals, I would say that eye contact and maybe even a little physical contact (like rubbing the other's hand) would be useful. But this is not a dual neurotypical relationship so – although it would be good for the Aspie to try to make a little eye contact and maybe a gentle fond touch to their neurotypical partner, you probably cannot expect it.

> You will need a different pattern, as below…
>
> Advise this person ahead of time that you want a conversation
> Tell them what the main topic is
> Don't blindside an Aspie
> (Actually, don't blindside anyone!)
> Do not stare in your Aspies' eyes
> Do not touch your Aspie unless they ask
> Stick to one subject until you are finished
> Talk in a quiet safe space
> No noise, bright lights, running children, swings moving in a playground
> No sickly food smells or perfumes
> No shouting – a low quiet voice is best
> No time pressures
> Then give your Aspie time to think and process
> Agree to meet again and finish if need be

Starting a Relationship

The movies are full of romance scenarios. In half an hour, the time of an average sitcom including advertisements, a couple meet after having never have met before, soon they kiss and then they have sex. Quite predictably. Culturally, in most TV shows, we have also shifted from the male taking the lead role in this romance game, to women mostly taking a dominating role at times (also in under 20 minutes) and like some of the old male roles, the woman are aggressively pursuing the man sexually. There are many issues with this scenario, but the main ones are that:

- Relationships in reality do not happen that fast.
- Consent is not present – although everyone behaves as if this is a consensual process, do not assume that this is so.
- Aspies, especially females, often use movies as *how to do relationships* guides. This then opens them to many risks and sometimes in compromised situations.

How utterly confusing for any young relationships, but even more so for Aspies – especially females.

In reality, research shows that genuine relationships take:

- Being in the same space at the same time
- Some sort of healthy initial conversations and mutual interest
- Time
- Compatibility
- Agreement
- Authentic interest at most levels
- Understanding of each other and learning about each other
- Learning to share resources
- Learning to share lifestyles
- A genuine mutual friendship
- Similar goals
- Some testing of faithfulness and character
- And ultimately, forgiveness at times.

We can't do all of that in 21 minutes and 33 seconds (the time of that ad-less average sitcom) and have a wild sexual relationship. Additionally, even with all of the above key ingredients for a good relationship, a good relationship still cannot be totally guaranteed even if all the other conditions are met.

Aspie girls can sometimes intuit if someone is interested in them, but they cannot filter out an unhealthy person, a manipulator or a predator necessarily. It seems that a significantly (from statistical analysis on the subject) larger proportion of Aspie women than neurotypical women are sexually abused or assaulted, or are forced to have non-consensual sexual relations. Sometimes they do not read the warning signs in the behaviour of the other; sometimes they are simply naïve and are quickly taken advantage of. Sometimes they feel that they have somehow contributed to the situation and the social rule that they have made for themselves is that they need to see it through as they had come this far. On the other hand, I have met men on the ASD spectrum aged up to 30, who have never managed a committed short, or even less likely, a long-term relationship. Their few fumbling attempts are awkwardly explained, and a couple of men even recalled, with enormous embarrassment, how they had been led on by a pretty young woman to the hilarious amusement of her friends who were all secretly making fun of him. For a few men, they had had sexual contact through a sex worker that they had paid.

> I met one man, on the spectrum with a low-ish intelligence. He was aged in his early forties. He had been hiring sex workers weekly since his twenties. He had never had a relationship outside of family connections, other than these. His social skills were appalling and he could not relate to people at all. He had come to see me as he was an otherwise devout Christian man, and he suffered enormous guilt for his *sin* as he perceived it. He also longed for a healthy relationship. Getting him a job at a local supermarket seemed to help him with some social skills. He belonged to a small church group at which there were no single women. It was a very difficult situation for him. We explored him changing over to a bigger church. We also explored maybe some basic hygiene as he needed a bit of cleaning up. Unfortunately, there were some other socially uncomfortable habits that I could not get him to break, and he firmly resisted any changes except for getting a *trolley boy* job at the supermarket (which he maintained until retirement).

Despite these stories, not all Aspie men and Aspie women are as described as above, and I would not like anyone to get that negative picture. Most are well presented and spoken and have a level of social skills that can be developed.

Early Stages of a Relationship

Important message! Remember that everyone is unique! Just as one rule does not identify and classify all neurotypicals, one person on the ASD spectrum does not reflect all people on the ASD spectrum. Neurotypicals and spectrum people are all human beings – the two groups just have some differences in the brain wiring.

Research consistently shows that people in relationships generally report that they are happier and appear to have less issues with mental and physical health, and report less loneliness. The few research projects done, report similar results for Aspies, despite many Aspies having a need to have a lot of time alone too.

Neurotypicals have hierarchies and protocols, multiple subscripts and agendas in their communication. They have layers called subtexts in their conversations. They give subtle cues, clues, and signals when a taboo topic is raised, meaning they do not want to participate in that conversation anymore. Aspies miss most of these, sometimes all of these (especially the males on the spectrum). So in the early stages of a relationship, some important conversations can be missed or misunderstood, which would probably block that conversation going forward.

When you are starting a relationship, the initial contact is important. There needs to be a:

- good level of hygiene (clean teeth, breath, no body odour, clean clothes)
- using space appropriately – not standing too close to a person nor too far away, face the person you are talking to, try to be aware of surroundings and not knock things over, try not to block other people.
- talking appropriately about subject matters common and pleasant, or important, to both such as ready-made pre-prepared topics like: "How was your day", and "Did you finish that assignment your group was working on?"
- try to dress appropriately: for example, don't wear your lucky childhood yellow and orange beanie that your grandma knitted because you always loved the sparkly pompom to your new girlfriend's graduation ball.

It appears that neurologically different parts of the brain are activated (often referred to as *light up* from the terminology used in brain scans in which an active part of the brain *lights up* on monitors) in conversations between Aspies and neurotypicals. In one study, the same story was read to Aspies and neurotypicals. The story intended to explore Theory of Mind, so that the subjects of the study had to use Theory of Mind to work out what the protagonist of the story was thinking and intending. On the scans, the neurotypicals *lit up* in the prefrontal cortex, which is the part of the brain that uses insight, reason, and understanding around relationships. In Aspies, the frontal cortex *lit up*, which is the part that does problem solving and the manipulation of data or information.

This shows that Aspies and neurotypicals process relationships differently – *and should therefore both have an understanding and respect that the other works differently neurologically. Once we understand that, a lot more progress can be made more quickly!* Basically, an Aspie uses their maths [or STEM] brain for relationships! Yet I have helped neurotypical people with maths over the years, and they often responded emotionally! Neither of the above makes any sense, but that's what people do – people are not robots that their workings should make sense!

> Years ago, I was teaching my very intelligent, very empathetic, colleague the PWI [Personal Wellbeing Index] and WHODAS [World Health Organisation Disability Assessment Schedule] measurements. We needed these simple statistics for a major insurance organisation, for clients that were referred to us from them. This colleague struggled with them and was considering not working for the insurance company anymore but as a last resort asked for help, and so I happily met with her. These tests use very basic, uncomplicated arithmetic and repeatedly follow the same process. They are basically looking for an average, an arithmetical process that a ten-year-old can probably achieve. As I started explaining the PWI (the simpler of the two tests), the tears started rolling down her cheeks. I stopped – utterly confused and tried to work out what was happening for her. She said that she was terrified of anything to do with numbers. She calmed herself down, and we started again. She immediately became more stressed. She calmed herself down again. She then started having a mild panic attack. She remembered struggling with maths at school and feeling ashamed. We calmed down her panic attack, got her breathing and self-regulating again. After a few more attempts at trying to teach her to understand the simple processes, I changed tack. I suggested that she do this like a recipe. She didn't have to understand how the ingredients worked or worked together, or why. I wrote out two *recipes* for the two above statistical processes and left a happy lady who could now cope. Her whole response to maths was emotional!

So back to relationships…

Aspies cannot assess complex relationship situations. They are better at more limited group numbers. Aspie women can do social gatherings and parties, but they do have difficulty with the give-and-take of conversation, small talk, and managing multiple relationships in a larger group. They are more likely to find a smaller group of no more than three other people although they would probably prefer one-on-one neutral conversations. If opportunities to escape arise, they are quite likely to absent themselves and help with the chores, disappear to help the children (they are often very good with children) or sometimes cuddle or play with the family pet. These small coping behaviours just squeaks them through the social minefield without drawing negative attention. For a couple, he needs to ensure that she is feeling safe and comfortable and to make allowances for her needs as she will desperately try to please him by participating to the best of her abilities. She is less likely than a male Aspie to make social gaffs but more likely than a neurotypical. If your partner is male, he will find the social scene even more difficult. Be kind and compassionate to him and make a plan around his difficulties.

> A small group of nursing students were discussing the upcoming placements with each other, after class. One young man, who was already doing some practical time in the hospital theatre, mentioned how much he was enjoying theatre. The Aspie nurse turned to him and asked where he was performing and that she would get tickets and come and support his show! The group went silent and stared at her in shock. She had completely missed the whole context of the group discussion and had only picked up on a few words!

In discussions reflecting on the early stages of their relationship and what they found attractive about their Aspie partner, people explained as follows. Women with Aspie males report being attracted to their non-aggressive, fairly placid, even submissive at times, ways. Men with Aspie females report they enjoyed the lack of mind games, there were no ulterior motives nor subtle hints to understand, their independence and their apparent lack of neediness.

If you are an Aspie, being aware of some habits that you may have, that affects neurotypicals, is very helpful. This may be the habit of interrupting conversations or talking over people, possibly picking at your toenails in public, or even maybe blocking your ears midsentence as your potential partner is speaking because you find the background too noisy. These are all early warning relationship *off-putters*! This may well mean that the person will not follow up with a subsequent date.

> I met a young man on the spectrum who wanted to have a relationship with a female. He had had three rather brief relationships of a few months each, since leaving school. He was 36. He presented well initially, was quiet and polite, attentive, well dressed, was intelligent and was financially quite secure. Although he was employed out of home part time, he also owned a small farm that needed management and care. He liked animals and thought he would like a couple of children one day (said in the same sentence as he did). In a sense, a matchmaker's delight! As we talked and he relaxed a little into the session (we were using his problem-solving brain about relationships), he suddenly startled. I couldn't understand this as the office was quiet, softly lit, soft-coloured walls with no sensitivity-triggering distractions. We continued the conversation as I pondered this. Suddenly again, for no reason that I could understand, he did another major startle response. After the third one, I asked him why he did that (it was very distracting, to say the least!). He was actually oblivious of it so we agreed that I would point out the next one that he did. Again, he was oblivious of it when the next one occurred. He moved onto talking about his main obsessions, which were wrestling and global spiritualities and religions – with many more startle responses as he relaxed into his happy places. All of this was at our first 50-minute meeting in the safest possible environment for an Aspie – I could only imagine how a date at a busy restaurant with music in the background would go for him!

Most Aspies, male and female, through research, report that their initial attraction to a person is not usually physical or sexual. They had usually connected over a common topic or sometimes an interest. The connection for the Aspie is usually a mental or intellectual connection.

At the beginning of a relationship, the Aspie male just wants to please. This is not uncommon in neurotypical relationships either, but there seems to be a higher drive to please from Aspies.

> One man, who invited his new girlfriend to dinner with his mum and dad asked what food she liked. She said roast. So he went home and insisted his mother only cook a roast, in order to please this new girlfriend. (Just as he demanded, his mum followed his instructions and later in the relationship, the man had the same expectation of his partner. He was very intelligent and could make very cutting remarks when he was displeased with her non-compliance!)

When an Aspie discovers an interest, they can be very focussed, sometimes almost obsessively so. Some Aspie men are described as flirts, especially if they have an interest in a person, because of the intensity of their look, how close they may stand, and how they consciously try to get the other's attention whether with words or gifts (or both!). *I have heard the expression that there is nothing more amazing than coming under the gaze of an Aspie man or woman – especially if he or she is interested in you.* For a season, this attraction for the Aspie can replace their obsessive interest and be a temporary obsessive interest in its place – only temporary though! This intensity can be, and often is, mistaken as attraction and has led to many misunderstandings and confusion later on.

Alternatively for example, at parties, Aspies can sometimes inexplicably stand too close and gaze too intensely at a person that they have met. They are *not* flirting, but the other person will not know that. Either a flirting situation will evolve and probably end up as a misunderstanding, or maybe move to a stage that an Aspie never foresaw, or the other party may become uncomfortable and remove themselves.

> A friend of mine had an Aspie brother who attended a social gathering with her. She had a close relationship with him, could manage his occasional indiscretions, and he respected and listened to her. I chatted to him because he was starting to look distressed. Unfortunately, he took this as a personal interest and invite to a relationship and would then start arriving randomly at my house and want to be very physically close to me. I had to ask his sister to please discourage him from visiting me.

Often, Aspies have great *off the wall* jokes. They are funny. Probably because humour employs creativity, intelligence and makes use of creative lateral thinking. Also because they think of multiple things at once (because of their lateral thinking), they sometimes deliberately present the ludicrous, which is usually funny.

Aspies can sometimes have an unusual definition of what constitutes an intimate relationship.

> One Aspie man had a relationship and what he believed to be a deep and committed friendship, or at least he perceived it that way, with a woman online, who had a chat site, which seemed to me to be mildly pornographic and erotic. He sent her as much money as he could and spoke to her most days. He had never met her, did not know her real name or where she lived, had never physically had sex with her, and knew that she was doing some online porn for other men as she complained to him about their demands. He had come to see me as he had had three relationships end dramatically – this relationship he considered as one of them. He considered this online relationship as equally a full and legitimate relationship as his first two with physical people were.

Aspies are not usually ego driven. A rare few become narcissistic but that is a comorbidity and unusual – and this rare touch of narcissism can appear ego driven.

Aspies seem to be unaware that they have communication and social issues. Many have told me that they are wonderful communicators, when they are blatantly and obviously missing cues and relating skills.

They may not get the facials or body language right so a statement may come across as sarcastic, especially if they are glaring at you in an effort to make steady (but difficult for them) eye contact.

An Aspie can talk for hours but not about personal feelings or their relationship. Unless you directly question an Aspie (who will usually answer truthfully and not mind being questioned), one can leave a long conversation with an Aspie with lots of facts and knowledge of their interests but not having found out much about the person at all. A neurotypical will then walk away, in their mind not feeling a *connection*, which is important in neurotypical relationships.

Aspies find it difficult to hide their sensitivities so after a while – sometimes even on the first meeting or date, their sensitivities will become obvious. Be compassionate – these difficulties are genuine!

> I used to think that I was very clever and would jokingly say that the old legend of the princess and the pea was obviously an Aspie story. After all my reading, others have made similar comments. I am not that clever it seems!

Couple Relationships (Long Term)

We live in a neurotypical world that significantly outnumbers the Aspie world. If you are in a relationship with an Aspie, at some point the differences will become noticeable.

Introduction

This is about those differences. It is a fault of Aspie books, and a fault of this chapter too, that Aspies are usually compared to neurotypicals, which suggests that neurotypical ways of doing things is the right way. It is not, but neurotypicals are the dominant hegemony, which is why comparisons happen this way. The hegemon, in this case, are the neurotypicals. Neurotypicals do many things that an Aspie is unlikely to do. They are more likely to be unfaithful; they are more likely to have varying and subtle levels of meaning in every conversation; they are more likely to convey their meaning through body language than through words, and they are more likely to be bullies.

A further important addendum that needs to be brought to attention here is that most of the literature on relationships is based on heterosexual relationships. It seems though that regardless of the type of couple relationship, most relationships that have an Aspie in it have slightly other differences than relationships in which both parties are neurotypical (again, the dominant relationships worldwide).

Gestalt philosophy is underscored by the principle that *the whole is greater than the sum of its parts*. In the paragraphs below, I have put down multiple examples so that any reader can get a better and more significant whole picture and understanding. It is a multiple mix of behaviours and situations, and social applications, which wear both parties down over time.

Finally, all the elements and misunderstanding described below are common in neurotypical relationships too but usually in a more diluted form. I have found that in most discussions when comparing Aspies to neurotypicals, that the behaviours are more at either end of the spectrum of behaviours, rather than in the middle range of behaviours (or misbehaviours) that are common to neurotypicals.

Neurotypicals often do poorly in relationships with Aspies too, mainly because they keep assuming that the Aspie will behave like a neurotypical. The neurotypical in the relationship with their lovely Aspie needs to completely reframe their expectations and behaviours and look creatively for better and healthier options around their relationship.

The remainder of this chapter is done in a series of bytes – each byte adds another aspect so that *the whole becomes greater than the sum of its parts*.

Finally, in most of the comments below, the reverse is often the true effect of Neurotypicals on Aspies!

Social and Communication Effects Where ASD Is in the Relationship

- Neurotypicals usually bear the burden of socialising, communication, and all the intra and extra family interrelationships. Neurotypicals need these anyway – even if they are introverted neurotypicals. Aspie female partners or wives are usually aware of social responsibilities and will follow through with that quite dutifully rather than socially. For example, they might be good cooks and the extended family then expects them to cater for functions and they take up the duty. Aspie women are also sensitive to social rules, so will try to apply them particularly if her partner or spouse is introverted or unsocial, despite being a neurotypical.
- Aspie men and women seem to desperately want to make their spouse or partner happy, but because of their various cognitive differences and social issues, they often get things wrong. The partner or spouse becomes angry and disappointed over time. They try harder. It is a cycle that is hard to break and needs help from a very experienced counsellor to straighten out.
- Aspies don't do subtexts and games. Neurotypicals are always looking for that other or deeper social meaning which can trigger an uncomfortable conversational cycle particularly if one speaker is on the spectrum.

- Aspergic men often appear kind, gentle, and are often quietly still. This often makes them quite attractive to women. They do not appear to be predisposed to being sexually driven. They are usually attracted to strong, independent, highly socially wired women.
- Many Aspies, especially males, will not communicate with their partner, spouse, or a family member if they do not think that this is necessary. How they formulate what is and is not necessary is often the problem. This can lead to many misunderstandings and hurts. When the Aspie is calm again, confront this process and discuss how as a couple you need to handle this better.

- Aspies need their partners to help with social stuff. If you are neurotypical in a relationship with an Aspie, then don't assume she/he knows what to do in a social situation – even if they have done it before.
- Conversations with Aspies can sometimes be monologues. It could be a series of bytes about his day. One woman was frustrated because her husband came home after work every day and talked at her. He felt that he was responding to the *tell me about your day* conversation that they had once had. It seems completely egocentric. It's not, so please be generous with your Aspie who is trying very hard to meet your neurotypical social needs. They are usually not capable of many words at the end of a day at work!
- There may actually be no plan to a day because it is a couple or family rest and recovery day. Sometimes even these have different meanings.

> One woman thought that they would have a *chill* day as a family. She had not clarified to her Aspie husband what this meant to her and was furious that he happily went off to play a computer game on his own. Not only was she left minding their several children, she had imagined a family day doing something relaxing together – a rarity in their busy lives.

- One of the effects of mind-blindness is a lack of awareness of how one's actions will affect the other person. This is very important when living in a relationship as people need to realise that there are consequences for their loved one or partner or even children.
    - One man and his friend call these mind-blindness moments *a Spergs moment*. That's the word-tip for the Aspie man from his friend to then take a hint and check the effect that he is having socially.
- Aspies can be generous, thoughtful hosts if they put their mind to it. They can also be interesting, even if their topics of conversation might be a little quirky. They generally do not enjoy conversations around emotions or abstracts, but fact-based conversation will usually engage them delightfully.
- Neurotypicals may often lie, because in reading the social communication, they see that this is often what the other person's neurotypicalness wants to hear. They do this because the strand of the

communication that is most important is about wanting to feel good, not about the truth. Unfortunately, Aspies will never get this, which leads to the Aspies arguing that they *only told the truth* after somebody has stormed out. That somebody may be deeply hurt, mortified or angry. We may thank someone for a lovely dinner, when in fact it was quite horrible.

> One couple were invited to lunch by a lady in their church. They had a big family, so invites were rare. When they got there, the host had made soup that contained rice to obviously extend the meal, but the rice was badly burnt and black. It was revolting. The kids politely struggled through the meal as their neurotypical mum told them to be polite. Everyone turned down second helpings, but the Aspie husband was so rude about it that they were never invited out to dinner there again.

- Aspies are often bullied. As a partner if you do nothing when your loved one is being bullied, then you are complicitly bullying too. Don't let the neighbours, your friends or your family (or even *their* family) isolate and attack her with their subtle social rules and demands.
- Socialising: Some Aspies resent their partner's socialising – especially if it interrupts their routine. They may also demand that their partner focus primarily on them only.

> One man would come home and be very rude to his wife's guests or his children's friends and demand that they leave immediately so that he could have quiet! The family were often and obviously, very embarrassed. He had to learn to share his home when necessary and they were more cautious about having friends over when he was expected home.

- Aspie males can be particularly insensitive in many social situations. They may ask a larger lady whether she is fat or pregnant. It might be the question that everyone is wondering especially if the lady in question was considering having a baby – the Aspie though is more likely to blurt out that question! Another Aspie male used to mock people who had unusual surnames, thinking he was being conversational.

- Aspies can be great communicators at work; examples include teachers, lecturers, accountants, journalists, or lawyers. This is because they are communicating facts. When they come home, they appear to often switch off their communication button (metaphorically, of course). They need time to process and change into their new environment headspace. Once they have unwound and been prepared for an important conversation or event, they can generally manage quite well.
- Aspies can be very interesting conversationalists and can have some robust arguments. They can make excellent debaters!
- If you are playing games at a social event, such as Taboo or Poker – then you definitely need an Aspie at your side. They remember the rules, do not take on the emotional pressure and they think at such speed that they are quick and responsive. The Aspie team will usually win!
- Neurotypicals often struggle with relational resentment. They often feel like they are always doing all the emotional and social work in the relationship.
- Aspies can be so very blunt and direct. There are no mind games there. Conflict happens when neurotypicals in the relationship put their own, usually emotionally slanted, interpretation on what the Aspie has said. They may perceive the Aspie as being sarcastic, smart, rude, or even hurtful. Of course, usually the Aspie never intended this. Without understanding each other, the Aspie and the neurotypical will find it difficult to resolve these moments.
- Many Aspies, especially male Aspies, have difficulty reading social situations. This can cause embarrassment to the neurotypical spouse or partner, and of course to others in a public setting. It can certainly cause a huge argument when the neurotypical gets home after such a social event and wants to tell their partner how difficult the situation had been for them. (Plus of course, the partner wants to *fix* the other and prevent them from making such blunders again.)

> A woman accompanied her Aspie husband to a dinner at the house of one of her husband's work colleagues. Another couple from work was also there. Their host offered her husband some *forcemeat* from the chicken, but her husband heard that he was being offered the *foreskin* of a chicken! For the remaining two hours, he could not resist coming back repeatedly to this hilarious (for him) mistake of the host and never once got that the other guest and his wife cringed with embarrassment repeatedly, with cold polite smiles. He took the smiles as the company enjoying his humour, so he kept coming back to the subject.

- Aspies seem to be self-contained and live in their own world, yet often needing to make occasional people-contact. They may do this social withdrawal with lack of eye contact and closed body language – the non-verbal communication that can say that I am not interested in you. Of course, the Aspie is usually totally unaware of this body language. Of course, all people need time alone too, and Aspies even more so. The important message here though is that as a neurotypical, don't rely on their body language – ask them what they need. Also encourage them from time to time to have social contact if you are in a close relationship with an Aspie.
- Neurotypicals may need to find additional emotional outlets and fulfilment elsewhere, in appropriate healthy relationships such as friendships and relating to extended family and siblings. Aspies can be wonderful partners and spouses. It is important to remember all the strengths that they may bring to a committed relationship. I have heard of situations in which the neurotypical partner has had affairs on their Aspie partner, but I do not believe that this is a healthy option and do not condone it!
- With social rules, sometimes Aspies, particularly males, have to be taught basic hygiene. Others of course are immaculate and perfectly clean and tidy.

- Aspies are very sensitive to perceived criticisms and can perceive criticisms that were never there. Part of this can be attributed to not being understood most of their lives, the other part is the lack of insight and ToM, so that they try to solve the relationship issues with logic. As the two parties will appear to continually misunderstand each other, the situation could possibly become highly inflammatory.
- Aspies are literal and logical, so a question that may require a gentle and insightful answer from them, can sometimes draw a response that is blunt (some say 'brutal') in its honesty and frankness.

- Aspies are not good at empathy although they are very good at sympathy (often referred to as emotional empathy and cognitive/intellectual empathy). Aspie men often lack insight and may try to find a logical solution to the problem that he perceives his neurotypical partner is having. The illustration on the previous page clearly describes a typical pattern between couples that usually does not end well...
- Because of mind-blindness (which is the difficulty to accurately read non-verbal communication and intentions of others) combined with the speed of their thinking, Aspies often interrupt and will then proceed to talk over others.

> One woman was talking to her adult son who had returned to university. Although living separately and independently, finances were tight for him, and she helped him out from time to time. She noticed that his car's licence was about to expire. In New Zealand, a vehicle requires periodic overall checks done by a registered mechanic to make sure it is safe, before getting the full roadworthy licence and annual registration renewed. She mentioned the licence (as he was notorious for forgetting to do this over the years) and his immediate and loud response was – *I am not going to that [particular mechanic]. I don't like him.* Actually, she hadn't even considered any mechanic and what was actually on her mind was that she was offering to pay for the costs and renewing his licence and that process. She was nearly annoyed enough at his rude and loud outburst to withdraw the offer. This is an example between a mother and son but couple relationships can often have a similar pattern.

- It appears that a significant number of neurotypicals in an unhealthy, long term relationship with an Aspie, often struggle with depression too. Neurotypicals need their emotions acknowledged and given a validity within the relationship. Many neurotypicals in relationships with Aspies complain primarily about not *feeling* emotionally connected, which concepts Aspies often cannot comprehend. When I deal with couple relationships in which only one partner may be on the spectrum, I often have to deal with the overlay of depression for them first.
- Because of the many Aspie misunderstandings, neurotypicals in long-term relationships with an Aspie may commonly develop the habit of

over-explaining everything to everyone, to mainly prevent misunderstandings. Any signs of offence in another person that they are with or communicating to, will often trigger them to either shut down or draw further explanations. One daughter patiently said to her mum one day, when her mum wavered and struggled to say something: "Just get to the point, Mum. It's okay to say what you mean." But that's what she saw her mum do with the dad in the relationship, trying to steer a conversation about an important matter that would not lead to a blowout in some way by him.

Context Blindness and Its Effects on Relationships:

- Generally, they do not say *I love you*. They have said it once and that is usually sufficient. Some Aspies learn to say it as a rote at times, like saying goodbye and going to work. Others say it because there is a rule to say so. One lovely Aspie man tells his wife that he loves her every time they have finished making love. Generally speaking though, Aspies seem to find this a difficult statement to say to their loved ones, whereas neurotypicals can say it quite easily and flick off this statement often. Unfortunately, neurotypicals need to hear it being said often too, especially female neurotypicals.
- Aspies are not good at giving praise. They don't understand that need for affirmation, which neurotypicals have. Their praise can be stilted and false sounding when forced – such as when a rule is made that they have to deliver praise in a particular situation. If you are on the spectrum, then make a list of compliments neurotypicals like and praise that you would be comfortable about expressing, for example, praising a well-cooked meal or a child who does something good or correct. An example could be: "That was a delicious lamb korma" or "You stroked that little dog so carefully that he seems to like you" (if you see a child being kind to a puppy).

> It would be good to check with someone that your praise is appropriate. One Aspie man would complement the cooking of a host by pointing out which parts of the meals were cooked better than the way his wife cooked it! And she was at the table sharing the meal!

- Aspies can often miss the context of where they are when they are speaking. They can speak overly loudly and not be aware of being heard. They also miss the self-consciousness of the neurotypical when they are doing this, so continue boldly on the same course. Sometimes a neurotypical partner will need to warn them, especially if the message being broadcast is of a sensitive nature!
- Aspie partners can be hypercritical, often cruelly so, although the seeming cruelty and bluntness is generally unintentional. Their need to get things right is a major factor that plays into their being hypercritical. They will bluntly speak out the facts of a matter, regardless of either the appropriateness of that, simultaneously with the inability to read how the other person (or persons) is receiving those bald statements. Of course, these are the reasons that they make great lawyers, surgeons, and engineers. They are factual, on task and not easily distracted.
- If she is still socially mimicking, then she will see what famous people do with their hair, clothes, and home design and try to imitate that. It would be loving in a relationship then to have a discussion about what works for both of you and make some new couple rules.
- Attending parties: a drunk Aspie is difficult to deal with, as of course is any neurotypical drunk at times! Alcohol often removes inhibitions, which is a well-known fact. An adult will have many inhibitions about social behaviour. These inhibitions help to make most social situations glide along fairly amicably and smoothly. A drunk neurotypical is difficult to deal with. A drunk Aspie can also be difficult for other reasons – it seems that any gating of their Aspieness slowly disappears. One man may talk to everybody about his specialist interest area; another may become extroverted after a few drinks and may make very loud, crude, and inappropriate jokes.

> One quiet teacher that I knew would become very loud and extroverted after a few drinks at a party. He would want to dance but being quite dyspraxic, it was difficult to dance with him. He would then jump up and down on the spot and insist everyone *pogo* with him, and sometimes, he could get a whole dance floor to cooperate – until they had had enough, although he had not. Eventually, party after party, year after year, other people became sick of this, but he never noticed

> and continued pursuing the matter. His embarrassed wife told him very firmly to *back off* and that he was annoying other people. He was mortified as he thought it had been such fun and thought that others had enjoyed his invented dance as much as he did.

- Aspies can be very literal. They often miss blatant contextual or emotional cues. Explain clearly what you want done or what you need from them.
- There can be multiple issues around context blindness.

> One woman told her husband a fact that had been given to her confidentially about a friend who had an embarrassing health issue. He didn't realise that it was confidential, so he blurted it out in a public setting at another time. He thought he was acting interested and was being conversational.

- An Aspie will often cause relationship issues by recalling a specific, detailed memory, but the contextual memory is hazy. This has caused many arguments between couples.

One Aspie man was married to a neurotypical woman who was a teetotaller. The Aspie had over the years of their marriage become an alcoholic and this caused issues for his wife (and family). In a counselling session, when his drinking was challenged and the wife said that she could no longer live with *a drunk,* he furiously responded that she had had a whole bottle of wine all by herself and she would also have been drunk. This completely confused the wife as she could not see how he had come to this conclusion. Knowing he was usually truthful; she knew there had to be something he related his statement to. She then recalled that on one occasion, more than twenty-five years previously as a young woman of 19, they had spent the day with two friends. Their friends had insisted that the wife try a particular local-estate glass of red wine. This was over an early lunch. She had a sip and did genuinely enjoy the flavour, so she had a glassful. The couple helped their friends set up for the night for a party to celebrate an event that neither of them could recall. The party finished about in the early hours of the

> morning. The couple were staying the night. At about 1.30, she had a third glass of wine, which finished the bottle the friends had insisted she have as she had enjoyed the wine so much. So over a period of about 14 hours she had three 250 ml glasses of red wine with food, which constituted the 750 ml bottle of wine. She did not recall being drunk nor any behaviour that indicated drunkenness on her part. Apart from that one bottle of wine (which she had genuinely savoured and enjoyed), she had never had alcohol again. Yet he held onto that justification that she had had a bottle of wine to herself and *was drunk herself* (as he assumed) more than 25 years ago.

Talk about context blindness! This is of course an extreme example, but is a stand-out, typical display of how an Aspie can argue their facts.

Managing Emotions around Aspies, Including When They Become Overwhelmed – and the Effects on a Relationship:

Of course, neurotypicals are emotional. They also often make disastrous assumptions and then act out on them. They are infuriating and complex in other ways. They are also wonderful in many emotional ways too, with empathy and expressed compassion and a full range of expressed emotions.

- Neurotypicals are often subtle and hint and gently get to the point. Aspies don't get that delicate conversational dance, so often they will shut down the conversation early because they cannot see where it's going. This leaves neurotypicals confused, angry, and unheard.
- Aspies are not good at either emotional awareness, self-awareness, or the build-up of their or other's emotions. They don't seem to easily verbalise their emotions. The first you may hear these emotions is an explosion of them during an Aspie meltdown.
- Aspies often do not get the emotional and physical exhaustion of others, particularly male Aspies and particularly of their partners. It is good to be specific when you need help.
- Aspies often do not engage because they cannot sense the moment with either empathy or body language, and often, they may not be making appropriate eye contact either. (It is a useful skill to make eye contact because this is partly how neurotypicals *sense* or *read* the right moment.)

This seeming lack of engagement makes Aspies sometimes appear cold and detached. Generally, they care very deeply but have difficulty showing that they care in an appropriate social manner.

- Aspies can be extremely trusting if they commit to you. Don't abuse it. Once lost, you probably will not get the trust, the Aspie, or the relationship back. Trust is precious.
- Aspies do get better at interpreting and translating.
- Frustration conversations: if an Aspie is interrupted, they will often start at the beginning of the story again or at least come to grips with their story again. This is more common to male Aspies, but female Aspies often react similarly. They can often only hold an interruption for a short while. If they re-tell the story, they need to get all the details correct so they will keep checking their story details and clarifying it aloud. This has nothing to do with intelligence but everything to do with how much stress they are managing and part processing of the day around other things, which are all running through their head. Like a laptop – it depends how many programmes are running simultaneously. Neurotypicals seldom (metaphorically) run more than two programmes at a time, and then they seem really pleased with themselves and call it *multi-tasking*.

- Many Aspies have huge difficulties prioritising (often referred to as difficulties with reticular formation in the brain). I have seen this over and over again. Plans that are unfinished. Tasks that are unfinished. This is not unessential hobbies – this is related to chores or necessary work expectations. There is the theory of reticular formation being a major player in the symptoms, particularly the sensory functions. What the reticular formation does is to help make a priority of functions in the brain, whether a sound is important or whether a task is important. Reticular formation occurs in the lower brainstem and has an important function in organising and coordinating information. It is thought that this is the part of the brain that makes it difficult for Aspies to stay focussed in areas that are not an obsessive interest. It is also this part of the brain that makes it difficult to ignore sensory stimulation, as their brain cannot prioritise or rule out a stimulation.
    - So in couples, the Aspie gets overwhelmed and cannot filter or prioritise important information: couple time or that annoying flashing light on the TV that needs to be repaired?
    - Or the Aspie mother can't relax because the children are still awake when they should be sleeping.

> One man that I know has several barns full of intended jobs. One barn holds over a hundred bicycles, slowly rusting. He intends to use these for spare parts and make new bicycles from old worn ones. Another man has a house full of computer related paraphernalia that he can use to make new computers or screens or accessories. He and his wife have a narrow path through their lounge.

- He needs time to stim. She needs time to stim. Stimming is more than doing hobbies or relaxing. It is not a *chill* process, but it is a process – a very important one. Stimming helps the reticular formation organise the day, thoughts, events, and the environment in the brain. Give your Aspie partner or spouse time to stim, and then see how beautifully they bounce back and how they can relate again. They need time to stim because you love each other and want this relationship to work better.
- When some Aspies are overwhelmed, they may shut their eyes for a period or simply walk away. To the neurotypical, it seems like they are

not listening. The neurotypical feels frustrated, invisible, and ignored, which can then lead to anger. Unless there is an emergency, give them space. They are not usually good at explaining how they feel especially when they are stressed. As a neurotypical, you know that feeling and can express it – they can't. Recognise the symptoms and get back to them when they are ready.

- Aspies may seem selfish when they might stop you mid-conversation – and walk away. She is not being rude. She is overloaded. Give her space to process, and she will come back and talk. An Aspie male may need a bit more coaxing to come back and explain themselves. Learn to make it a rule that explanations are usually important if a non-explanation can detrimentally affect the relationship.
- They like time alone – let them select the social occasions to be with you. Neurotypicals think *if you love me, you will love what I do*. This is not logical to Aspies.
- To us neurotypicals, it seems like Aspies dispose of people. It seems like an Aspie can just drop a person. It is because they only seem to manage one main relationship at a time. Mothers can be hurt. Best friends can be hurt. Aspies care deeply about these other relationships; they just can't juggle them all. They care so deeply although you may rarely see them, but if you have a need (an illness, just had a relationship break-up, are moving to a new house, or short on money) – they will be the first ones on the scene. Don't assume that your social rules are theirs. Despite seeming to drop people, they are the most faithful and loyal friends or family you can have!
- Aspies are generally not spontaneous, even the few that are extroverted. They need lots of warning and planning and time to get their head around an event or decision. Holidays and time away can be a bit of a nightmare with Aspie men – Aspie women are more amenable to trips but with warning.

> One neurotypical wife eventually resigned herself to booking and planning all the holidays by herself, with her husband distressed and constantly carping in the background about how unnecessary trips and holidays were. She packed the car, packed the children in the car, locked up the house and did all the necessary shutting up the property for going away. On the day of the trip, he would get in the car huffily, refusing to drive, and would sit with crossed arms and glare out of the window in a sullen silence. After a couple of hours of driving, he would start unwinding and begin enjoying himself. A few hours later, he would start saying that they needed to do this more often and it was such fun. By the next day, he was convinced and then convinced the children that this fabulous trip was all due to his efforts and how they should do such trips again in the near future. To add insult to injury, she was also the family photographer. Never did he consider that she needed to be photographed with the family or the children. All the holiday photographs showed him off as having fun with the children and she was absent. Of course, when holiday time or a day trip for the family came up again, she would have to go through the whole drama again.

- You may help your Aspie have time out at social events and cover for them. You may have a series of friendly platitudes to cover the gap. This is of course really hard work to maintain. Don't expect your Aspie to appreciate your efforts. They did not see you doing this; they did not ask you to do this, and they certainly would not understand why you had to do this.
- Some have poor emotional regulation when overwhelmed. They might laugh inappropriately or not be able manage their emotional responses. One man I know grins inanely when he is feeling very stressed, for example, his boss, who had threatened to fire him, became increasingly angry by the Aspie's seeming attitude because of the wide inane smile. For a couple, this can be very upsetting and difficult to manage especially for the neurotypical who is dependent on various nonverbal communications and this type of communication does not match the situation.
- Sometimes, under various circumstances such as being overwhelmed or being socially uncomfortable, an Aspie can be very distracted and

unfocussed. I have found they need to fiddle to focus. In counselling, I offer sensory cushions or something to manipulate like a Rubik's cube, or simply a pen to toy with. One woman took a book to read at her partner's graduation. Another man likes to have a short piece of rope in his pocket and makes various knots as we speak. One woman likes to look at the rotations of a square box fan. Another Aspie man I know likes to count the minute squares on my carpet and do multiplications in his head. They tell me that having something to focus on seems to dim the clamour in their head and they can focus more easily. Most neurotypicals focus best on one thing at a time and become offended by their partner fiddling and fidgeting. It's best to accept that to make a conversation or an important discussion work. I would advise though that they do not fiddle with anything related to their obsessive interest. The obsessive interest will win over the important conversation unfortunately.

- Research shows that the fight or flight response is easily triggered in Aspies. In such cases, they will often react in anger. Research has shown that sometimes in Aspergers syndrome and High Functioning Autism, the amygdala (freeze, flight, or fight centre in the brain) is often larger in Aspies. In other (more rare) ASD presentations, it seems that the amygdala is smaller, so the behaviour of the person is seemingly reckless and fearless at times. One young man ran across the top edge of a waterfall which had a long sheer drop and slippery rocks. It is once again that extreme either/or response common to ASD.
- Aspies generally cannot deal with sudden stressful situations. Whether this is because their amygdala is generally more easily stressed is not known. (When the amygdala is triggered in the brain, the frontal and prefrontal cortexes are often partly or fully disabled. What this means is that the Aspie cannot think clearly, which of course affects their behaviour.)

> In one small city, a hurricane swept through. A middle-aged couple lived on the third (the top) floor of a building of apartments. The wife of the couple was suspected to be on the ASD spectrum. The hurricane ripped off half the roof, with a subsequent rain shower that came directly into their apartment. An adult son and his wife were also in the apartment, visiting at that time. With the rain pouring, the

> mess of timber and roofing and debris, broken glass from one smashed window, the smashed or sodden furnishings, and the storm still raging, the situation was extremely stressful, to say the least. The three of them immediately threw themselves into making the apartment safe again. The Aspie woman phoned her sister and for the next couple of hours wept aloud on the phone and retold the drama repeatedly.

- When Aspies are overloaded, they may lose chunks of information.

> After a stressful day, an Aspie man was on the way home. His wife called and asked him to pick up milk as he passed the local shop. He agreed. He arrived home with the milk, having forgotten to pick up their son who was still waiting at the school gate with a frustrated teacher who wanted to go home herself.

> One Aspie man in a marriage was overwhelmed that his job was to take him to a new country, and he could not think about it. His wife agreed to handle everything: the documentation, the sale of their house, sorting out their taxes, packing up the family, and the final flight. Now he likes to joke that, "It is easy to change countries – just let your wife do everything. All I had to do was get on a plane!" When he says that, she feels again the trauma and lack of support during that time – of which he is oblivious.

- Angry Aspies in relationships can be verbally abusive (as can anybody be, but Aspies seem to be unaware of how abusive they can be and can also not stop the flow of verbal abuse once they start). Anger is often about a breakdown in communication or a ritual that has not been followed. Usually, the Aspie is overwhelmed. Because Aspies often show no expression, there is usually also no warning of the looming anger. Also because Aspies often have poor emotional regulation when upset, they can become inappropriately over-the-top-raging-angry, seemingly almost instantly. Once they have fully vented, they can then walk away, satisfied at having expressed themselves. The other partner is usually left reeling. The Aspie then cannot understand why the

neurotypical takes so long to come around again and acts as though the explosion had never happened.
- Aspies cannot deal with confrontation. Dealing with social situations alone are difficult when all is going well, but when it isn't, they are even worse. Most Aspies tend to shut down when confronted (due to cognitive issues), although a few may become mostly angry.

> One neurotypical wife was mortified by her husband's behaviour and thought that he would be arrested. They had come from New Year's Eve celebration, in which there had been a large bonfire and fireworks. The meal included all of her husband's favourite foods, and they had had a very pleasant evening. The children were asleep in the back of the car on the drive home. Neither adult had drunk alcohol because they had a long drive home and also knew that there would be plenty of police road checks and breathalysing. Inevitably, they came to a police checkpoint and were directed to stop for breathalysing. Although the husband, who was driving, was completely sober, the licencing and registration of their vehicle was all legal and they would be almost instantly waved through, he could not bear the police officer approaching him. His anxiety mounted and as the officer came near the window, this man became confrontational, abusive, and non-compliant. The officer then started proceedings to call for back-up support and have the husband taken in. The wife struggled but managed to calm the situation down and explained to the officer that her husband was on the ASD spectrum. To soothe over the officer and to prevent it happening again, she took over the driving. Of course, they sailed easily through the next checkpoint and eventually got home safely. She reported that not only had the pleasure of the evening been destroyed for her but also she had been so stressed by her husband's behaviour that she couldn't get to sleep that night.

- When stressed or in an argument, the Aspie partner will often shoot off a whole volley of words with no filter and leave their neurotypical or Aspie partner reeling. This is especially typical of female Aspies. Such an attack of words is a meltdown of major proportions, enough to meltdown oil, lead, and paint (metaphorically) all together! Look at the meltdown and not the individual parts, as difficult as this is to do. Then when things have calmed down, a healthy dialogue over what transpired

is important and remedies need to be put into place so that this sort of behaviour is not repeated.
- Generally, men solve problems in a more factual manner, but women need to have their feelings met. This is so for Aspie women too, although it can be thought to sometimes be obsessively so.

> I was working with a couple on their relationship. The Aspie wife wanted her husband to know how she had felt over some careless incident that had occurred because of him. She would not let the subject go, because she was convinced that he did not get it – which referred to her emotional state. He felt so browbeaten and annoyed that he walked out of the counselling room and went to the local soccer field to emotionally cool down.

- Overwhelmed Aspies can be resentful, as can any human being who was overwhelmed, except that Aspies can then make some unrealistic demands and expectations. It is not their level of resentment that is the issue but how they react out of it.

> One Aspie was overwhelmed by his work and was the main income earner for the family. His wife was looking after their four children and doing her master's degree papers. One child was a baby and the toddler was suffering from a head injury (the symptoms of which the father described as *being naughty*). She also worked part time and home schooled the two older children. She managed all the housework and care of the children and employed a gardener, as these strategies were best *for the sake of peace*. Every day, he came home and harangued her about getting full-time employment and pulling her weight to contributing to the household as he did *everything*.

- Aspies often solve emotional problems with logic. They have very meaningful but practical solutions. Work with them. They are usually quite easy to follow.

> One lovely Aspie wife wanted a little romance from her very blokey husband. He floundered as to what this meant. She helped him by suggesting that he

> bought her a card occasionally, in which he stated that he loved her or something equalling endearing to her. He forgot repeatedly, and she became resentfully impatient! He tried on occasion but could never find the *right* words. She told him that he could buy a whole batch of blank cards in advance, and every few days he could write something in it and was even willing for him to repeatedly write the same thing – just as long as he did this act which demonstrated his care for her. He balked at the thought that this was, in his view, lacking spontaneity and could not accept that she didn't care if every card had the same picture and words. He scrawled a rough message in a card and gave her one every few days. She was deliriously happy and felt really loved – especially because in following all her rules, it showed that he cared. Then the cards ran out and the saga started all over again.

- Sometimes in a relationship when couples argue, Aspies often are left reeling themselves with overload, but they can also quite often have no idea how insensitive emotionally they can be to the other partner. The lack of Theory of Mind (ToM) is very obvious at times.

> One Aspie man had been unfaithful to his partner and had been discovered. He did not deny it when accused, because true to form, Aspies tend to be quite truthful. First of all, he thought he had not been unfaithful because he had been having sex with women who were prostitutes, both of which conditions, in his eyes, did not constitute unfaithfulness. As he had not had sex with neither the same person repeatedly, which would constitute a relationship in his definition and also not with a man (he was in a gay relationship); he considered it a business transaction to meet an immediate need. Apart from hurt, his partner was angry and devastated and everything else one would feel emotionally when cheated on. After the argument, the Aspie man felt that he could never please his partner and would end the relationship. His partner found him hanging in the garage and managed to cut him down and save him just in time. When they were both in the counselling room talking about this, the partner tried to express how he felt about this, having developed PTSD from the trauma of finding his partner in the garage. I needed to check if the Aspie man himself still had suicidal ideations. There were many safety issues in the counselling room that day. The Aspie man said he would not try suicide

> again and especially not hanging himself with a rope. "I won't do that again because it #%?@*# hurt [my] neck too much!" He said this in a tone of voice and a sneer that suggested he was contemptuous of us for asking the question – it was a stupid thing on our behalf to ask such questions. Apart from himself, he was oblivious of the effects his actions had had on his partner. That final statement left both his partner and I in shock in the room, again which the Aspie man did not pick up. This huge emotional situation was dealt with completely logically by this Aspie man, unlike his neurotypical partner.

- Aspie meltdowns are terrifying if they are aimed at you – regardless of the social situation but especially so in a relationship. Someone once described it as feeling as if a garbage truck had dumped a full load of putrid emotional waste over them.
- When Aspies do have a meltdown, whether it is anger or distress, they have problems modulating emotion. When overwhelmed, Aspies will usually react in what looks like an angry manner (a few will shut down completely for days). I have seen an Aspie woman crying and beside herself with stress while she tried to pull chunks of hair out of her own head and was scratching and ripping down her face with her long nails. Aspie women who have meltdowns can look and behave in a psychotic-seeming manner and many women have been placed in mental-health care because of this. Their behaviour and words can also impress onlookers that the Aspie is not safe. The long-term effect on both parties in the relationship when this happens is extremely dangerous: at the very least, emotional trust is broken on both sides.

> One Aspie man I know does not allow himself to be angry so he shuts down completely into mute silence for several days, until he is able to process his anger and the issues that had caused it. Then he *comes back*, as he describes it, *from some remote place*.

> One Aspie man did not believe that he should do domestic chores. He saw himself as the provider and his wife as the domestic maintainer, despite the fact that she herself worked and managed their children. One night, she told me, she was exhausted and knew that she still had the

> dishes to do once she had settled their children in bed (which she was just about to do). She asked him to please help and wash the dishes (not expecting anything more than just the wash-up). In front of the children, he responded that he would get a gun, put it in his mouth and shoot his brains out rather than do the dishes! He never did get how this comment could cause distress in his neurotypical wife, at many levels!

- I have noticed that in some cultures, especially third world ones, that people may say yes but mean no during language confusion, with the simultaneous desire to be pleasing and hospitable. My Filipina neighbour would often do this as her English was extremely sparse and I have absolutely nil when it comes to any of the dialects of the several languages of the Philippines. Aspies seem to do the same when they are overloaded with language or sensory issues. They may under periods of stress say *yes* in agreement and later deny that they had even said that.
- Many neurotypicals often stop telling their spouse or partners their thoughts and feelings, as the Aspie gets it so very wrong sometimes. The Aspie will often try to argue their neurotypical partner's feelings logically or they may become defensive because they may perceive a criticism or a possibility that is not there. One ASD specialist refers this to as *emotional deafness*.
- Aspies are prone to depression and that fact is well documented. Temple Grandin speaks frankly about her own depression, which she appears to consider to be an organic failure in her brain neurology. She has experimented with antidepressants (under medical direction of course) and has found that long term a low dose antidepressant taken consistently is very helpful to her emotional wellbeing. Some people do resist antidepressants, but one should be realistic about the quality of not only one's life but also how one's depression affects their partner.

Routines, Familiarity and Special Interests, and Their Effects on Couple ASD Relationships:

- Research indicated that many people get into relationships with Aspies because ASD is in the family tree and is therefore familiar, and this is the same for Aspies marrying neurotypicals.

- Most days, Aspies need a plan and a focus in order to achieve. Some are very good at self-management in this way, although they then do not like their plan to be interrupted. Others need to have an external structure sometimes put in place for them otherwise they don't seem to function.

> One of my female Aspie clients asked me how I did my housework and in what order, as she felt that she could not get through the day's work. As she usually did her chores and housework after the children went to school, she described her attempts at creating order: she would pick something up and take it to its place in another room, see something there, see two things elsewhere, get distracted sorting those, would then put one of the two things down, forget that she had done that only to later find the washing powder besides the dog food bowl and the potatoes all brown because they had been peeled and left on the kitchen bench for a few hours. She continued with a long list of her days, in detail and crying with the sheer frustration of her days as she recalled her story. Sometimes the female Aspie distractibility often sees the females being mistakenly diagnosed as ADD or ADHD. This difficulty prioritising tasks is due to a malfunctioning of the reticular formation within the brain, as discussed earlier in the chapter.

- On the other hand, some Aspies are extremely tidy and organised and can find what you need immediately whether it is the warranty of that new kettle or the hair-tie that you left on the bathroom shelf. (These are not the Aspies who struggle with OCD, which is another level of anxiety altogether that interferes with their lives.)
- Allow their special interests where possible. It allows a viable distraction which helps them to stim, which is necessary for processing and calming their emotions down.

> Some special interests are not always possible! One lady (who self-diagnosed herself to be on the ASD spectrum) discovered that she loved being pregnant. Her husband worked this out at their eighth child. Once the baby became a toddler, she seemed to lose interest and would fall pregnant again. After the 11th child, he had to take more serious steps. She grieved for a long time that she would not have any more children with her husband.

- One couple had a shared interest in travel, which brought them very close together. She did the research and organising. He did the driving.
- Another couple had a shared interest in puns.
- Similarly, another couple had a shared interest in crossword puzzles, which they enjoyed doing together.
- Some couples have had a shared interest in rescue animals, endangered animals, and various worldwide environmental issues.

- If she is comfortable in her own skin, she will have a unique individual style of dressing and arranging her home. It usually is stunning. And unique. If it works, then let the matter be. The alternative is relative chaos. Which do you want?
- Another couple were both shift workers. The Aspie partner would often neglect to do certain chores such as the laundry, feeding their dog, watering the plants or preparing their evening meal (which he would take to his night shift). This was mainly because he seemed to be *pretty hopeless at organising [himself]*. They resolved to work together using a structure written up on a whiteboard. Although he participated, he preferred her to fill in the noticeboard with all of the relevant household chores that day and week. It worked reasonably well unless he got lost on his computer games (when he should have been sleeping). They agreed no games until he had checked off everything on the board. It was a system that worked for them, and they were both involved with it.
- Aspies are homebodies! At home, they have more control of their environment and therefore feel safe. They have adjusted the home around their sensory issues. When deciding to share a home, think deeply and respectfully about these ramifications for both of you.
- There are extremes around finances. The neurotypical partner will often handle the finances because some Aspies can be so casual and careless with money. On the other hand, some Aspies are excellent financial managers, both in work and at home and often handle family finances and pay the bills on time. Some Aspies are a bit more obsessed regards financial management.

> One Aspie man that I know keeps a spreadsheet and every docket has to be explained and handed to him. Even their loose cash is micromanaged

> One neurotypical wife gave her husband cash to pay their rent to the landlord. Being a generous man, he bought her gifts instead as he did not remember why he had so much money in his wallet. She got a lovely leather handbag and a couple of silver bangles. (And an angry landlord!)

- Some Aspies with poor financial management have got themselves helplessly entrapped with credit cards and the resultant debt.

> One Aspie man had caused serious relational distress with his credit cards and impulse buying. When his card maxed out, he would simply apply for a different card. Their financial issues came to a head, and he agreed with his wife that there would be no more credit cards and he would only use what was in his cash card. Unfortunately, their money for their mortgage was in the joint account, and he would keep drawing out the mortgage money and so his wife had to refine their system once again when she discovered that the mortgage payments had bounced and the bank had alerted her that their mortgage account was in arrears.

- For some couples, their routines increase their security with each other and with all that transpires through the day.
- Often there is only one way to do anything – the Aspie way. There is a way the dishes are done, what is eaten, and how it is eaten. One Aspie man insisted that at every dinner in what turned out to be throughout his very long life, that the meal be accompanied by a potato in one form or other. Every dinner!

> One Aspie husband insisted on having fresh tomatoes in his salad and it always had to be cut in slices – not chunks and not cubed. Years after their divorce, the neurotypical ex-wife told me that she still felt guilty if she cut the tomatoes in anything but slices.

- Moving to a new house can be overwhelming for Aspies, and the changes can bring about significant cognitive rigidity in many ways.

> On Aspie woman I know has had to move to a new home a few times in her career. She is rigid about her process. She has to unpack and set up on the same day and make a home. She will just keep working at it! She won't eat or do anything till it's all done. Once she has made her home, she can settle very easily.

- Aspies often do not get the reciprocal nature of relationships. Neurotypicals often have the feeling that *I do this for you, but you don't do anything back for specifically for me*. I used the example earlier of tomatoes needing to be consistently cut in slices and never in chunks – as in *never* in chunks!
- The career male Aspie is usually only focussed on his job. If he has a career wife, she has to manage that and all the household jobs including care of any of their children. Some can be taught rules not to do this.

> One Aspie man I know enjoyed cooking, so he always came home to cook the family meals. He is a great cook. He also preferred the family to eat their meals in silence. Then, completely stressed by the day, he tucked into his wine or whiskey throughout the evening and generally ignored the family.

- Aspies in relationships usually love their routines.

> One Aspie husband made a home routine that his wife and later their family followed. The children grew up and left home, leaving the routine behind them, of course. He maintained the same routine. When his wife went away on a course, his routine fell apart (mainly because she maintained all the domestic needs around his routines and expectations). She returned home after four days to find him in bed and very depressed, not having eaten for the four days she was away. He was unable to manage on his own as she was such an intrinsic part of his routine.

> One lady has clothes pegs with individual colours, which she uses for matching together for various laundry. One colour for socks. One for undies. All the socks are hung together. All the undies are strung up alongside each other. She is very unhappy when her partner hangs up the washing and cannot settle until it is done the right way in her view. She and her partner have had a few arguments about this, and she has now accepted that this peg colour coordination is her problem and not his.

- I have worked with many couples who have issues around the placing of cutlery in the cutlery drawer, household paraphernalia and tool shed arguments – all of which lead to an abundance of arguments about placed or misplaced items. Either one person is fastidiously tidy, or extremely untidy. I have occasionally done couple counselling where both parties are extremely tidy or extremely untidy, but because they were on the same page about this, so to speak, that was not the couple issue that was presented.

- Rules play an important role to Aspies – even if they themselves often do not follow their own rules. They will often have rules about hugs and kisses. A lot of Aspies also do not like PDAs (Public Displays of Affection). This can be confusing, because in the beginning of the relationship, they seem to accept and participate willingly in many of these. But as time goes on, some of the Aspie traits take over again.

Sensory and Cognitive Issues, and Their Effect on Couple Relationships:

- As a couple, sensory issues can be a strength or a weakness. He might notice that the gas is leaking and save the family's lives, but he can't sit next to you because your perfume is overwhelming. She can spot a tax error quickly in the accounts but can't bear your shared bedroom because your collection of boyhood cars on all the shelves is visually overwhelming. The noise of the birds, the neighbour cleaning his boat motor, the traffic in the distance overwhelms him, but he knows the sound the roast potatoes make when they are perfectly ready to be removed from the oven. Make the sensory issues work for your relationship.

- A romantic meal out is often difficult to organise with an Aspie, who might focus on the food, the lights and noise, and the surroundings! He may complain all the way through, be rude to the staff, and manage to ruin an evening, and not once notice his wife or compliment her efforts to dress up for the occasion. Talking about feeling like the invisible partner in the relationship will help – but only once the dust settles. In the meantime, try to find a quiet restaurant or café that works for both of you.

> Over time, Aspies can make immense progress as they get to know people. One Aspie man said to his neurotypical wife, to whom he had been married many years, that although he knew he couldn't often read her expressions, he knew when she was wearing her *American Red Indian expression* [as he labelled it]. It was an expression she realised that she had adopted when he exasperated her, and she did not want him to know how she was feeling.

- Some Aspies can be chaotic and disorganised due to poor executive function and the effects of ineffective reticular formation. Their intentions may be good but are often not completed. One woman I know can afford organisers, employed to come into her home and set it right, tidy, and functioning effectively. Then slowly, the state of her home slips back again and in come the paid organisers.
- Aspies, especially males, rarely make plausible liars. This is obviously a good thing if you are in a relationship with an Aspie. Of course, if you are wanting your Aspie not to tell the truth in a public situation, this may be a little more difficult to work with! And don't ask them to lie for you – they do not do that very well. If you want them to do this to cover you, and they fail, you will feel disappointed and let down, and possibly angry with them. This is not their fault!
- A neurotypical can complement and praise their spouse or partner, but because of context difficulties, mind blindness, and poor executive function, the Aspie often never *hears* the full message and only hears what appears to be negative bits when taken out of context.
- Aspies often struggle with insomnia. Of course, insomnia affects every facet of life, with its resultant tiredness that intrudes on relationships and

effectiveness at work or even on concentrating. If both partners struggle with insomnia, then the relationship needs some genuine care and perhaps some medical support for the nocturnal struggles.

- Sensory issues can overwhelm an Aspie. In one family, the Aspie husband and father could not cope when eating if people talked. Eventually, the whole family, as the family grew, had to eat in silence.

- There can be a circuitous communication issue when talking to an Aspie. They remember dialogue, sometimes literally and perfectly and often months later. At some point, they then, perhaps in a disagreement, may recall the dialogue back but out of context or having missed the nonverbal language parts such as the tone of voice or the subscript. They then argue selective bits of this historic dialogue verbatim back to their partner with the *but you said* prefixed. The neurotypical then feels this has changed into an intellectual argument about semantics and gets frustrated as the whole point has been missed.

- Proprioception: Aspies often do not have a conscious awareness of how they use space around them or around other people. They can at times appear quite clumsy. Or they can at times, particularly males on the spectrum, stand too close to another person and invade some personal space.

> One woman I know loved to play the sport of squash, which her Aspie husband also enjoyed. He stood right in the middle of the court, a third of the way back from the front wall. It was very difficult to hit the ball often, as she did not want to strike him. Despite her many remonstrations, despite her many explanations of the game of squash, he would hog that space, as he felt it was his only way of winning. She eventually stopped playing the game with him. She was also completely unsympathetic when he came home with a couple of welts on his arm, as his new squash partner had struck out at a ball expecting her husband to stand back to avoid being struck.

- Lack of empathy in Aspie men particularly can make them seem uncaring. It is another effect of lack of Theory of Mind.

> One female neurotypical client said that she felt the empty nest really badly and despite being glad for her very successful children who were making their own healthy way in the world, she missed her nurturing role and the family times she shared with them. Her Aspie husband responded that she could focus all that attention she had given the children back on him and that he was glad that they were not around because they were so distracting. He also patiently advised her to enjoy the quiet in their home. He appeared pleased to have solved the problem for her and never understood her emotional grieving and longing (or her anger at his seemingly selfish and unsympathetic comments).

- In Aspie/neurotypical relationships, the neurotypical partner can often shoulder most of the work around the household and their social needs, and they don't take many breaks. They have to focus on the bigger picture. Ironically, Aspies can sweat the small stuff (in neurotypical eyes) – a lot!

Couple Sexual Relationships

There is a bit of a fallacy probably created by the media that everyone should enjoy sex, and across the board, research actually shows a wide range of interest and disinterest. In our Western culture, there is also the Victorian residual thought in older people that men are primarily sexually driven and women are not. Our Western culture is also sadly peppered with childhood sexual abuse, which can have significant effects on later adult sexual activities, both physically and emotionally. (A current statistic is that one out of three women and one out of seven men have had some form of sexual abuse before the age of 16 in our Western society, and that statistic may be even higher with the current online availability of pornographic material.)

Most neurotypicals settle somewhere in the middle. Generally, making love in a relationship is described as satisfyingly enjoyable. At times, they enjoy sex, and on some other occasions, they may engage only because their partner feels like it. Some people always enjoy it; some people avoid it. I met a couple who had had sex on their first honeymoon night and then never again for the next ten years, because they had no interest. There was no desire for children so any sexual activity as a procreating necessity was not pursued by either party. There was just no interest (and they were both neurotypical). Most neurotypicals can recall enjoyable sexual occasions, which was about the sexual act but also the emotional connectedness that sex brings.

Statistically, it appears that couples who have regular consensual sexual activity describe themselves as happier and more connected with their partner. It also helps that in sexual activity, particularly with a longer term relationship (but can also be so in a brief affair too), the hormone Oxytocin is released. It is the hormone that bonds us to the person we are with when the hormone is released. At birth, mothers release Oxytocin, which also floods the baby through the umbilical cord, and the two of them have a good bonding time during those first few hours after birth when the baby is being held and loved.

Aspies appear, as in most other human behaviours which typically reflect the neurotypical stance, to be more at the outer edges. Aspies are not generally initially attracted sexually to others but usually through an intellectual connection a relationship starts. Possibly because the sex act is an emotional connection too and has very complicated, subtle non-verbal cues, that the Aspie does not respond sexually initially. Most enjoy healthy and appropriate sex, but they have told me that initially they were sometimes confused by the range of emotions they felt and were unaware of before.

In sexual relationships, there again seem to be extremes in Aspie behaviour. Some respond with delight to sex because they are so sensitive and will seek out the intense pleasure repeatedly, while others respond with distaste at the physical closeness, the smells of the other's body, breath and sex, the intensity, the sweatiness, and the raised emotions – and will only engage reluctantly at another point.

Dr Jeroen Dewinter from Tilburg University in the Netherlands has done a lot of research on youth, autism, and sexual behaviour. He completely debunks the myth that ASD youth aged 14–16 are slower to sexually develop and has found that their sexual experiences closely matched neurotypicals of that age. This included young people in care. This was from his research presented at The European Autism Conference in 2019.

Dr Dewinter's further research showed slightly different outcomes for young adults. Late adolescence shows lower incidences of long-term relationships – 47% of ASD women were in relationships (7% with another woman) as opposed to 80% of neurotypical women. Male statistics were similar with 50% ASD males in long-term relationships (5% with another male) as opposed to 86% of neurotypical males. In terms of abuse and deviant sexual behaviour, people on the ASD spectrum were significantly more likely to be abused. I suggest that these later statistics are affected by the mind-blindness that people with ASD have, so they do not read flirting signals, or predator signals, well.

Much of the older research is based on reports from caregivers or parents of Aspies. On the above research by Dr Dewinter, it is interesting that caregivers and parents reflect the same observations as the outdated research – which indicates that parents of teenagers are often unaware of their children's sexual activities (a common finding across the board of all teenagers).

- Another problem with the research to date is that it is limited, and that the groups of subjects are often very small. There is still a lot of research to be done in this area.
- A further problem with the research is that people with variations on the ASD spectrum are often *measured* together. Specifically, Aspergers or High Functioning Autism are not attended to in isolation.
- A final problem in research is the language of sexual discussion with Aspies is different to neurotypicals. A research question that reads *How often do you touch yourself* can have several meanings to an Aspie, although the neurotypicals will know immediately and automatically that the question refers to masturbation.
- Sex is primarily about the lead up: it is eye contact, body language, visual sexual arousal, dozens and dozens of various non-verbal cues. Very little is about words, and often consent is not even in those words. These important cues are why Aspies miss the initial flirting, the build-up, and the outcome (positive sexual intimacy or sexual assault).
- A couple may argue because one party is aware that the Aspie is subject to some flirting – but usually, the Aspie is unaware of the flirting.
- Aspies also often do not understand neurotypical jealousy. The Aspie may be intellectually attracted to another person and not be aware that they are perhaps being flirted with. Temple Grandin herself, an expert on ASD and herself on the spectrum, said once that she did not understand the concept of being jealous.

- Young Aspies are often unaware of how to have sex and are often shocked at the time. They have asked for more specific sex education than that taught to neurotypicals.

> One Aspie woman was rescued by her husband when he noticed her disappearing up the steps at a large work party. He assumed that she had gone to the upstairs toilet. When she didn't come back in a suitable time period, he went to look for her. She was in a man's room, and he was attempting to sexually assault her. She had taken him literally when he asked her to come up to his office as he had something up there that she might be interested in. She had missed all the danger signals and subtle cues.

- Many Aspies, the larger majority, report satisfaction with their sex life. If they are coming to see me for couple counselling, they commonly tell me that this particular part of their relationship is not an issue. And as the counselling progresses, this statements remains consistent and true.
- Most Aspies feel emotionally connected and very close to their partners, through sexual intimacy.
- For some male Aspies, they describe sex as the only time they feel deeply connected to their partner emotionally. This thought and statement can often cause some problems and misunderstandings in the relationship.

> One woman, after a forty-year marriage, soothes her husband when he is stressed by simply leading him to the bedroom like a little child, and making love to him the way he prefers the most.

- Infidelity is very rare in Aspies. One research sample showed that 90% of affairs and unfaithfulness are committed by neurotypicals.
- Infidelity is a problem if the sexual act itself becomes an obsession, where the actual sexual partners are indiscriminately chosen.
- Sexual intimacy involves a lot of sensory issues. Sometimes these sensory issues may overwhelm them during a sexual act, and they may then refuse to have sexual intimacy again.

- Couples need to make conscious efforts to work on the sensory issues and carefully find a path around them or through them. In the last Netflix series of *The Good Doctor (Series 3), Dr Murphy* (who is autistic) has a love interest and they work through his sensory issues, episode by episode, as they try to become more physical and intimate. It is a fairly good depiction of some of the issues, for both the Aspie and the neurotypical.
- Because of mind-blindness, Aspies can sometimes speak out an observation, which definitely destroys the moment. In a scene from *Doc Martin,* the doctor eventually has his first intimate kiss with his love interest. After the kiss, he reflects on the several chemicals from her mouth that he can taste, and he suggests that her monthly period is imminently due to start. He is completely blindsided by her angry response and her furious (and embarrassed) immediate departure.
- Consent in a sexual relationship is essential! A lot of problems have been because the neurotypical perceived consent but the Aspie had not intended for sex to occur. Females particularly, often end up at that wrong place often at the wrong time and then don't know how to back out.

> One woman told me that it was her fault that she was raped by her flatmate. He had ordered a burger, which had been delivered to their residence, and she had taken it into his room as an act of kindness. She had knocked on the door, waited for him to respond, and when he did, had opened the door and walked over to him to give him his food. Obviously, that is not a reason for rape, but she felt that it was. I initially met her months after this had occurred, when she was so depressed since that episode which she had told no one because of her sense of shame. She had dropped out of university and returned home, very depressed, almost mute, and considering suicide.

Sex is so personal and intimate and couples need to explore and find their own ways that work happily for both of them. If there is no conversation around sex, both parties can become resentful as they are increasingly left unsatisfied sexually.

One Aspie woman never got that her husband doesn't initiate sex because of her filters and Aspie mechanisms. He has simply given up trying. Then she is angry that she has to schedule it two times a week (her routine) and initiate intimacy every time.

Sensory issues hugely affect sex. These issues can be visual, sounds, smells, touch, taste, the setting, the texture of the bed sheets, the environmental surroundings, and many other issues.

> One neurotypical could not have sex with her husband as he was so unpleasant regards his body odour. He refused to shower. He also was not generally interested in sex. She had to schedule a shower and sex night weekly with him. He was indifferent to both.

Many people are shy about getting help for sexual issues. Males will generally refuse to see a professional about sexual help – even more so Aspie males. My personal opinion is that many people think that sex is such a *normal* act that they should naturally and instinctively be able to navigate it. There seems to be an element of shame in what they perceive as their ignorance. (Interestingly enough, many women feel similarly about breastfeeding and are shy to ask for a lactation professional, because they feel that they should instinctively be able to get this correct.) Unfortunately, a lot of internet sexual advice is often at a level of pornography, and often does not include consent discussions, so that even there many people cannot find the correct answers.

Some Aspies make this sexual intimacy an expression of all their love. They go out of their way to explore and research how to sexually satisfy their partner. One neurotypical woman told me she felt overwhelmed and suffocated by the intensity of the act with her Aspie partner. He was always the same deep intensity, and she eventually started withdrawing sexually because she could not cope with the intense spotlight mentally that he placed on the act.

> Another woman had a husband who was very loving during the sex act. In fact, he was so obsessed about getting everything *just perfectly right* that it would take him up to three hours to prepare. He had to have a scented, candle lit bath with her, then champagne in the room that was spotless and at just the correct temperature that he had calculated, rose

> petals on the bed and so on. She said she loved sex with him and initially it was all very romantic, but when he now suggested sex, she usually fell asleep on their bed while he was still setting up the bathroom. She couldn't wait three hours and then still have to get up to go to work the following day!

- For some rare Aspie women, pregnancy and childbirth and having a baby to care for was so overwhelming, they withdrew from having sex altogether – despite contraception being available. These women generally did not have a second child!

Some Sexual Relationships Can Become Unhealthy or Even Risky:

Despite all these fairly rare examples below, Aspies are generally honest, kind and faithful. Their outcomes when things go wrong is because of their different way of thinking and processing information than to the way that neurotypicals do.

> A young woman was flattered by a truck driver. He was the father of a friend of hers. She was 14. He was 38. He coerced her to come for truck rides and convinced her she had to pay for it through sex. As her own father was absent, and as she was afraid and simultaneously rapt by the attention of this older man, she continued to regularly skip school for the day and drive to another city and back with him. She was 30 before she realised that this was statutory rape, as she recalled this first of a series of rapes to me!

- There appears to statistically be a higher proportion of Aspies who are transgender, compared to neurotypicals. I have worked with quite a few who had got themselves into risky sexual situations and have been abused, raped, and badly assaulted or violated.
- Some Aspies are not aware of how their part of the sexual act is unpleasant for their partners or spouses, because they ignore nonverbal cues, or because they can be quite egocentric about the act and only

focussed on their own needs and satisfaction. They may even ignore that their partner is unwilling or even in some pain. I have sadly heard of one religious man who believed that it was his biblical right to force his wife sexually whenever he wanted – which to me seems to go against the very basic scriptural principles of love. He treated her as if she were his possession and he would often remind her that she was *his*.

- Some Aspies build a specific routine around sex often and refuse to change. When talked to, they will often break down their sex act into steps. Do this, then that, then that until it's finished. Why vary something that works for them, they often query.

> One man had read a book on sex and was determined to find his partner's clitoris – believing that if he could find this magical *button* they would have great sex. He forced her legs open and roughly pulled apart her labia and significantly hurt her, while she begged him to stop. He was so earnest in his pursuit of their mutual sexual pleasure, yet he missed and completely blocked out some very loud cues that she was hating what he was doing.

- Some Aspies have worked out their own meanings of unfaithfulness. Aspies sometimes do not consider it being unfaithful if they have sex with a gender that they are not attracted to.

> One man thought having sex with another man was not being unfaithful as his wife was only concerned about him being unfaithful with another woman.

Going From Bad to Worse in the Relationship

Some relationships do break down and end. This is amongst neurotypicals as well as in relationships that included a partner on the spectrum. Again, the difference is that the Aspie way of thinking can often put a different slant on the breakdown, and the mind-blindness, communication, and cognitive difficulties, all add fuel to the fire.

> One neurotypical woman was trying to resolve things with her Aspie husband. She decided to give him space and wait for him to come back to her to resolve the issues of their relationship as she felt that she had no tools left. Despite the many discussions they had had around his behaviour towards her, he seemed to not have insight or understanding and continued the same destructive patterns. Imagine her delight when he said he was ready to talk about this issue that concerned them. He then stated that he had worked out that she now showed all the symptoms of depression, and he gave her some leaflets that he had collected and some advice about medication that he had researched! Imagine how angry she was that he got it so wrong!

Neurotypicals can often fire attack statements especially when the relationship is under duress. It is wise to use *I* statements and not *you always/never* statements. Communication needs to be clear both ways and neurotypicals are more likely to be at fault with their subtexts and hidden messages, their sarcasm or pointed barbs, their tone of voice and body language. All of this usually leaves Aspies quite confused.

For some neurotypicals, there are significant, profound detrimental effects of living long term with an Aspie. These effects are sometimes called Cassandra syndrome, Mirror syndrome or Ongoing Traumatic Relationship Syndrome. The symptoms are similar to PTSD in which the sufferer feels that no one understands the level of trauma they are experiencing within the relationship nor the loneliness of it. Diagnosis can bring help and healing. Diagnosis should not make the situation at home worse.

One of the unique traits of Cassandra Syndrome, is that the neurotypical begins to mirror the Aspie's behaviour. Another is the profound loneliness of the neurotypical despite living together, in a relationship, in their home. Other signs include depression, anxiety, and not being believed by outsiders. In small doses and in initial contact, Aspies often appear to be the healthy one as they act out their positive social skills and factual content, both of which they can maintain for a small time. That's how the neurotypical got into the relationship in the first place. Outsiders do not see some of the constant undermining, slow insidious effect of the Aspie behaviour on the esteem of the neurotypicals and their thinking. One Aspie husband always staged washing the dishes when visitors could see him, and the wife was not believed when she told her friends how unhelpful he was with their domestic chores. Such patterns of this kind is akin to living with a narcissist, and many of my neurotypical clients come in having diagnosed their spouse or partner as a narcissist because of their patterns of behaviour, from their online Google search.

Some neurotypicals seem to lose themselves in their relationship with their Aspie partner. I know one woman who has been in a relationship for over 60 years with her Aspie husband, and she now seems more Aspie than him. Her anxiety to not offend him, and her desire to please him, resulted in her taking on his Aspie rituals, and she adheres to them as if they are her *normal*.

In another relationship that I worked with, the Aspie man accused his wife of having an affair. Their relationship had broken down and was disintegrating, and his lack of emotional engagement precluded her from wanting to have a sexual relationship with him. He said that he came to this deduction because it was the only explanation that fitted their situation. She frustratedly told me that she didn't have the interest or the energy for another relationship!

I have had a few experiences of Aspie breakdowns, where the female was on the spectrum. A generalised reflection is that for the women, they seem to have changed the rules of the relationship and are dissatisfied with their spouse as the spouse has *never* met her needs, as one woman told me. Another told her husband in a counselling session that she had never loved him, which he could not comprehend because she had historically said that she had loved him; her response was that she had had the wrong criteria for love and that she now had the correct criteria. Another said that she had *simply fallen out of love* with him. These women all had a common thread of having made cognitive decisions around emotions. On rare occasions, I have worked with women on the spectrum who have been unfaithful, which lead to the relationship breakdown.

After a separation, the Aspie still not understanding his contribution to the breakdown of the relationship came back to sombrely tell his now ex-wife that he understood. His understanding would hopefully lead to some reconciliation if only she could view the matter the same as him. This was a man interested in nature and biology, with a great belief that humans were simply another biological species. He solemnly told her that he had been researching about female spiders and how some eat the males after mating. He had come to the conclusion that human females were like spider females. After the human female had enough sperm and children, they dismissed the male, and it was dangerous for him to come back to the family *nest*! He sincerely wanted her to view her behaviour in this light and to make efforts to overcome the natural behaviour of all female species – which would lead to their reconciliation. So much for reconciliation!

When Aspie men are stressed, they may sometimes smile and often not talk, particularly if they have been in a confrontational situation. This can make neurotypicals furious or they might feel patronised or suspect arrogant sarcasm. The smile is an unchanging forced one. As they often have difficulty with understanding communication, it may be very helpful to ignore the smile if the other party is neurotypical, as difficult as that is, and work through the issues factually and one-by-one.

Neurotypicals often mourn the lack of natural affection in their relationship. They often enjoy touch and intimacy that is non-sexual. Over time, this often leads to a sense that their Aspie partner is not interested in them and the slow decline in the relationship often begins.

As the relationship declines, many an Aspie is very lost and frightened and has greater difficulty in understanding and fixing the problem. They too will often disappear behind a silent emotional wall, with intermittent, occasional meltdowns. This only adds further fuel to the fire, and the neurotypical withdraws even more. And the cycle continues...

Trying to Fix the Relationship

What helps the relationship when it has started to break down? I believe that diagnosis and understanding the ASD diagnosis is an essential start.

> Years ago, a friend of ours collected his daughter who was playing at my house with my daughter. He rarely drank alcohol, but I was surprised to see him stagger a little as he walked, and he was slurring some of his words. I was worried about him driving home. After he left, I phoned his wife. "O dear," she said. "It's becoming that obvious. He didn't want anyone to know, but he has been diagnosed with motor neuron disease." This news was very saddening for this lovely family, but it helped that I understood his behaviour. Once he knew that I knew and understood, he too relaxed and was comfortable around our family again – because we understood each other.

I think it is critical that if ASD (or alternatively known as Aspergers Syndrome or High Functioning Autism or other similar terminology) is suspected, that a diagnosis is important and is really the first step! The Aspie finds and accepts the diagnosis and the neurotypical or other Aspie partner accepts it too. They then do research into how to make their strengths work for the relationship and to determine the issues that stress the relationships, especially those around Asperger's – and find a way to be healthily conscious to work around this. The *issue* is not ASD. The issue is the clash between ASD and neurotypical, or even ASD with a partner with different ASD symptoms. *The neurotypical behaviour can be as much of an issue as the ASD behaviour within the relationship*. Finally, a little bit, or a lot if necessary, of counselling can help. Counselling that explores the differences between the Aspie and neurotypical is a constructive and great practical way to move forward. An expert on ASD can make a lot of difference and counselling can be very beneficial.

Sometimes Aspies are strong in their demands in relationships. Neurotypicals often surrender. At other times, neurotypicals make the demands and the Aspies surrender or yield to those demands. This leads to stress, distress and maybe even resentment, all of which are really unhealthy contributors that make for a very negative relationship. An unhealthy co-dependent relationship can also ensue either way.

A Smorgasbord of Options for Relationships in Which One At Least One Party Is on the ASD Spectrum (not in any order):

- Seeing a counsellor
    - Couple counselling: Get a counsellor who understands ASD. Some of my clients call me their *translator*, as I often re-interpret their conversations to each other in a way that is clear to both.
    - The ASD partner can present very well in initial meetings with a counsellor and even seem to completely cover the situation and make the neurotypical look bad – especially if they reflect back on remembered dialogues!
    - In counselling, I am often asked by a male Aspie to *just give me the rules. I will keep them all to keep the marriage*, at which point, I have to stop the frustrated neurotypical from walking out the door. I often have to let the partner know that this is a very well-

intentioned loving statement and commitment from the Aspie, phrased as best as they know how at the time.
- Make sure that you have a well prepared few items and examples before you both go to your first appointment with a counsellor. I think it's best if both parties come together as the picture develops far more quickly that way – in my experience anyway.

As counsellor, I once erred badly in this regard. I asked a married couple (an Aspie wife and neurotypical husband) an opening question regards the most difficult issue for them regards this marriage, that day. The Aspie wife exploded in a peeve of anger, saying that her husband had left *skid-marks* down the toilet that morning, and that he did it every day and she was tired of cleaning the toilet after him. That session nearly ended in under three minutes, as a very red-faced husband got up to walk out! He probably wanted to run away in embarrassment. He did resettle in the session, despite his wife not letting that issue go for nearly the whole session – which was quite a perfect enactment of how situations often got to in their relationship.

Other Practical Ways to Work on this Yourself.

- Mutual respect is critical. Without respect, it is very difficult for anybody to move forward.
- Being open and honest is very important to any relationship. If you suspect you or your partner (or spouse) is on the spectrum then tell him or her and explore that together, with an open mind and all blame withheld.
- Only discuss one topic at a time.
- If you have a shared spiritual faith – it often helps to bring that into the relationship.
- Get a book with diagrams on body language and go through this together. One Aspie lawyer that I know is excellent at reading physical body language. She has a phenomenal memory and has learnt it all as a list of rules (it also helps that she can intuit very well too).
- Meet the needs of the Aspie but also the neurotypical partner.

- Neurotypicals, you cannot expect Aspies to fill all your emotional needs, nor to necessarily empathise with you. Make sure that you have an amazing circle of friendships where you can get this. Your Aspie partner has strengths that your friends do not have, but in this area, you need to actively look elsewhere.
- Both partners or spouse remind each other of why you are together and how you are still pledged and committed to the wellbeing of the other. Take an effort to show that you are dedicated to your relationship. Make a conscious effort to reassure each other, especially in difficult times. Sometimes these simple basics can make a significant difference to each person's confidence in the other and in the relationship.
- Share your successes and accomplishments with each other!
- If pregnant, go to pre-birth classes together where possible.
- Aspie males are more likely to have difficulty knowing what is and isn't confidential. Remind him that certain topics are not to be talked about outside of the relationship.
- With Aspies, they sometimes need some direct, clear, unambiguous, forthright speech with no waffle from their neurotypical partner if the matter is important. Don't beat about the bush!
- Speak in a way that you will understand each other. Use the style that best suits the person you are talking to if you can. Be clear about what is important to you.

Years ago, in the early 1930s and 1940s, there was a significant problem on the public busses in London, in which many people would hoick and projectile their phlegm on the floor or across the bus. The spread of germs from this was not yet fully understood, but the cleaners certainly didn't want that job afterwards! The bus companies then put up a sign in the bus which read: *expectoration prohibited*. Of course, many people could not read, and certainly, many people would not have understood the terminology. It certainly did not stop the behaviour! Eventually, a sensible person realised this error and new signs went up that simply read: *no spitting in the bus*. Problem solved! Moral of the story: speak clearly in a way that others will understand you!

- If either party in the relationship has an issue to raise, don't blurt it out in the heat of the moment. That will only make things worse. Ask the other party to make time to discuss this important issue with you. Make it a habit to not blindside each other. One person may have been thinking about the issue for months, whereas this matter may be brand new to the other.
- Neurotypicals need to learn a whole new way of communication. Speak factually, directly, use short sentences, stick to one subject at a time, and explain factually what you mean. Just saying you feel sad to your Aspie partner and expecting an empathetic warm response is unrealistic. Express a bit more clearly what that is like and ask for what you want from your partner, particularly if you require some sort of physical comfort.
- Because neurotypicals are wired differently, they might need a counsellor themselves to process with. Or find the social support outside of the house such as a club. One woman left her Aspie husband at home to give herself a break from the relationship stress and threw herself into the local theatre company. (she obviously needed more drama in her life!)
- Offer ways to actively help your Aspie in social situations – which may often be a major issue in your relationship. Aspies cannot generally function in as many social situations as a neurotypical can and also may not want to (even if they are the more extroverted kind of person). Many of the couple arguments that I hear is about too many social activities and commitments for the Aspie.

Aspie women can sometimes (understandably!) try to escape social gatherings by being the chief cook and bottle-washer – over time, this may become her job in the extended family and she can become understandably very upset. Help her with this and be respectful. Socially arrange some appropriate help that your Aspie can cope with, such as standing by her side socially, or arranging other people to take on the many tasks that have devolved to her.

- If he or she becomes inappropriate at social gathering or parties after a few drinks, then it may be a good idea to set rules by agreement about these before the party, or leave early! (This includes neurotypicals behaving badly!)

- Some Aspies may simply walk out of a social gathering when overwhelmed, with their spouse looking for them or their vehicle and having to train or bus home, only to find a satisfied Aspie fast asleep with their phone switched off. Again – have a pre-arranged agreement before the event so that you can discuss this appropriately when your Aspie is overwhelmed, or even help them leave early.

- Neurotypicals may want to be sensitive to their Aspie partner and occasionally reduce their social need or the time they want to spend at an event, or even compromise on the expectation that their Aspie wants the same as they do socially. Obviously, an introverted neurotypical will be less social.

- If your male or female Aspie partner has been taken advantage of at a party or an inappropriate attempt has been made on them, agree to stick together at parties. It's always good anyway to look out for each other at social gatherings, for all sorts of reasons.

- Once an Aspie discovers and realises their many social gaffs, they can be socially quite frozen and unresponsive afterwards. As a partner, or spouse, step into the gap appropriately and also work before a social situation and help prepare your spouse for a positive social meeting with factual and constructive helps. Break these helps down into do-able steps. Then remind your spouse that you will be there at their side throughout. Don't leave your Aspie spouse alone with strangers or even family that they do not know very well if they feel insecure about these social situations.

- If you have a big social event to attend or in your home, then you and your Aspie partner need to work out ways to help the Aspie quietly escape from time to time if they need to. Some examples could include getting something at the store, cleaning the swimming pool, checking the pet's water bowls, getting out the cutlery and preparing the table, or handing out the drinks – just to give the Aspie a little headspace.

- Neurotypicals need to monitor their often impulsive social gestures, such as inviting the squash team home after a game. Aspies need warning and also their agreement (or their non-agreement respected.)

- Aspies do well in small groups, socially.

- Reduce sensory issues when talking in your important couple time.
- If your Aspie has difficulty because of the light or brightness of the room, difficulty reading or watching TV, it may be helpful to contact an Irlen specialist and maybe work towards getting some Irlen lenses (often non-prescriptive).
- If either of you are suffering from depression or any other mental health condition, please get it attended to so that the impact of this on the relationship is minimised and managed.
- Communication skills in Aspies are often poor when it is not around facts and can be very literal. Communications often fall down especially when involving subjects around emotions.
- Reflective listening skills are really important – develop these intentionally! And then use them attentively with each other. Listen. Digest the information. Think about it. Reflect it back. Important conversations and subjects need to be thoughtfully, respectfully, and delicately managed.
- Negotiate new routines or less routines or different ways to do ordinary everyday things so that your mutual life around each other is simplified.
- In a relationship, Aspies often like rules; they like the predictability of rules and the order and structure that they offer. Neurotypicals often hate the rigidity of rules and occasionally want some spontaneous, in the moment, maybe even impulsive, stuff. But for the relationship to work, there has to be some rules. The rules help make a context for the Aspie. I often read that neurotypicals want empathy and a conversation that involves some healthy reciprocation. Within an appropriate context, they may get the Aspies to have a little empathy and reciprocation that is more neurotypical in nature.
- Life often in a couple relationship, revolves around the needs and issues of the Aspie partner. This may make the Aspie partner seem to be controlling, or sometimes they can even be bullying as they are steadfast in resisting anything except their own way. Confront this behaviour in a healthy way, and it's essential to refuse to be bullied. Take this issue to a counsellor to sort out if need be, to find better ways to manage circumstances.

- If the Aspie partner is feeling stressed, a pressure touch can be helpful. You and your Aspie partner will need to negotiate what works for them. Often, they cannot bear light, feathery touching.
- Don't punish each other for a perceived offence. Not subtly. Not overtly. Talk about it! Fix it!
- Have healthy time apart if either of you need space – as long as you are open and honest about this. The Aspie may need space to defrag; the neurotypical may need space to re-engage with their neurotypicalness! Both will be refreshed.
- Writing is often an easier way for Aspies to express themselves, which also limits non-verbal cues. I have met a few couples who negotiate difficult issues primarily through writing (emails or texting or some form of private media channels).
- Some things are just better in writing. These could include shared diaries, chore lists with time limits, written (typed) letters or even joint journaling.

> Some cultures create symbols of respect while someone else is talking. In traditional American first nation's peoples, they developed the talking stick. Whoever holds the stick, regardless of age, has a right to express their opinions. When they signal that they have finished, they hand over the stick and the next person may speak, uninterrupted, and express their reflections and opinions – whether in agreement or disagreement.
>
> It is similar on (New Zealand) Maori Marae (meeting houses where important tribal or family discussions are often held). Whoever has the podium has a right to respectfully express their opinion until they are finished. In this way, everyone is respectfully heard without interruption.
>
> In counselling, especially where there are many rude interruptions and people talking over each other, I often apply these principles, and by agreement, everyone cooperates more fluidly. They all express their own understandings and perceptions, their agreements and disagreements are all heard, and eventually, they are able to negotiate some sort of middle ground.

- Aspies are faithful, funny, and genuinely care deeply (although they may need to be taught to express that).

- Admire the Aspie problem-solving skills – one woman said her husband can fix anything and gave me multiple examples. I actually think she is correct!
- Aspies learn to speak *neurotypical*! Admire some of the neurotypical strengths that your partner brings into the relationship.
- Learn to focus on the many good and wonderful things that you both bring into the relationship. These far outweigh the negatives in a healthy relationship.
- Learn to do at least one thing together that you both either enjoy, or have as a shared goal.
- Remember your early relationship and re-ignite those things that brought you together.
- Or maybe just focus on and remember what it was about this other person that attracted you in the first place, and use it as a positive stepping-stone to rebuild the relationship.
- A common couple failure is the cessation of praise. Say positive things about each other. There is an old rule that says that for every criticism, we need to apply eleven positive attributions to negate that negative effect from the criticisms. Don't take the rule too literally, but remember that a long litany of your faults is really painful and unpleasant. When relationships break down, only the faults are present. Change that pattern to help save this relationships.
- Learn to listen with an open mind. Don't interrupt a genuine attempt at healthy communication, no matter how clumsily it might be presented. When the person is finished, then add your bit. Don't interrupt.
- Focus on the good and the strengths that you bring to your relationship.
- Learn to love unconditionally, as you did when you first met.

Chapter 9
Counselling and Autism

This moving quote from Dr Lianne Holliday-Willey (whom I have already mentioned several times in this book) is a great summary of that Aspie stranger who first comes into your counselling rooms…

> "Simply put, within AS, there is a wide range of function. In truth, many AS people will never receive a diagnosis. They will continue to live with other labels or no label at all. At their best, they will be the eccentrics who wow us with their unusual habits and stream-of-consciousness creativity, the inventors who give us wonderfully unique gadgets that whiz and whirl and make our life surprisingly more manageable, the geniuses who discover new mathematical equations, the great musicians and writers and artists who enliven our lives. At their most neutral, they will be the loners who never know quite how to greet us, the aloof who aren't sure they want to greet us, the collectors who know everyone at the flea market by name and date of birth, the non-conformists who cover their cars in bumper stickers, a few of the professors everyone has in college. At their most noticeable, they will be the lost souls who invade our personal space, the regulars at every diner who carry on complete conversations with the group ten tables away, the people who sound suspiciously like robots, the characters who insist they wear the same socks and eat the same breakfast day in and day out, the people who never quite find their way but never quite lose it either."
> — Liane Holliday Willey, Pretending to be Normal: Living with Asperger's Syndrome (Autism Spectrum Disorder) Expanded Edition

She writes about the ones that are *most noticeable*, but mostly, our clients are not always necessarily immediately noticeable as she describes, and the counsellor will need to work a little harder to discover the very noticeable, likeable person within their client. These patterns are noticed over time and within a safe relationship.

Definition of Counselling

This was taken from the website for the New Zealand Association of Counsellors and is acknowledged as belonging to them:

"Counselling is the process of helping and supporting a person to resolve personal, social, or psychological challenges and difficulties.

A professional and well-trained counsellor helps clients to see things more clearly, possibly from a different view-point, and supports clients to focus on feelings, experiences or behaviour that will facilitate positive change."

Who to Choose as Your Counsellor?

Generally, one would find a counsellor that is experienced and meets a specific counselling need or needs, such as managing anxiety or stress, coping with change, dealing with grief or trauma, dealing with domestic abuse, or resolving a relationship or family issue. Generally, counsellors have preferred areas in which they work and therefore make it a more specialised interest. Most counsellors either have a website or are listed on an agency website at the very least, and one can read a detailed description of their expertise and also the preferred methodology that that counsellor may use in therapy.

Once you have found a counsellor that you think may suit you, check that they are professionally registered with a recognised professional board – or you might just go to the relevant board and scroll through their registered counsellors. Being a registered counsellor means that those counsellors have to adhere to a particular standard of training, professionalism, and ethics. You may have a short list of three or so counsellors, psychotherapists or psychologists in your area that you think may suit you – check them all out. That means phoning or emailing them and asking about their ability to see you, and also their capacity to take on a client. Ask about their payment structure and also how long you may have to wait between appointments before you can get a follow up booking.

If you are on the spectrum, or the issue in some way involves someone with Aspergers or HFA [High Functioning Autism], then I highly recommend that you look for a counsellor who has experience, skills, and knowledge in this field – as well as lots of the other above criteria. You might want to work on your anxiety issues, but because Aspergers is in the picture in some way, I would still recommend that you seek out someone with expertise in the ASD area. If it is not on their profile description, then give them a call. Ask them if they have skills in this area and then also ask about how long you will need to wait for an appointment if they are skilled in working with ASD clients…

Also discuss how the billing works so that does not come as a surprise. And while we are on the subject of billing, there are not usually subsidies for most people on the spectrum directly, but there may be some other agency funding which the professional that you have chosen may know about. In New Zealand and Australia, there is some government counselling funding available at the discretion of your local doctor (although these funds are limited, they are a possibility). These funds focus on issues such as depression or anxiety and is available to anyone, but if ASD spectrum issues are involved, you would need to see a counsellor that does both. The Social Welfare (known as *Work and Income New Zealand*) agency in New Zealand may subsidise some counselling sessions, under their criteria, so if you are on a Work-and-Income Benefit or a retirement or government pension, you can talk to your relevant case manager. Some counsellors have a late-cancellation fee or a fee if you miss an appointment.

- Choose a registered professional, whether a counsellor, or a psychologist
- Check out their modalities and strengths
- Ask about their experience with Aspergers
- Check their appointment schedule and invoicing processes

Counselling and ASD, Particularly Aspergers

You may be wondering why I am harping on and on about getting a counsellor who understands Aspergers. Well, the secret is out! The majority of therapies in counselling and psychology are based on the majority of the population which is – guess what? Neurotypical, of course! Most standard therapies are *not* successful with ASD clients because their ASD wiring is different. Remember that ASD is a neurological, social developmental disorder.

This means that the processing of social and emotional issues are quite different to your standard neurotypical clients.

Many of my ASD clients have a history of trying to get help and wandering from one counsellor to another, feeling increasingly unheard and unsupported, or sometimes even criticised. I have had clients that were told, for example, that separation may be the only option for dealing with their *rude* [Aspie] husband. I have not yet met an Aspie (male or female) who had been to well-meaning highly skilled counsellors, who have not come away feeling that they were the problem in the relationship, both in their personal relationship in couple counselling therapy and in the relationship between the client and the counsellor. I am amazed at many of my clients who kept on trying to get help, despite the obstacles! Occasionally, I meet an Aspie who has had a bad experience elsewhere in counselling, who is anxious and frightened at having to meet a counsellor again – and I have heard some shocking stories of how they have been spoken to or treated! Some, of course, have met a skilled counsellor in ASD and have found it so helpful that when they have moved, they have tried to find another with similar skills as the experience was so satisfying.

To ASD clients potentially looking for a counsellor, please find one who understands your different, wonderful, wiring.

For any counsellors who are reading this, please can we change the way we do counselling for our Aspie clients? Of all professions, counselling should be the one on the forefront of inclusivity. It is Module 101 of our training, after *do no harm*. I am writing this book partly so that no more harm can be done from us in the helping professions and services. If a significant statistical chunk of our population are on the spectrum or showing traits, we really need to be brushing up on our skills.

In regards to sexual abuse, we (us counsellors and in the helping professions) know that (in first world countries) statistically one in three girls and one in seven boys will have faced some level of sexual abuse by the age of sixteen, and we are highly trained and aware of that. In New Zealand, roughly twelve percent of our population is Maori, and we (New Zealand counsellors) are all trained to be highly respectful and understanding of the Maori culture and are appropriately expected to honour and uphold the Treaty of Waitangi, which respects our Maori community in all ways. Surely, with these statistics for ASD we are needing to do some added training as we have a significant population base. At some stage, every counsellor is going to have an Aspie walk through the door (not literally – for Aspies) to attend a counselling appointment.

Are there counsellors on the ASD spectrum? Yes, there are. Some are known internationally and have written their own books on the subject: Rudi Simone is a registered counsellor and author and is on the spectrum, according to one of her books that I have read. I know a very sound counsellor who is on the spectrum. I also met and tried to work with one who was very rude (for a counsellor) and with whom there was no relationship building at all.

> All counsellors have a debriefing process, which we call supervision. Some years ago, my then current supervisor had retired and I thought I would try out a lady who had moved into town. I had phoned ahead for an appointment, and at the time, she said that she didn't know any locals so it would be good to meet up. I arrived a few minutes early and sat outside her office, in her waiting room. At exactly on the dot of the appointment time, she pulled open her door, and loudly, without eye contact or introduction, demanded loudly and strongly that I came in immediately. (This of course and understandably put me a little on edge!) Usually on this first session, there is a bit of discussion about mutual expectations for our roles in this supervision/debriefing process. Instead, she fired a barrage of questions at me about my work, still without introduction or eye contact. She obviously had a mental list that she was running through, but I was quite flummoxed at the randomness of her interrogation (that is how it felt). She then said that she wanted to talk about the last client I had dealt with (this is of course not the process at all – I needed to bring in my issues around clients). I started discussing a matter that was resolved for the very last client that I dealt with. She then asked me how I intended to proceed with that client (ignoring that the client issue had been resolved). I started answering, and she interrupted me with: "Time's up! You have terrible time management and need to work on that next session." She gave me a pre-written invoice as she was talking and then got up and opened the door brusquely and waited for me to leave. I thought that I would give her the benefit of the doubt and tried to meet twice more after that and she continued in the same vein, so I gave up and met with someone else (remember that in this instance I was the client and needed that professional support). I heard after about another three months that she had upped and left town, seemingly overnight. I also heard later of a string of upset clients that had seen her briefly.

Aspergers Is Not...

- A disease, therefore *it* is not catching
- A mental health condition
- Criminal. It is not deviant
- An excuse to avoid natural consequences
- An intelligence issue. Most Aspies intellectually range from average to very intelligent.

A Refresher on ASD, Particularly Aspergers (For Professionals)

The Main Criteria Include:

- It is a social development disorder. This means that social communication is particularly difficult for someone with Aspergers. This includes reading social cues such as body language and eye movements, recognising different tones of voice, recognising when sarcasm is being used, or even when a rhetorical question may have been asked.
- It is a neurological variance, or some may call Aspergers a neurological disorder. Better phrased, it is known as being *neuro-divergent*. Most of the population is known to be similar neurologically; that is, most people have their brains wired in the same way. This makes them *typical* of most human beings. Hence, they are referred to as neurotypical. People on the ASD spectrum are neurologically a-typical. (Neuro means *relating to the nervous system or the way the brain is wired*). So their ASD brain is wired differently to the typical, majority population.
- There is a struggle with theory of mind, alternatively also known as mind-blindness. This means that someone on the spectrum cannot understand what the other person may be thinking or trying to express. Mind-blindness means not picking up signals that another person may be offended or angry or may be even preparing to bully the person with Aspergers. They may also miss sarcasm or irony and most times will not get the punch line of a joke particularly if the joke involves innuendo, for example.

- They may have an obsessive interest. In this regard, they will be very singularly focussed.
- They have delayed processing because they take in more detail than neurotypicals. They need much more time to process a situation than any neurotypical may ever need.
- There may be some cognitive rigidity. This mean that they cannot easily change from subject to subject. Neurotypicals can flip through several subjects in a short time – Aspies will become lost in this kind of transaction and will slowly disengage more. This is often why they (Aspies) are poor at small talk, that social and often meaningless chitchat that neurotypicals do, and they do it even if they don't know each other. This completely messes with any minimal social understanding that an Aspie has.
- Usually hypersensitive, resulting in sensory difficulties and possibly sensory overload.
- They often have difficulty staying focussed and appear to have multiple thoughts often running at the same time – what we would refer to as a distracting stream of consciousness (this can be found in ADHD as well).

- There is difficulty recognising and expressing emotions.

Some Other Conditions that You May Find with Aspergers:

A client may present with one or many of the following, over and above their diagnosis. Some may be considered a comorbidity, whereas others may be linked to the different neurology often already found in Aspergers. (The list below is deliberately not in any particular order.) The incidence of these conditions below does seem to be more highly represented in people on the ASD spectrum (Autism Spectrum Disorder, which includes Aspergers). But that may be a result of statistical errors and measurements to date – or it may signify the enormous difficulty those on the spectrum face as a minority group in a largely neurotypical society – or certainly a society that is chiefly managed and run by neurotypicals. A lot more research to these links still need to be undertaken, to complete clarification.

It also needs to be stated that having one, some or a collection of these symptoms, does not necessarily, in reverse, diagnose Aspergers.

- Alexithymia: difficulty or sometimes inability to describe one's emotions. Mostly, cannot even recognise one's own emotions. This may result in a flat tone of voice when speaking
- Anxiety (it is estimated that 40% of ASD people suffer from anxiety, whereas the general population stands at 15%)
- Depression
- ADD or ADHD (Attention Deficit Disorder, Attention Hyperactive Deficit Disorder)
- Dyspraxia: a difficulty that affects gross motor control (like walking, running, and playing sport) in which the person is often uncoordinated and has difficulty with physical activities
- Dyslexia: having problems, with various levels of difficulty, of forming or reading words or making sense of words, letters, or symbols
- Tourette syndrome: it is a rare condition in which tics and involuntary muscle movements cannot be controlled. Sometimes speech also cannot be controlled in which the person utters words without any seeming self-control. Often these words are offensive or obscene. Although it is rare, it is seen proportionately more with Aspergers than in the general population.
- Narcissism: extreme self-centeredness and indifference to others but not necessarily manipulative or retaliatory for rejection when seen in Aspies.

It is *not* Narcissistic Personality Disorder, which has different and more deliberate and conscious malicious and malevolent traits.
- Misophonia – a hypersensitivity to a particular noise that can affect the ability to think or concentrate and may even make one nauseous – some even find it physically painful. It could be a simple noise like someone popping gum or crunching potato crisps.
- Face blindness, or Agnosia, is a neurological inability to recognise and read faces. Many of my Aspies tell me that they cannot remember people's faces. Some tell me that they can see a round blank with hair but cannot describe any facial features. It is as if the face is *fuzzed out* – so remembering a person and identifying them later is often near impossible.

> I was once standing at an airport barrier to check my son onto a flight, when a current client, a well-known local accountant, walked right past me, looked me full in the face with absolutely no recognition. At our next session, I mentioned this to him out of curiosity and apart from him being embarrassed and hugely apologetic (which was not my intention), he explained that he often did not *see* faces despite looking directly at them. He said if he were expecting to see me, it was easier to recall a session with me in it, and then he would be pre-prepared to recognise my face.

- Synaesthesia: a different kind of sensitivity to sounds, so that they make a visual pattern. The New Zealand (and now, international) composer and singer, Lorde, describes openly how she uses this condition to help her write music. She is satisfied with a piece of music that she has written when the sound matches the visual synesthetic visual pattern that she perceives in her mind. Interestingly, there are so many versions of this condition, such as colours having taste and various other combinations; it is thought that there are over 80 different types of synaesthesia.
- Misokinesia: a hypersensitivity to a repeated visual or body movement that causes distress such as the consistent flapping of a flag (even if it can't be heard), or the maneki-neko (the Japanese *beckoning cat*).

- Hypochondria: an obsessive interest in one's own health usually combined with a fear of illness, resulting in many visits to doctors usually with negative results.
- Sexual identity and gender: These issues are more highly represented in the Aspergic community. There are multiple reasons for this.
- There may be addiction issues and higher use of alcohol and/or marijuana than the general population. Alcohol abuse can be an issue for older, single Aspie men particularly. The Aspies that I have worked with where this has reached a level and issue of abuse, say they use alcohol and/or marijuana to calm their anxiety or to help them sleep.
- Abuse, meaning verbal, physical and/or sexual, seems to be experienced by a surprisingly large number of Aspies, and these being social issues, it can be seen why Aspies may miss the warning *red* flags early on.
- A significant number of Aspies have been bullied, at school and at work, and sometimes in relationships too.
- Because the employment environment has social elements too, many Aspies struggle at work, and a large proportion are either unemployed or in low-income work. This excludes those who have reached a professional status and to a large degree are either in situations in which they are working one-on-one largely or have a level of control and management over their work environment.
- Insomnia: this is very common to Aspies and the large majority I have met and worked with, have struggled with one of the forms of insomnia. The ongoing effects of sleep deprivation are well known, but it is always good to check with an Aspie as to the quality and regularity of their sleep, and their general sleep patterns. I know many who may be overwhelmed in the day and will shutdown and literally go to sleep on the couch on one or many afternoons – and then wonder why they cannot sleep at night.
- Suicidal thinking and ideation: this is much more highly represented proportionately across the Aspie population too.

> Professor Simon Baron-Cohen said: "It is totally unacceptable that autistic people are born into our society as happy individuals and that by the time they reach adolescence or adulthood many of them have felt so battered by society that they no longer see any point in living. It is not for autistic people to change: it is for *society* to change, to become more welcoming to people who are neurologically different, neurologically more sensitive, and who struggle with disabilities related to socialising, communication, and coping with unexpected change. This urgent change has to start from preschool onwards. A single death by *suicide* of an autistic person is a tragedy and is one too many."

- Aspies over 55 may begin reverting to the sensory issues of early childhood, that they have learnt to manage as adults. They are also prone to sensory overload again and to increased cognitive rigidity. Their obsessive interests will often get stronger, as it may be the way that they soothe themselves. This is over and above all the other common physical health issues that all people in this age range increasingly face.

Preparing for Counselling for ASD Inclusiveness

If you are the (Atypical or Aspergic) Client:

Do your homework on the professional person that you are meeting before you come in, so that you are well prepared and do not have to deal with surprises. Do wear your most comfortable clothes, that are familiar to you and that especially does not irritate any sensory issues you may have. Make sure that you do all that you can to remind yourself of the appointment.

> Aspies might remember the names of all the trees and insects in their country and be a skilled ecologist – they might be the most knowledgeable in the country – but the Aspie may not remember that today is rubbish day, or that they have an appointment that they have only remembered after the message left in a tight, clipped voice from their therapist, on their answerphone came through about two hours after they got back into a cell phone reception area.

It is really rude and thoughtless to leave your chosen professional person waiting for an hour for you, having to chase after you, being unable to offer somebody else that appointment slot, and the loss of income – their profession is their job and therefore their income, so please be considerate. If you have to cancel, please give them at least 24 hours' notice.

Once you are in the office, after greeting your counsellor, please ask them to give you a moment to look around the room and get your bearings. Remind them again that you have Aspergic traits (or maybe the person with you has these traits if you are accompanying someone on the spectrum). If the room is too bright or too noisy, please ask to have the curtains or the sound levels adjusted. Remember that you have checked that they are aware of your Aspie traits and sensory issues, so if they haven't asked, then they are probably waiting for you to express your needs – within limits of the professional's capacity of course.

If you need to stim, or have a comfort item, whether it is a weighted blanket, or your Aspergic son needs to fiddle with his Star Wars Lego man, then bring those items with you. The more relaxed you are, the more successful and quicker you can begin to process the issues that you have brought into counselling.

Expect a few introductory questions if it is your first session. Tell your counsellor about you: how old you are; what your family structure looks like; what is important to you, and what you want from counselling. If you are on some later counselling sessions, then come in prepared and tell the counsellor what you need to work on in that session. If you know your counsellor well, then you may also at some time ask your counsellor if they have noticed anything that they think you might need to also work on. A counselling hour is traditionally what we call *a fifty-minute hour*, but if you think you will need longer than that, then please pre-arrange that with your counsellor. The counsellor may have other clients after you, so that appointment timeslot need to be respected for several people and cannot be easily adjusted to your needs during your session. You may need one session or you may need a few counselling sessions to deal with your issue – depending what it is and how much you are affected by it. Once that is resolved, you can finish with the last issue-related session, or you can initiate another topic, if there is more than one thing that you are dealing with. Counselling overall is finished when you have satisfactorily dealt with that issue that you took into the first counselling session.

For the Professional (Counsellor, Psychotherapist, or Psychologist):

The most important part of this preparation of course is your training. Get your qualifications and become a registered counsellor with your national professional board. Then get some good public experience for a few years. You will be mainly working with neurotypicals. Hone your therapy skills.

Then start some specialist training work in ASD. Make it a goal of your professional development. Read books, blogs, and YouTube clips on the subject and people's first-hand accounts, volunteer in a centre for autism, link up to the national ASD centre in your country, find a supervisor who specialises in the field. Learn, learn, learn! Make sure that out of this you learn to generally expect or treat an ASD client like they are wired unlike a neurotypical client. Once you have met all other professional criteria, get some practical experience as part of a team until you, and your supervisor, feel that you are competent to work one-on-one.

Many professionals and writers on the subject believe that it helps that you have a few acquaintances and maybe even family on the spectrum!

Now, if you think you are ready...

Do have a quiet office with plain walls and soft lighting. Make sure you are able to shut the curtains or blinds if need be. Make sure that phones and other distractions are muted, and if you have a radio on to avoid being heard outside of your rooms, then please keep it low and with the sound going out to the waiting room, not blaring into and bouncing around your office. Avoid a busy décor, or a busy office. Maybe have a couple of sensory cushions, or a Rubik's cube, or even a clicky pen for fiddling with – meaning the client and not the counsellor! (Surprisingly, Aspies cope far better if they have a distraction, especially if trauma or emotions are the subject for the day). Be aware of sensory issues – so don't wear perfumes or colognes, don't have strong room deodorises or burning incense, or bubbling little ornamental water fountains.

> I have an unusual designer shirt with uneven patterns and trimmings, although it is in grey and white. It has a few little sequins on it. One Aspie client, throughout our session would startle, much like the Moro Reflex in new and young babies. After a few of these episodes, I asked her what was triggering these reactions. She said that if I moved even very slightly, the light would change and the sequin would appear to flash dazzlingly at her like a spark

> towards her eye (she said), giving her quite a fright. I fortunately had an old black poncho in my car, and while I was overheated in my shirt and hot poncho my client was able to comfortably complete the session. That was a lesson to step up my awareness even further, about what I could wear if I had an Aspie client on that day in my diary!

Do ask your new client if there is anything that you can adjust to make the office more comfortable (and safe) for your possibly sensory overloaded client. Do not expect eye contact. In fact, I have found that the minute I tell my Aspies that for this session they do not have to make eye contact with me, they often seem to have a huge sigh of relief – and we are off to a good start. [Remember that your client may have come in about their particular issue – and eye contact may be your issue!] I also regularly ask every session anyway, if there is anything we need to adjust in my office that will make it easier for my client to settle and get into the work.

Do not try to do a neurotypical *read* of their expressions, tone of voice, lack of eye contact, and body language in general – they mostly do not play by those social rules.

> One Aspie woman told me of a shocking rape from her new boyfriend when he was high on drugs, which had left her with broken bones, and her vagina and anus torn and bleeding. She had afterward hidden in this state in a cupboard in a dark basement so that he couldn't find her until she could eventually escape and get herself to a hospital. This shocking tale was told with no flinching, a gentle smile on her face, her blue eyes alert and clear, and her facial feature and body were both completely relaxed. To all intents and purposes, she looked like a neurotypical who was recalling a happy family birthday party. She was completely traumatised but not dissociated – in fact, she was very present in her story.
>
> One couple came in in for relationship therapy. They had decided to work on their marriage of about 15 years. A few sessions in, the neurotypical wife blurted out that she had had an historical affair, which had lasted for quite a while. I tried to contain this emotional missile that just landed in the room. The Aspie husband felt he had a right to ask some questions (which I knew would be factual) especially as he felt my office was a safe place for both of them to talk about this difficult topic. They agreed to continue the session and

> she agreed to answer his questions, which were of the who, what, when, where nature, and the final question asking whether she still loved this man she was having an affair with. She answered that she did not love him and was not emotionally connected to him. He never stopped smiling warmly during this whole shocking revelation. We continued the session for a short while longer and I put some safety strategies in place. I then booked him an appointment on his own for the following day, knowing that the emotional overload would hit him dramatically and painfully once he had processed this revelation in his own quiet time. I actually booked a double session, which was absolutely necessary as it turned out, to help him process the effect and affect this revelation had had on him. (A short note – they did reconcile fully and as far as I know have for many years continued in a healthy relationship.)

If all of this makes you uncomfortable as a professional, then you should perhaps not be considering working with Aspie clients.

If you want to continue with the work, then take the matter to supervision and also do your research thoroughly. If you are uncomfortable with doing conversations their way, then have some sympathy and empathy for those who have struggle a lifetime to do it our neurotypical way! And in your discomfort, tell them kindly that you are not trained to work with autistic or neurodivergent people but would love to refer them to a skilled practitioner. They have chosen to come to us for therapy, they trust us, so let's make it a safe place for them to get in and deal with those issues that they have had the courage to come in and face!

If you are a counsellor that is naturally a neurotypical, then make sure that your skills with neurotypical clients are well honed first. That leaves you with plenty of *space* then to focus on your Aspie clients, whether they come in singly or as part of a family or a couple where there are neurotypical elements.

Some Good Rule-of-Thumb Strategies When Counselling or Working with Aspies are:

- Don't use neurotypical rules. This is probably your worldview. Try to begin to think of the Aspie's worldview and the way in which they think.

- Stay focussed on their concerns – remembering that an obsessive distraction with say a vase facing in the wrong direction can be sufficient to either upset them or stop them proceeding.
- Give them time to think and process and keep still and quiet to allow them the space for this. Don't fill every space with your words.

> Often clients have complained of how their previous counsellor kept on and on talking and didn't give them enough time to answer or even consider the counsellor's questions.

So don't rush in during silences, especially if they look like they are thinking. While they are thinking they will probably focus on an object, possibly fidget or they may stim.

- Don't chatter or make unnecessary small talk. Excuse the rather crude analogy, but small talk for neurotypicals is like dogs sniffing bums – it is about gathering social information about the other and where they fit into the group. Aspies cannot do small talk:
  o Because they have a social development disorder
  o Because they have neurological differences
  o Because they have some cognitive rigidity and jumping from subject to subject will overwhelm or exhaust them before they have even started a counselling session.

Some adult Aspies may expect small talk as they have lived in a neurological world all their life but be gracious and let them off the hook this time please, neurotypical counsellors. It is about your Aspie client, not about you.

- Avoid distractions where possible.
- Don't read their body language and make interpretations. They don't do the majority of the neurotypical behaviours.
- Aspies may appear to become suddenly angry or start crying. They have probably been feeling that all along but have not expressed it the neurotypical way. Don't be surprised as the emotional dam bursts – and go through that journey gently and safely and warmly with them.

- Often a counselling session is about helping them to process and understand an event. Remember that they have very concrete thinking and imagination is weak. I refer it to allowing our Aspie clients to metaphorically unpack a messy pantry, wipe everything down and then re-arrange the various items tidily back into the pantry (their mind) again. It is lovely to see how relaxed an Aspie is once they have been able to *process*.
- Check that they are ready for a counselling session.

> One young woman was woken late from her sleep by her driver, so that she arrived groggy, hair uncombed, and very distracted mentally. She could not focus on that session at all, and she asked and we agreed that she leave early.

- Don't solely use neurotypical-focussed therapies, such as Rogerian Therapy (although please remain client centred) or IDT (Interactive Drawing Therapy) or the popular Gestalt Empty-Chair-Technique. Ask an Aspie to draw their feelings or talk to an empty chair, and they will probably high tail it out of your office (remember that there is an issue with imagination and cognitive rigidity, let alone Alexithymia). Rogerian therapy relies a lot on accurate reflections and rephrasing, but this poorly done will seem to the client like they are simply being mimicked or echoed, and this may be distressing. Also, much as I enjoy Rogerian or person-centred therapy, by its very nature, it is non-directive and Aspies often need support to find direction.

- If they suffer with sleep issues or insomnia, then try to make appointments work for them – within reason of course. If they cannot fall asleep until 4 am, then an afternoon appointment consistently given would work best for both of you.
- Don't use clichés and idioms.
- If you and they both understand how they *stim*, then try to put into place stimming opportunities where they need it. Stimming is a self-soothing repeated action, which helps them to process information and/or feeling, and the outcome is often that they reduce their stress, anxiety or distress – they appear externally to calm down.
- See what works for your client.

> One of my client's emotions and memories are tied together in what she perceives as a multi-dimensional lattice. New lattices and events can be created and added. We have explored using her lattice to remove pain from memories, to simplify memories and so forth. Sometimes she is successful at doing this and sometimes she is not, but we are trying to make this work for her as it has been a very successful coping resource for her all her life. Her lattice is also her normal, and I may not fully have grasped it yet, as she tries to explain to me how she processes and files, all of which helps her to cope with social life. If she has a lattice for an event for example, and the lattice is clear, she can cope as she has a framework. She also sees diseases, like cancer, in animals, and it has its own particular lattice and colours within the animal lattice; this in particular is a useful tool for her as her work relates to animals.

- Be literal and concrete in your communication (you may have to learn this skill). Neurotypicals are full of abstractions and generalisations. Joni Mitchell, the singer and songwriter, has a line in one of her songs that I often reflect on when thinking of neurotypicals: *Friends were calling up all day yesterday, all emotions and abstractions.*
- Be literal in your explanations to Aspies and break actions down into literal practical tools. For example, if you are helping a client with their insomnia, then explain that coffee contains caffeine and explain the effects of caffeine on insomnia. Don't (vaguely) tell your clients that they may need to cut back or reduce their intake of coffee but actually work out a programme with them towards reducing coffees from say eight cups a day to two cups a day before 12 pm. Create a diagram or a chart with an actual formula for reduction, e.g. Day 1 [information], Day 2 [information] and so forth. And of course, work with your client and don't yourself slip into talking *at* your client! Invite your client to suggest a formula that may work for them.
- Don't stop their stim, even if it irritates or annoys you (providing of course it is not harmful). They are stimming because they have to put up with you too.
- Ask specific questions. They cannot seem to generalise very well, and it then seems like they are withholding information. They generally are not, but they do have difficulty expressing some of the information.

- If you know their obsession (the Titanic, trains, beetles, astrology – whatever it is), make an agreement that if it is not relevant to counselling, you will not exceed a time limit for talking about this subject – no matter how interested you are. Agree to a time limit with them (e.g. five minutes at the end of the session – a little like a reward and stim at the same time as they leave. Then you will both end on a happy note).
- Some reminders:
  - Aspies often have poor executive function in the brain. (Executive functioning deals with problem solving and self-monitoring or organisation.) Planning and making priorities are very difficult for Aspies.
  - Aspies often have difficulties with brain flexibility (being able to change subjects, or perspectives, or focus).

Some More Useful Tips and Reminders for Counsellors, Once You Actually Have a Counselling Session with a Client

(Assuming you are working one-on-one with an Aspie)

These tips are not in any order; however, the first one is a total priority.

- All neurotypicals are wired similarly, and Aspies are wired differently to neurotypicals but are similarly wired to each other. All neurotypicals are individuals, and you will never, in all your life, have met a neurotypical identical in every aspect (not even monozygotic/identical twins). With neurotypicals, everybody is different too, with different beliefs and personalities and ways of processing emotions. Aspies are all unique individuals too – please don't box all Aspies into your single framework and then become patronising and all-knowing. Aspies too have their own individual personalities, beliefs, and emotions. Get to know your whole client.
- I do a lot of drawings, involving simplified flowcharts and sometimes lots of stick figures to help with explanations. This often works better combined with the words spoken in therapy. Just talking with your Aspie client is often not enough.

- If you are familiar with neurology, as pertinent to counselling, then explain to the client the science of your processes. I find that this works very well with my clients. It is a good solid information and easy to understand. It also offers a great background for any later work or therapies that you may want to introduce.
- Most people are stressed and anxious when they come to therapy at first. This is normal. They and I know we are going to be talking about the hard stuff in their life that has brought them here. On top of this, most Aspies suffer from an elevated anxiety anyway and this is a social interaction that they do not feel confident to manage. If they remain anxious, they may trigger their fight-or-flight response (referred to as an action of the amygdala). Once the Amygdala is switched on, the frontal cortex is often partly or fully disconnected, which means that your Aspie client is partly or even fully unable to process at all. Everything you do or say in therapy will probably not stick and the Aspie will feel worse. So make sure that you have helped them to completely calm down before you begin. Some of their stimming or your introduced, adapted mindfulness exercises could work well here. After a few sessions, Aspies are fine as they understand the process.
- Because of the alexithymia, mind-blindness, and cognitive rigidity, it is sometimes difficult to engage an Aspie client, and it may take a good half hour or so to get them focussed and into the groove, so to speak. Help them get focussed on the subject. Once focussed, the work can usually proceed much more quickly. But because of this sometimes slowness to get into the counselling session, it is often a good idea to maybe schedule a session that is an hour and a half, for your first appointment especially with an Aspie client.
- Reminder: Fiddling helps them to focus.
- Aspies and emotions: The article below say it all. Although it is referring generally to AS (Autism Spectrum), these couple of paragraphs are particularly relevant to Aspies, and even more so to male Aspies.

[The National Centre for Biotechnology Information (NCBI) in the US, has a journal article on their site that explains the emotionality of Aspies very well. I quote from the article: Treating clients with Asperger's syndrome and autism, with authors Alisa G Woods,

> Esmaeil Mahdavi, and Jeanne P Ryan, published 11.9.2013, and can be seen in full, as cited, at:
> https://www.ncbi.nlm.nih.gov/pmc/articles/PMC3851204/]
> "Emotion and emotional reactions may be difficult for individuals with AS to process and discuss. This can include the expression of emotions, understanding the emotions of others, and emotion regulation. Individuals with AS may not have diminished emotionality; however it may be more accurate to say that individuals with AS have greater difficulties in understanding and compartmentalising their own emotions or in conveying these to others.
>
> Neuroimaging studies have indeed shown that in people with AS the amygdala and hippocampus—interconnected brain regions essential to processing emotions and emotional memories—appear to have differences in their neuronal and lipid composition relative to non-AS controls. It may be that emotions overwhelm people with AS, increasing their inability to manage them. Depression and anxiety is higher in people with AS than in the general population [sic]. Depression and anxiety may be further exacerbated by the fact that people with AS are often victims of bullying and abuse, likely due to their social awkwardness. Therapists treating individuals with AS may therefore consider screening for mood disorders as part of the therapy initiation process. One study has suggested that individuals with autism in general tend to express anxiety through changes in their behaviour rather than verbally. Therapists may therefore note that depression and anxiety will not always be verbalised by the client but may become apparent through behavioural changes."

- Remember that *alexithymia* is common to most Aspies. Alexithymia means difficulty or sometimes inability to describe one's emotions.
- This first strategy is useful for Aspie clients who want to deal with feelings and emotions, or who want to learn social skills for interacting with neurotypicals. Assuming that I am working one-on-one with an Aspie client, I begin by trying to teach them to recognise and name their emotions.

I might download one of the many free downloads of emojis online and print it off on card and present it to my client for discussion. This helps with the naming of emotions. Ironically though, I have found that my Aspie clients and children are excellent at remembering emojis but then do not cross-relate that to actual emotions or their emotions. I first drew a list of my own emojis, with the same result with my Aspie clients. Then I tried to draw more life-like faces, with a sudden significant successful outcome as they started to understand that faces showed emotions.

> One Aspie jokingly told me that it was a secret code of NTs [Neurotypicals] that I was sharing, and would I get arrested for divulging this big obviously *state* secret.

I have attached a simple few sketches below, as I try to illustrate to clients how expressions vary and that facial expressions give very good tips about what a person could be feeling.

DOODLES OF EYES, EYEBROWS & MOUTHS CHANGING FOR DIFFERENT EMOTIONS

If the Aspie client is a child, I have on occasion drawn emojis on ping-pong balls and have turned that into a game.

- Another very helpful strategy if the client is needing help to *fit in* socially is to spend time teaching my Aspie client *the basics of body language* and the meanings of tones of voice. Because they generally avoid looking at eyes, I teach them to look at the point on the bridge of the nose of the person that they are talking to, which point is midway between both eyes. In this way, they appear to be making eye contact without the discomfort of direct eye contact. They will naturally glance briefly at your eyes, or over-stare, but the relaxed neurotypical eye contact is not present. Or I teach them to say that they are Aspie and eye contact is difficult and could they look away but assure the other person that they are listening. If they can bear eye contact, I teach them that expanding pupils mean that you are liked; dilating pupils means the other person is not enjoying the conversation. I teach them the dull-eyed distracted look when someone is bored. I teach them to watch feet – if a person is heading out in a hurry and doesn't want to talk, their feet is faced away in the direction they want to go. If their feet are pointing at you, they are probably enjoying that space with you and the conversation. Not looking at neurotypicals in the eye with good strong eye contact means that you are hiding something or being dishonest and sneaky (this always, without fail, shocks my Aspie clients if they have never known this before). The list goes on and on, but I think that you get the gist of it.
- Counselling ASD people is more directive than traditional neurotypical therapy (except for sex therapy!). I will for example say to an Aspie client, "You have interrupted me seven times in the last five minutes, which has meant that I have not been able to answer your question. Please let me speak and I will tell you when I have finished." Aspies often have great difficulty recognising when it's their turn to speak. Some communication training is very helpful. Remember that their interruptions is a guileless, delightful, enthusiastic engagement with you, with usually no negative intent, and they are certainly not trying to annoy you. But it can be frustrating to begin to answer their question,

and they are already asking another and may ask you three more before you have finished your sentence!

Possible Therapy Tools

- *Many standard counselling therapies do not work on Aspies* because the therapies are mostly tried and tested on neurotypicals, who are more emotionally and socially based. The therapy usually does not work for the Aspie, but the Aspie feels bad because that therapy works for so many other people – doesn't it? So by deduction, they think that, once again, they are the problem. Also, a lot of therapies do not make sense to them. Now I have made a broad sweeping statement, so let's see what is needed, and what does work?
- Aspies will often come in for counselling but many may need help with processing too. The two are slightly different. Many are relieved to just talk aloud and process their issue – sometimes just their talking is enough. It is a mental and emotional pressure relief.

CBT (Cognitive Behavioural Therapy): Aspects of this work very well with Aspies, and other Aspies tell me it was an embarrassing nightmare in which they felt humiliated as they could not make the expected connections that a CBT specialist expected from them. The *Cognitive* part of this therapy refers to your thinking and how your thoughts relate to and affect your feeling and/or your behaviour. Although many therapists seem to remark that this therapy tool is not useful for Aspies, I have found *aspects* of it very useful. Aspie clients can have a lot of unhealthy thoughts (just as neurotypicals can). By changing your thoughts and thought patterns, you can often change how you feel about a situation or how you may react or behave in a given situation. This is often referred to as a reframing technique. Just use eclectic bits of the therapy to help your clients. Don't do the whole intensive cross-questioning process – they will simply be overwhelmed and then embarrassed (and then probably won't come back).

Unhelpful (and poorly done) Rogerian strategies for Aspies

- Aaron Beck in 1976 came up with the theory of Cognitive Distortions (still part of CBT), and in the 1980s, David Burns added to this work, which he published in his book *Feeling Good*. Although there are many variations, diagrams, and resources around these cognitive distortions, I tend to favour the following with clients:
    - All or nothing thinking
    - Over-generalising: *always* and *never* come into this often
    - The mental filters that taint our perceptions
    - Ignoring the good (which can often be linked in with the *all or nothing* type thinking)

- Jumping to conclusions (usually through unconsidered, hasty processing)
- Responding (inappropriately) out of our emotions
- Making a drama about nothing, or minimising a factor that is significantly important
- Playing the blame game
- Playing the labelling game
- Should-a/would-a/could-a: I think is a favourite theme among all my clients, regardless of whether they are on the spectrum or neurotypical. I tell them that *should* (and all variations of it) are the worst swear words and we agree in a fun way, to not use that word in our therapy for a session. Clients are often shocked at how often they think the word *should*. We also have a *swear-jar* for the should word and see how many times a client bumps into the *should* – thoughts in a counselling session. Eventually, *should* triggers laughter of recognition, followed by some repair work.

It is all about retraining our brain to think healthily and about training ourselves to be self-aware. Most people respond automatically to given situations, but over years, that automatic response may be inappropriate or outdated. For example, we can tolerate and understand to some degree that toddlers have tantrums, but as adults when we are thwarted or cannot get our own way, we learn that it is socially inappropriate to have tantrums (especially public ones).

(If you are interested in learning more about this, then perhaps purchase the book by David Burns. This is not a full counselling tutorial but a suggested list of what I have found helpful when working with Aspie clients.)

- Aspie clients do struggle to understand the dynamics and interactions of thoughts, feeling, and behaviour in CBT. I usually draw an interactive triangle on the board to show this graphically. It helps to explain the inter-relatedness of the thought/feeling/behaviour aspects and how one affects the other.
- A strategy that I have found, that works very well with the Aspie mind that likes to classify things, is Transactional Analysis [TA], particularly the application. TA works very well in teaching clients how to take the

appropriate and healthy option in any given social interaction – and many have used this TA filter with very good outcomes. In TA, clients are taught that there are three primary roles or categories that we take on socially, or in our thought processes – that of parent, adult, or child. We need to be aware of the role that we are in and the role of the other person. The interactions between two people are called *Transactions* in this theory. It becomes a simple framework for appropriate social behaviour in most circumstances, and it may be the first framework that an Aspie may ever have had. Once confident in this, the client can expand to learning how to transact in a group situation and also to learn subtle variations.

- Relationship counselling works very well for couples where one or both parties have ASD. There are some important things to consider here:
    o Couple counselling is fraught with tension for all parties when they first meet the counsellor. It is good to never forget that this is a hurting couple in the counselling room. It will be good if all parties can acknowledge that.
    o Your counsellor needs to speak *Aspergers*. By that I mean, the counsellor must be able to communicate in a way that the Aspergic partner can relate to. My clients often call me their *translator* and jokingly suggested that they will pay me big money to move in permanently with them so that I can do this with them all day long – and forever!
    o The counsellor, and maybe the client too, need to be aware that at the point of engaging a counsellor, the neurotypical is usually extremely resentful, and the thought of doing *anything more* for the Aspergic partner is often an anathema for them at this stage. So tread gently with the neurotypical too. Neurotypicals in this situation often suffer from Cassandra syndrome, so being aware as a counsellor of both clients and their needs is very important
    o Aspie men, in particular, will often demand a set of *rules* that they will diligently apply to the relationship. (Of course, there aren't really that many concrete rules – it is a relationship after all, which is both a social and emotional engagement.)

- With Aspergers, as with all people, the learnings and new habits need to be repeated, repeated, repeated...so that new habits can form. There is a teaching somewhere that says that a new habit takes 11 repetitions to start the habit and 21 to entrench the habit. Of course, take this thought lightly and not too literally, but there is a helpful point to it.
- Make sure that the counselling focuses on the relationships and not the individuals and that both parties have to do the work – what I call the *business* of a relationship. This *business* does not have a *silent partner* and is equal opportunity focussed (another one of my phrases and metaphors that I use commonly in counselling).
- And finally, the Aspie has to learn to *speak* neurotypical, and the neurotypical has to learn to *speak* Aspie. They need to be fluent in their communication and emotional connecting and understanding, both ways.

- REBT (Rational Emotional Behaviour Therapy) is particularly helpful in changing behaviour, particularly where there are mental health issues – such as depression – that have become inherent in the client. REBT therapy is also a variation of CBT. It is the work of Albert Ellis and was first published in 1956, although there are now several re-workings of this therapy. The core of the therapy is to change unhealthy *beliefs* which negatively influences unhealthy behaviour. A client may have been the subject of bullying and has developed an unhelpful and irrational belief that *the world is out to get them*. They may have then become reclusive and aggressive if the safety of their hermit-styled life (the unhealthy secondary behaviour from the belief) is threatened.
- DBT (Dialectical Behaviour therapy) is another arm of CBT (combined with mindfulness), which focuses on changing unhealthy thoughts, beliefs, and behavioural patterns. It is particularly helpful where there are mental health comorbidities such as Borderline Personality Disorder, suicidal ideation, and self-harming. It is particularly helpful for teaching acceptance of one's life, developing healthy tools for emotional regulation, and for practising useful, *appropriate-to-Aspies-mindfulness-strategies*. This therapy works well where anger is a primary issue for Aspies.

- EMDR (Eye Movement Desensitising and Reprocessing) works well where an Aspie has experienced trauma. Out of the trauma experience, there may be naturally occurring fight-or-flight-type thinking to ordinary everyday events. The client has in effect developed PTSD (Post Traumatic Stress Disorder). We are all familiar with the PTSD of returned servicemen, especially where they have experienced fierce front-line type battle in a war. The backfiring of a vehicle for one of these war veterans, for example, can often make them dive for cover under a desk and then they may cower there and break out in a sweat. Other Aspies may have experienced a rape or any of a series of types of trauma. A colleague who has vast experience in this work, and me, both agree that our Aspie clients are particularly responsive to EMDR. Basically, when using EMDR, we are helping the client shift the trauma to a safe part of the brain, where it not only becomes inactive and in the past tense, but no longer has triggers. Current PTSD has triggers and the sufferer is affected in day-to-day life as if the trauma is happening repeatedly in the present. I say to my clients that PTSD is metaphorically like a brain injury, and we have to fix the brain. My Aspie clients appear to like and understand the metaphor. They also like the factual explanations that I give them about brain neurology and the science behind the understanding of PTSD.
- ACT therapy (Acceptance and Commitment Therapy): apart from helping a client accept a past event (or events) that had happened, they can then process and *move on* from it, and the client commits to maintaining consciously their positive values and not the fears or inhibitions steering their lives. It is also a fabulous tool for teaching emotional regulation particularly where there are comorbidities like major anger issues or a Borderline Personality Disorder. It is also great for dealing with stress, anxiety, and depression, as it uses its own range of mindfulness strategies to help the clients relax, come back to the present and focus positively.
- Gestalt: this is helpful when teaching clients to see the bigger picture. Gestalt philosophy is "the whole is greater than the sum of its parts." I draw a smiley face with two down strokes for eyes, and the half arc underneath – which symbolically is always the smiley face quick-draw. I tell my clients that they are focussing on one of the lines and not the

whole picture. But please don't use the Gestalt *empty chair* and role-playing with them, until you have at least done a lot more work on understanding their emotions. This empty chair appears on the surface to work with some Aspies who are extroverted and enjoy drama (acting and stage work) and are usually female. However, I have found that they are very good at finding the script that the counsellor wants or expects, rather than expressing themselves in a healing manner that alters and removes those distressing emotions.

- Solution focussed therapy is a practical strategy that helps the client towards a solution in the future and explores clients' strengths and aims to assist in achieving this. Compared to CBT, which is more focussed on problem solving, this form of therapy looks at solution building. *Solution-focussed brief therapy* has a more practical application. Although it is brief and comprehensive, the effects are often long lasting.

UNHELPFUL GESTALT STRATEGIES FOR ASPIES

This short list is by no means complete. There are many (many!) therapeutic tools not listed here and most of them hold some useful technique or strategy that may be applicable on an individual by individual basis. The tools are by no means categorically successful, although an eclectic skilful assortment of therapies will do the job best for your client. For your Aspie client, it may be one of the few occasions in a lifetime in which somebody has sat down and listened to them and tried to meet their emotional and psychosocial needs. (And by the way, I think we have that many therapeutic tools for neurotypicals, and not all of them work for everybody. It's great to have a selection to choose from then! One mould does definitely not suit all!)

- Integrative therapy is a concept and approach named so primarily in psychotherapy, in which a deliberate attempt is made to combine a selection of strategies that may work for a client. In counselling and psychology, a similar concept is used; it is called being therapeutically *eclectic* while at the same time being aware of the whole person (the physical, emotional, mental, spiritual components of their *being*) and integrating the two. There are a combination of about 500 therapeutic strategies in counselling and psychology, so there is quite a smorgasbord to pick from for our clients.

On the whole, I find that Aspie clients often do not need a single therapy tool or approach as such, but they do need to learn how to process their thoughts and emotions and manage their different wiring. I use psycho-education a great deal. I also teach them ways in which they can help themselves and express themselves in all appropriate and healthy ways. I have had clients, years later (when I have bumped into them somewhere), tell me that when they get stuck, they often still "hear [my] voice in [their] head", from which they extract the relevant tools they need at the time, and so directly apply it and help themselves. I find it so very encouraging in my work, to hear that our counselling has worked for them, in both the short term and the long term!

I understand that there are 20 major therapies in psychology, 200 minor ones and another 300 that are a combination of the first 200 or so. I remember reading of one research experiment in which I think 12 of the major therapies were compared in terms of efficacy, cost, length of time required and so forth. The idea was to order the therapies from the best down. In the end, it was found that regardless of the therapeutic tool used, the primary and most effective *tools* consisted of:

- Good listening skills and
- Unconditional regard for your client.

Be Prepared for Possible Unexpected Surprises

My neurotypical clients have certainly given me many surprises over the years, both positively and negatively. This section is focussed on my Aspie clients in particular. My female Aspies are more socially aware and often wear their neurotypical mask in the beginning, but my male Aspies have little of such an influence. Regardless, I have often suggested to clients that they come as comfortable as they can be so…

> One came barefoot to every session. He never wore shoes anywhere, and it was the first time he could come to counselling because he was allowed to come in his calloused, roughened bare feet. He also never washed his hair on principle and always wore the same pair of jeans, which were getting decidedly slimy. One of his issues was the hope of finding a shop that sold the identical jeans and he would buy six so that he could never run out again. Unfortunately, he had bought them at a surplus store, and they were of Chinese origin with no known label and were irreplaceable, so the old slimy ones stayed. His intellect was absolutely brilliant and his entrepreneurial skills through IT was like none that I had met before. Unfortunately, because of his cognitive deficits, he was unable to maintain consistency and the follow-up needed. I suspect that he will still succeed in that area one day. He also had a wife, who was not on the spectrum, of many years and who adored him and accepted all his quirkiness, and she remained the singular focus of his life.

The men particularly often walk in with their heads down, their fists bunched, and they have a stiff-legged brisk walk. I remember one person writing that her clients often presented *as if they were outsiders, as if they did not belong.* (I apologise as I can no longer remember who said this, but it has stuck with me.)

> One had eczema and struggled with hay fever, which particularly affected his eyes, he continually picked on his eczema, and the corners of his eyes and ate the findings. He had a complete lack of social awareness.
>
> Another ten-year-old girl picked at her toes and ate the dead skin and dirt from between them. She always slowly tore up bits of tissue from the tissue box, sometimes sucking on a bit. Her mother was in the room, and although I raised a concern, she was not concerned and did not stop her daughter. She always wore baggy track pants and would hide many tissues and sheets of toilet paper (she would need the bathroom several times in a session) in her pants, so that she was quite bulky when she left.

Some clients have had difficulty with the light and requested that I turn off the lights and almost shut the blinds, so that the room is comfortably dim. Another cannot bear the quiet hum of the heat pump and asks to have that turned off. Another suffers terribly from extreme heat and asks that I turn the heat pump down to the minimum that it can go, while I wear a thick jumper that I have especially brought in for his session (if I forget my jumper, he suffers through a mutually agreed 20°C).

I have many stories and have also seen the weird and wonderful in many of my neurotypical clients, so any oddities are not linked only to my Aspies. Maybe those stories will end up in their own book one day, like the warm and wonderful stories told by the neurologist, Oliver Sacks. He actually dedicated a fascinating study on Temple Grandin, a significant scientist herself and a well-known *voice for Autism*, which book was called *An Anthropologist on Mars*.

Despite the unusual oddities described above, most of my Aspie clients present quite neurotypically in general and present appropriately. As the session continues, the evidence of their different wiring becomes more apparent. Aspie clients are willingly engaged, enthusiastic, responsive clients, and a pleasure to work with, especially once they feel safe and accepted. That acceptance, unconditional regard, and our listening skill is the best way to respond to all our clients, whether they are on any kind of spectrum or not.

Chapter 10
Contributions

Several people have wanted to make a difference and show aspects of their experience with AS in any form, and have offered a contribution. Knowing that personal stories are impacting because this is real life and not just theory, I have included stories by Aspies, people who have Aspie relatives, people who have experiences with Aspies and even a few creative pieces to show the wonderful creativity of Aspies. All the stories are used with permission and as they have been written by their respective authors. Some people chose not to be named to protect the identity of others.

My Story
Author: Crystal Lundon

What can I learn about Aspergers?

I have learnt that Aspergers was the answer that I have needed all my life.

My name is Crystal, and I am a 33-year-old mother of two children aged seven and six. My family relocated from Auckland to Whangarei in October 2012. I have known my counsellor for just over three years now, and in that time, she has mentored me through a journey of self-discovery. A journey I would like to share with you.

When arriving in Whangarei, I was apprehensive as I felt my whole life had been uprooted and everything and everyone I knew for 30 years had been left behind in Auckland. Even though I was feeling apprehensive, I knew that it would probably be best if I approach life in Whangarei with a positive attitude and try to make our family integrate into our new community.

In the early months, I learnt that this community was very different from the West Auckland community I grew up in. It was already hard for me to socialise to start with and when I found roadblocks wherever I turned (socially), I became very discouraged. This in turn let me down a very dark path of depression and anxiety. The worst I had experienced thus far.

I knew that the best thing to do was to reach out for help as I had done previously in January 2010 after my daughter was born and I was misdiagnosed with postnatal depression. The local District Health Board's mental health services got in contact with me, and in a matter of weeks, I was talking to a psychiatrist.

I had a few appointments with this psychiatrist, and he had given me yet another misdiagnosis of bi-polar II. When I was given the diagnosis, I had a pile of literature to peruse. I can honestly say that the information was so general that most people these days could be diagnosed or misdiagnosed very easily.

A couple of weeks later after researching the information presented to me and also researching online, practising therapy called CBT (recommended by the psychiatrist) I still found that I was not making any headway emotionally.

In the ditch effort, I contacted my local GP and asked for a referral to a counsellor. A week later, I had a call and an appointment was up. Once again, I was sitting in front of someone telling my story, but this time, it was different. I finally found someone who was listening, someone who cared, someone who would take the time to see me for who I am. It was such a wonderful feeling.

In our sessions, we touched on difficulties I had had through my life from as young as seven right up to the age of 30. On top of social confusion through high school, I also found that reading was hard. I once asked my mother to read a novel for me and then tell me about the story/plot and characters once she was finished in order to complete a school assignment. These are the types of things that I would do to help myself cope because I found reading quite laborious and frustrating. It was a clear indicator of dyslexia and I wish that it was realised earlier.

In May 2014, I visited an ophthalmologist in Auckland as advised by my counsellor. She thought I needed to discuss whether I might need Irlen lenses. He diagnosed me with not only dyslexia but also photosensitivity. He informed me that 1 in 20 people who need prescription glasses also need some form of coloured filter for their lenses. And out of that 1 in 20, I was the most sensitive to light that he has ever treated in his career.

A couple of months later, my counsellor had had an inkling for a little while and asked me if it was okay to try an AQ test. "Sure, why not," I answered with a hint of curiosity and excitement in my voice. After taking the test, her inkling was a reality. With this new information, I made yet another trip to the GP and was referred to a psychologist who specialises in ASD, and I was officially diagnosed in January 2015. It was ultimately validating.

Now looking back, I have come such a long way in fields of self-development. I have put a lot of effort into building self-autonomy, learning how to look at things from other people's perspective, building solid friendships, learning to trust people (and whether to trust them), and how to be happier on a whole.

Learning that I am AS was the beginning…

The beginning to all the answers in my past, present, and future.

Insight into who you are and accepting who you are can be freeing. It can be comforting. It can be empowering. It is something that you have to work at and chip away at bit by bit. But when you do, you will find someone (within yourself) who can give you something that no one or nothing has ever given you before.

I delved with my counsellor into the subject of Aspergers and Autism Spectrum Disorder (ASD). I found myself becoming immersed in it on a daily basis over many months. It was so fascinating to me. With a click of a button and a few taps on the keyboard, I could find a connection to many others out there telling their own stories. I could find information that became so relevant to myself that it became thought provoking as well as reassuring all at the same time.

With all my newfound knowledge, I decided to look back on my life and analyse it.

In childhood, I remember climbing trees and sitting on an outstretched limb above all the chaos. The sounds of the leaves rustling in the breeze was comforting. It was a lot easier than listening to the constant noise coming from humans.

In adolescence, I would flit from social group to social group. Sometimes it was easier because I could choose to be there or not. There weren't many expectations that way. I guess I learnt from a young age that if I didn't get too close to any one group, they wouldn't know who I really was, and then I couldn't scare them away, or I wouldn't get hurt when they found out they really didn't like who I was. It was definitely a defence mechanism.

By my late teens, I had finished school. I enrolled in a business administration course. I then moved on to a career in print media and eventually found a boyfriend who had a large extended family who also doubled as his best friends. I was part of several new social circles in a matter of two years.

I wanted so badly to fit in that I began to mould my behaviours, speech, and actions to become what was socially acceptable for everyone else. I needed to be someone they felt comfortable being around (or spending time with).

From the age of 18 to 27, I held a full-time job, and I would socialise at least once a week (to keep up appearances). The strain that I placed on myself would manifest as crippling migraines or meltdowns of varied sorts; anger, withdrawal, uncontrollable crying, and even panic attacks.

I have learnt that the more an autistic person takes on artificial NT traits, the more stressed they become. It can be very detrimental to themselves as they are trying to be someone or something they are not. I have learnt who I am is enough and being NT should not be my goal in life. Forcing yourself into something else makes you miserable!

Some of the most eye-opening information I have found are the various aspects of ASD I possess. I have particularly noticed these aspects in myself:

- Dyslexia
- Order and routine – OCD
- Scattered thoughts – ADD
- Depression
- Anxiety
- Fatigue
- Sleep issues
- Sensory overload
- Stimming

With these core aspects, I have been able to notice them and how they apply to my everyday life. Once I learnt what each trait was, I was able to combat them by introducing coping strategies, which helped me to progress through each minute, hour, day, week, month, and now years. It is still a work in progress, but I am very proud of the strides that I have achieved thus far.

The Strain

I would like to touch on the strain that I spoke about earlier and the struggles I go through on a daily basis. Hopefully, I can convey it in a way that you can imagine yourself in each situation.

Imagine waking up one morning and the volume has been turned up on every noise you hear and you are able to hear every noise no matter how near or far. Someone follows you around shining a lamp/light in your face while reciting what you have to do for the day over and over until you have completed each task successfully. Your sense of smell is heightened, and it smells like your clothing has been saturated with perfume. Being touched becomes very uncomfortable and even the slightest touch can be painful because it sends a static shock through your whole body, which also makes the hair on the back of your neck stand up. A slight humming or ringing is forever present in your ears, and in fleeting moments of silence, it becomes as loud as static heard when trying to choose a radio station.

Daily chores like cleaning, shopping, working, or even conversing are interrupted by an uncontrollable pull and tug in your thoughts like a small child demanding your attention. The journey your thoughts take is very similar to branches on a tree. There is one main thought that then branches off into three different paths and those branches split into two more paths and those branches split into two more paths. Each branch or path ends with different scenarios and outcomes, some outlandish, some rational, some irrational. Some outcomes may even affect you emotionally and you could feel the emotions that you are picturing or playing out in your scenario. The mind is a brilliant thing!

The strain of the above combined with usual daily living and functioning would often become too much to bear, and my sensory system would overload similar to a computer and would force itself to shut down. This presented a debilitating migraine. My migraines would be so debilitating that I would lose my sight and then be bedridden for the day while my body would shut down. Recovery took up to two days while my system tried to reboot. While rebooting I would become dissociative and numb on the inside and out. I would trudge around like a zombie, and I was only able to perform the minimum functioning requirements. It often felt like I was only working on a quarter of my so-called normal brain capacity.

People often ask me why I'm so tired all the time. If you experience the few stimuli shown above on top of your normal day, you would feel exactly the same. I equate it to running a 10 km marathon in my mind every day.

Dyslexia

As stated earlier, I have always had difficulties with reading. After leaving school, the extent of reading for me was picking up a magazine and only reading headlines, small captions regarding a photo, and at a push reading a short one-page story. I found any reading hard on my eyes and brain.

Dyslexia has many different ways of presenting itself. Mine is when reading I tend to start off reading and then re-reading the first line at least 2–3 times. If by some miracle I get to the end of the paragraph, I am rarely able to retain any of the information I have only just read. Then one of two things happen, I either start all over again or throw the book across the room yelling "Bloody hell! …I give up!"

I tend to read word to word hoping to retain as much information as possible, whereas others read word after word. I concentrate more on each word and its meaning rather than reading all the words in a sentence and knowing what has happened or what is being said or understanding the circumstances being explained. Sound confusing?

Just to top it off when I am reading sometimes, my eyes go all haywire. My eyes zoom in and out just like a camera lens on automatic trying to focus on a subject. Not only do I lose my place when I am reading and have to go back to the last piece of information that I have been able to retain, I also have pain in my eyes and brain. It is really weird and annoying!

My counsellor informed me that I may have dyslexia and how some people can combat it with coloured lenses. With my newfound information, I armed myself with multiple transparent coloured plastic sheets and a novel to trial each colour. I discovered I responded well to or with the colour blue, and I achieved something I hadn't in a long time… I read a book. I did not have to re-read as many times, I did not feel tired afterward, and most importantly, my information retention was a lot better.

As stated above in May 2012, an ophthalmologist equipped me with a new pair or Irlen lenses, which aid me every day with not only reading but also my photosensitivity (or sensitivity to light). The moment I was fitted with the lenses, it opened me up to a whole new world. One in which I was able to literally open my eyes, my face muscles were relaxed, and there was no strain being put on my eyes or brain. It felt like a total relief in all ways.

Order And Routines

With most things, I need to have order, routines, and uniformity. If I do not have these, it seems to invade my thoughts all day or all weekend until I have put it in its place or order.

When hanging out the washing, each item is hung a certain way and then pegged using one type of peg. And no, the pegs don't need to be all the same colour… I'm not that bad. My kitchen tea towel has its place hanging on the right-hand side of the oven door handle next to the oven mitt, folded in half lengthways. My children's coloured drinking cups are stacked one on top of the other making sure no one colour is ever stacked upon itself. I mean it just looks wrong having a blue cup, then a pink cup and then two yellow cups. Am I right? A couple of my routines are that I always do my grocery shopping on Tuesday mornings and my favourite is going to see my counsellor on Wednesday mornings and my bestie on Friday mornings.

Routines help take a lot of uncertainty out of each day or week. Order is my own personal preference on how things should appear, and it is usually visually appealing to me. The combination of these two things free me from having yet another or more thoughts racing through my mind each morning, hour or even day.

NTs may place a label of OCD on a case like this, but OCD is driven by anxiety.

It may seem excessive to some, but for me, it's yet another tool that helps me through my journey. I'm glad that I am able to know that for me, it is not an anxiety-based trait. I know it would not be the worst thing ever if I found two cups which are the same colour sitting on top of each other, and I know it would not be the end of the world if I was unable to do the shopping on Tuesday.

I also know that if one or more of these routines would be unable to be followed, it does not make me a bad person, partner, or mother.

Scattered Thoughts – Add

There are many thousands of thoughts running through my mind on a daily basis. Some or most of them are recurrent thoughts, and these can be some of the most difficult to harness. This is referred to as Feedback Loops of thoughts.

My thoughts also lead me down different thought pathways each time I think of something new. My mind flits from thought to thought. Some thoughts are dwarfed by other incoming ones. Some distract me from what I am physically doing. The age-old example is that you remember you need a pair of socks from your room. On your journey, you have been pondering over a thought and when you arrive, you can't remember why you were even there. I even do it when I'm talking. I find myself saying, "What were we talking about?" or "Where was I going with that?"

It is definitely challenging and still a work in progress, but I have noticed that the thoughts do not consume me as much. And the thoughts do not always lead me down negative thought paths anymore.

I started letting the thoughts in but at the same time assessing each thought carefully to make sure that it was a valid one. If it wasn't, I was able to tell myself that it was not healthy, and I had to let it go, or even delete it from the thought hard drive. If it ever arose again, I would tell myself again that it needed to be removed.

Anti-virus software for your mind. Helps weed out unhealthy thoughts.

Depression And Anxiety

These are two of the easiest traits to become immersed in. If your thought processes are negatively inclined, you have absolutely set yourself up for a very uncomfortable ride.

I took that ride for years. I still even have the odd day or week where these affect me.

Changing thought processes can help exponentially. Knowing who you are can help too. Knowing that I am a good person and that I matter, absolutely aided in myself getting through some dark moments.

Catching a thought before you branch off in negative thought combats both anxiety and depression.

Surrounding yourself with people who see your worth leads you to see it within yourself.

I think it is key to have a support person that you have access to at least once a week. I have found that having a trustworthy person or two make a huge difference in helping you through tough times and/or situations. Once you have established trust with this or these people, conversations become easier to have and ideas or opinions can be challenged in a healthy manner. Your support person or people may even become vulnerable and tell you one of their own stories. Depression and anxiety are very common and most people will experience one or both within their lifetime.

On dark days, I tend to look at my life and voice what I am grateful for, or all the good things I have: two beautiful children, a healthy family, roof over our heads, food in the cupboards, the car starting…and the list goes on.

Fatigue And Sleep Issues

Before learning about AS and its traits of sensory overload and ADD, I would struggle through each day because by 10 am every morning I was completely drained of energy. By 1 pm in the afternoon, my eyes would become heavy as a thumping headache would form. I would feel guilty about resting during the day and so would busy myself with anything just to stay awake. By 8 pm each night, I would fall asleep exhausted on the couch. Just to give you a visual; sitting upright, head back, tongue out, slight drool, and snoring as loud as the TV.

I knew I needed help and so started researching AS and sleep issues.

My sleeping patterns are all over the show. Most nights, I want to stay up till at least midnight. Now I know that this really isn't the best idea for someone like myself. The less sleep you get, the more fatigued you become, right? Well, take that and then times it by 10 and that is how I feel. I'm tired; I'm in pain physically; I'm still having to process sight, sound, smell, and I also have an internal script running in my head.

Going to bed at the same time each night may not be able to cure me of fatigue. But if my sleeping patterns or lack of REM sleep keep me from being well rested, at least I would have been in a resting position for eight hours.

Now that I know why I am fatigued, I know the best thing to do is rest or sleep when I feel the need. Doing this helps alleviate fatigue from the daily challenge. I have even noticed there is a usual or regular time of day that the fatigue sets in, so I have organised daily chores and/or errands around it.

I have had and still have days where I overexert myself mentally and/or physically. I find that I can function throughout the day but pay the price the following day. I am so tired the following day that I am only able to lie and watch TV all day. If I take each day slowly and apply myself skilfully to tasks, I am able to function the following day also. I have learnt not to stretch myself too thin and too wide. My ratio of good to not so good days (relating to fatigue) would now be 5:7, a huge improvement considering I was pretty lucky to get 1:7 three years ago.

Sensory Sensitivity

From the first moment I open my eyes to the moment I fall asleep, I live in a world of constant stimuli.

As I sit here writing in the dim light, I can hear the dog breathing, the TV show playing in the background, the clicking of the computer mouse under my partner's finger. I can also feel the soles of my feet on the floor, and I can still taste my dinner on my tongue.

Everyone knows that there are five human senses: sight, sound, smell, touch and taste. Almost everyone would experience at least three or more of these every day. My experiences with these senses are quite intense. My eyes are very sensitive to almost every type of light. My ears are sensitive to loud noises, especially high tones. It hurts when I am touched unawares; it feels like a pulse of energy shoots through my body from the point of contact.

One of the reasons that Aspies are so sensitive to stimuli is because of our Reticular Formation. The Reticular Formation is a region in the brainstem that is involved in multiple tasks. One of those tasks is filtering incoming stimuli to discriminate irrelevant background stimuli. For people with AS, their Reticular Formation does not work properly and therefore does not filter out background stimuli.

I have no control of what enters my brain all day every day. When I was younger, I experienced meltdowns as stated earlier in the chapter. I am now making a link between my sensory overload to my dysfunctional Reticular Formation.

My new sensory equation:

Dysfunctional Reticular Formation + no filtering stimuli − no time for processing x 16 hours per day, seven days a week = Sensory Overload

Nowadays, I try to protect myself by having time to myself, whether it be quiet alone time or what I call *adult time* after I have put the kids down for the night. I might write, watch TV or even listen to music. I wear my Irlen lenses daily. I have restricted my exposure to certain noise levels (I only wish my kids had a volume level that was adaptable). I also avoid certain places or stores like the plague at certain times or days when I know it may be busy. That way I can get away without being touched or electrocuted, as I would say.

Understanding yourself and how your body works can ultimately help you find a plan that suits you and your lifestyle.

Stimming

To those of you who do not know what stimming is, it is a ritual that you perform in order for you to process information.

Funnily enough, one of my stims is to sit and watch TV for hours and hours. Who doesn't do that, right? It's amazing the information I process effortlessly each night. A quick fix of mine is staring aimlessly at an object. I can even do that and hold a conversation at the same time.

Some people stare off into space and look quite vacant for what seems to be a long time (especially if you just asked them a question). Just so you know, they haven't checked out of the conversation. They are merely processing loads of information in a matter of seconds.

Some people retreat into bedrooms with curtains closed, jump into a duvet, and proceed to roll themselves in it until they are cocooned within the duvet. I gave it a go once…and only once, I couldn't stop giggling the whole 30 seconds because my mental picture of doing it looked nothing like the real thing. It actually felt like I was a human burrito that was hiding in the nether regions of someone's fridge.

Stimming is a way of processing or sorting information so that it can be filed in a way that makes sense to ourselves and in turn can be recalled when needed. It also is a form of download. Once the files are downloaded, there is space made for tomorrow and so on.

Another stim that is very therapeutic for me is actually what I am doing right now…writing. The words seem to flow out of me and once they are ink on paper, space clears in my mind. It is no longer a thought. It becomes visual/physical and the process of putting it all into words frees it from being intellectual. The really interesting part is that because it is physical, your brain does not file it away in such detail. What's the need to if you could access it in physical form whenever you need it? Ink and paper takes the place of intellectual filing cabinets for me.

Conclusion

So, as you can see, I have learnt a lot about Aspergers. You could even say that I have made it my special interest.

I have learnt to be kind to myself and that it is okay to take things slowly, to physically only give what I can, that it is okay to fail, and that taking care of myself can lead to becoming a happier and more balanced person.

I have learnt that there is a person out there that will accept you for who you are. When you find this person, they will see you for the creative, honest, and upstanding person that you are, and they will praise you for making their lives richer.

I have learnt that Aspies are very special people who have the ability to see the world in a different light. It's just another thing that makes us interesting.

I have learnt that when needed an Aspie can adapt to any situation if they have been given the time to process all information presented to them. It would be analysed and nit-picked until all the bugs had been worked out or worked through. If it will make life easier for the Aspie, they will move heaven and earth to implement change. I am living proof.

I am proud that I am Aspie and I am proud that I am able to adapt myself to better my life…not only for myself but for my family too. Like I said earlier, I am still a work in progress, but I am a long way from where I was when I started my journey. I have seized the challenge of self-discovery and self-improvement. Truthfully, I don't think that I will ever stop learning and evolving. It is absolutely going to be an interesting life!

All the best to you on your journey.

Friends
Author: Name withheld

Over time, we became friends and did what friends did; we got together; we chatted; we shared similar interests; we raised something interesting from work or the news; we mulled over future plans; some historic life stories got a grumble; we shared books and some movies; we went to different theatres and the opera; we explored art galleries and a few antique shops extensively (the latter of which she initiated and loved doing); we walked my dog on the beach or went for bush walks; we occasionally went shopping and had regular coffees together for years, working steadily through the cafes in town, sharing birthdays, and occasionally going out for a meal together. We were introduced by a mutual friend who later moved out of the district, and on our breaks, it would be the two of us meeting instead of the three of us, usually about twice a month as our busy lives permitted. She came to my book review and opening night. I took her shopping to find a suite for her office, necessities for a wild animal she rescued; she needed to buy a dehumidifier or sometimes just to buy her groceries, as she had no car. Like all people, we both had interests outside of the friendship, but we also had quite a few in common; we were both professional women, ran our own successful businesses, were involved with our relative communities, and were single (through choice), plus all the activities we did together over a few years, as described already.

From my own work, I knew almost immediately that she was on the spectrum. She knew there was *something different* about her; she had once confided. She gave her perceived condition a (self-diagnosed) name which was not on the spectrum, and she had developed a diet and routines that gave her optimal capacity to live her life. She had funny (peculiar) little mannerisms in coffee shops or ordering meals, or the order in which she absolutely needed to do things, and certainly in the way she treated people. Because of her need for a certain order and layout of her plans, I would often try to adapt around her (I just saw it as important to her). She once told me she found this a particularly *disappointing* habit of mine and that I needed to have more structure myself, which would help [me] be more *inflexible* as she *saw* that I often went against what I really wanted to do! Considering that I was a businesswoman, with several children (she was childless), that I had no external help and therefore needed to be very structured to make all my jugglings work; I found this statement particularly startling and rather humorous. I shrugged it off as her Aspie thinking and her inability to accurately read and relate to others and her *lack of theory of mind*, which is often the first of the diagnostic criteria in most textbooks on Aspergers.

Most people, despite her strongly socialistic thinking, were treated by her as objects, and she talked at them – while at the same time being sincerely and very genuinely concerned always for others and extremely, deeply, respectful of *humans as* she referred to people. She would note that a kind and patient waiter was *a good human*, for example – and would then say that directly to them. People – who were mostly strangers – would often look at her in mild surprise and puzzlement as she talked, albeit always kindly and respectfully, at them. The only exceptions were the few people she become fond of, and with these she would have a more confiding type of relationship, and she was more relaxed and possibly less intense. She had a deep spirituality (and yielded to her own cluster of gods), which understandings she would use mainly to interpret the behaviour of other people. She also had a huge dependence on astrology, which she applied vigorously to her relationships as it helped her to get a framework in which to operate (she did not like my particular zodiac sign she had told me, although it was apparently compatible to hers, and then was annoyed that I did not behave as people in my star sign ought to do). She also had an intuition or sixth sense so that she operated from some place of instinct and would often try to intuit the intentions of another, often having complex hypothesis and interpretations (she usually had no factual information) of a social situation in which she may have become involved. I found her way of viewing life interesting albeit curious, as it was so different to what I knew.

She continually sought order and structure and would hire work staff she would call *assistants* (whom she paid very generously in line with her socialistic thinking, principles that she personally and admirably upheld in her own life), to then manage her housework, post her work mail or even to collect her library books that she had ordered – and this system was a useful adaption for her, and worked well for her, as it meant she could get to things she intended to do. Without assistants, she lived in a vague disarray with mounting stress as she was unable to achieve all that she felt that she needed to do, and she certainly could not manage everyday chores and basics independently as she could never stay focussed long enough to complete anything; she was easily distracted, then frustrated, then distressed, and went in repeated circles. Unfortunately, her assistants did not last longer than a few months, and she would be searching for the next perfect assistant who would really *get her* – I have no idea why they left, but I was just aware that these people were briefly in her life and then gone and would not come back. She did tell me her interpretation about vibes and feelings and spiritual conflictions and zodiac signs, but I could never work out the facts and did not pursue those discussions.

Despite her quirks, I enjoyed her honesty and intelligence and how she tried to live true to herself, and our time together was almost always pleasant and social and interesting. She seemed to sincerely and genuinely engage and was very chatty – leading many of the conversations. We would enjoy a coffee, a walk outdoors, or brainstorm ideas or just chat, as one does in any friendship. We were friends, and it was good to just escape work and just *be* in the moment.

Then two surprising things arose and changed everything. They came, proverbially *out of the blue* as it often does with Aspies.

The first was my *fault* originally – I committed the heinous crime of forgetting her birthday in the first year that I knew her. I took her out to lunch nearly three months later as a light-hearted compensation. After that, she became extremely anxious as her birthday approached. She was estranged from her extended family and was herself both single and childless. She would talk of unhappy birthdays and being overwhelmed by birthdays but her strong need to be acknowledged remained quite obsessively – so I tried to remember and to my knowledge got it right for a few years there (that's where diaries are useful!). I understood that the acknowledgement of her birthday was deeply important to her. Apparently, her birthday went by every year in the past, for many years, completely unacknowledged, and this had become a major issue in her life – and evidence of her increasing sense of isolation and aloneness. Earlier in that last year of friendship, we had been to an antique shop that was closing down, and she had fallen in love with an exquisite little teacup set. I returned to the shop later and purchased it about six months in advance for her birthday – not my usual pattern of purchasing gifts, but the opportunity was great to get her something that she had so openly and gleefully delighted in.

Just a little over a month before her birthday, we were having coffee and she expressed a longing to do something special for her birthday. (She would never reveal her age, but I understood that this was one of the *big ones*, some sort of significant mid-life age and milestone). I offered to support her in that and we decided that she would think about it and would let me know. It seemed that she only wanted to go out to dinner, so that was quite easy for me to arrange to meet with her. Because of her dietary restrictions and her need for things to all line up for her, I left it to her to choose the date, place and time, albeit I had commitments as well. About two weeks later, I sent her a text to ask what she had decided, and she said that she would get back to me, which was the first conversation we had had about that topic after her decision originally. She would occasionally drop a text about other matters, like work or a book she was enjoying. A week before her birthday, we had a coffee again, and I brought it (her birthday intention or plan) up casually when she mentioned her coming birthday, and she thought of a local restaurant that she enjoyed. It had views over the water. She would book and get back to me. She planned to book on her birthday, which was on the Friday.

That Thursday night before her birthday, she initiated contact about the matter and said that she could no longer make the dinner and postponed the birthday dinner saying that she was overwhelmed with work and would spend the day at work and out with clients on her birthday. She had misjudged her work commitments and would not be free as she had previously thought. I had no problem with that and could certainly relate.

The following morning, I sent her a text to wish her a happy birthday. She thanked me. I had a work meeting at midday and would have had to go directly past her house to get to my meeting, so I popped in and left the wrapped parcel on her front porch (knowing that she was out with clients as she had indicated the night before in her text message). Later that evening, she had found it on her arrival home and had texted to say how delighted she was with it and that she was keen to have a discussion with me as to where I had made such a great find! (She had obviously forgotten our visit to that little antique shop, which was great!) She suggested a coffee at lunchtime the following Wednesday when she would be free. I had a client cancellation, so we teed up a time. All good and normal.

On the Monday evening, she texted me to say that she needed to have a serious discussion about our *relationship*, which she would do on Wednesday evening. She sent a second text to say that she "did not want to blindside [me] and hence the warning". I responded that this sounded very serious, and she responded that "yes – it [was]". I then sent her a follow up message to say that as this was serious, she may prefer that we talked this evening and I [was] willing to come over. It was obviously important and distressing to her plus I certainly did not want to wrack my brain to try and fathom what she could be thinking!

She replied rather brutally with: "Pull yourself together. You are a professional woman who works with people. Stop making a drama of this! You are now harassing me. You harassed me on my birthday. I will see you on Wednesday at my house for coffee. Do not contact me again until then."

I was completely shocked. I laughed because it was so untrue and ridiculous that I was not even going to respond to it. I *chose (and had to work hard at that choice)* to put it out of my mind as I did not want to now become distressed myself. I knew it was classic Aspie behaviour and thinking, and that it was pointless to try and ameliorate this situation in any way, as she was not able to. I knew that she had a complex code of rules by which she lived and I assumed that I had broken one of her invisible, unwritten rules and offended her in some manner. I could do nothing until I found out which rule it was.

On the Wednesday, it was pure curiosity that took me to her house, to see what she was actually thinking and what she was going to say. I declined a cup of coffee so that she would not have to become anxious by doing the *manners and hospitality thing*, which usually stressed her and would certainly increase her stress in this situation. She then proceeded to make what was a clearly rehearsed speech and which I did not interrupt.

(If Aspies are interrupted during a serious speech, they are often flustered and distressed and often have to start over again at the beginning, or they break down and are unable to complete what they intended to say. They can then become a bit disoriented and may thrash about verbally, and sometimes may show emotional distress and/or aggression -ed.)

She said that she wanted this space to express her feelings about us and that I had to hear her through and not respond. I was aware that she expected to be taken literally, so I made not a single comment throughout and only listened.

She then stated that the *relationship* was not working for her for the following four reasons:

- She had always wanted a *playmate* and she *had discovered that [I] was not [her] playmate and never would be*! "A playmate was a person you had lots of fun with like road trips and holidays," she explained carefully, almost a little patronisingly – except that she did not recognise that that was the tone of voice that she was using.

I wondered if she had a delusion that we could be a Thelma and Louise type of relationship, or if this was what she thought a framework for a friendship was. She based a lot of ideas about people around movies that she had seen. I thought of the several road trips we had taken to the big smoke *about two hours' drive away, where we went to the opera and other shows. Personally, I don't enjoy opera very much, but I was willing to go with her. We had a lunch one particular day, walked around, and then attended the opera and drove home, chatting, and enjoying ourselves. We had had other similar experiences none of which I assumed were relevant in her current thinking.*

- She explained that [I] had no idea how to be a friend! She said that she needed to explain to me how friends worked as [I] obviously had no idea! She proceeded to explain that friends had a common hobby and goal, and that they would work together to achieve this. "We had never made such a goal," she said disappointedly. "When we got together, we just talked about different things and this was not how a friendship worked in [her] eyes," she explained further. She thought I needed to work out how to make friends and how to keep them. She said very kindly that she hoped I would take this word of advice to heart and apply it in the future as she only wanted to help me!

Again, I was astounded as I have many friends, and some of those friendships have been around for longer than twenty years! I knew that she had no other friends in the community. Also, as discussed in the first paragraph, we had behaved like friends in many areas – so I was confused as to how she saw friendship!

- She felt that I would always put my children before her.

This was a friendship (or not – apparently!) and not a couple relationship in any way, where children might possibly be an issue. My astonishment was beyond words at this statement and as she continued with that thought further, I again did not interrupt her or even mentally respond to such thoughts that she was expressing.

- Finally, she concluded that I gave her *no energy* and that friends gave each other *energy*. As [I] would obviously never give her energy, she therefore felt that she had to *end the relationship*.

Just in case there is any confusion or misperception here for the reader, this was purely a friendship between two middle-aged heterosexual women; there was never a physical or sexual component or any type of commitment that moved this from a friendship to a relationship!

I stood up. I said, "I have heard your feelings. I am leaving now." And I walked out the door.

And I never returned.

To protect the identity of the parties who are both professional women in a small town, this story was dictated to Dee as the editor of this chapter, and the author needs to remain anonymous. The author felt that her neurotypical experience of a friendship with this Aspie needed to be described for others who may have had similar confusing events that had happened or would happen to them.

Editor's note: This neurotypical had obviously adapted a fair bit to the needs of her AS friend because she understood AS and could therefore accommodate to some of the AS needs, and the friendship had gone on a lot longer than perhaps it would have had if that understanding of AS wasn't there. The friend had obviously felt that she too had done all she could to make the friendship work, within her own understandings.

Mother of AS Daughter
Vixxen (pseud)

Hello, I am a mother of an autistic daughter. She was diagnosed when she was around three. A speech language therapist picked up on it while we were having a meeting. It was a bit shocking to hear at first, but I did already have some concerns as she had gone from talking quite well to hardly at all. She would cry all the time and we were struggling. Getting a diagnosis so early in her life helped I think, as I was able to do some courses that helped me to better understand, teach, and discipline her in a way that she would understand. Yes, I think discipline is a vital part of growing up, and I think that there's a stigma that if a child is special needs, you have to wrap them in cotton wool because they will not be able to handle it. Well, I think the more you introduce them to things, they start to adjust and become more independent, but if you don't allow them to experience life because you are struggling, then it's just going to hinder them. When there are services out there you can access, like the ASD plus course, the incredible years parenting course and Northable too, then use them. My daughter is 10 now, and she's high functioning on the spectrum. She talks a lot better though still has some trouble with her sentence structure. Most people don't even realise that she is autistic because she is very social and loving. She has very high sensory needs where she always wants to be tickled, and she tippy toes, but she has met or exceeded all milestones at school and makes me so proud and happy. I think for most parents, it's hard to even think that there may be something *wrong* with your child, but there isn't even if they are diagnosed with autism or Aspergers or any of the other neurological disorders. It's your acceptance and understanding that will make all the difference to your child. Thank you.

My Story
Sharlene Liggett

From day one, I knew something was different about my baby son. He wouldn't be comforted easily; he would stare into the distance, blank face; he would scream for such a long time if there was a loud noise such as me blending his food or the Velcro strap on his safety sleeper making that ripping sound. I called in my midwife and the GP, the Plunket nurse, and various friends who had new babies; everyone said there was nothing wrong with him. He was interactive and content; why was I trying to find fault with him? I knew, but now I seriously doubted my instincts as a mother.

As time went on, he often acted like a regular toddler. I decided I was wrong, and everyone else was right. He was a normal little guy. But why didn't he start walking and talking when he should have? And why, oh why, did he scream so much when there was a loud sound? Why was he such a fussy eater? Why would he cry relentlessly when I tried to introduce him to day care where there were a lot of kids and noise? No one had answers. Everyone thought it was me with the problem. So I adapted to taking him to a home-based childcare where it was much more peaceful. I made no loud noises around him, and we had our own way of communicating or I simply tried to guess what he wanted.

The moment I became pregnant with my second son, he went off my breast milk. The crying of the new baby terrified him. I didn't know who to comfort first, my terrified toddler or the new baby. I only had two arms. He was fearless, would run head on giggling into the waves at the beach. I would get him out of his car seat and he would take off running. He would always take off running with such reckless abandon. My outings were limited, and usually with a friend,

I would convince to tag team with me to attempt to contain his disappearing acts. My life became more and more confusing and isolated. My relationship with the children's dad broke up very quickly. Even though we had teacher aides in kindergarten for him and speech language specialist working with him before school, the paediatricians declared him just lazy; he had nothing wrong with him. My memory is of when he was about four and there was of a panel of a multidisciplinary team consisting of an occupational therapist, psychologist, speech and language therapist, and a paediatrician. I was sitting on the other side opposite them, anticipating a conclusion to their assessments of my son. Now I would finally understand him and get my answers! I couldn't stop crying when they told me there was *nothing wrong with him*, and I needed to have a look at myself to see why I was always trying to find something wrong with my son.

That is where I burnt out with my plight. I tried making him be a regular kid; I expected it. The great health professionals en mass said so. We just muddled along somehow. A few years later, I met a woman who encouraged me to revisit an assessment for my son. She had a similar story with her now adult son who was diagnosed with autism. Should I? I was beaten into submission years before, so could I muster the strength to try to get answers for my son. I knew he had autism. I had done my research but kept it to myself. I wanted so desperately to understand him, to support, and guide him! Should I? Some people condemned me with comments like *why try to label your son*? That's not what I wanted.

I made my decision, I saved up my money to go and see a specialist in Auckland. I once again filled in the forms about his behaviour, etc. I finally had enough money, and we made the trip to Auckland. Words cannot describe the emotions I went through on that trip. I was so scared that I would be told once again that I was a neurotic mother with something wrong with me again. I was told by the specialist that he could tell as soon as my son walked in the door that he was on the spectrum. I stayed with a friend in Auckland as I needed to break the trip up. I wish I hadn't. I was so emotional and didn't know what to think!

Eventually, it sunk in. I was right! I then felt terrible as for a number of years I had expected him to be *normal* and to fit in. Now that things had become clear, I could work with his school to get the support and understanding he needed. It was not an easy road, but it was much less of an evil than trying to fit a square peg in a round hole.

It has never been an easy road with my darling son. He is 13 now and what a roller coaster! I love the analogy the *Welcome to Holland* story. It explains it perfectly. I have learnt so much. One thing is to always trust my instinct as a mother. I have learnt how to advocate for my son. I had no idea I had such a mother bear inside me! I have learnt to keep asking for help.

We're in a good place now. I understand why he does the things he does now and so does he. That has taken MANY years and with the help of our amazing counsellor who is guiding us and teaching us. I also admire my son so very much – he is amazing how he overcomes the challenges he faces in his life. He has to learn to fit into this neurotypical world with our weird rules and social expectations, when the rest of us just know it. This is no easy task for him. I love my son's fascinating mind, his creativity and resilience. I know he will do well in his adult life because I finally got the answers and support we needed.

My Story
Tracy Bucknell

Growing up, my little girl watched first and analysed the situation before participating. She had one best friend but was never part of the group and was happy not being so. She had her own groove and purpose. She didn't know what *you're not coming to my party* meant, when little girls didn't get their way.

When she started school, she was labelled an *elective mute* by one of her teachers because she didn't participate in group situations or put her hand up in class for help. She started working one-on-one with a reading recovery teacher and excelled past the standard reading level within six months and the same happened with maths tutoring. When the school brought in a speech language therapist, at six years old, she negotiated games prior to testing with the therapist and was seen to have no problem with speech at all. In fact, when cross-country came around and I wouldn't write her a note to get out of participating, she came home very proud that she talked the teacher in to not making her run and letting her hand out the medals.

When I enrolled her in primary grade soccer (because everyone said group sports would be good for her), she was very hesitant but would only do the individual warm-ups for training during the week, with a lot of encouragement. The first day of soccer on Saturday morning at Kensington Park, she saw all the people watching and the size of the field with its volume of voices and flat-out refused to play and wouldn't go back, ever!

My baby has always been *no frills*. She says things the way they are. She doesn't have time for things that don't interest her or have no purpose. The people in her life mean everything to her, but she finds it hard to express her emotion and gratitude. I love her dry sense of humour and logical thought pattern. I love that I know she will always correct my grammar and remind me *not to wear shoes on the carpet* because that is what I always tell her. She has the most amazing memory and a brain for numbers. What some see as *difficult* or *rude*, I see as just my little girl expressing herself honestly, with the tools she has and the truth she sees.

I know that she needs to know in advance about change, and so we plan and take away the unknowns in the situation, where possible. In high school, this meant walking the route to her new school a few times before she started and having her uniform in the closet two months before school term. She spent the first few weeks navigating the way to all her classes, by going to the next class during break and waiting by the door to make sure she was there on time.

Unfortunately, high school also meant that this *veil* that covered her, her unique, wonderful way of not caring what people thought and being content to be her – suddenly was gone. It's like she woke up one day and just saw all the *ugly* in the world for the first time and was devastated about being her and feeling different.

If this sounds like your child, I hope that you encourage and praise them for their differences; I hope that you accept them and the fact that *normal* comes in all shapes and sizes and that regardless of people's perception, everyone needs love and support to be their very best self. So push past people saying, *they can't cope* and *wouldn't it be easier to go to a special school*. People are always afraid of what they don't understand – dare to challenge their thinking and motives; follow your gut and advocate for your child. If you don't, who will?

Fiona Green Is Setting the Agenda for Disability Pride By Fiona Green

I am standing for the Whangarei District Council in the Okara Ward 2019. If successful, I will be the first Māori autistic female in New Zealand to be elected to a district council.

When I was diagnosed with Asperger's syndrome (a high-functioning form of autism) five years ago, I finally got my answer to a lifetime of wondering why I was so different from everybody else.

I'm proud with what I have achieved in my life with Aspergers. I am proud because autism defines my uniqueness.

Some see disabilities, I see my abilities – and so do others who have an open mind.

Aspergers syndrome is not a mental illness. It affects the way those who are afflicted with it socialise and communicate. Motor skills may appear uncoordinated – walking might be awkward, clumsy or just slightly different.

It is a collection of symptoms that occur together with the condition. We are simply physiologically wired differently. Labelled by some as a *clumsy r*#$!&*, *a delusional ideologue* and a *physically incapacitated lump of meat*, I have proven these comments are unfounded, and I have campaigned hard in my local and business community to change that conversation.

I am a proud and strong voice for the disenchanted and disenfranchised.

I am a social justice (business) and autism advocate. I have a Bachelor of Education (teaching degree) from Massey University; a business management qualification, and I have completed various administrative studies. I've written a number of children's books in Te Reo Māori: I Te Rangi (2006), Taika (2006), Manu Taratahi (2006), Te Punua Kekeno (2006), E Rua nga Weta (2006).

My poems in Te Reo – Ka Pai Nga Tau, Te Kairuku toa, Pitakataka, Kotahitanga, Matariki have featured in He Kohikohinga Publications via Learning Media. I established Business Crisis Support NZ (18 June 2018) to fill a much needed support gap – from my own experience of being treated *differently*, losing a business (due to ill health at the time and entrusting the wrong people to look after it during that time), and experiencing the mental health fall-out – post-loss. I am not alone.

People who have been through this – suffer alone, because of the unforgiving stigmas. They need to find others – for support, comfort, encouragement, and healing, etc. They need to be around those who have experienced similar – in order to gain a semblance of order.

My Bachelor of Education (teaching) degree helps with research, investigation, analysing, writing, presenting information and educating. Aspergers syndrome and my accompanying physical challenges never stopped me – or even others who have it – from running a business and contributing to the local economy. It has not stopped me from using my initiative to fill a much needed support gap which has attracted people at differing levels of entrepreneurship.

My dabblings as a published author – required creativity. Creativity is a skill I draw on in my business and autistic advocacy endeavours.

Events leading up to, during, and after I lost my business, impacted severely on me. Due to a culmination of tragic events – mainly through ill health. I was also diagnosed with an adjustment disorder (similar to PTSD); experienced anxiety, depression, etc.

I worked with an occupational therapist who finally got me motivated again and speaking after I went mute. When it comes to helping others, *lived* experience of mental health is considered relevant experience by the mental health sector – and for this reason, I have used my *lived* experience of business loss, my own life journey with Aspergers – to help others effectively, empathetically, and relevantly.

I proudly initiated the first petition in a move to Change NZ Accounting Law – as a move to ensure accountants support business owners better rather than exploiting their lack of financial and economic literacy.

The Gifts and Strengths That Asperger's Syndrome Brings to My Advocacy Work Include:

- Being hyperfocussed – ability to focus on one objective over long periods of time without becoming distracted. Allows Aspies to accomplish large and challenging tasks.
- Unique global insights – ability to find novel connections among multi-disciplinary facts and ideas which allows them to create new, coherent and meaningful insights that others would not have reached without them.
- Independent thinking – their willingness to consider unpopular or unusual possibilities thus generating new options and opportunities, thus paving the way for others.
- Internal motivation – rather than being swayed by social convention, other's opinions, social pressure, or fears, Aspies can hold firm to their own sense of purpose. Their unique ideas can thrive, despite naysayers.

- Attention to detail – their ability to remember and process minute details without getting lost or overwhelmed gives them a distinct advantage when solving complex problems.
- 3-Dimensional thinking – their ability to utilise 3-dimensional visioning gives me a unique perspective when designing and creating solutions.
- Cutting through the smoke screen – their ability to recognise and speak the truth that is being *conveniently* ignored by others can be vital to the success of a project or endeavour.
- Logical decision making – their ability to make logical and rational decisions and stick to their course of action without being swayed by impulse or emotional reactions. This allows Aspies to navigate successfully through difficult situations without being pulled off-course (source: Coaching Asperger www.coachingasperger.com)

In Breaking Down Any Kind of Stigma Including Disability, I Work on the Principle of:

a) talking about these subjects openly and publicly,
b) letting people know how common these subjects are,
c) speaking out when there has been an injustice.

As one of my friends (85% disabled) remarked recently, "If one moves forward, everyone moves forward."

I am proud that my disability has made me persist in the face of adversity. I am proud that my disability has helped others see their strengths. I am proud that my disability has brought me into contact with others with similar challenges.

I am proud to simply be me.

I am standing for the Whangarei District Council in the Okara Ward 2019. If successful, I will be the first Māori Autistic Female in New Zealand to be elected to a district council.

The only obstacle standing in my way as an autistic candidate is opportunity. Thank you Whangarei District Council for taking me and others who are different, over that line of inclusivity. If I am not elected, my messages of solidarity, acceptance, inclusion, diversity, tolerance across the board will have still resonated throughout Whangarei and Northland.

I am also a proud member of Disabled Persons Assembly (DPA) New Zealand.

My Story
Cherry Knight

Being someone, that it's become evident doesn't have a neurotypically wired brain, has a lifelong feeling that I didn't fit.

Constantly feeling and over thinking…

Why am I so different?

Why don't others speak my language?

Think like me?

See what I do?

Know what I intuitively know?

Perceive life the way I do?

I don't fit; I don't have a sense of belonging.

Those thoughts only cognised where I could put that into words in my fifties. Before that I only had feelings and a lot of negative self-talks about feeling a misfit – but that was before I started engaging with ASD through a work opportunity.

I began engaging with children diagnosed with ASD, and I instantly felt at home, at ease. I seemed oddly to fit. Life became more easeful in their company. I intuitively understood – and the odd obsessions, the high states of anxiety, the over thinking, and profoundly deep conversations were all too familiar.

Seeking to understand more about these children's behaviours, intuitive feelings, their brain wiring, abilities to cope better, I contacted a counsellor who became my counsellor. Before that I had a person that had been mentoring me with my work, with ways to engage, build rapport, to use the technique of (OWL) Observe-Wait-Listen to be better able to see the person and not their behaviours.

In those sessions with my counsellor, I had a profound self-insight as a lot of those symptoms were my natural way of existing, and it was news to me others weren't having the same experience.

After those sessions, a greater self-acceptance slowly grew, and in that acceptance, I am different, it's okay.

Slowly understanding that when the negative self-talk came, the overthinking happened and my anxiety levels were high. And breathing and re-affirming *I Am Okay* brought me back to fundamentally that at my core I am perfectly okay.

The differences, the not fitting, the not belonging were only layers on top of that core person...

List of My Symptoms
Crystal Lundon

Aspergers
Sensory Overload
Mental Overload
Anxiety
Chronic Fatigue
Fibromyalgia
Migraines
Dyslexia
Dyspraxia
Tinnitus
Synaesthesia

Other
PCOS, Hair thinning, Hirsutism
Chronic Lower Back Pain (perhaps from my dyspraxia)
Sleep Apnoea
Gut problems

Sensory Overload

<u>Sight</u>

- Pain in the eyes
- Photosensitivity – sensitive to all types of light: natural, fluorescent, laser, camera flashes
- Fatigue

- Spots in my vision
- Momentary blindness
- Migraines

Sound

- Pain in inner ear
- Pain also travels all the way to brain
- Loss of concentration
- Disorientation
- Become anxious – Amygdala, living in flight-or-fight mode
- Loud noises can evoke emotions like anger and crying because of pain experienced
- Noise like sitting in a classroom results in a headache that will last the whole day
- Fatigue

Touch

- Can feel like I am being electrocuted if touched unawares
- Need sufficient space around me to feel comfortable
- Become anxious – Amygdala, living in flight-or-fight mode

Smell

- Heightened sense of smell
- Some odours can make me feel ill/nauseous
- Headaches
- May need to leave abruptly to escape being overwhelmed by emotions

Mental Overload

- Become easily frustrated
- Brain function slows – can only act on one thing at a time
- Fumble/stammer words

- Hard to communicate simple words and phrases – forget some words
- Dyspraxia – fine motor skills are hard to perform, clumsy
- Mental confusion – brain fog
- Hard to understand what people are talking about or what they want from me
- Have to always ask Does that make sense as I am not sure if I have said what I am thinking

NB: Hard to deal with these effects because it feels like everything is impaired, and I know I am capable of more mentally and physically. It is very frustrating knowing that I have to be like this for some time so my brain can reboot. The longest I have experienced this was 5–7 days straight.

ANXIETY

- High levels of Cortizol daily
- Panic attacks
- Mood shifts/sudden change in emotions

Chronic Fatigue

- Mental fatigue – from sensory overload, anxiety, scattered thoughts, feedback loops
- Physical fatigue – aching muscles
- Always tired – Need lots of rest or even sleep during the day
- Sleep is always interrupted – I wake 4–5 times minimum each night

Fibromyalgia

- Random sharp pains in arms, legs, nose, chest, and stomach
- Tendons feel loose and I cannot perform things like opening jars or lifting heavy items
- Muscle fatigue – aching muscles, mostly arms and chest
- Joints ache or feel enflamed – usually accompanies muscle fatigue

NB: Sharp pains in the upper torso has led to doubling over in pain. Breathing makes pain worse. I have to take shallow breaths until pain subsides.

Migraines

- Tunnel vision that leads to blindness
- Vomiting
- Minimal functioning for two days
- When working previously would suffer a minimum of one migraine per month

Dyspraxia

- Fine motor skills are hard to perform
- Lacking in spatial awareness – walk into doors, doorways, people
- Balance can be impaired
- Trip over things – mats, own feet
- Clumsy

Tinnitus

- Random ringing in ears – high frequency (one ear may even shut off)
- Never quiet in moments of silence – low buzzing

Chronic Lower Back Pain

- Weak muscles
- Easily reinjure myself

Sleep Apnoea

- Wake 4–5 times minimum every night
- May sleep nine hours but awake still tired and even exhausted

- Usually yawing by 10 am and feel I need to sleep by 2 pm

Steps I have taken to help myself:
- Counselling
- Irlen lenses to help with photosensitivity and dyslexia
- Not exposing myself to too much light
- Not exposing myself to too much noise
- Not spending too much time on computers, laptops, or tablets
- Resting during the day
- Sleeping during the day
- Not overexerting myself physically
- Trying to eat gluten-free breads
- Maintaining a balanced diet
- Trying not to have too much sugar
- Taking magnesium in the evenings before sleep
- Setting a bedtime of 10.30 pm

Family Blindness
Dee Jones

(I was told this story so I turned it into a poem.
This family had not yet come to terms with this little boy's possible diagnosis.)

She laughed at her grandson's

- *Cuteness*

As related by her daughter
He'd searched his mother's hair
Closely, carefully
Splitting hairs
To find the

- *Eye*

At the back of his mother's head
She said – no, son

- No eyes
- Just a story to make you behave

He said – that's okay

- Cause Daniel's mum has *two eyes*

At the back of her head
Mother and daughter laughed fondly –
Blind to the eight-year-old
Aspergic boy
Trying to gain *sight*

- And insight.

(The next four contributions were written by the same contributor, with some very real experiences. I loved her insights, awareness, and understanding!)

Some of My ASD Spectrum Traits
"D"

Lack of recognition of faces
Recognising people by clothes or accessories. Conscious cataloguing of people
Social behaviour by rote learning
Sensory overload
Lack of recognition of social cues
High anxiety and exhaustion
No recognition of or common bond with other Aspergics

The Party
"D"

I went to a party recently.

My host introduces me to someone: female, middle-aged, expensive hair, sickly perfume. We talk. Weather, hometown, I love your shoes, where did you get them? Safe, safe, safe. As I desperately move my face in what I hope are appropriate expressions, I try to gauge my effect on her. I can't. Am I frightening her? I decided against using humour – too dangerous.

Someone else moves up. Female, middle-aged, hair a different shade of blonde, different sickly perfume. Introductions. Lull in conversation. Do I move away? Do they both want me to move away? The perfume combination makes me feel sick. The man in the neighbouring group laughs loudly, and I can't hear what either woman is saying. They are both talking at the same time. I really feel sick now.

I move away. Neither woman notices I'm gone. I go to the kitchen counter, which is doubling up as a bar. Red or white? Any alcohol would be a disaster, but it's easier than explaining I don't drink. An awkward looking young man is standing alone by the bar. Kindred spirit? I smile at him. He looks like I am about to take a bite out of him. I grab a glass of white wine and smile and wave to an imaginary person across the room, and go to meet them.

When I get there, a half drunk man is propped up against a wall talking to no one. Dirt under his fingernails, cracked hands, chronic sunburn on his forehead. A farmer? Too much to hope for. I ask him how the grass is doing, and that sets him off on another soliloquy. Yes, a farmer. Excellent. You can say anything about the grass, and it takes ages. I stand under the umbrella of his talk and gaze intelligently at my untouched wine.

A woman grabs my arm.

"I thought you looked like you needed rescuing," she hisses. Bloody hell. Is it the first woman I met, or the second? The two shades of blonde hair are too similar to use as a guide without both women standing together. The first woman was wearing a purple scarf with a gold and amethyst brooch when I met her, but it looked hot, and she may have taken it off. Okay, don't use names.

"Thank you," I respond.

"What did you think about what Lila was saying before?" she says.

What did I what and which one was Lila?

"Oh, I think she has a good point." Hopefully, Lila wasn't just discussing murdering her husband.

"Really, after what's been going on with the Fundraising Committee?"

"Well, yes, that's true. But I still think she has a good point."

"Hmm, I s'pose she does." Lila, if only you knew what I just did for you. "Oh, look. There's Corinne. Corinne darling…" She flits away.

My half-drunk farmer is now fully drunk and snoring in an armchair. No refuge there.

There are no books in the house except a nice leather bound set of Charles Dickens on the mantelpiece. I take down *Great Expectations* and the whole set falls off the shelf. It is a cardboard decoration. No one takes any notice.

I consider making an unnecessary visit to the toilet, but at this time of night, there's probably a queue, and I might have to talk to I someone should remember meeting. You can't just leave a toilet queue.

Two children are trying to strangle each other under the coffee table. No one takes any notice. Maybe their parent hopes they'll finish each other off.

Then I consider the amount of mayhem that is going unnoticed might mean everyone is fairly drunk. Excellent, I find my host.

"Rebecca, I have to leave. I think I'm getting a migraine."

"Oh, you poor thing. So early in the evening too. We haven't had a chance to catch up."

I really am getting a migraine.

I'm not going to another party unless someone gets a court order and makes me.

How right you are?
"D"

"…your selfishness, rudeness, and complete lack of consideration. I don't feel I can take any notice of you until you have apologised." She concluded her litany of my faults with, "My sister says you're creepy."

My best friend had just subjected me to a verbal tirade. I had not seen it coming. Apparently, I *should have tried harder* to like our other mildly obnoxious flatmate. I thought I had been a good friend, supporting her through a breakup with her boyfriend (very boring), and sharing my precious chips when I had takeaways.

I was eighteen years old and had left home a year before. This was my first student flatting situation, and I was finding it tough going. The dirt, disorder, noise, unwashed dishes, and the leak in my roof of my room combined to make my life a misery. The people surrounding me every day baffled and frightened me. I didn't even feel human, let alone part of the activities that my peers delighted in.

It would be a full decade before I realised that my friend was possessed of a self-absorption that only a beautiful eighteen-year-old can have. Her deep sense of *rightness* automatically made *me* wrong. I believed her. Her self-assurance that she was correct was an extreme example of what I have come to think of as *self-marketing*.

Self-marketing is a deep-seated belief that one's own way of doing things is the only right way, and the presentation of that belief. An instinctive understanding of the subtle cues of other people and an ability to judge where one fits in a social situation *should* be the normal way of operating. I know that my inability to grasp concepts is *wrong*; it has been proved to me many times. Many people never doubt their own correctness.

I have spoken with many other Aspergers syndrome sufferers, and that feeling that *something is wrong* with them is a common finding. Conventional counselling and psychotherapy serves to highlight the gaps without acknowledging the extra facets of an Aspergic mind. I had several well-meaning therapists who tried to train me to *feel properly*. This left me with a keen awareness of my own defects.

I was 41 years old when I first (self) diagnosed my Aspergers syndrome. Suddenly, the world made sense. I wasn't broken; I was different. I will never know what is going on in a room crowded with people. On the other hand, I can find four leafed clovers as I walk past them and recognise individual sheep from across a paddock.

Everybody who told me I was wrong can go jump in a lake. I am fine.

Stimming
"D"

Emotion. Don't know which one. Try to identify it. Maybe anger. Yes, its anger. Try to feel angry. Sort of angry. Fades after a few seconds. Try expression? No, last time I did that it was disastrous. I don't get it. Identification and expression are supposed to work, my counsellor said so. Emotion still there. Internal friction, like tectonic plate pressure. Earthquake would be a relief but impossible. Lasts for days. Tighten up the rules, helps with living with the friction.

Finally, peace and quiet. I can stim. Guilt rises, remnants of being punished for this as a child. I really want to do this. The carpet pattern floats. The almost vertical lines the curtains make with the window frames shimmer. The intersections are fantastic. I look at them over and over again; each time they are the same and different. Things start to move. The carpet pattern vibrates while remaining still. Wonderful. I start to rock my whole body. Sometimes side to side, sometimes back and forward. Today, side to side is better. Harmonises with the movement of the carpet, amplifies it, nullifies it. Sensory input to my brain fades. I can hear the clock ticking and the birds outside, but they lose their importance. I stop looking at individual things and can see the whole. Peace. The world is soft, uniform. I am aligning with the underlying patterns of the whole universe.

Slowly, individual sounds and objects reform. I stop rocking. The world comes back into focus.

Wonderful. I look at the clock. Twenty minutes. A good session. The tectonic plate pressure in my mind has eased.

That was better than an earthquake.

My Story
"Jan"

"Do the best you can until you know better. Then when you know better, do better." – Maya Angelou

If only I had known! That first ten years of our marriage could have been so much easier. I spent so much of it confused, self-doubting, over-compensating, and over-giving trying to fill the gaps that undiagnosed Aspergers can cause on a couple and a family. It wasn't until my brilliant, quirky, and anxious oldest daughter was in her first year of intermediate school that she self-diagnosed as Aspergers. With a little digging and speaking to those in the field, my husband also recognised himself in the criteria and our crazy world started making sense. The sense of relief that I was not mad, that there was some reason behind the inconsistency of our relationships, was mixed with a grief that still sneaks up on me eight years later.

I am a therapist. One of those overly attuned types that lets her intuition guide her, creative, freedom loving, and spontaneous. So yes, the complete opposite of our loved ones on the spectrum! I think I was attracted to my husband as he felt solid to my fluid, logical to my intuitiveness, organised to my chaos. I adored (and still do) my quirky, imaginative girl whose playhouse turned into a laboratory, who at five wanted to be an archaeologist, and, with her little sister in tow, would go on adventures in our garden. It took me a while to realise that it was the packing for the adventure – her special interest at the time – that took most of the day while the garden ramble was all of five minutes! She was so lucky to have a little sister who was her opposite in every way (and still is). Emotionally wise, warm and happy to take the back seat and do her big sister's bidding – until the age of four when she found her own voice and would pack the bags no more!

I have learnt so much from the strange combination of needs, traits, and personalities of this family. Once the understanding of the diagnosis and its impact on daily life sunk in, our world changed. The Aspergers didn't change, but our way of being a family did. My expectations lowered, then morphed, then grew again but in a different direction. I understood we were not like other families at the school or the sports ground. We needed more downtime. At times, I've felt stretched in every direction with the opposing needs in the household. My older daughter's need for quiet and withdrawal, my youngest (not ASD) with her need for friends over, my husband exhausted from a career dealing with people all day, and of course, my own needs to go out dancing or being with friends. There is a certain loneliness living with people on the spectrum, something deep within us that does not get attended to with an Aspergers partner or even child.

But now we know better, and so we do better. I adore my family. I love difference and people who challenge the norm, I always have. That's why I do the work I do. My husband is one of the best people I know. A truly *good* man. But as a partner – that's been a bit harder. He has learned and has been open to learning, and my daughter has had the benefit of his example and learning. He often says, "If I had known what she did when I was her age, life would have been easier." I am not sure I could stay with a partner that was not willing or open to learning and accepting they had an Aspergers diagnosis. I don't know where else there would be to go from there.

Here are a few of the things that have helped me along the way:

- One or two sets of good family friends. We are lucky enough to have a few families with their own quirky kids that we socialised with from when the girls were little. Slightly odd behaviour was okay and accepted; the kids and adults got to practise their social skills, and no one was offended if someone left early. Not too many surprises or new people to relate to each time and lots of outdoor adventures in nature that avoided over-stimulating environments.
- Lots of downtime: I had to learn to accept that there was not much energy left over after a day at work or school and allow people to retreat to quiet rooms for a few hours before we could gather together again or talk about the day.
- Holidays: For us this was essential to break away from the routine of life, and my loved ones with Aspergers loved it. For some reason adventures away were an escape for all of us, and I think this helped us stay together in the hard times of the undiagnosed days.
- Movement: I can't stress this enough. People with Aspergers are not good at the emotional processing stuff – they HAVE to do it through their bodies. If my two don't get to boot camp or be active for a few weeks, they are completely different people (and not in a good way!) Good for us also.
- Regular food: I know it sounds obvious, but they both forget to eat. Ditto with putting on a jumper, feeling pain or taking pain relief, knowing they are hot or cold.
- Ask for what you need: Be clear and stop waiting for your Aspergers loved one to *just know* things – they don't. You are the one with the emotional insight, and you will be right in matters of the heart. If you want flowers, ask for flowers. If you want a hug, ask for a hug. If the

way they are talking to you is not okay, tell them it's not okay. If they are shouting or talking loudly, tell them they are shouting. There is very little introspection on their part. It is not their fault, and they are not trying to be rude or hurt you. I wish I had known this one earlier as it would have saved a lot of hurt feelings on my part.

- Common interests: I think this is a big one in terms of maintaining a relationship in general but especially with a few people with Aspergers in the family. Board games, puzzles, quiz nights, escape rooms (we do these when we travel) are all the perfect side-by-side social stuff that helps create social occasions with a bit of structure and less intensity than dinner or a party. Any side by side doing – fishing, diving, hiking, travelling with others is a good way to take care of your own social needs and support your loved ones on the spectrum.

- This one you will have heard before – work I love, my girlfriends, my dance, walking on the beach, music, reading, hands in the soil planting flowers, yoga, walking the dog. The *you* stuff, I'm much better at it now. Sometimes it can be very energy draining living with people with Aspergers. Have a space somewhere to call your own. We had a big tree in the garden of our home, and when it got too much, I would sit and lean my back into its trunk and ask for strength. A strong spiritual life and a strong connection of that spirit through nature has held me all the way through.

- Outsourcing – anything you can. This means getting support and help for all the small things in life. It may look like swapping skills with someone to get something done in the house (projects don't get finished quickly in my house). My first work pay went on someone to clean as it was always such an energy drain for me. I think energy is the greatest commodity in our house, and we have to be mindful to have things and systems in place to make things as easy as possible. We moved into town when the girls reached intermediate age, and it was the best move we made as the everyday logistics were easier. Whatever your easy is – do it!

- Getting the right support: That means counsellors, doctors, research, support groups. Ask for help – no one is supposed to do this stuff alone.

- I was watching Greta Thunberg, the 16-year-old climate change activist leading the charge worldwide, who also happens to have Aspergers. It's no surprise to me. Autism genes are game changers in our world. The ability to see things differently and the courage, the enormous courage to speak their truth (because there is either truth or nothing in my house) amazes me. We need these clever minds and these new ways of seeing. And we need to make our world a place where these ways of seeing are accepted, encouraged, and supported. My daughter has experienced first-hand the price of seeing the world differently and yet she courageously continues being out in a world that is not always kind. I am incredibly proud of my family. All four of us. We have had to grow beyond ourselves to a place where the four of us can dwell. It has not been easy. But there are so many versions of love. I may not have the one I thought I would have, but this family has taken me to a much bigger and broader definition of what big love might really mean.

Now I can differentiate between what is the autism and what is the person. And have learnt to love and accept both for what they are without losing myself in the process. That took a lot of time and has been a very bumpy ride, but I keep my eye on the big picture and hold the belief that we all have value and contributions to make. Courage and kindness – somewhere between the four of us, these things have grown and our Aspergers journey continues to be part of this. And maybe that's what the world needs a little more of – the courage to be different and the kindness to be accepted for it.

Kia kaha on your journey

Nga mihi nui

Jan

My Personal Account of Being a
Wife of an Aspergic Man
Shelley Head

When I first began a relationship with my husband seven years ago, neither of us were aware that he was Aspergic. Although I didn't realise it at the time, he displayed some classic Aspie traits.

1) He was extremely polite.
2) He had a pun for almost every conversation (very clever but became a little annoying at times)
3) His workspace was a chaotic mess (a trait that I still struggle with today).

In 2012, his counsellor suggested that Anthony may be Aspergic. He was 43 years old. It didn't come as a surprise. He had very few close relationships and didn't really know how to do *family* – I learned that he wasn't in contact with any of his cousins and didn't feel a close connection with his sister or parents, for that matter. What I DID see was a fabulous father to his two children. He was/is a very loyal person and jealously guards those that he loves.

I fell in love with Anthony very quickly. He insisted on building our friendship first, and in that time, I witnessed a deeply caring, generous and supportive man who also enjoyed going on adventures as I did. We were both desperate to spread our wings, and it was lovely to have someone to do that with.

Over the years, anxiety has been an everyday struggle for Anthony, as well as a sensory processing disorder which makes going to church or large functions virtually impossible for him to cope with. Anthony is unable to drown out surrounding stimuli and is therefore easily startled or distracted. Some restaurants/eateries have a TV playing music videos or sport. Anthony has to sit with his back to the TV or well out of eyesight otherwise he will fixate on the images and less on me. If he has to go to the supermarket, we try to time it for the quietest time of the day, usually near closing.

Medications have helped to keep his anxiety levels to a more manageable state, and needless to say, Anthony is most comfortable being at home with me and our menagerie of cockatiels and backyard chickens.

Not long after his diagnosis, I came across a book called *Mozart and the Whale – An Unexpected Love Story*, and I identified greatly with the couples' love for cockatiels. By this stage, Anthony and I had begun our collection, and it was delightful to read of another Aspie couple who shared our love for these feathered friends. To quote from the book: "Who needed TV when you have a home filled with cockatiels?" and "It didn't take a psychiatrist to realise that Jerry and I doted on our birds as though they were our children." We have found a safe place in each other and in our feathered love nest!

It has not been an easy journey but one I would not hesitate to go on again. The way I see it, I just had to learn Anthony. There are men out there who wear a false bravado, and internally, they are a mess! My Anthony is real about his struggles; he wears his heart on his sleeve, what you see is what you get, and I'd choose him any day over the great pretenders. I have learned so much from him, and I am not joking when I say that we are still in honeymoon mode after four years of being married.

My Story of Our Family
A.M.

Meltdowns. That's what I called them. And then I read about them in a book. A children's picture book that I came across in the library when I had taken the kids there one day. My son was having them. Regularly. Almost every day after school. Until you learn to do everything, you can to avoid them. To minimise them. To protect the little sister from being collateral damage. Not to mention getting out of the house in the morning five days a week. Exhausting. Come to think of it…I was about to say, he didn't have meltdowns as a pre-schooler…let's say, he didn't have as many meltdowns as a pre-schooler – there were a couple of doozies I can remember…and I *do* recall keeping an eye on things if several kids were playing together from say 4–10 years old.

As a baby/toddler, other mothers would say things like: "You're so lucky…he's so quiet…he would just sit and observe the others, sucking his lip and twiddling his hair…"

"Mummy, why do I have to go to kindy?" he calmly asked – just wanting to understand why he had to go somewhere he did not want to be. Somewhere boring. Noisy. Could never join in freely with others. A tide of boys running backwards and forwards through the playground – and one little pre-school boy just standing in the middle, sucking his lip, twiddling his hair into a propeller on top of his head, following them as a tennis crowd follows the ball. (His hair was not overly long, but it was cut shorter for school – you can't go to school with a propeller on your head.) This and many, many other social awkwardness issues. Years of loneliness and sadness at not being able to join in with the other kids at school – not helped by the fact that we moved cities three times during his school life and then after school, moving to another new city. From kindergarten, through the school years, tertiary study, and starting out working, having to go flatting in a city where he has no friend networks. Heart breaking for a mother to watch. There was a really good patch of about 4–5 years at high school when there was a really good group of about five or six boys with similar interests (i.e. smart and loved gaming).

Picking him up from kindergarten when the first time he ever experienced paint, the teachers could not believe how he used multiple colours and maintained clear lines and colours even though they went over each other, unlike most other children they said. Or the day when they could barely contain themselves until I got there to tell me about the amazing building/city he had constructed from wooden blocks – they had never seen anything like it.

He was happiest at kindy sitting inside with a girl with Down syndrome and her caregiver, quietly doing *table things* – puzzles, books, drawing etc. The time when he was about five years old and covered the floor of a bedroom with a grid of A4 paper that he had drawn on with pen – small, detailed, patterns, shapes, repetitions.

When he was six, someone told me about their grandson who had been having some issues…long story short, he was tested and turned out that he was *gifted* and they encouraged me to have my son tested – yup, also *gifted*. Many years later, it turns out that they are both Aspie. I always suspected he was *on the spectrum*. At one stage (about 10 years old), I had taken him to a psychologist connected with Autism NZ for an assessment. My recollection is that the moment I answered that I had not noticed him having issues with labels on his clothing, she decided that he was just stressed. (Do neurotypical 10-year-olds really flap their hands from shoulder-height while they walk around in public?) It was a short time after that meeting that I found him at home in a brand-new T-shirt with the scissors behind his head trying to cut out the label. The lights went on – I asked him why he didn't wear a particular shirt that looked really nice on him; he said it wasn't comfortable – it had some trims and seams.

Once when the weather had started getting cooler, I had changed the kids' beds to fleecy sheets but didn't tell them because I thought it would be a nice surprise for them when they got into bed. There is a saying, something like: "You've met one Aspie, you've met one Aspie." Well, the daughter loved the sheets. The son didn't get to bed until about 10 pm. "What have you done?" he wailed out of his room. He could not stand the feel of the sheets, and the bed had to be re-made with summer sheets. (He was at high school and often couldn't sleep well/much. He stopped having daytime naps before he was two, unlike the daughter who would often fall asleep even after getting home from kindy and school – even while sitting at the table drawing.)

The daughter seemed *fine* – sociable and happy...until intermediate (again, a move involved making new friends) but also happy in her own company – in fact needed it. When dropping her brother off at kindergarten, he would be asking why he had to go, and she would need to be physically removed – yes, sometimes kicking and screaming – because she wanted to stay. Also assessed and found to be *gifted*.

Always tended to have stomach pain issues, from birth – by high school, it was common to be unable to get up Monday to Friday and then be perfectly fine on Saturday and Sunday. This turned into a number of issues that finally led me to take her to a psychologist, after a visit to the doctor who said that she needed more than counselling. It turns out that she is Asperger...a whole lot of information that she and I had been unaware of its significance started coming out of the woodwork...walking on tiptoes as a pre-schooler...how she looks between people's eyes or past the side of their head when talking to them...how she can feel when she is overloaded and has to get home to a safe place, etc...how *stupid people make my throat hurt*. Compared with her brother and father she seemed *normal* – we had never even considered that she might be on the spectrum.

It wasn't until answering questions with the psychologist, telling her about the son and the father that we found out that the father is on the spectrum. Major realisation time. As many people seem to be finding out these days, after the diagnosis of a child, often at least one of the parents is also on the spectrum. It turns out that the father, prone to anger, shouting, smashing things – in a word, meltdowns – is also on the spectrum. While at first offended: "I'm not autistic!" the realisation and understanding of how and why he processes things in a certain way was enlightening and freeing, and he knows why he can't have too much social time, and why he needs to be anti-social most of the weekend so that he can function during the work week. I used to get frustrated that he would sometimes sleep half the weekend away – now I understand that the social interactions of the week can be exhausting, and he needs to recharge. He would often cancel a social commitment at the last minute – frustrating and embarrassing to live with and to explain to others, until you realise that if it was some other kind of special need or boundary, it would be acceptable for the person involved to say, "No, I can't do that."

Tension was rife in the family while the kids were growing up – particularly between the husband and the son. In one instance, the son got so angry at the tirade coming from the father that his nose *burst* – blood everywhere. I have never seen him angry again since that day, over ten years ago now. I've asked him about it – how can someone go from having meltdowns to no signs of outbursts or anger? He said he just realised that it didn't achieve anything and therefore was pointless. No more anger.

Mealtimes were particularly tense times. Yes – they say, "The family that eats together stays together." The goal, that would be *my* goal, was to have dinner as a happy family time, conversation, no TV. Over the years, it was better to have the distraction of the TV, and with four of us at an eight-seat table, I used to put as much space as I could between the husband and the son. I hated mealtimes.

Both kids were highly sensitive to movies and programmes that other kids had no trouble with – kid's movies – Disney, Pixar. Even very simple pre-school shows could be stressful. I found it was best to watch everything they watched so I could answer the inevitable questions and/or calm the fears.

Awareness has helped with management for the daughter and the husband. The son (now 24 years) sometimes acknowledges that Asperger is there, but he does not believe it is an issue in his life – in spite of mother and sister seeing its impact and talking with him about it and trying to encourage him to see someone who works with it and would understand some ways of dealing with life that could help him. Social awkwardness, lack of friends and relationships is depressing.

One day soon after the husband's realisation of being on the spectrum, we were driving into town to do the weekend grocery shop; he was explaining some of the ways he processes and reacts to things – I reached across and held out my hand. "Hi, I'm Xxxxxx. Nice to meet you." It was a whole new journey of discovery for both of us.

In the shop, there were people chatting with the deli-counter staff – he wanted to request something but had to wait. He came back to where I was waiting with the trolley, hands buried deep in coat pockets and started rocking from foot to foot. I said, "What are you doing?"

His reply, "I want to get served, but they won't go away."

"No, I mean, what are you DOing?" And indicated the rocking.

"I'm always doing this in my head," he replied. Now he knows why.

Watching TV one evening, wife makes comment to Aspie husband – a comment, not a question – one that any *normal* person would have responded to, you know, *engaged in conversation*. Silence. "Are you deaf or are you Aspie?" she asks him.

"I didn't hear anything that required a response," he replies.

Weekday mornings – getting everyone out of the house – were dreaded.

In the afternoons coming home from high school, the son would go to his room – best conversations were frequently at 1 or 2 in the morning when he might be up cooking – never a conversation after school. The daughter on the other hand would need a couch session – we'd both get a hot drink and sit on the couch for anything from 20 minutes (rare) to an hour or more while she downloaded her day. Now in her twenties, she has recently commented that she doesn't know how she would have coped if we hadn't been able to do that.

Bedtime was always another *talk time* – for both of them – more off-loading of the day; the time when troubles seemed to need to come out. The trouble with that was that it was also time when the Aspie husband wanted the wife watching TV with him. Lots of tension.

Son has completed a degree and has a good job. He started a couple of years after his school friends who went to uni straight from school. I knew there was no point making him go straight away – he had to be ready and make the decision himself or it would have been a waste of time.

Daughter is just finishing her *third first year* as she calls it. She has started three different degrees – sciences, English, accounting and is now on anti-depressants. She is really good at study – but hates it. Top of her class in first year web design…only went to two lectures. She had already taught herself most of it off the internet. She has an admin job now – loves it – frequently runs out of work so tries to find ways to slow herself down. I told her to just do her thing and blow them away…she's started tidying up their database…loves efficiency – minimising the number of steps required to achieve the outcome etc… I remember the son used to be big on that too.

Being spoken to harshly in public by your spouse – not fun. But they're oblivious to that. They just don't get it.

My Journey That of a Neurotypical… Possible Living with an Aspie Farmer

She took my hand, encouraged me to embark on what was a most memorable journey – it was breath taking…I had met the love of my life, and I felt so lucky and empowered and energised. Everyone saw it, and they equally rode on that journey with us. Amazing.

Then one day, eight years down the track, it ended…kinda abruptly…more on that later.

Talk about a rollercoaster ride of emotion and excitement. This is my ride on that roller coaster – not right, not wrong, just my perspective.

I have never actually been on a rollercoaster but looking back on marriage, and on reflection, I think I had that rollercoaster ride with my wife. In hindsight and having done some research, I think she is on the spectrum, which is why I offer these thoughts in case they can help others.

The randomness and illogical thought processes that I was confronted with (particularly as our highflying romance disintegrated) to me seemed Jekyll and Hyde to the nth degree.

Now none of these words are designed to hurt or pour scorn. This is simply a deeply thought-out and frank appraisal of my reality and journey.

So life with a potential Aspie you ask. Perplexing – yes. Confusing – yes (for both parties, I have since learned). Malicious…I finally worked out not at all…they are great people. Random – check. Tiring and exhausting…very much so. Mentally and emotionally draining…yes. Always on guard expecting another random conversation, logic or activity – absolutely. Frustrating – yes.

And always wondering *where did that come from*? What sign did I miss? How did I misunderstand the obvious…or did she misunderstand my obvious? And how did I never see all of these signs, threads, mannerisms over the years …looking back, I started to piece some of the puzzle together and realised that there was a trend…if a little random.

Yes – mannerisms and conversations and logics I had at times viewed as illogical in our time together had actually been far more prominent, constant, and regular than I had realised… But clearly completely logical to her. I just had not made the connection until I began to research the spectrum upon the advice of someone more knowledgeable than I on the subject. We can always learn!

When it all ended, it felt like I had been kicked to the curb…that I was now surplus to requirements…clearly, I had missed what requirements I should have been providing or meeting, and so over a period of time, I was struck off. Had broken too many of her rules and there were no more chances allowed. So I was gone. Well, she was. I did not realise many of those rules existed in her mind. Her – I guess it was a given that I should know there were unwritten rules and associated ways to respond, act, think, apply logic. I guess I missed the bus…and missed it too late.

I think I was struck off so she could continue her journey to experience the next best thing. To tick some new boxes…whatever those are…and so many that appear random to me, but it is her journey and her right of passage to do what she feels is best for her. I once suggested the concept of Aspie to her… That she could have that tendency. She was very angry at the insinuation.

She seems happy now – despite for many years suggesting reconciliation…even when in another relationship with another man – again to me…illogical thought. She has created a new life (told me she had no option) but seems to lurch from one fad to the next… And often forgets about the previous fads, just like she does forget about previous friends (despite their loyalty and humility and patience) as she finds a favourite new friend…only one or two every few years. They seem very much on same wavelength as her in thought pattern and logic. Then every few years seems to go back and revisit past friends despite cutting contact for many years – again nothing intentional to my mind – just the way thoughts and memories and stimulation work in the mindset.

Amidst all of this, I receive random photos, social media posts of memories past… Our memories… Married with children…well, married with child.

And at times, it is all as random and illogical as that 1980s TV show (minus the sexism). No right – no wrong.

I wish her well. To this day, I still feel somewhat sad for us, and her, and me, because I feel she is on a crusade for something she may never find or fathom…whatever that is I hope she does. We were soaring, and we created a beautiful baby, which I know she loves but picks her moments for contact and input (as is clearly her mindset... Always with absolute justification, as suits, when challenged or feeling the need to justify actions or rationale or logic). Needless to say, our journey was amazing – from hero to zero.

I have learnt that some conversations are simply not worth having...or better off dropping, saying to her there is no point anymore and walking away...because her mind is made up...and/or we are so far unmatched in thought pattern and logic that spectrum discussing will result in a merry-go-round of indecision/disruption/disagreement/confusion that will create un-needed angst.

If she decides something is white (even if it is clearly black), there is simply no swaying her from that viewpoint. And that's okay. That's her right and her reality – just as my reality is mine... On a completely opposite (again – as I have learnt...I am a neurotypical).

It's ironic really given we were once so in love and so utterly connected (heart, mental, physical) and on the same page.

Now we are not even part of the same book – go figure. But we are part of the same story...we were together...we created a beautiful baby who we both love...and we will be forever linked.

Some days I breathe a sigh of relief that the exhaustion and (attempted) understanding is not my obligation anymore. And that lifts an immense weight. Again – I wish her well in her journey.

Steve

My Thoughts on My Experiences during My Teaching Career Working with Children and Families Living with Aspergers and ASD Marja Smith

My twenty-five-year teaching career has spanned the early childhood, primary and secondary school sectors. I have had the eye-opening privilege and challenge of teaching children living with autism, many with extremely high, challenging needs, both within mainstream classrooms and specialist schools.

When I was asked if I wanted to contribute some thoughts, the Maori way of viewing Autism came to mind: *takiwatanga...his or her own time and space.*

And I thought, *How can I summarise what being involved with the lives and hearts of children and their families living with autism has left me with?* It is too big and beautiful an impact. I am left with forever imprinted memories of the distinct faces, goodhearted personalities, and long-awaited accomplished milestones of these special children and young people. Of their innocent, child-like joy. Of their incredibly honed specific abilities, each and every one of them possessed due to having one or more of their main senses sidelined. Of the mothers and fathers and caregivers whose lives and priorities have changed pace and place due to the greater kaleidoscope of colour these creations have brought into their lives. Their courage, rawness, and determination to cut to the chase and target what is real and most important to and for their child. I remember all these children by name and face and the smiles on their faces, how they transformed the people around them whose senses were supposedly *intact* to valuing different (and I would say even more beautiful in some aspects) ways of *being* in the world. Jordan, who couldn't help but interrupt to take the mickey out of every situation and didn't get how his teachers thought it so inappropriate when it really was quite funny! Sarah, who could recite every native bird and who said it like it was… "Pooh, you stink," when I thought my secret smoking habit with perfume spray was well hidden from my teaching colleagues! Alexis, who found such delight in working out the cause and effect of the shaving foam can and who after years of working with a core-board finally asked for a drink instead of ranting and raving and tearing the classroom cupboards apart to find one (with six teachers tearing our hair out playing frantic guessing games trying to figure out what she wanted!) Six-year-old Lana totally trashing a classroom after being triggered from post-traumatic trauma and abuse, finally falling asleep in exhaustion under a table then accepting being held in an hour-long tight embrace. (All names changed). Children with police tracker anklets because they could scale any height to escape into what their other senses were calling them to, with no fear and perfectly poised, sensed balance and timing. Those who learnt to sit with their lunchboxes without throwing them and feed themselves with a spoon after many years of patient, consistent teaching. To give and receive a hug without suddenly pulling the hair out of the one whose arms they were in or poking the eyes of the person they were staring at…because they had learnt to regulate themselves, birthed from trusted, time and tested, honouring relationship. These are the profound experiences of honour that have touched my life.

If I was asked to choose between teaching a classroom of children living with autism or a mainstream class, I have often chosen the former. The milestones are often far longer awaited and hard won, but I find them by far the most rewarding.

My relationships with these children, their parents, and my teaching colleagues are by far more real, much deeper and both personally and professionally more life impacting.

When I was faced with the possibility of raising a child living with special needs, due to a later in life pregnancy with one whom would rather not if given the choice (due to lack of experience I believe), I knew for me there was no other answer but a full-hearted yes. Because those living with *special* needs and abilities such as autism teach us so much about what really is important – about beauty and patience and love and courage and how to laugh through the frustration and the tears. They gift us this.

Two examples of creative pieces.

This next piece is actually an impressive couple of creative pieces, by an anonymous author. I have included it to show the incredible creativity that some people have!

One of the Nameless

On this land, there is a hill. On this hill, there lies a man. Through this man, there stabs a pole. On this pole, there hangs one tattered flag.

The slain man lies still. For hours, he does not move. His cheek rests on the ground; the grimace of pain on his face softened only by the slackening of a dead man's muscles. His body is twisted, his knees bent under him at an uncomfortable angle. His hands are loosely wrapped around the stake imbedded in his abdomen, slick with blood. His blood.

An eyelid flutters slowly open. There hints a deathly pain in his eyes. Young eyes. For a moment, there is no other movement. Then there is a hint of laborious breath, shallowly taken. The breathing quickens. Movement begins. Hands grapple unsuccessfully with the pole. His legs attempt to uncurl themselves and his back is arched in a wordless scream.

There is other movement. He looks up. There is a man in blue, his menacing shadow over the fallen other. The man on the ground opens his mouth, so wide – *it hurts so much* – that unwelcome tears brim around his tired eyes. The standing man grasps the pole. He wrenches it out of the youth's body with a furious look.

The fallen man stands to his feet. He is in red. He looks at the man in blue. There is no glory in the fight. He is frightened. Now he is angry. They grapple for the post. He wins and with it, hits the blue man. But the blue man is big. Very big.

The red man runs away from the blue man. All the way. Down the hill. There are others here. In either blue or red. Many of the blue are half red now. Dripping, panting, cursing, dead. Many of the red look like they are sleeping, except that this is a nightmare. There are so many.

– It is scary –
– What can one man do? –

The red man turns and is confronted by another blue man, a different one; an older one. The red man readies the post. It is a short fight, but it is a hard one. The blue man is pierced through his stomach. The lance is withdrawn again.

The red man turns. There are hundreds of men. They are everywhere. There is no order. He stabs and hacks at whom he can. He ducks from whom he cannot. It is exhilarating. He is fit. He is young. The red are good. The blue are bad. Run and fight.

– Glory will be won! –

The man in red runs back up the hill with all the other men in red. They are his friends. They are his brothers. The pitiful blues are down below. The true of heart cannot fail to succeed. The reds have the advantage!

– Charge! –

The sun sets slowly in the east.
On this land, there is a hill.
On this hill, there stands a man.
This man stands and clasps a pole.

On this pole, there
flies one triumphant flag.

(Editor's note – this story is written in reverse, as the reader will have noted that the sun setting in the East, not the West. This is a particularly powerful concept and piece of writing. I love the lateral creativity of it! Go through it again and see it like a movie in reverse. Or, it is okay to put your own interpretation on any piece of creative writing!)

Editor's note – the story below is written by the same previous person, except that this it is a creative, cynical recounting of an actual, factual experience. Enjoy!

Lawyer (Fact-Based Writing)[1]

It was towards the end of the year, when we start seeing more skin from the ladies and having occasional festive celebrations that this particular happening happened. One such celebration (perchance a Christmas party – celebrating the life of a boy-child with excessive encouragement from various beverages) was in full swing and had been, at the beginning of the night, themed on a fashion lost over a century ago (presumably because this would help the revere the birth). Here were an equal amount of men and women.[2] The women were revelling with feather boas, black cocktail dresses, red lips, and strings of pearls (which were real – depending on who you were).[3] The men, on the other hand,[4] had donned the plain (but expensive) suits that they wore every day, other than the occasional extrovert, James, and those with wives who *had insisted*. The alcohol came with the compliments of The Firm, so it was rapidly being done full justice to. The dinner was a full buffet and the hall historical.[5]

"It's gonna be a good night!" From Joe to William, eyeing a couple of girls walking by, who were dressed in skirts a good few inches shorter than they wore at work.

"Indeed." William had his wife on his arm, which meant that there was technically only chance for a very proper exchange of greetings between the two

---

[1] Note: Although the characters are real, their names have been changed

[2] Those invited had been allowed to bring their wives.

[3] Or, in many cases, *weren't*

[4] Because this wasn't *that* sort of party.

[5] Note: The hall was historical *before* the party, although of course the party significantly contributed to its proud past.

groups. But while Carol was engaged in being introduced, Kylie had looked a little too flirtatious and a little too full busted for him not to notice.

William Seeker was a Lawyer – with a capital letter. Not only was William Seeker a lawyer[6], he was also a partner[7] of the prestigious law firm, Ebbers & Burrows.[8] This thusly ranked him within the twenty Most-Important-Persons[9] of Auckland city, and he was accordingly modest about it.

As dawn crept steadily closer, Carol had come to him unsteadily from the bar, to which she had been affixed for most of the evening.

"Darling, I have a headache and am feeling a trifle tipsy." She appeared not to notice how close Kylie's chair was to William's, nor that as she made her way to them, Kylie had hurriedly removed her hand from resting on his leg. "I may have to go home and sleep it off."

Not even a hint of a blush suffused his face. "Of course, dear." He made no offer to take her himself[10] but instead took his bulging wallet from his pocket and with Kylie's eyes affixed to the shiny brown leather, handed his wife enough for a taxi home. "You put yourself to bed, and I shall make sure not to disturb you in the morning."

Because you won't be there. The silent words hung in the air as her eyes gave an involuntary flicker towards Kylie's direction.

"Thanks," she said quietly. She turned and treaded her way through the crowd to collect her belongings.

Seeker[11] was not a man too overly proud of his profession[12] and even mingled on occasion with the common people,[13] discussing menial things like property, money, cars, and women.[14]

It was difficult talking to Kylie. Not only was she at least two generations younger than him and popular with the young males her age, he had nothing to say to her other than one request, which he knew if he asked openly, would have

---

[6] With a capital.

[7] As above.

[8] Which actually had capitals.

[9] I think you get the point.

[10] Because he understood.

[11] As he was known by his equals.

[12] He did not have something so crass as a *job* or *employment*.

[13] That is, non-lawyers, such as dentists and surgeons.

[14] All of which, of course, was his.

to be refused and leave him lonely[15] for the night. He knew it was his power that attracted her, so there was mutual consent. It was his power that wanted to know he could still make the conquest.

He was an understanding man, without bias against riches or status. He was sympathetic with the plight of the poor[16], which he showed by freely volunteering the services of his firm[17] to organise trusts and funds for charities and churches and considered himself in no way a bigot of race or gender.[18]

Kylie he understood. While he couldn't converse with her, they both knew that Kylie fitted snugly into the social hierarchy; that is, she tried to sleep her way to the top and those at the top encouraged her efforts. But there were others that he was unsure about. Specifically, there was James. It was shocking. As far as he could tell, the boy was good looking, popular, rising quickly to the top, *and possibly a gay*. He had tried to hint at this to the other partners[19], gently pointing out some observed peculiarities such as –

"Quite friendly with the ladies but never see him with one of them, eh, Bill?"

"Bit effeminate isn't he, Tom?"

"Fuck! I can hear his bloody fashion parade from two floors away!"[20]

But the partners either didn't want to hear, or they lived so far in the past that they thought it was an impossibility that they should have handpicked someone with such a disability.

To make matters worse, he appeared to be close friends with Kylie and insisted on hanging around in a vaguely protective way – rather like she was a weaker sibling and not a fully grown, well-busted young woman who knew exactly what she was doing.

After a widely theatrical yawn, however, with his arm seemingly unconscious as it curled around her shoulders and feeling the shudder of anticipation run through her frame,[21] he finally succeeded in losing James.

"You tired, honey?"

---

[15] Or at least slightly cold.

[16] Such as teachers, builders, and politicians.

[17] For a small fee.

[18] Both he and they knew their place – and his was significantly higher.

[19] Note: the derision he felt was such that I feel forbidden to honour them with the capital William claims.

[20] This was to anyone that would listen.

[21] For what else could it have been?

She nodded mutely. James (again hovering) said, "The rest of the girls and I are heading to the Bongo. You want in, Ky?"

William gave the boy a sharp look. "She's obviously tired, son. You spend your energy at the club. I'll see her home safe."

James lingered uncertainly, looking at her determined eyes and carefully smiling face. "You sure babe? I don't wanna leave you stranded."

"She's *fine*," William retorted, knowing[22] that she wanted him to take complete control. He stood up and helped her stand too. "She's just had a few too many. Leave her now." His voice change to the authoritative one he used in the office.

James knew for a fact Kylie was not anywhere near her limit. He also knew that he himself was far past it. He shrugged and reluctantly turned away. Being rude to a partner[23] was never wise.

"I guess I'll see you at work then. Good to see you, Mr Seeker." And he attached himself to the tail end of the group trooping loudly outside, with only one glance back at his friend.

Seeker waited until this group had left before they followed discreetly.

"Honestly. It's as if he's not even a man," he muttered to himself, leading the way out the door. He opened the front door of the taxi for himself and sat in the seat, listening to her climb in behind him.

William Seeker was a Lawyer. With a capital letter. And in no way did he regret his choice.

The poem below was one that I had written, when I was contemplating the book. I had had a vivid dream, symbolically about the difficulty of fitting in when you are not the same as everyone else. I wrote the dream down and turned it into a poem. For a long time, I even considered the title as the book title as well, but realised that some would not understand the context and may be offended. Dee Jones

The Rhinoceros in the Room
(How some just don't fit in)
It was always this calm
Peacefully predictable

---

[22] In his instinctive way.
[23] (Capital)

The long lawns stretching down to
Meet and greet the curious waves where
The sunkissed toddler splashed as
The squirming baby on my hip watched
The scrawking, darting, dipping gulls.
Further down, another house
Kept an eye on the sea,
While the backyard stretched smoothly
Over the uneven paddocks
Where a clutter of children cantered as
A motherly neighbour minded the motley mix.
With the sun at its midday zenith
Over the staid yellowed bungalows

– it was time (the others already gone)
– time for the children to nap
– time for the games to end

When the ground RUMBLED and TREMBLED
When the GRINDING SHRIEKING of armour SCREECHED:
Vicious breathing SNORKED from the broad nostrils
Of a METAL RHINOCEROS
POUNDING heavily up to my house

The terrified toddler ran into the house
The baby froze on my hip, not even breathing

I stood across the access, between the exit and entry
Play now the rhinoceros SHOUTED.
Play little boy
No! You can't! Speak nicely first!

Pause. A little STOMPING and CLATTERING.
Let me in!
Let me play in the room!

The rhinoceros ripped up the turf with
His rough fore-hoof : WRIP WRIP RAKE
TOSSING his big fibrous horn dangerously
SWINGING his large head from side to side
The rivets of the metal plates
JANGLING and SCRAPING.
You don't fit in our house. You don't fit through the door!
He just didn't fit.
His head dropped
His forelegs turned in, near collapse
His tail tucked in down behind him
He seemed to collapse into a small small teary rusty heap
I just want to be with people –
Like other people
Tell me how...

—Dee Jones

Appendix 1

Tool for women to indicate ASD

Background:

Between my colleague and I, we can confidently say that we have close to fifty, if not more than fifty, years of working with ASD, between us. As a clinical psychologist, my friend Dr Yvette Ahmad, has diagnosed many on the spectrum as well as clinical work, and I have done clinical work for all that time. We often liaised professionally regards client issues and checking how comorbidities and other issues like trauma or narcissism, could impinge on ASD.

Our biggest gripe has always been the misdiagnoses of females on the spectrum. After several years of this, we considered doing something about it. So back in early 2018, we started our research on all available tools for women (and most were the same as that for men), and looked at why they did not work for women. We put together our thoughts, and designed a couple, but we were not satisfied that they were any better. We were operating within the same pattern, and as they say proverbially – that if you keep doing the same thing, you will keep getting the same outcome. One day, I felt that I had a new way of looking at the matter and took my brainstorm to Yvette – and we were away!!! We donated many many many hours of our lives to working on our test, researching and developing it, and then repeating the process. We refined and catalogued. We met in all available gaps between our clients and commitments, often in cafes halfway between our offices. We invested a tidy sum into decaffeinated coffees. Eventually, we liked what we had! It was time to test it.

First, we had to test the test: did it work, could it compile data, how long did it take, what was the feedback? We had a few, random local community volunteers – regardless of diagnosis – who did the online test. We listened to their feedback and refined the test. We got our professional and ethics clearances, and then requested volunteers within our criteria. In essence, we had two groups: Neurotypical women and formally, officially diagnosed women on the spectrum. We started locally and then went nationally. Then through contacts, we went international! We had a universal set of women from every continent, regardless of ethnicity!

Our first set of data was a simple chi-square test – and the results simply blew us away!!! As the results started to roll in, we felt that we were onto a winner. As the statistics came in, we knew we had a fabulous test. Then more research, a bit more tweaking, a battery of statistics from a statistician of international repute, and we were satisfied. But we are still doing ongoing development and refining this test for public use.

So while Yvette is writing a professional article for a journal and doing all the professional *stuff* around that (like detailing our research and methodology and the long list of statistical tests undertaken), I simply wrote this non-academic blurb.

Please be aware that our tool is simply an indicator, and as such is not, absolutely not, meant to be used as a diagnostic tool.

I have included two graphs, that show some of the outcomes:

Total score for both subgroups
Total score
144
125
100
75
50
25
0
NT
ASD

Logistic regression
Predicted chance of ASD
100%
75%
50%
25%
0%
0
25
50
75
100
125
144
Total score

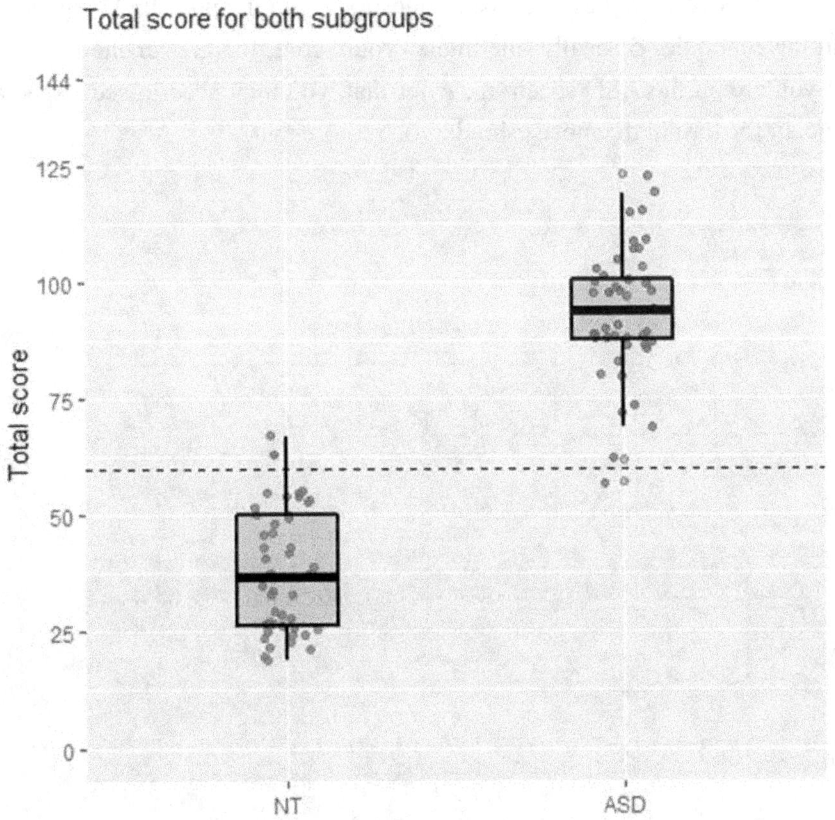

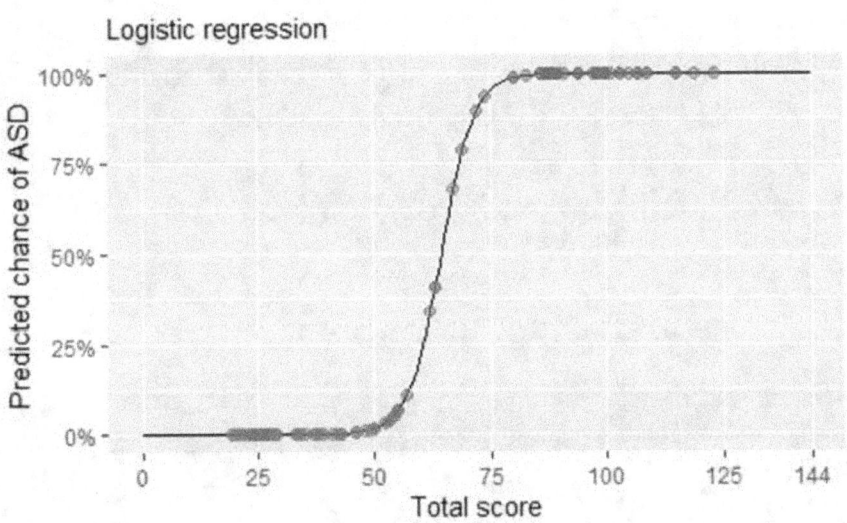

Or in Appendix 2, we have the list of questions, and in appendix 3, we have the marking schedule. Basically, the higher your score, the greater the probability that you are on the ASD spectrum. After that, you may need to see a specialist clinician for formal diagnosis, should you require that.

Appendix 2

Female ASD questionnaire

Copyright: Dee Jones and Dr Yvette Ahmad
Disclaimer: This is not a diagnostic tool. It could merely give you a possible indication that you may or may not be on the spectrum.

Question Number	Consider the following statements and circle either Y=yes, or N=no in the right hand column.		
1.	I often feel socially isolated	Y	N
2.	I often miss social 'cues' [social cues are what others are saying in body language and tone of voice]	Y	N
3.	I read other people's intentions well	Y	N
4.	I read other people's cues through their body language	Y	N
5.	People are often negative towards me	Y	N
6.	People are often dismissive of me	Y	N
7.	I have a best friend that I have known for several years	Y	N
8.	I have a few close friends	Y	N
9.	I feel like I know lots of people but not any that I could confidently call a "friend"	Y	N
10.	I often do not notice when someone is talking to me	Y	N
11.	I often do not notice someone is talking to me when I have sensory overload	Y	N
12.	Others find me unaffectionate	Y	N

13.	I have sometimes been described as non-emotional or cold or detached	Y	N
14.	I mostly feel confused about whether to hug someone or not	Y	N
15.	I have been accused of behaving inappropriately	Y	N
16.	I have been told that I sometimes make unusual sounds	Y	N
17.	I often find social formalities difficult and confusing	Y	N
18.	People close to me often get annoyed at how I speak to them	Y	N
19.	Others are surprised when I get angry	Y	N
20.	When I get angry, I feel like other people understand why I am angry	Y	N
21.	I have alexithymia (difficulty expressing my emotions]	Y	N
22.	People often look at me without saying anything, then look away	Y	N
23.	If I am employed, I like to work in a busy place as part of a team (mark "no" if not employed)	Y	N
24.	If I were asked to lead a team, I would feel stressed	Y	N
25.	I prefer to work on my own	Y	N
26.	I believe that I am a good communicator	Y	N
27.	If I am in company, I prefer to only be with one person at a time	Y	N
28.	I mostly enjoy being in a crowd	Y	N
29.	I sometimes do not understand the punch-line in jokes	Y	N
30.	People often laugh at a joke and I don't get it	Y	N
31.	I have often felt that I am not normal	Y	N
32.	I am told that I can be too direct, rude or to the point, by people close to me	Y	N
33.	I have been found to be aggressive or too confrontational, by people close to me	Y	N
34.	I find it difficult to make friends	Y	N
35.	I find it difficult to understand why people do bad things to others	Y	N

36.	I often have sick days from my work (whether it is work of my own choice, school work or paid employment).	Y	N
37.	If I were to work, or am in employment, I accrue sick days as I do not take sick leave usually	Y	N
38.	I often do not go to work although I am not sick (whether work is of my own making, school work or paid employment).	Y	N
39.	I have many long term friends	Y	N
40.	I often drink alcohol	Y	N
41.	Others often misunderstand what I say to them	Y	N
42.	I often feel like people do not understand my explanations or comments	Y	N
43.	I often feel different	Y	N
44.	I often forget to bath/shower or wash my hair	Y	N
45.	I have been in compromised sexual situations	Y	N
46.	I have been interested for a long time in some hobbies like anime, cosplay or steampunk	Y	N
47.	I have an obsessive interest	Y	N
48.	I like to teach my pet to do tricks (if you do not have a pet, respond No)	Y	N
49.	I am good at copying or imitating voices so that I sound identical to them	Y	N
50.	I like animals	Y	N
51.	I would prefer to work with animals rather than to work with people	Y	N
52.	I would prefer to do gardening or cooking rather than be with, or work with, people	Y	N
53.	I am good at sport	Y	N
54.	I fixate on tiny things that other people do not seem to notice	Y	N
55.	Visually stimulating rooms distract me	Y	N
56.	I often feel like I can't find the words to explain something, and then people don't follow or understand me	Y	N
57.	I often feel stressed	Y	N
58.	I try to follow rules exactly	Y	N
59.	I try to follow rules exactly for sport and games	Y	N

60.	I have lots of rules that only I seem to adhere to	Y	N
61.	I have been told that I am very literal	Y	N
62.	I am very black-and-white in my thinking	Y	N
63.	When something (that others would think is trivial) has happened to me, I find it difficult to stop thinking about it and move on	Y	N
64.	I make lists but often lose them	Y	N
65.	I often have attention difficulties	Y	N
66.	I keep multiple lists	Y	N
67.	I often forget what people that I have recently met, look like	Y	N
68.	It is difficult to remember facial features of strangers that I have recently met	Y	N
69.	I dislike change	Y	N
70.	I like it when I come into the classroom/workplace and everything has been changed around	Y	N
71.	I keep routines	Y	N
72.	I am upset if my routines are interrupted	Y	N
73.	I need lots of downtime, alone	Y	N
74.	I often feel like I am not coping	Y	N
75.	I get upset when people move my things, e.g. the pens on my work desk	Y	N
76.	I like to categorise my belongings e.g. laundry pegs need to match	Y	N
77.	I mean to be tidy but always seem to go in circles and seem to remain untidy	Y	N
78.	I would describe my humour I as different to others	Y	N
79.	I seem to be disorganised despite that I want order and structure	Y	N
80.	I have difficulty making priorities in my life	Y	N
81.	I have difficulty keeping my priorities	Y	N
82.	I often do not finish my work, as expected of me (whether it is work I planned for my day, school work or paid employment)	Y	N
83.	I was bullied at school	Y	N
84.	When I changed schools or moved house, I was still bullied in the new place	Y	N

85.	I am still often bullied	Y	N
86.	I found school boring	Y	N
87.	I am often bored with my work (whether it is work of my own choosing, paid employment or studies I have undertaken)	Y	N
88.	I am often bored at school or in my studies, but can spend hours doing my own research	Y	N
89.	I started having romantic relationships much later than my friends did	Y	N
90.	I had a boyfriend/girlfriend just because I thought I had to, to be normal	Y	N
91.	I went through a period, particularly as a child, of selective mutism [selective mutism means choosing not to talk or respond to certain people or in certain situations]	Y	N
92.	I had a phase in which I wanted to be a boy	Y	N
93.	I have had doubts about my sexuality	Y	N
94.	I describe myself as asexual	Y	N
95.	I find the conversations with my peers about their intimate relationships, pointless and a waste of time	Y	N
96.	I have learnt to drive	Y	N
97.	I was/am scared of learning to drive	Y	N
98.	I worry about my health	Y	N
99.	I am good at paying my bills on time	Y	N
100.	I am disinterested in money	Y	N
101.	I am careless with money e.g. I often lose money	Y	N
102.	I often forget to pay my bills	Y	N
103.	I have been seriously deceived more than five times	Y	N
104.	I have been financially disadvantaged by someone more than five times	Y	N
105.	Where I can, I avoid talking to people on the phone	Y	N

106.	I think that I am hypersensitive/over-sensitive to noise, or smells, or tastes or touch or any physical senses	Y	N
107.	I often suffer from sensory overload [being over-stimulated by my environment]	Y	N
108.	I like to be touched	Y	N
109.	I am oversensitive to noise	Y	N
110.	I am oversensitive to light	Y	N
111.	I am oversensitive to taste and food textures	Y	N
112.	I am oversensitive to labels and seams on my clothes	Y	N
113.	I often feel irritated by clothes touching my skin, or by some fabrics	Y	N
114.	I like to be hugged	Y	N
115.	I am emotionally very sensitive	Y	N
116.	I sometimes have a "meltdown" when I am overwhelmed	Y	N
117.	I sometimes "shutdown" when I am overwhelmed	Y	N
118.	I am uncomfortable with direct eye contact	Y	N
119.	Stimming helps to settle me when I have sensory overload. [Stimming is a repeated action that helps to soothe (for example, bouncing a leg or twiddling with something like a strand of hair), Stimming also aids the processing of information when overwhelmed]	Y	N
120.	I can do my Stim in public (if you do not Stim then respond No)	Y	N
121.	I experience synaesthesia [Synaesthesia means that you might 'see' or 'hear' colours for example, or sound can present in a series of colours for you]	Y	N
122.	If I do experience synaesthesia, then I do use it effectively in my life – especially because I am creative	Y	N
123.	I experience misophonia [Misophonia means that noise, like somebody crunching an apple or	Y	N

	eating crisps loudly, can affect your ability to think or even distress you]		
124.	I am picky about my food and what I will eat	Y	N
125.	I dislike it when different servings of food on my plate touch each other	Y	N
126.	I eat methodically, eating one serving before going on to another	Y	N
127.	Certain colours upset me	Y	N
128.	There are certain colours of food that I don't eat (or don't like to eat)	Y	N
129.	There are quite a few food textures that I cannot bear, and will not eat again	Y	N
130.	I experience misokinesia [Misokinesia – for example, when other people make repeated body movements that annoy you]	Y	N
131.	I often enjoy sex	Y	N
132.	I often avoid sex	Y	N
133.	I can sense it when people don't like me	Y	N
134.	I struggle with dyslexia [Dyslexia – having difficulty in reading, interpreting words, letters and symbols]	Y	N
135.	I struggle with dyspraxia [Dyspraxia- having difficulty compared to your classmates for example, in walking, drawing, writing and coordination in sport]	Y	N
136.	I suffer from anxiety	Y	N
137.	I struggle with depression	Y	N
138.	I get obsessive	Y	N
139.	Other people tell me that I am obsessive	Y	N
140.	I often feel that I am physically a bit clumsy	Y	N
141.	I have been accused of being a hypochondriac?[Hypochondriac- do you often find that you get aches and pains and physical symptoms but the tests that come back are negative]	Y	N
142.	I have been diagnosed with ADHD (Attention Deficit Hyperactive Disorder) or ADD (Attention Deficit Disorder)	Y	N

143.	I experience or have experienced repeated gut issues such as bloating, diarrhoea, constipation or gut-pain	Y	N
144.	I have once, or still do, struggle with gender issues	Y	N

Appendix 3

Scoring the Female ASD questionnaire

1) If you have scored "No" for the following numbers, then give yourself one point for each "No":
3/4/7/8/20/23/26/28/37/39/40/53/70/96/99/108/114/131/133
2) Add all the "No" answers from 1) and get a total.
3) Thereafter, for the remaining questions, give yourself one point for all the remaining "Yes" answers and make sure that you exclude the above numbers in 1).
4) Add all the "Yes" answers from 3) and get a total for those.
5) Add the totals of the "No" answers from (2) and the "Yes" answer from (4) together. That is your final score.

Compare your score to the outcomes from our original research below:

- score below 45 there is 0-5% chance of ASD
- score between 45 and 60 there is a 50% chance of ASD
- score above 60 there is 95-100% chance of ASD

A better way to frame it:

- 95% of women who score below 45 are NT
- 50% of women who score between 45 and 60 are NT/ASD
- 95% of women who score above 60 have a statistical diagnosis of ASD

If you scored in the 60-above range, then you may want to get an official diagnosis through a clinical psychologist. This is not a diagnostic test, but an indicator only.

Glossary

ADD: Attention Deficit Disorder

ADHD: Attention Deficit Hyperactive Disorder

Alexithymia: Not being able to either know or describe one's feelings, or both.

Allistic: The closest meaning is neurotypical but the general meaning is non-autistic

Allodynia: is a heightened sensitivity to touch. This is also known as tactile sensitivity

Anxiety: when overwhelming thoughts and feelings unhealthily interfere with daily life; a state of extreme worry leading to distress, around a perception that does not align with reality

AS: Autism Spectrum

ASD: Autism Spectrum Disorder

Asperger Syndrome: is sometimes also referred to as Mild Autism, or alternatively, High Functioning Autism. It is also referred to in different writings as Asperger's syndrome. Now, since the publication of the DMS-V, it is referred to as ASD, or Autism Spectrum Disorder. It is often shortened fondly to Aspie but not in official documents.

Asperger, Hans, Dr: first identified a form of milder autism, which was named after him [Asperger syndrome]

Aspie: Fond reference to someone on the ASD spectrum

Cassandra Syndrome: a person usually in a relationship and living with an Autistic person in a relationship for a long time, who is not believed when they describe that private relationship. The term can be used to describe the mental and emotional negative effects and possible damage when living with someone who is neurologically wired differently to you.

Cognitive empathy: thoughts about what something may feel like for another person but lacking an emotional component of empathy and is possibly more similar to sympathy

Cognitive rigidity: mental inflexibility in thought, difficulty to change quickly from one thought pathway to another

Cognitive: refers to our thinking and processing. In children, this happens primarily in the frontal cortex as the prefrontal cortex is not fully developed until the early twenties in most adults

Comorbidities: A comorbidity is usually another major problem that exists along with a main first issue or may even be a result of the first issue

Context blindness: a lack of awareness of one's environment, in which a person may speak or act inappropriately to the situation

Counselling: "Counselling is the process of helping and supporting a person to resolve personal, social, or psychological challenges and difficulties." (taken from the website with permission of the New Zealand Association of Counsellors)

Depression: a persistent disorder in which mood is low and thoughts are predominantly negative, which can significantly interfere with the functioning of daily life

Developmental disorder: This means that a child is thought to be born with a particular condition, which remains or is apparent through most of the developmental stages as the child is growing

DSM: stands for the Diagnostic and Statistical Manual of Mental Disorders. The DSM is put together by the American Psychiatric Association. These are updated every few years and reprinted under a numbered and sub-lettered system. The latest edition is known as the DSM-5. Psychologists use a number of diagnostic tools, one of which includes the DSM-5

Dyslexia: Difficulty with words, symbols and letters despite normal intelligence

Dyspraxia: there are usually issues around gross motor control. This means controlling the muscles in your body leading to difficulty when coordinating movement and coordination. They often have poor posture, have limited stamina; they generally do not have good balance and have poor muscle tone.

Eating disorders: these include anorexia, bulimia, and difficulty with certain foods or food textures. There are unhealthy or inappropriate issues around food consumption.

Emotional empathy: a deep feeling that connects with the same feelings that another may have and respond appropriately

Exteroception: An awareness of external factors on your body such as the wind, people pushing in a crowd, smells and so forth

Frontal cortex: is the part that does problem solving. It is metaphorically like a computer hard drive which stores all our unique information and *programmes*. It is one of the main areas activated in the brain when a person is thinking.

Gender issues: difficulty relating to the gender roles culturally assigned around one's gender. A non-acceptance at times of one's gender

Hapa Aspies: a term coined by Kathy Marshank and refers to a person that may have many symptoms of Asperger syndrome but not enough for diagnoses. The term means half-an-Apie. This may be due to genetic, environment or other (undefined) causes. The suggestion is that this is commonly found where at least one parent is on the Autism Spectrum Disorder and the other is neurotypical

Heterosexual: attracted to people of the opposite gender, particularly a relationship and sexual attraction

Hyperosmia: means having an abnormally acute sense of smell.

Identity: how one perceives one's *self*, whether independently or as a part of larger group

Interoception: awareness of the internal signals of your body such as becoming ill, tiredness, hunger and so forth

Kanner's Autism: Dr Leo Kanner first identified autism in children in 1943, and one form of Autism was named after him. Kanner's autism is more severe than Asperger syndrome. All forms of autism are now classified under ASD (Autism Spectrum Disorder) and are generally not differentiated anymore

Limited executive functioning: cognitive organisation is often poor because the brain circuitry that does not seem to be fully connected. Lorna Wing, the earlier pioneer in Asperger syndrome, suggests that Aspies have incomplete pathways and poor screening activity in the part of the brain that is known as the Reticular Formation

Mind-blindness or Theory of Mind (ToM): Both in the context of ASD, refers to the difficulty that people on the spectrum have in reading the emotions and intentions of others and responding appropriately or empathetically. This means the inability or difficulty to perceive another person as having their own thoughts and emotions and that others are self-contained human beings (not moving, emotionless objects). Another symptom of mind-blindness is lack of empathy lack of empathy particularly towards other people.

Mirror cells in the brain: These mirror cells act like mirrors when one is learning a new skill and is the tool by which children often mimic behaviour. As we get older, the cells are less dominant in our visual learning, as we develop other forms of learning.

Misokinesia: means being intensely aware of repeated movements that can annoy and distract and may even cause distress, such as a flapping flag, or the pendulum of a grandfather clock, or a Neko ornament (the Fortune Cat that often waves its paw and is found in Asian stores).

Misophonia: Repeated noise (like chewing) causes anger and affects the ability to think

Neurodiverse: All humanity is on the neurodiverse spectrum: technically we are to some degree neurotypical, neurodivergent or possibly somewhere in-between

Neurodivergent: the brain is not wired like the majority of the population of neurotypicals. This includes Autism, ADHD, Tourette's syndrome and other examples of this different wiring

Neurological: this refers to the *wiring in the brain*, or how the brain works

Neurotypical: The majority of the population is neurotypical. Neural reflects on the how the brain and the nervous system is wired. The most common way a brain is wired in any general population

Nosological: The WHO ICD-10 reference terminology to Asperger syndrome

Obsessive Compulsive Disorder (OCD): Obsessive and unrealistic thinking that leads to feelings focussed intensely and anxiously on extreme details, which incapacitates a person's life. A particularly debilitating form of an anxiety disorder

Pervasive Developmental Disorder and sometimes PDD-NOS (Pervasive Developmental Disorder – Not Otherwise Specified). These diagnosis, with the additional one of Rett syndrome, are now all classified together under the diagnostic title of Autism Spectrum Disorder and is a presentation of the same condition with additional aspects

Photophobic: means having an extreme sensitivity to light

Prefrontal cortex is the part of the brain that uses insight, interpretation, and reason, often in social contexts and particularly in developing understanding around relationships

Proprioception: Aspies often do not have a conscious awareness of how they use space around them or around other people

Prosopagnosia: is a neurological disorder characterised by the inability to recognise people by their faces. It is also sometimes called face blindness. Sometimes the term Facial Agnosia is used, which means the same as prosopagnosia

PTSD: Post Traumatic Stress Disorder. Stress reactions triggered long after a trauma has occurred, which disorder may endure for years or even a lifetime

Reticular Formation: Reticular Formation is near the top of the brainstem, not far from the Amygdala (the fight-or-flight system) and runs down the back of the brainstem for about 4–5 cm. If this were a fibre-optic cable, then it would be an extremely dense and highly complex filtering system. If the filter works optimally and efficiently, then distractions would be able to be filtered out. It seems to also help to prioritise information. Aspies can have difficulty in concentrating and focussing when faced with a lot of stimuli simultaneously

Selective mutism: this occurs predominantly in childhood, in which the person chooses selectively to not speak although they are physically capable of speaking

Sensitivities: this is usually an aroused awareness of the environment, often unpleasantly or even painfully so at time. Hypersensitivity can be a hyper-awareness to sound, textures, light, tastes, movement, and other sensory areas

STEM: refers to Science, Technology, Engineering, Maths subjects. Some academics refer to STEMM subjects and add Medicine

STIM: self-stimulatory behaviour that soothes or helps processing as they do the repeated behaviour

Synaesthesia: a stimuli that can manifest in a different sensory area such as sounds can make a visual pattern, or tastes can be visual

Theory of mind or Mind-blindness: Both in the context of ASD, refers to the difficulty that people on the spectrum have in reading the emotions and intentions of others and responding appropriately or empathetically. This means the inability or difficulty to perceive another person as having their own thoughts and emotions and that others are self-contained human beings (not moving, emotionless objects). Another symptom of mind-blindness is lack of empathy particularly towards other people

ToM: Theory of Mind, or mind-blindness

Tourette's syndrome: unwanted body movements or sounds over which the person seems to have little control. These may include tics or offensive language

Bibliography

Ariel, C. (2012 Loving Someone with Asperger's Syndrome : Understanding and Connecting with your Partner. Oakland: New Harbinger Publications.

Aston, M. (2001) The Other Half of Asperger Syndrome. London: Jessica Kingsley Publishers

Aston, M. (2003) Aspergers in Love: Couple Relationships and Family Affairs. London: Jessica Kingsley Publishers

Aston, M. (2012) What Men with Asperger Syndrome Want to Know about Women, Dating and Relationships. London: Jessica Kingsley Publishers.

Attwood, T. (1998) Asperger's Syndrome: A Guide for Parents and Professionals. London: Jessica Kingsley Publishers.

Attwood, T. (2008) The complete guide to Aspergers syndrome. London: Jessica Kingsley Publishers.

Attwood, T. (2003) Why Does Chris Do That? Some Suggestions Regarding the Cause and Management of the Unusual Behaviour of Children and Adults with Autism and Asperger Syndrome. London: AAPC

Attwood, T., Grandin, T et al. (2006) Asperger's and Girls. Arlington: Future Horizons.

Baron-Cohen, S. (2003) The Essential Difference: Men, women and the Extreme Male Brain. London: Penguin

Baron-Cohen, S. (2012) The Science of Evil : On Empathy and the Origins of Cruelty. New York: Ingram Publishing Services

Bentley, K. (2007) Alone together: Making an Asperger Marriage Work. London: Jessica Kingsley Publishers.

Birch, Jen. (2003) Congratulations! : It's Aspergers Syndrome. London: Jessica Kingsley Publishers.

Bonker, E. M. I Am in Here: The Journey of a Child with Autism Who Cannot Speak But Finds Her Voice

Booth, L. (2014) When Fraser met Billy. New York: Simon & Schuster

Boyd, B. (2003) Parenting a Child with Asperger Syndrome : 200 Tips and Strategies. London: Jessica Kingsley Publishers.

Carter, R., Aldridge, S., Page, M., and Parker, S. (2014) The Brain Book: An Illustrated Guide to its Structure, Function and Disorders. London: DK Publishers

Chorpita, B.F., and Weisz, J.R. (2009) Match-ADTC: Modular Approach to Therapy for Children with Anxiety, Depression, Trauma or Conduct Problems. Florida: Practicewise.

Colson, Emily. (2012) Dancing with Max : a Mother and Son Who Broke Free, Grand Rapids: Zondervan.

Craft, S. (2018) Everyday Aspergers : A Journey on the Autism Spectrum. Lancaster: Explainer HQ

Dillon, Jayne. (2013) Jessi-cat : the cat that unlocked a boy's heart. London: Michael O'Mara Books Ltd

Evans, K. and Swogger, J. (2016) Something Different about Dad: How to Live with Your Amazing Asperger Parent. London: Jessica Kingsley Publishers.

Finch, D. (2012) The Journal of Best Practices: A Memoir of Marriage, Asperger Syndrome, and One Man's Quest to Be a Better Husband. New York: ScribnerBook Company

Fleischmann, Arthur. (2012) Carly's Voice: Breaking Through Autism. New York:Simon & Schuster.

Gardner, Nuala. (2013) All because of Henry: my story of struggle and triumph with two autistic children and the dogs that unlocked their world. Edinburgh: Black and White Publishing

Grandin, T. (2006) Thinking in Pictures. London: Bloomsbury

Grandin, T. (2008) The way I see it: a personal look at Autism and Aspergers. Arlington: Future Horizons Inc.

Grandin, T. (2012) Different…Not Less: Inspiring Stories of Achievement and Successful Employment from Adults with Autism, Asperger's and ADHD. Arlington: Future Horizons Incorporated.

Grandin, T. (2013) The Autistic Brain: Thinking Across the Spectrum. Boston: Houghton Mifflin.

Grandin, T. (2014) The Autistic Brain : Helping Different Kinds of Minds Succeed. Boston: Mariner Books

Grandin, T. (2015) The Way I See It : A Personal Look at Autism andAsperger's. Arlington; Future Horizons Incorporated.

Grandin, T. and Panek, R. (2014) The Autistic Brain. London: Ebury Publishing.

Grandin, T. and Johnson, C. (2009) Making Animals Happy. London: Bloomsbury Publishing.

Grandin, T. And Johnson, C. (2006) Animals in Translation : The Woman Who Thinks Like a Cow. London: Bloomsbury Publishing

Grandin, T. and Johnson, C. (2010) Animals Make Us Human : Creating the Best Life for Animals. Boston: Houghton Mifflin

Grandin, T., and Barron, S. (2016) Unwritten Rules of Social Relationships. Arlington: Future Horizons Inc.

Hagland, C. (2010) Getting to Grips with Asperger Syndrome: Understanding Adults on the Autism Spectrum. London: Jessica Kingsley Publishers.

Hawkes, Hilary. (2009) Asperger Syndrome: The Essential Guide. Peterborough: NEED2KNOW

Heinrichs, Rebecca. (2003) Perfect Targets: Aspergers Syndrome and Bullying: Practical Solutions for Surviving the Social World. Kansas: AAPC

Henault, Isabelle, (2005) Asperger's Syndrome and Sexuality : From Adolescence Through Adulthood. London: Jessica Kingsley Publishers.

Higashida, N. (2014) The Reason I Jump: one boy's voice from the silence of autism. London: Hodder & Stoughton

Higashida, N. (2018) Fall Down Seven Times, Get Up Eight. London: Hodder & Stoughton

Holliday Willey, Liane (ed). (2003) Asperger Syndrome in Adolescence: Living with the Ups, the Downs and Things in Between. London: Jessica Kingsley Publishers.

Holliday Willey, Liane. (1999) Pretending to be normal. London: Jessica Kingsley Publishers.

Holliday Willey, Liane. (2001) Asperger Syndrome in the Family. London: Jessica Kingsley Publishers.

Holliday Willey, Liane. (2011) Safety skills for Asperger women: how to save a perfectly good female life.

Hoopman, K. (2006) All Cats Have Asperger Syndrome. London: Jessica Kingsley Publishers.

Hoopman, K. (2015) The Essential Manual for Asperger Syndrome (ASD) in the Classroom : What Every Teacher Needs to Know. London: Jessica Kingsley Publishers.

Jackson, Luke. (2002) Freaks, Geeks and Asperger Syndrome: A User Guide to Adolescence. London: Jessica Kingsley Publishers.

Jackson, L. (2016) Sex, Drugs and Asperger's Syndrome (ASD) : A User Guide to Adulthood. London: Jessica Kingsley Publishers.

James, L. (2017) Odd Girl Out: An Autistic Woman in a Neurotypical World. London: Bluebird (an imprint of Pan MacMillan)

Kidd, Ann. (2009) You're a Dick, Mummy. Motueka: NZ.

Lawson, W. (2003) Build Your Own Life : A Self-Help Guide for Individuals with Asperger Syndrome. London: Jessica Kingsley Publishers

Marshank, K. (2009) Going over the Edge: Life with a Partner or Spouse with Asperger Syndrome). Kansas: AAPC Publishing.

Marshank, K. (2013) Out of Mind- Out of Sight: Parenting with a Partner with Asperger Syndrome (ASD) North Charleston: CreateSpace Independent Publishing Platform.

Miller, J. K. (2003) Women from Another Planet?: Our Lives in the Universe of Autism : Our Lives in the Universe of Autism. Bloomington: AUTHORHOUSE

Montgomery, S. (2012) Temple Grandin: How the Girl Who Loved Cows Embraced Autism and Changed the World. Boston: Houghton Mifflin.

Morena, S., Wheeler, M. and Pakinson, K. (2012) The Partner's Guide to Asperger Syndrome. London: Jessica Kingsley Publishers.

Muggleton, J. (2012) Raising Martians from crash landing to leaving home: how to help a child with Aspergers syndrome or high functioning autism. London: Jessica Kingsley Publishers

Newport, J., Newport, M. and Dodd, J. (2007) Mozart and the Whale : An Asperger's Love Story. New York: Touchstone Books

Nicholls, S. (2009) Girls Growing Up on the Spectrum. London: Jessica Kingsley Publishers.

Notbohm, E. And Zysk, V. (2004) 1001 Great Ideas for Teaching and Raising Children with Autism or Asperger's. Arlington, Texas: Future Horizons.

Ortiz, J. M. (2008) The Myriad Gifts of Asperger's Syndrome. London: Jessica Kingsley Publishers.

Pap, L. (2018) Being with Aspergers: "So that's how it's done!". Bloomington: Balboa Press

Paxton, K. and Estay, I.A. (2007) Counselling People on the Autism Spectrum: A Practical Manual. London: Jessica Kingsley Publishers.

Pease, A. and Pease, B (2006) Why Men Don't Have a Clue and Women Always Need More Shoes. London: Orion

Pease, A. and Pease, B. (2006) Why Men Lie & Women Cry. London: Orion

Pease, A. and Pease, B. (2017) The Definitive Book of Body Language : How to read others' attitudes by their gestures. London: Orion Publishing Company

Pease, B. and Pease, A (2003) Why Men Can Only Do One Thing at a Time Women Never Stop Talking. London: Orion

Pease, B. and Pease, A. (2001) Why Men Don't Listen & Women Can't Read Maps : How We're Different and What to Do About It. New York: Harmony.

Pease, B. and Pease, A. (2010) Why Men Want Sex and Women Need Love : Unravelling the Simple Truth. New York: Random House

Pyles, L. (2001) Hitchhiking through Aspergers Syndrome. London: JessicaKingsley Publishers.

Robinson, J.E. (2008) Look Me in the Eye: My Life with Aspergers. New York: Random House.

Robinson, Ricki G. (2011) Autism Solutions : How to Create a Healthy and Meaningful Life for Your Child. Sydney: Harlequinn.

Robison, J. E. (2011) Be Different : Adventures of a Free-Range Aspergian with Practical Advice for Aspergians, Misfits, Families & Teachers. New York: Crown Publishing Group.

Sacks, O. (1995) An Anthropologist from Mars. Sydney: Pan MacMillan Australia Pty Ltd.

Sacks, O. (2011) The Man Who Mistook His Wife for a Hat. London: PanMacMillan

Schnurr, R. G. (1999) Asperger's Huh? : A Child's Perspective, London: Anisor

Simone, R. (2009) 22 Things a Woman Must Know If She Loves a Man with Asperger's Syndrome. London: Jessica Kingsley Publishers

Simone, R. (2010) Aspergirls: Empowering Female with Asperger Syndrome. London: Jessica Kingsley Publishers

Simone, R. 2012) 22 Things a Woman with Asperger's Syndrome Wants Her Partner to Know. London: Jessica Kingsley Publishers

Slater-Walker, G. and Slater-Walker, C. (2002) An Asperger Marriage. London: Jessica Kingsley Publishers.

Smith Myles, B. , Tapscott Cook, K. , Miller, N. E., Rinner, L.A. (2001) Asperger Syndrome and Sensory Issues: Practical Solutions for Making Sense of the World. Kansas: APC.

Stefanski, D. (2011) How to talk to an autistic kid. Minneapolis: Free Spirit Publishing Inc

Tammet, D. (2007) Born on a Blue Day: a Memoir of Aspergers and an Extraordinary Mind. New York: Simon & Schuster.

Weston: L. (2010) Connecting With Your Asperger Partner : Negotiating the Maze of Intimacy. London: Jessica Kingsley Publishers.

Winter, M. and Lawrence, C. (2011) Asperger Syndrome – What Teachers Need to Know. London: Jessica Kingsley Publishers.

Young, R. (2009) Asperger Syndrome: Pocketbook. Hampshire: Teacher's Pocketbooks

www.ingramcontent.com/pod-product-compliance
Lightning Source LLC
Chambersburg PA
CBHW072142070526
44585CB00015B/987